Creating Images
and the Psychology
of Marketing Communication

Advertising and Consumer Psychology
A Series sponsored by the Society for Consumer Psychology

Aaker/Biel: *Brand Equity & Advertising: Advertising's Role in Building Strong Brands* (1993)

Clark/Brock/Stewart: *Attention, Attitude, and Affect in Response Advertising* (1994)

Englis: *Global and Multi-National Advertising* (1994)

Goldberg/Fishbein/Middlestadt: *Social Marketing: Theoretical and Practical Perspectives* (1997)

Haugtvedt/Machleit/Yalch: *Online Consumer Psychology: Understanding and Influencing Consumer Behavior in the Virtual World* (2005)

Kahle/Chiagouris: *Values, Lifestyles and Psychographics* (1997)

Kahle/Kim: *Creating Images and the Psychology of Marketing Communication*

Kahle/Riley: *Sports Marketing and the Psychology of Marketing Communications* (2003)

Kardes/Herr/Nantel: *Applying Social Cognition to Consumer-Focused Strategy* (2005)

Mitchell: *Advertising Exposure, Memory, and Choice* (1993)

Schumann/Thorson: *Advertising and the World Wide Web* (1999)

Scott/Batra: *Persuasive Imagery: A Consumer Response Perspective* (2003)

Shrum: *The Psychology of Entertainment Media: Blurring the Lines Between Entertainment and Persuasion* (2004)

Thorson/Moore: *Integrated Communication: Synergy of Persuasive Voices* (1996)

Wells: *Measuring Advertising Effectiveness* (1997)

Williams/Lee/Haugtvedt: *Diversity in Advertising: Broadening the Scope of Research Directions* (2004)

Creating Images and the Psychology of Marketing Communication

Edited by

Lynn R. Kahle
University of Oregon, USA

&

Chung-Hyun Kim
Sogang University, S. Korea

Routledge
Taylor & Francis Group

LONDON AND NEW YORK

First published 2006 by Lawrence Erlbaum Associates, Inc., Publishers

Published 2022 by Routledge
2 Park Square, Milton Park, Abingdon, Oxon OX14 4RN
605 Third Avenue, New York, NY 10017

Routledge is an imprint of the Taylor & Francis Group, an informa business

Publisher's Note

The publisher has gone to great lengths to ensure the quality of this reprint
but points out that some imperfections in the original copies may be apparent.

Cover design by Tomai Maridou

**CIP information for this volume may be obtained by contacting the
Library of Congress**

ISBN13: 978-0-8058-5216-5 (hbk)
ISBN13: 978-0-415-64707-6 (pbk)

Contents

V. INDIVIDUAL CHARACTERISTICS AND CULTURE

FOREWORD

C. W. Park
University of Southern California

Image may be researched in many different ways, depending on the angle from which one approaches it. This book offers many different approaches to the research on image—its memory structure, formation and change, the role of mental imagery, the conceptual link between image and experience, and measuring and understanding the role of different types of image, such as country image, individual and celebrity source image, and corporate image. A conceptual structure for research on image is offered here that both includes the topics in this book and identifies future research implications. This structure is arranged in three parts: determinants, role, and outcome of a powerful image. Each part addresses different research issues on image.

The first research issue involves identifying determinants of a powerful image, factors that must be present for a strong positive image to form. These factors serve as guidelines for any image-building communication activities. The second issue concerns the type of relationship a powerful image may offer to consumers. Regardless of its type and contents, it may be useful to identify the most desirable relationship form that a brand image can create between consumers and a brand. The third issue concerns the effects of a powerful image on the perceptual, attitudinal, and behavioral responses of individual customers. So as to justify the marketing investment made in creating a powerful image, firms should strive to create images that have far-reaching impacts on the highest possible rung in the customers' response hierarchies.

It is possible to examine these three parts of image research under the theory of brand attachment. I have been working on this topic in collaboration with Professor Deborah J. MacInnis at the University of Southern California for some time. Attachment theory offers a fresh perspective to image research, expanding its scope and depth as well as enhancing its relevance to both academics and practitioners. I discuss each issue and then describe how brand attachment differs from brand attitude. Differentiation of attachment from brand attitudes is critical given the implied centrality of the latter in extant brand image research.

As to the first research issue, I propose that three factors serve as important ingredients to a powerful positive image, regardless of the nature of that image: (a) trust, (b) expertise and (c) affective brand–self connection. As elaborated later, I postulate they determine the degree of consumers' attachments to a brand. The higher they are, the stronger consumers' attachments to a brand become.

A fundamental basis for a positive brand image is the effort of the firm to create or enhance consumers' trust in a brand. Although in marketing, trust has been understood in terms of both benevolence and competence, I define trust in terms of benevolence and treat competence as a separate construct, as the two are quite different in their core meanings. The more trust a consumer feels toward a brand, the more positively predisposed he or she becomes to that brand. A brand should also possess a certain level of competence or the ability to satisfy a consumer's needs. Hence the stronger the relationship between a brand and its capability to satisfy the needs of the consumer (simply stated, expertise), the more favorably predisposed consumers become to the brand. In fact, the ability to satisfy one's important needs has been identified as the major force for the decision to sustain or dissolve an attachment relationship.

Although trust and expertise are critical for creating an image, they may not be sufficient to exert the strongest possible impact on consumers. For an image to have a strong impact on consumers, the image needs to be self-relevant to the consumer on an affective basis. In other words, an affective connection between the brand and the self is critical. Although trust and expertise may elicit certain affective feelings toward a brand, these feelings are not as strong as those that are also accompanied by a self-relevant emotional connection between a brand and a consumer.

Several means are available for creating the affective brand–self connection. Autographical memories, referencing idiosyncratic or individual events in a person's past, trigger nostalgic feelings, which lead to a brand–self connection. Aesthetics is still another means to create a brand–self connection. Here, the brand–self connection is based on one's appreciation of the aesthetic qualities, attractiveness, and association of the brand with certain emotional feelings. Sexual attractiveness and artistic appreciation of an object are the basis to create affective connection to a brand. Identification is still another way to provide an emotional refuge or safe haven in the sense that it provides reassurance that a given value is admired and respectable. For example, many owners of Harley-Davidson motorcycles report being deeply attached to their Harleys because they resonate the values of freedom and machismo—values that are intrinsic parts of the owners' desired selves.

Whereas trust, expertise, and affective brand–self connection each facilitate a positive brand image, their combination has a synergistic impact on brand image valence. In addition, although trust and expertise are important elements for establishing a strong brand image, the affective brand–self connection seems to be even more important for a brand image to become strong and sustainable. Consider, for example, *Consumer Reports*. We trust its information, and we also highly value its expertise in judging the quality differences among various brands. Yet we do not seem to have developed any strong affective relationship with it or strong affective feelings toward it. Therefore, our image toward *Consumer Reports* appears to lack passion or emotional commitment.

As to the second issue, the kind of relationship an image should establish between a brand (firm) and consumers, I propose that the desired image should create a strong emotional bond with a brand in the minds of consumers. Regardless of what the image is, it must elicit affect-laden and emotionally significant feelings toward a brand in the minds of consumers. The three determinants of a powerful, positive image lead to the formation of strong brand attachment. Attachment is a theoretical construct that has a rich history in psychology, describing one's innate need to develop and sustain an emotional bond with others (Bowlby, 1979; see also Reis & Patrick, 1996 ,for an excellent review). The desire to make strong affectionate bonds with others serves a basic human need, beginning from a child's attachment to the mother and continuing through adulthood, including romantic relationships, kinships, and friendships. In a marketing context, we regard it as a relationship variable between customers and a brand that is based on the functional, psychological and emotional relevance of the brand to customers. For example, consumers may form an attachment to any object that elicits nostalgia, reinforces one's self-identity or desired image, renders a feeling of connectedness to a group through a group membership, or offers sensory (experiential) pleasures. Perhaps the most vivid examples of attachment may be found in our preoccupation with sports teams and celebrities. Emotional attachment is defined as the affectionate bond that a given consumer has with a specific brand. Emotional attachment to a brand varies in intensity or strength, with some consumers exhibiting strong attachments to brands and others exhibiting weak attachment or none at all (see Thomson, MacInnis, & Park, 2005, for conceptual and measurement issues regarding brand attachment).

Finally, as to the third issue, identifying the most desirable effects of a newly created brand image on individual customers' responses, I believe that we need to examine such effects with reference to a consumer response hierarchy, starting from basic responses such as perceptual recognition to higher order behavioral responses, such as paying a price premium for a brand. I propose three hierarchical stages of the customer–brand relationship on the basis of the intensity of attachment. They are the brand preference stage, the brand commitment stage, and the brand investment stage, which correspond to three levels of attachment: weak, moderate, and strong attachment, respectively.

Consumers' attachment intensity to a brand is associated with three hierarchical stages of the customer–brand relationship, from a low level of simple preference to brand to higher levels of commitment to the brand over time to actual investment in the brand. At a low level of attachment, consumers reveal a mere brand preference without necessarily revealing a pattern of stability or commitment. At an intermediate level of attachment intensity, consumers are committed to the brand despite pressures to switch. At a high level of attachment, consumers invest something of themselves (e.g., money, time, reputation) to protect, defend, and promote a brand. The brand investment stage represents the destination stage for any brand. It symbolizes the most successful relationship between customers and a brand. If brand preference, commitment, and investment represent three hierarchical stages of customers' relationship with a brand, it is important to define and provide behavioral indicators of each stage.

Beginning with the brand preference stage, consumers are assumed to have favorable attitudes toward and preference for a brand. Although they purchase a brand, their behavior does not guarantee repeat choice. At the brand commitment stage, consumers have strong attitudes and preferences. The response tendencies at this stage may include loyal patronage, resistance to competing alternatives, and forgiveness of mishaps. Commitment makes individuals more likely to forgive mishaps that occur with the brand to which they are attached. At the brand investment stage, consumers reveal several behavioral response tendencies associated with high levels of attachment. Moderate levels of attachment induce both brand preference and commitment, and at higher levels of emotional attachment consumers may go beyond preference and commitment to make sacrifices and invest something of themselves in the relationship. In the psychology literature, willingness to make sacrifices is characteristic of relationships where emotional attachment is high (van Lange et al., 1997). Brand investment includes time investment (e.g., search), monetary investments (e.g., willingness to pay a price premium), and reputational investments (e.g., word-of-mouth referrals).

Attachment is a theoretical construct that explains the relationship phenomenon that has been central to recent work in marketing (e.g., developing and maintaining relationships with consumers). It is different from the attitude construct. Attachments, as emotion-based responses, have effects above and beyond those of attitudes, as evaluation-based responses. As indicated by Mikulincer, Hirschberger, Nachmias, and Gillath (2001) and Thomson et al. (2005), attitudes represent cold affect whereas attachments include hot affect. Attachments have evaluative properties but also include the property of the relational bond.

In addition to this definitional property, the two constructs seem to differ in their effects on behaviors (see Thomson et al., 2005). As indicated earlier, attachment has strong motivational and behavioral implications. An individual who is highly attached to a person or object tends to be committed to and willing to invest in, protect, and preserve interactions with the attachment object. On the other hand, favorable attitudes do not necessarily imply such strong motivational or behavioral manifestations. The link between attitude and behavior is contingent on a number of situational and dispositional factors and is quite inconsistent. Because attachments are not only evaluative but also emotionally responsive, they have considerable behavioral implications. These implications become highly critical in consumer behavior when brand loyalty, willingness to pay a price premium, willingness to forgive the mistakes, and word of mouth are the ultimate behavioral outcomes for brand managers. In contrast, in the selection of appropriate dependent variables for the effect of persuasive communication, the attitude literature has traditionally limited its focus to attitude change, behavioral intentions, or behavior itself, without further developing the hierarchical stage of behavioral commitment such as brand loyalty, word of mouth, and paying a price premium. I believe that attachment serves as a useful construct to account for the higher order effect of the impact of persuasive communications.

Finally, I reiterate the importance of affective brand–self connection as a critical determinant of attachment. When a brand is highly self-relevant to consumers, particularly when that self-relevance involves hedonic dimensions such as sensory pleasures, aesthetics, or value expressiveness, the attachment construct may become a much more useful construct than attitude in explaining consumers' consumption and purchasing behavior. I therefore suggest that image research be conducted with an eye toward creating, strengthening, and maintaining strong brand attachment.

REFERENCES

Bowlby, J. (1979). *The making and breaking of affectional bonds*. London: Tavistock Publications.

Milkulincer, M., Hirschberger, G., Nachmias, O., & Gillath, O. (2001). The affective component of the secure base schema: Affective priming with representations of proximity maintenance. *Journal of Personality and Social Psychology, 81,* 305–321.

Reis, H. T. and Patrick, B. C., (1996). Attachment and intimacy: Component processes. In E. T. Higgins & A. W. Kruglanski (Eds.), *Social psychology: Handbook of basic principals* (pp. 523–563). New York: Guilford.

Thomson, M., MacInnis, D. J., & Park, C. W., (2005). The ties that bind: Measuring the strength of consumers' emotional attachments to brands. *Journal of Consumer Psychology, 15*(1), 77–91.

van Lange, P. A. M., Rusbult, C. E., Drigotas, S. M., Arriaga, Z. B., Witcher, B. S., & Cox, C. L., (1997). Willingness to sacrifice in close relationships. *Journal of Personality and Social Psychology, 72,* 1373–1395.

PREFACE: INTRODUCTION TO CREATING IMAGES AND THE PSYCHOLOGY OF MARKETING COMMUNICATION

Wei Shan Chin, Lynn R. Kahle, and C. H. Kim

In the age of television, image becomes more important than substance.
—S. I. Hayakawa

Image marketing is one of the fastest growing areas in marketing communications. In the fall of 2003, *Time Magazine* published a special supplement entitled "The Business of Image Marketing." The publication is timely and clearly illustrates the public's growing interest in the making and application of image. Although the emphasis of the supplement was on style, fashion, and design, the concept of image marketing also encompasses brands, individuals, and countries. Image creation provides a unique vehicle for communicating with consumers, one that does not necessarily follow traditional marketing rules. Image creation can also be applied to different areas of interest such as branding of products, organizations, and countries. For businesses, a powerful brand image created by strong brand associations can to some extent influence consumer buying behavior. More important, image has the ability to evoke unique psychological patterns of behavior in consumers and influence the information processing of individuals; hence, this topic is highly relevant to researchers in the area of consumer psychology and marketing communications.

Image is a key concept in consumer psychology and has been studied extensively from different areas within consumer psychology. Although image has been studied extensively, no consensus on the definition of image has emerged. Instead, the concept of image is broad, and there are many ways to conceptualize, categorize, and evaluate image. Image can be described as an abstraction of associations related to a thing, person, or place. Here, it is important to distinguish between visual aspects of image and mental representation of image. In advertising research, image is often characterized as a persuasive form of the visual metaphoric rhetoric by the mind (Scott, 1994). However, in this book, we are explicitly interested in the abstract and mental representation of image, which goes beyond visual information to include other experiences and symbolic benefits. Consumer researchers have long been interested in the information processing and cognitive representation of image, an interest that is evidenced by the many theories on the creation of image and brand image, storage of images in consumers' memory, and other applications of mental imagery in consumers' minds. For example, brand image has been described as a category (Boush, 1993; Boush & Loken, 1991), a schema (Bridges, 1990), and part of an associative memory formulation of brand associations (Keller, 1993). More recently, emphasis on the mental representation and abstract nature of image has increased. For example, Fournier (1998) examined the metaphor of interpersonal relationships of consumers with brands. Thus, we see a shift of research interest moving toward the mental representation and abstract nature of image, one that encompasses many different attributes (concrete and abstract), benefits, and values.

In this book, we embrace the multidimensions of image and approach image as a holistic form of mental and abstract representations in consumers' minds. Drawing upon Keller's (2003) Multidimensionality Model of Brand Knowledge, we approach the study of image in a similar holistic and synergistic manner; however, we expand on his definition of image where he describes it as "visual information, either in concrete or abstract in nature" (p. 596) and propose that his other elements of brand knowledge (i.e., thoughts, experiences, feelings, benefits, and attributes) can also be used to enhance the representation of image. Hence, image is broader and encompasses more abstract and symbolic meanings. This mental representation includes abstract and symbolic elements like thoughts, experiences, attributes (both concrete and abstract), attitudes, values, and other symbolic benefits.

Consumer research insights play a critical role in the understanding of image and consumer behavior. Recently, the growing interest in image by the public and organizations has created a surge in consumer research activity in this area. In personality and social psychology, research activity for image-related findings has increased. The relation among human personality, social identification, and consumer behavior has been widely studied. The personality construct in marketing, in the form of the Interactional Personality Model (Endler, 1983), used psychographics to improve the prediction of consumer-related behavior. In this regard, psychographic characteristics have been defined as "intrinsic psychological sociocultural and behavioral characteristics that reflect how an individual is likely to act in relation to consumption decisions" (Schiffman & Kanuk, 1991, p. 233); however, studies of specific brand personality have only recently emerged. Recently, Aaker (1997) summarized five basic dimensions of personality in an attempt to measure brand personality of consumers. In social psychology, there have been studies on organizational identification (which is the special expression of identification with an organization) and social identification (which is the sense of belonging to certain groups of organizations). Another area of research that is picking up interest is the study of consumer identification with a brand (Kim, Han, & Park, 2001).

Due to the increased managerial relevance and priority placed on branding in recent years, academic research into consumer branding has surged in recent years. Much attention has been devoted recently to the concepts of brand equity (i.e., the net asset of a brand) and brand knowledge (i.e., the combination of brand awareness and brand image of a product; Aaker, 1991; Keller, 1993). A positive brand image increases the brand knowledge of a particular product or service and enhances customer-based equity and satisfaction (Keller, 1993). By enhancing customer satisfaction and loyalty, a positive brand image can prove to be advantageous for companies on a long-term basis. However, in an increasingly networked and competitive marketplace, firms can no longer rely solely on the success of a particular product or service. Companies should continue to use their brand images to differentiate their products and services from other firms and to extend the brand images to new markets. As the cost of entering new markets is increasing, it is important for firms to use brand extension techniques to offset cost and reduce the risk of failure (as brand image is already established in consumers' memories). On a larger scale, brands can also be leveraged to another person, place, thing, or brand (Keller, 2003). By linking their products to other entities as a means of leveraging knowledge, there is increased brand recognition and awareness. Keller (2003) also explained that the extent of leverage knowledge is important (i.e., how well consumers know the product, how meaningful the product is, and the transferability of the knowledge) to create an optimal positioning in consumers' minds. An application of leveraging knowledge can be used for pairing country image and tourism, celebrity image and endorsements, corporate image and sponsorships, and so on.

The purpose of the book is to advance the understanding of the concept of image as it is applied to various areas of interest. This book also serves to meet the growing interest in image-related studies by the public and academics and provides an innovative and holistic approach to the study of image. A significant development in brand image research is the growing importance of brand leveraging strategies to increase brand equity by linking a brand to other entities (Keller, 2003). This book reflects the importance of brand leveraging as the sections cover in-depth discussion on cross-country and tourism images, corporate and sponsorship images, individual and celebrity images, and cultural and social images. Currently, academic literature on image studies is broad, covering multiple areas within consumer psychology and marketing communications. Furthermore, the literature is characterized by diverse empirical findings and conceptual frameworks. This book provides a comprehensive and holistic look at the concept of image: The topics range from theories of image creation to other image studies on a country, corporate, and individual level. The sections cover the major topics currently being debated in image marketing and the psychology of communications. Several new and innovative concepts of image creation are also introduced in this book. In the first section of the book, Boush and Jones introduce a new conceptualization for the synthesis of brand image in a managerial context. Other innovative concepts in image studies, such as the schema correspondence theory and social constructionism perspective, are also discussed in the first section. Interestingly, the rest of the sections can be seen as an application of brand leveraging processes of image. We see how brand image is applied to countries, corporations, individuals, and culture.

This book is primarily intended for academics and scholars (including students) in the interdisciplinary fields of consumer psychology, marketing, and communication. In addition, scholars and professionals interested in image and communications will find this book useful. We are proud to showcase the work of eminent researchers in consumer research from all over the world in this edition. As an added feature, a high percentage of scholars are from universities and professional agencies outside the United States. We are fortunate to have attracted the participation of these leading researchers from Asia and other parts of the world from the Image and Advertising conference held by The Society of Consumer Psychology in Seoul, Korea. This group of researchers is exceptionally international: The researchers hail from diverse countries such as South Korea, United States of America, Japan, Taiwan, Australia, England, New Zealand, India, and Singapore. In addition, these researchers (who include academics and practitioners) are also multi-disciplined and wide-ranging in the scope of their work and their journeys of discovery bring us through various aspects of consumer mental imagery, from country image evaluation to individual values and culture.

OVERVIEW OF CONTENTS

This book is divided into five sections, with individual sections focusing on various aspects of image.

Part I—Theories of Image

This section provides an overview of the theoretical and conceptual frameworks on the mental representation and creation of image from various perspectives. The authors discuss the creation, processes, and constructs of mental imagery and seek to understand image and consumer behavior. The chapters illuminate past studies in the particular area of image study and present innovative new conceptualizations and approaches to the study of mental representation of image.

Part II—Country Image

Globalization of markets and an increasing networked world have emphasized the need for the study of effective country image and cross-country implications for tourism, products, and people. Authors in this section discuss various aspects of country image research, such as measurement and process of a country image, destination image and tourism implications, and evaluation of country products. Academic literature on recent country image related findings (such as COO effects) are also discussed in detail. More important, the chapters cover new approaches to the conceptualization, processes, and measurement of country image and the impact on image-related consumer behavior.

Part III—Individual and Celebrity Source Image

Cornwell (1995, p. 15) described sponsorship marketing as the "… orchestration and implementation of marketing activities for the purpose of building and communicating an association (link) to a sponsorship." In the last two or three decades, the practice of commercial sponsorship by companies for marketing programmes has increased at an exponential rate. In accordance with the growth in interest, research into the area of commercial sponsorship has surged. By leveraging on a successful celebrity brand and establishing a good fit between product and brand (i.e., "the celebrity"), marketers can improve the brand image and appeal of their products or services. This section discusses the leveraging of individuals (i.e., celebrities, models, etc) to endorse products for advertising purposes. Also, topics on celebrity source image (i.e., the process and implications of endorsements for the celebrity and endorser), cross-cultural studies on advertisements, and individuals and individual source expertise are discussed.

Part IV—Corporate Image

A positive and superior corporate image is important for enhancing the competitive advantage of any organization or business. Corporate image is multi-dimensional in nature: There are multiple stakeholders, and corporate image can be observed from different perspectives such as from that of consumers, employees, or other shareholders. Furthermore, corporate image can be enhanced by sponsorship marketing, and there is a positive effect if the sponsorship is valid to the brand. In this section, the first two chapters examine the conceptualization of corporate image from various stakeholders' perspectives (e.g., customers, employees, shareholders, etc). The last chapter provides a new theoretical framework based on information processing for the conceptualization of corporate sponsorship.

Part V—Individual Characteristics and Culture

Image can be related to individual characteristics and culture in a number of ways. For example, personal values and culture of an individual can affect the individual's perception of a brand and influence consumer behavior in purchase decisions of various products or services. This section covers the implications of individual characteristics and culture in consumer buying and consumption behavior in various settings. This section also discusses cross-cultural studies on individual characteristics (i.e., individual brand personality), cultures of different groups of individuals, and consumption patterns in different countries.

PART I: THEORIES OF IMAGE

In the first chapter, "A strategy-based framework for extending brand image research," Boush and Jones present an original framework that synthesizes previous conceptual frameworks and empirical research relevant to managing brand image effectively. Boush and Jones analyze the information processing of brand image as it relates to brand image content and structure and propose that a synthesized framework for brand image is more effective in utilizing the benefits of brand image for all stakeholders. This model is unique in the consideration of the strategic functions of the brand for all stakeholders and hence provides important managerial relevance for the research. This chapter illuminates past research on brand image conceptualization and provides a useful reference for additional research on brand image frameworks.

In the second chapter, "Measuring prototypicality of product categories and exemplars: Implications of schema correspondence theory," Brannon and Brock extend their well-known work in the schema correspondence theory (Brannon & Brock, 1994) to demonstrate that people represent products, brands, and advertisements as fuzzy (i.e., poor representative) and prototypical (i.e., good representative) exemplars of personality constructs. Using a new measure of prototypicality, they found that gearing persuasive appeals to the type of product proved successful for prototypical products. Their research contributes to the understanding of personality and schema construct of products and brand image in the academic sense. A practical inference for advertisers is that gearing certain persuasive factors is beneficial when representing certain product categories.

In the third chapter, "Emergence and change of consumer product image in social constructionism perspective," Junko develops a framework for ethnomethodologically informed social constructionism in the legitimacy of consumption and investigates methods in which people believe in the legitimacy o f a product and actualize it by developing and keeping established practices. He builds his case by studying the Christmas cake consumption phenomenon in Japan and finds no realistic propriety for products or Christmas cake in Japan; it is the "continuous accomplishments of actors" that constitute product image or "Christmas" image in Japan. His findings give companies and marketers practical advice on the changing realities of product cycles and the importance of communicating with consumers.

In the fourth chapter, "Understanding the role of mental imagery in persuasion: A cognitive resources model analysis," Mazzocco and Brock propose a new model (called Cognitive Resources Model or CRM) of attentional resources in the processing of imagery in persuasive communications. Utilizing the resource capacity of the processing system (i.e., the central executive), the CRM is effective in predicting some attitude change in the processing of a persuasive message. Their findings illuminate existing research on persuasive communications and contribute to the further understanding of the complex effects of mental imagery to consumer attitude change.

In the fifth chapter, "From image to experience," Schmitt explores the important concept of experiences in consumer behavior. Although prevalent in advertising, Schmitt finds that very little attention has been paid to the use of experiential appeals and affects. The author proposes a new holistic and adaptive approach to experiences; by embracing the integrated nature of experiences (from the use of the mind and body processing), he distinguishes mind modules (i.e., sense, feel, think, and act) that can create unique experiences. His discussion on the conceptualization of experiences provides critical insights to the world of experiences and paves the way for more research on the processes and determinants of experiences.

PART II: COUNTRY IMAGE

In the first chapter, "Building a national image with words: The role of word-of-mouth ("WOM") in establishing Korea's international image," Na, Son, Kim, and Marshall explore the power of WOM as a vehicle to effect the image of a nation. The authors find a clear mandate for the power of WOM and find that WOM also varies cross-culturally. Their findings demonstrate the importance of WOM in country and tourism image. The chapter also provides a review of relevant COO effects, WOM literature, and emerging tourism literature to support their findings.

In the second chapter, "Measuring country image: The case of S. Korea," Cho and Suh attempt to measure 16 national brands, including S. Korea, and examine the characteristics of S. Korean national brand. The authors also approach the study of a national brand in a slightly different manner from the conventional products and consumer manner, choosing to use three components (i.e., national competitiveness, psychological proximity, and national brand strategy) for a more effective and comprehensive evaluation. By adopting a macro and holistic approach, this study strives to measure the real value of national brands.

In the third chapter, "The social construction of destination image – A New Zealand film example," Larsen and George bring us on an enlightening and fascinating journey to "Middle Earth" or rather, New Zealand, to study the impact of film on destination image of a country. Larsen and George point out that despite the emergence of widely studied literature on destination image, no theoretically based conceptual framework remains. A new perspective, which views destination image as socially constructed (Young, 1999), has recently emerged. Larsen and George identify five further topics of interest within the destination image in Gallarza et al's (2002) conceptual model of destination image and use the New Zealand film example to illustrate their findings and also the social construction perspective in general. Although they only performed an exploratory study, their findings on the impact of film in New Zealand provide supporting evidence for Gallarza's model and also for the social construction perspective.

The fourth chapter, "Chinese consumers' evaluation of hybrid country of origin products: Effects of decomposed elements of country of origin, brand name, and consumers' ethnocentrism" by Jung and Kau, is a comprehensive and in-depth study of hybrid products, which is an emerging topic in country-of-origin (COO) literature. Hybrid products are the combination of various processes such as products manufactured in one country with key components sourced in another. This study examines the decomposed elements of COO and brand name, together with the effect of ethnocentrism on the evaluation of hybrid products from a developing country. Overall, this complex and exhaustive study contributes to COO study in myriad ways, from brand image effects on product evaluation, ethnocentrism effects, and COO decomposed elements.

PART III: INDIVIDUAL AND CELEBRITY SOURCE EFFECTS

In the first chapter, "Managing celebrities as brands: Impact of endorsements on celebrity image," Parulekar and Goa examine the applicability of various celebrity source models to determine the effect of an endorsed brand on the image and brand equity of a celebrity. This focus on the celebrity viewpoint in endorsements is a sharp contrast to previous research on celebrity source effects, which typically evaluated the value-add of celebrity endorsers and impact of celebrity endorsers on advertised products or services. In this regard, celebrities are acknowledged as brands in their own rights and having their individual brand personalities. This insightful study provides a basis for determining the right fit between a celebrity brand and the endorsed product or service, which is crucial for the success of celebrity endorsed products or services and changes the way we approach celebrity source effects.

In the second chapter, "A cultural third-person effect: Actual and expected effects of source expertise among individualists and collectivists," Yoon and Vargas review third-person effects in the context of source expertise in advertising and persuasion. Building on previous research that suggests that differences in cultural orientation influence patterns of behavior, this study explores the cross-cultural differences (i.e., collectivists vs. individualistic values) in the persuasive communication context and provides implications for nations and individuals in the use of persuasive communication.

In the third chapter, "Sports celebrity image: A critical evaluation of the utility of Q scores," K. Kahle and L. Kahle investigate the effectiveness of the Q-score system in predicting athlete celebrity endorsement success and propose an alternative method of evaluating celebrity endorsement success. The authors argue that the traditional Q-ratings are obsolete and propose a second system for evaluating athlete celebrity endorsement success based on a more effective match-up hypothesis (of desired and actual image maps of optimal market positions) and other critical factors. In conclusion, the authors propose that this new system, together with Q-ratings, can provide the most effective means of testing athlete celebrity endorsement success. Their findings have specific practical implications for sport celebrity endorsers and the method by which sport endorsements are currently being evaluated.

In the fourth chapter, "A Range of female beauties: A cross-cultural analysis of cosmetics TV commercials," Han and Gregorio provide an interesting review of female beauty depictions and advertising on a cross-cultural level by examining the cultural gatekeeping functions inherent in advertising creators' selections of female models. The study showed similar patterns in the characterization of female beauty on a macro level. However, on a micro level, there were significant differences on smaller culture-specific variations in beauty patterns. Overall, this study contributes to the conceptualization of beauty found in advertisements and cross-cultural impact on beauty images, both topics that have received little research attention in previous times. A practical application will be for global marketers to examine carefully the specific cultural values that influence beauty definitions in local markets.

PART IV: CORPORATE IMAGE

In the first chapter, "Well-matched employees make customers happy: Effects of brand-employee congruence," Yi and La explore the effects of brand-employee congruence on employee satisfaction (ES) and customer satisfaction (CS). A significant contribution to brand personality studies, this chapter is the first to examine the personality congruence between employees and the corporate brand thoroughly, as previous research on employee research focused on employees' personalities, without regard to corporate branding. Furthermore, the empirical research showed that well-matched employees with personality of company can enhance both ES and CS.

In the second chapter, "Managing the multi-dimensionality of corporate image: From the stakeholders' multi-layered experience perspective," Kim and Suh review corporate image from a strategic perspective and attempt to conceptualize corporate image as an established, managerial concept based on stakeholder management (i.e., consumers/ public). The relation between overall corporate image and consumers'/public's multilayered personal experience are explored in this study, and empirical results suggest that particular attributes of corporate image can be influenced by the multiple facets of consumer experience with the situations of the company. Hence, this study demonstrates the importance of considering the holistic multidimensions of stakeholders' experience and identities when determining and implementing a successful corporate image for the company. The chapter also provides an in-depth discussion of the multidimensionality of corporate image and several theories on the conceptualization of corporate image.

In the third chapter, "Conceptualizing sponsorship: An item and relational account," Weeks, Cornwell, and Humphreys attempt to fill a void in the current perspective on sponsorship research, that is, the lack of a comprehensive psychological conceptualization of how sponsorship works to affect its audience. Based on

Einstein and Hunt's (1980) relational and item theory, the authors develop a theoretical framework of how sponsorship operates when used to achieve image-related and awareness objectives and to provide guidance for enhancing sponsorship practice. The study found that the perceived semantic relation between the sponsor and sponsee is crucial, as is the item-specific or relational specific of the relationship, as these affect sponsorship effectiveness. Thus, the use of item and relational information framework will strengthen the existing theoretical framework for future sponsorship research.

PART V: INDIVIDUAL CHARACTERISTICS AND CULTURE

In the first chapter, "Values, brands, and image," Kim, Boush, Marquardt, and Kahle provide an insightful study of values as an important tool to further the understanding of brand image and consumer patterns. As personal value is typically one of the factors contributing to image, the connection of a brand image to a strong consumer value is important. Hence, the concept of branding is discussed in terms of its relation to two key related concepts: namely, an image and a personal (or social) value. The effects of values and relationships are applied to the brand extension concept and various consumer models. Overall, this study contributes conceptually to Keller's (2003) holistic model of brand knowledge and image by expanding on the various relations of image, values, and branding. There are also practical implications of values and image, as discussed in consumer models.

In the second chapter, "'Image' attributes of automobiles and their influence on purchase price decisions," Powers expands on current consumer behavior research that shows that image attributes of products or the purchase environment can affect the consumer decision-making process and provides a real-life empirical study to test the relation between image attributes (e.g., color, engine size of car) and price in a consumer behavior context (i.e., automobile industry). As there have been few studies that explicitly investigated the relation between emotion/affect and price, especially with real market empirical tests performed, this study will provide much needed insight into the conceptual-level relation between emotion/affect and the consumer decision-making process. The result of the study shows that image attributes can be powerful tools for marketing strategies for automobile sales. The real market validation and results also provide strong implications for automobile and consumer products managers.

In the third chapter, "Assessing the influence of cultural values on consumer susceptibility to social pressure for conformity: Self-image enhancing motivations versus information searching motivation," Jung reviews the effect of certain cultural values in moderating the social conformity impact. Although social conformity is a widespread phenomenon, there is a current lack of studies on consumer conformity under social pressure. This chapter also provides extensive review on social psychology and marketing research on social conformity, from Asch's (1951) experiments to current research on the topic. In addition, this chapter also provides managerial implications for adapting to social conformity process in a certain cultural region.

In the fourth chapter, "The impact of media and culture on the consumption values of women in China and Taiwan," Liao and Bei explore the role of culture, societal norms, and mass media on the traditional Confucian values and the consequential impact of related consumption values for the women in China and Taiwan. Liao and Bei also provide an in-depth and insightful discussion on the economic change, social change, and foreign influence in the two countries in the past several decades and the consequential impact on the culture, values, and attitudes of Chinese women in the two countries. The chapter provides managerial implications based on the findings on the influence of mass media on consumption values.

In the fifth chapter, "Cross-cultural comparisons of a brand personality in print media: The case of mainland China and Taiwan," Shen, Bei, and Wu compare the brand personalities exhibited in print media for two Chinese cultures and the implications for different brand personalities. The authors found that excitement and competence dimensions are more greatly represented than other dimensions for both cultures. In recent times, there has been an increased interest in the concept of brand personality, and research has shown cultural differences in brand personality (Aaker, 1997). This study extends previous research on cross-cultural differences and provides fresh evidence for the case.

REFERENCES

Aaker, D. A. (1991). *Managing brand equity.* New York: The Free Press.

Aaker, J. L. (1997). Dimensions of brand personality. *Journal of Marketing Research, 34,* 347–356.

Asch, S. E. (1951). Effects of group pressure upon the modification and distortion of judgment. In H. Guetzkow (Ed.), *Groups, leadership and men* (pp. 177–190). Pittsburgh, PA: Carnegie Mellon Press.

Boush, D. M. (1993). Brands as categories. In D. A. Aaker & A. Biel (Eds.), *Brand equity and advertising* (pp. 299–312). Hillsdale, NJ: Lawrence Erlbaum Associates.

Boush, D. M., & Loken, B. (1991). A process-tracing study of brand extension evaluation. *Journal of Marketing Research, 28,* 16–28.

Brannon, L., & Brock, T. (1994). Test of schema correspondence theory: Effects of matching an appeal to actual, ideal, and product "selves." In E. M. Clark, T. C. Brock, & D. W. Stewart (Eds.), *Attention, attitude, and affect in response to advertising* (pp. 169–188). Hillsdale, NJ: Lawrence Erlbaum Associates.

Bridges, S. A. (1990). *A schema unification model of brand extensions.* Unpublished doctoral dissertation, Stanford University, Palo Alto. CA.

Cornwell, T. B. (1995). Sponsorship-linked marketing development. *Sport Marketing Quarterly, 4*(4), 13–24.

Einstein, G. O., & Hunt, R. R. (1980). Levels of processing and organization: Addictive effects of individual-item and relational processing. *Journal of Experimental Psychology: Human Learning & Memory, 6,* 588–598.

Endler, N. S. (1983). Interactionism: A personality model, but not yet a theory. In M. Page (Ed.), *Nebraska symposium on motivation 1982: Personality—current theory and research* (pp. 155–200). Lincoln, NE: University of Nebraska Press.

Fournier, S. M. (1998). Consumers and their brands: Developing relationship theory in consumer research. *Journal of Consumer Research, 24,* 343–373.

Gallarza, M. G., Saura, I. G., & Garcia, H. C. (2002). Destination image: Towards a conceptual framework. *Annals of Tourism Research, 29,* 56–78.

Hunt, R. R., & Einstein, G. O. (1981). Relational and item-specific information in memory. *Journal of Verbal Learning & Verbal Behavior, 17,* 175–187.

Keller, K. L. (1993). Conceptualizing, measuring, and managing customer-based brand equity. *Journal of Marketing, 57,* 1–22.

Keller, K. L. (2003). Brand synthesis: The multidimensionality of brand knowledge. *Journal of Consumer Research, 29,* 595–600.

Kim, C. K., Han, D., & Park, S. B. (2001). The effect of brand personality and brand identification on brand loyalty: Applying the theory of social identification. *Japanese Psychological Research, 43,* 195–206.

Schiffman, L. G, & Kanuk L. L. (1991). *Consumer behavior.* Englewood Cliffs, NJ: Prentice-Hall.

Scott, L. M. (1994). Images in advertising: The need for a theory of visual rhetoric. *Journal of Consumer Research, 21,* 252–273.

Young, M. (1999). The social construction of tourist places. *Australian Geographer, 30,* 373–389.

ABOUT THE AUTHORS

Lien-Ti Bei is a Professor at the Department of Business Administration, National Chengchi University. In 1988, Lien-Ti Bei graduated from National Taiwan University with a Bachelor of Science degree in Psychology. She earned her Master's and PhD degrees in consumer behavior from Purdue University. Immediately after completing her doctoral program, she took the position of Associate Professor at National Chengchi University in August 1995. In the years of teaching, she has won three Excellent Teaching Awards voted by students. Lien-Ti also devotes herself to research. Three Outstanding Research Awards from The National Science Council in Taiwan and more than 50 Chinese and English journal articles and conference presentations are evidence of her on-going devotion to research. Her research interests are consumer information processing, cross-cultural comparisons of consumer behavior, branding strategies, and brand personality. Lien-Ti is now also the Director of the Office of Student Affairs, College of Commerce, National Chengchi University.

David M. Boush is Associate Professor of Marketing at the University of Oregon. Research interests include trust, brand equity, consumer socialization, and response to advertising. His articles have appeared in such outlets as the *Journal of Consumer Research, Journal of Marketing Research, Journal of Business Research,* and the *Journal of International Business Studies.* He is a member of the American Marketing Association, the Society for Consumer Psychology, the Association for Consumer Research, and the Academy of Marketing Science. He is also a former marketing research analyst for Hallmark Cards. His visiting appointments include a stint at ESSEC, and a series of e-commerce classes for UC-Berkeley extension. He currently serves on the editorial board of the *Journal of the Academy of Marketing Sciences* and has served as Chair of the Department of Marketing at the University of Oregon.

Laura A. Brannon is Associate Professor of Psychology at Kansas State University, Manhattan, Kansas. She received her doctorate in social psychology from The Ohio State University. She has published articles and chapters on a variety of topics on the psychology of persuasion, including how consumers process scarcity appeals, counterattitudinal messages, and health communications. Some of this research has appeared in journals such as the *Journal of Consumer Psychology, Personality and Social Psychology Bulletin, Psychonomic Bulletin and Review,* and

Health Communication. Her research has been funded by NSF, NIMH, and the USDA. Brannon's ongoing research programs focus on persuasion and compliance/social influence theories. She has extended her research on the basic processes of persuasion and compliance to various applied areas. Much of her current research addresses social marketing and applies marketing and social influence techniques to the amelioration of social problems, in particular, to the fostering of health-promoting behaviors.

Timothy C. Brock is Professor of Psychology at The Ohio State University, Columbus, Ohio. He has published articles and chapters on a variety of topics in the psychology of persuasion, including effects of salesperson–consumer similarity on purchasing behavior, the role of cognitive responses in determining acceptance of persuasive messages, and the effect of cognitive tuning on attitude change persistence. His books include *Order of Presentation in Persuasion* (with C. I. Hovland et al.), *Psychological Foundations of Attitudes* (with A. G. Greenwald and T. M. Ostrom), *Cognitive Responses in Persuasion* (with R. E. Petty and T. M. Ostrom), *Attention, Attitude, and Affect in Response to Advertising* (with E. Clark and D. Stewart), and *Persuasion: Psychological Insights and Perspectives* (with S. Shavitt). He is a past president of the Society for Consumer Psychology and a recipient of the Society's Distinguished Scientist Award.

Wei Shan Chin received her degree in Psychology (Honors) from the University of Michigan, Ann Arbor, where she earned the Muenzer Memorial Award for Outstanding Psychology Honors student. After graduation, she worked in a Singapore-listed company, Health Management International, as a business executive. A research enthusiast, she has a diverse interest in all forms of business research.

Dong-Sung Cho is Professor of Strategy, International Business and Management Design at Seoul National University. He received a doctoral degree from Harvard Business School in 1976 and worked at Gulf Oil's Planning Group before joining SNU in 1978. He was a visiting professor at HBS, INSEAD, Helsinki School of Economics, the University of Tokyo, University of Michigan, Duke, and Peking University. Among the 42 books he published are *The General Trading Company* by Lexington Books (1986), *Tiger Technology: the Rise of the Semiconductor Industry in Asia* by Cambridge University Press (1999), and *From Adam Smith to Michael Porter: Evolution of Competitiveness Theory* by World Scientific (2000). His papers appeared in *California Management Review, International Journal of Advertising, Journal of Business Research, Journal of World Business, Long Range Planning, Organization Science,* and *Research Policy.* He was Dean of the College of Business Administration, SNU, 2001–2003, and Dean of the Graduate School of International and Area Studies, SNU, 1999–2001. He has been on the Board of

Directors at 15 multinational companies and research organizations. He is Honorary Consul General of the Government of Finland in Korea.

T. Bettina Cornwell (PhD, The University of Texas) is Professor of Marketing in the UQ Business School at the University of Queensland. She was formerly Professor of Marketing in the Fogelman College of Business and Economics at the University of Memphis in the United States. Her research focuses on promotion and consumer behavior, especially with regard to international and public policy issues. Articles on the topics of consumer behavior and sponsorship-linked marketing have recently appeared in the *Journal of Advertising, Journal of Advertising Research, Journal of Consumer Marketing, Journal of Consumer Affairs*, and the *Journal of Public Policy and Marketing*.

Federico de Gregorio is an Assistant Professor of Advertising in the College of Communication and Information Sciences at the University of Alabama. He has worked as both a marketing analyst and a copywriter. His research interests are in product placement, implicit cognitive processes, and emotional appeals in advertising.

Kyoo-Hoon Han is a doctoral candidate in the Grady College of Journalism and Mass Communication at the University of Georgia. He completed his Master's degree at the University of Missouri–Columbia. Before studying at graduate programs in the United States, he worked as a TV commercial planner and producer at Korad, Ogilvy & Mather, one of the major South Korean advertising agencies. His clients included Daewoo Motors, Daewoo Electronics, Julia Cosmetics, Haitai Confectionery, and Kumho Tires.

Michael S. Humphreys majored in Psychology, receiving his BA from Reed College in 1964 and PhD in 1970 from Stanford University. After serving on the faculty of the University of British Columbia and Northwestern University, he moved to the University of Queensland in 1979. In 1990 he was elected as a Fellow in the Academy of Social Sciences in Australia. He is currently Professor of Psychology and Director of the Key Centre for Human Factors and Applied Cognitive Psychology. He has published widely in the areas of human memory and attention including work on a) how to link individual differences and motivational states to human performance, b) the complexity of memory representations, c) the separation of current and prior memories, d) the creation of false memories, e) the role of cues in short-term memory, and f) the implications of connectionist models for human memory.

Scott M. Jones (PhD in Marketing, University of Oregon) is an Assistant Professor of Marketing at Clemson University in South Carolina. His research interests include how consumers perceive and interpret brands and brand partnerships, the marketing of sport, and entrepreneurship.

Heonsoo Jung is Assistant Professor of Marketing at School of Business, Konkuk University. He received a PhD in marketing from New York University and a MS from the School of Statistics at Stanford University. He received an honorary doctorate from New York University. His research interests are in marketing engineering, high-tech marketing, and international marketing, and he is actively engaged in research on them. Professor Jung's consulting clients include companies such as Samsung Electronics and LG Electronics.

Kwon Jung is currently an Associate Professor at the KDI School of Public Policy & Management in Korea. He received his PhD in marketing from the University of Illinois at Urbana–Champaign in 1996. He taught at the National University of Singapore before he joined the KDI School in 2002. His research and teaching interests include marketing/business research, cross-cultural consumer behavior, consumer lifestyles, and new product development & brand management. His research publications have appeared in the international and regional journals including *Psychology & Marketing, Journal of Cross-Cultural Psychology, Journal of International Marketing, Asia-Pacific Journal of Management*, and many international conference proceedings. He also co-authored the book, *Understanding Singaporeans: Values, Lifestyles, Aspirations and Consumption Behaviors* (2004).

Kevin E. Kahle is a student at the University of Oregon and works as a business consultant based in Eugene, Oregon.

Lynn R. Kahle holds an endowed chair, the James Warsaw Professorship of Marketing, at the University of Oregon. He spent the 2004–2005 academic year on sabbatical as a visiting professor of Marketing at Singapore Management University. Topics of his research include social adaptation, values, and sports marketing. He has published more than 150 scholarly articles. His books include *Social Values and Social Change, Marketing Management, Values, Lifestyles, and Psychographics, Sports Marketing and the Psychology of Marketing Communications*, and *Euromarketing and the Future*. He has served as President of the Society for Consumer Psychology, President of the City of Eugene Human Rights program, and Chair of the Department of Marketing at the University of Oregon. He was Founding Director of the Warsaw Sports Marketing Center, which *Sports Illustrated* (Oct. 7, 2002) called the "best sports management school." He served as Editor of *Sport Marketing Quarterly*. A recent ASA study classified him as one of the 50 most frequently cited marketing professors.

Ah-Keng Kau is a professorial fellow with the NUS Business School, National University of Singapore, and the Deputy Director of NUS Entrepreneurship Center. He received his PhD in business administration from London Graduate School of Business Studies, U.K. He has done and supervised many studies on services marketing. He has published extensively in various international journals, including the *Journal of Marketing Research, International Marketing Review, Journal of Business Ethics, Internal Journal of Small Business, Journal of International Consumer Marketing, Tourism Management, Psychology and Marketing, Journal of Travel Research* and *Social Indicators Research*. Presently, he is on the editorial advisory boards of *Management and Development, Journal of Asia Pacific Marketing*, and *Singapore Management Review*. He has also jointly authored three books: *Values and Lifestyles of Singaporeans: A Marketing Perspective* (1991), *Seven Faces of Singaporeans: Their Values, Aspirations and Lifestyles* (1998), and *Understanding Singaporeans: Values, Lifestyles, Aspirations and Consumption Behaviors* (2004).

Chung-Hyun Kim (PhD in marketing, University of Oregon) is professor of marketing/advertising at Sogang University, Seoul, Korea. His major research interests include integrated marketing communications, advertising, brand management, and consumer behavior. He has consulted with several corporations including SK Telecom, POSCO, and ad agencies in Korea. He is a former editor of the *Korean Journal of Advertising*.

Woo-Sung Kim received his undergraduate degree in English education from Seoul National University, South Korea. He received two masters' degrees in psychology and business administration from the University of Missouri and his PhD degree in marketing from the University of Oregon. He has been an assistant professor at Youngsan University, S. Korea, and is now the chair of the Department of Marketing. He has taught numerous courses including Consumer Behavior, Marketing Research, Marketing Communication, Service Marketing, Marketing Principles, Special Seminar in Marketing Management, and Research Methods in Business at the University of Oregon and Youngsan University. He published articles in *Journal of Consumer Psychology, Korean Journal of Consumer Studies*, and *Korean Journal of Consumption Culture*. His research interests are in brand management, consumer decision making, advertising effects, sports marketing and consumer behavior, and experiential marketing.

Suna La teaches at the department of management at Korea National Open University. She received her PhD in marketing from Seoul National University. Her work has appeared in *Psychology & Marketing, Service Industries Journal, Korean Marketing Review*, and *Korean Journal of Consumer Studies*. Her current research interests include brand personality, customer loyalty, dimensions of service quality, and internal branding.

Gretchen Larsen is a Lecturer in Marketing at Bradford University School of Management. Before joining the School of Management, Gretchen was a lecturer at the University of Otago, in New Zealand, where she also completed her PhD on the symbolic consumption of music. She developed and tested a model depicting the relation among the consumer's self-concept, the symbolic properties of music and the consumption context. Gretchen continues to develop her interest in music and arts consumption, alongside other research interests including consumer behavior, symbolic consumption, film and destination image, consumer policy and interpretive methods.

Tsai-Ju Liao is an assistant professor in the Department of International Business, Providence University. In 1996, she graduated from National Chengchi University with a Bachelor of Business Administration degree in statistics. She earned her MBA degree from National Central University. Her research interests include marketing, international business management, and strategic management. She has presented seven Chinese and English conference papers.

Adam Marquardt is a Marketing PhD student in the Charles H. Lundquist College of Business at the University of Oregon. He obtained his MBA from the University of Tennessee at Knoxville, with concentrations in marketing, integrated value chain management, and sports management. His research interests include entrepreneurial value proposition creation, self-image and brand image congruence, and the building of customer relationships through brand imagery and affiliation. He has had conference proceedings and presentations accepted at AMA and AMS.

Roger Marshall is Associate Professor of Marketing at Nanyang Business School, Nanyang Technological University in Singapore.

Philip J. Mazzocco is currently a PhD candidate in social psychology and a Lecturer in psychology at The Ohio State University, Columbus, Ohio. His dissertation, for which he was awarded the American Psychological Association Dissertation Research Award, examines factors that moderate the impact of text-elicited mental imagery on attitude change. Generally, his research interests lie in the areas of social influence and judgment and decision making. He is co-authoring a book summarizing and integrating work on the psychology of scarcity (with Timothy C. Brock and Geoff F. Kaufman).

WoonBong Na is a Professor of international business at Kyunghee University in Seoul, Korea.

C. W. Park is Joseph A. DeBell Professor of Marketing. Prior to joining the Marshall School of Business, Professor Park was Albert Wesley Frey Distinguished Professor of Marketing at the Katz School of Business at the University of Pittsburgh (1979–1997). He holds a BA degree in German language and literature from Seoul National University in Korea and an MS and PhD in Business Administration from the University of Illinois. Professor Park is an editorial board member of the *Journal of Marketing* and *Journal of Consumer Research* and a member of the board of advisors of *Journal of Market-Focused Management*. He has published numerous articles in *Journal of Marketing Research, Journal of Consumer Research*, and *Journal of Marketing*. His works have also appeared in many other journals, including *Organizational Behavior and Human Performance, Journal of Advertising, Journal of Consumer Marketing*, and *Current Issues and Research in Advertising*. His current research interests include the conceptual- measurement model of brand equity, mental budgeting of time and money, identifying extension boundary-breaking strategies in the brand extension context, and developing brand fortification strategies through brand extensions. Professor Park has conducted research in the consumer behavior area, concentrating on individual and dyadic decision making and choice, information processing, marketing communications, social influence, and branding decisions. Professor Park is internationally acclaimed and widely recognized as one of the most frequently cited researchers in the field of consumer behavior. He was an advisor for Samsung Corporation for many years, offering consulting services in marketing and corporate strategy issues. Professor Park co-authored *Marketing Management* (Dryden Press, 1987), with Dr. Gerald Zaltman from Harvard University. In 1987 he was the recipient of the Alpha Kappa Psi award for his article, which appeared in *Journal of Marketing*. Professor Park teaches marketing management and promotion strategies at the MBA level and marketing strategy and consumer behavior at the doctoral level. Since 1991, he also has taught marketing strategies to Samsung executives in the Samsung Executive Education Program.

Ajit Arun Parulekar is an associate professor of marketing at the Goa Institute of Management in India. He has previously worked as a brand manager in the pharmaceutical industry specializing in new product launches. His research interests focus on measurement issues related to brands and studying the impact of marketing communications on aspects of brand equity. He is also a member of the American Marketing Association.

Keiko I. Powers is the Senior Director, Statistical Analysis at Power Information Network, an affiliate of J. D. Power and Associates. She obtained her PhD degree in quantitative psychology/psychometrics from University of California, Los Angeles, in 1990. After completing her PhD degree, she worked at UCLA Anderson School of Management as an Associate Researcher conducting various academic and marketing research projects in consumer behavior, market response modeling, and public policy. Her recent academic research interests focus on application of advanced statistical approaches, such as multivariate time series modeling, correspondence analysis, and general linear modeling, to various consumer behavior topics. In particular, she has been investigating psychological and behavioral aspects of consumers' experience with automobile purchases. She has also been conducting research on sampling and projection methodology for the automobile industry.

Preety Raheja works with Sapient Corporation in Gurgaon in India as an HR professional. She finished her MBA from Goa Institute of Management in 2003. Prior to that she worked as an IT journalist for two years with Dataquest magazine. Preety lives with her parents, younger sister, and dog in Gurgaon (New Delhi suburb).

Yung-Cheng Shen is an assistant professor of Yuan-ze University, Taiwan. Having obtained the doctoral degree in cognitive psychology from Columbia University in New York in 1997, Yung-Cheng has been working at universities and marketing consulting firms since then. His major research interests are in branding, consumer decision making and attitude change. Specific topics include consumer evaluations of brand extensions, assimilation and contrast effects in branding and advertising. He also teaches consumer behavior, marketing research, and marketing management for undergraduate as well as MBA and EMBA programs.

Youngsoek Son is Associate Professor, Department of Advertisement and Public Relations, Hallym University, S. Korea.

Taewon Suh has been teaching at Texas State University since 2003. He received his degrees from Sogang University in Communication and from Saint Louis University in International Business & Marketing. His teaching and research interests span marketing communications, international marketing, and corporate strategy. He has published 14 research articles in academic journals such as *Journal of International Business Studies, Journal of Marketing Communications, Journal of Supply Chain Management*, and *International Marketing Review*, among others.

Yong-Gu Suh is Associate Professor of Marketing and Retailing at Sookmyung Women's University in Seoul. He received a doctoral degree from Oxford University in 1996 and worked for KIET (Korea Institute for Industrial Economics and Trade) as a research fellow before he joined the University. He has written five books, all in Korean, including *Mini Skirt Marketing* (2004) and *Creative Marketing Strategy* (2003). His papers appeared in *Journal of Consumer Marketing* and *Journal of International Consumer Marketing*. He is currently directing the brand-new Le Cordon Bleu–Sookmyung MBA program and has been a marketing advisor committee member for Hyundai–Kia Motors since 2002.

Patrick T. Vargas received his PhD in Social Psychology from The Ohio State University in 1997. He spent one year as a post-doctoral fellow at the University of New South Wales, and has been at the University of Illinois, Urbana–Champaign, since 1998. He has appointments in the Departments of Advertising, Psychology, and the Institute of Communications Research. His primary research interests are implicit attitude measurement, attitude–behavior relations, stereotyping and prejudice, and social cognition.

Clinton S. Weeks is currently a PhD candidate at the University of Queensland Business School and School of Psychology, in Australia. He completed undergraduate degrees in Arts and Business Management at the University of Queensland. His research interests are in the area of cognitive psychology (primarily memory and information processing) and marketing (primarily sponsorship-linked marketing).

Chih-Yun Wu is a PhD student in the Department of Business Administration, National Chengchi University. She earned her MBA degree from the same university and specialized in brand management and consumer behavior. Her undergraduate major, Chinese literature, though very different from MBA, helped her with her thesis, a cross-cultural comparison of brand personality in advertising, in many ways. Her research interests include brand personality and cross-cultural comparison of consumer behavior.

Youjae Yi is a professor of marketing in the College of Business Administration at Seoul National University. After receiving his PhD in marketing from Stanford University, he taught at the University of Michigan in Ann Arbor (1987–1993). He has published widely in journals such as *Journal of Marketing Research, Journal of Consumer Research, Journal of Applied Psychology*, and *Journal of Econometrics*. He was an editor of the Korean Journal of Consumer Studies and Seoul Journal of Business, and he co-chaired the Asia-Pacific ACR Conference in 2004. He has also served on the board of LG company, on the Advisory Council of ACR, and on the editorial board of several journals such as *Journal of Consumer Research*.

Sukki Yoon is a doctoral candidate majoring in advertising at the Institute of Communications Research at the University of Illinois at Urbana-Champaign, where he teaches classes in international advertising and advertising research methods. He received his MA degree in advertising from the Michigan State University in 2000. His areas of interest include advertising strategy and consumer behavior. As a freelance columnist and reporter, he writes regularly on advertising.

Part I—Theories of Image

This section provides an overview of the theoretical and conceptual frameworks on the mental representation and creation of image from various perspectives. The authors of individual chapters discuss the creation, processes, and constructs of mental imagery and seek to understand further image and consumer behavior. The chapters illuminate past studies in the particular area of image study and present innovative new conceptualizations and approaches to the study of mental representation of image.

CHAPTER ONE

A Strategy-Based Framework
for Extending Brand Image Research

David M. Boush
University of Oregon

Scott M. Jones
Clemson University

Frameworks for assessing competitive advantage (Day & Wensley, 1988) describe the brand image as a resource, a possible source of advantage. It is a resource that managers have long understood to be important. Aaker (1989) reported a study where, out of 32 potential strategic competitive advantages, managers ranked reputation first and name recognition third in importance. Recent activities in the marketplace show an increased interest in brand image as a resource both by reliance on brand extension for growth and by acquisition of well-known consumer brand names (Aaker & Keller, 1990; Tauber, 1988). Clearly it is not the brand name itself that provides a resource to be managed but the mental representation that has come to be known as brand image. Although the concept of brand image is among the most central in marketing, marketers are hard pressed to agree on what the term means (Dobni & Zinkhan, 1990), and its literature is characterized by a variety of interesting empirical findings predicated on a diverse array of conceptual frameworks. For example, the brand image has been described as a category (Boush, 1993a, 1993b; Boush & Loken, 1991), a schema (Bridges, 1990), and part of a belief hierarchy (Reynolds & Gutman, 1984). Taken individually, these structure-based perspectives offer theoretical consistency; however, many questions relevant to managing the brand are never addressed. The literature on brand image is also characterized by a narrow focus on the brand images held by consumers, excluding the way a brand image may influence decisions made by competitors, retailers, and other stakeholders. The purpose of this chapter is to synthesize what we know about brand image and to provide an integrated framework for conducting additional research. Such a framework should be comprehensive in the sense that

3

all important elements of brand image can be included within it and fruitful in its suggestion of untested relationships. The focus throughout this chapter is on what brand image can do for the firm. With that perspective in mind, a model is presented that relates the content and structure of brand image to the strategic functions brand image performs. After defining brand image, the model is presented first in an overview and then with a description of its components in greater detail. Because the focus of this chapter is the strategic functions brand image can serve, those functions are described first. From that point the components of the model are described so as to trace the content and structure of brand image back to its sources. The implications of changing brand image, and of explicitly considering market segments, then will be discussed. The final section will summarizes what we know and what we need to know about brand image to manage it better.

BRAND IMAGE DEFINED

A brand is widely defined as a "name, term, sign, symbol, or design or combination of them which is intended to identify the goods or services of one seller or group of sellers and to differentiate them from those of competitors" (Kotler, 1991, p. 442). Each of these components can prove to be crucial in laying the groundwork for the brand of a firm and its identity. A great deal of study has focused on the development of a strong brand (Aaker, 1991, 1996). Many of these studies are concentrated on brand development within traditional industries and product lines. However, as noted in several chapters in this book, the need for recognizing, developing, and managing a brand image is of importance to services, products, philanthropic organizations, geographic locations, athletes, and celebrities. We follow Newman's (1957) definition that "a brand can be viewed as a composite image of everything associated with it" (p. 101). More narrow definitions, such as those that confine brand image to the intangible or symbolic (e.g., Gardner & Levy, 1955) omit some brand associations (e.g., with quality or product function) that form a basis for strategic advantage.

    A point that must be made explicit at the outset is that, because brand image is a mental construct, there are as many brand images as there are perceivers (Bullmore, 1984). When we speak of a brand image, we refer to the extent to which perceptions overlap across individual consumers, competitors, channel intermediaries, or others who are influenced by the brand image.

OVERVIEW OF THE MODEL

The main components of the model are: (a) the sources of brand image, (b) the content of brand image, (c) the structure of brand image, (d) the uses of brand image in stakeholder decision-making, and (e) the key strategic functions brand image performs for the firm (see Fig. 1.1). Based on experience, marketing communications, and associations from brand partners, individuals form mental impressions that we

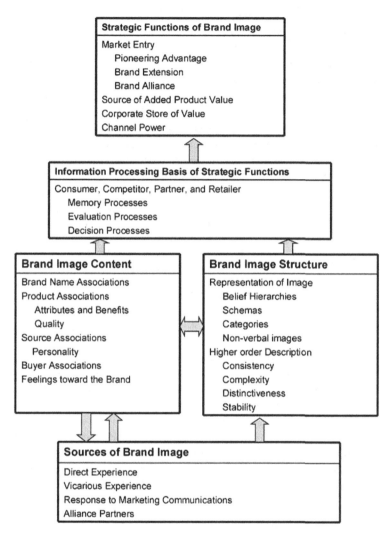

FIG. 1.1. Strategic model of brand image.

call the brand image. This image can be described in terms of both its content and its structure. The content includes the brand name, product associations, source associations, buyer associations, and feelings (i.e., affect). Frameworks for understanding brand image structure include belief hierarchies, categories, schemas, and nonverbal images. As we present later, it also is useful to discuss the structure of brand image using higher order descriptors such as consistency, complexity, stability, and distinctiveness. The arrows connecting the boxes in Fig. 1.1 indicate direct influence relations. Brand image sources influence, or create, brand image content and structure. Brand image content can influence its sources, for example, by providing expectations that may influence both the processing of advertising and product experience. Brand image content also influences its structure. For example, image consistency results from product attributes being perceived as highly correlated. Reciprocally, image structure can influence its content. For example, the perception that the products or product attributes of a brand are highly correlated may lead to beliefs about production expertise (Keller & Aaker, 1992). Both the content and the structure of brand image (which collectively amount to brand knowledge) influence the memory, evaluation, and decision processes that underlie consumer, competitor, and channel member actions and ultimately support the strategic functions of market entry, added product value, corporate store of value, and channel power. The ability of advertising to influence the strategic functions of brand image is mediated both by the brand image itself (i.e., content and structure) and by the processes by which it is used (i.e., information processing). Although the present model can apply to services, retail establishments, or industrial products, for simplicity the examples here emphasize manufacturer brands of consumer products.

THE FUNCTIONS OF BRAND IMAGE

Market Entry

Perhaps the most important functions of brand image center on market entry. Brands can permit a firm to enter a new market and simultaneously can inhibit market entry by competitors. Pioneering advantage, brand extension, and brand alliance are three important ways to gain and hold a place in the market.

Pioneering Advantage.   Many of the strongest brand names (General Electric, Coca Cola, Hallmark) were among the first to be strongly associated with their respective product categories. Brand images allow firms to cement first mover (i.e., pioneering) advantages (Bain, 1956; Urban, Carter, Gaskin, & Mucha, 1986). The first brand to enter a market can occupy the best position, leaving less desirable positions for later entrants. If these later entrants want to compete for the same position they must offer something unique (e.g., lower price). Taking on the pioneering brand can be even more difficult if the cost of switching to a new brand is high, either because trying a new brand is costly or because of knowledge that is specific to using the pioneer's product. Products without a brand identity, such as unbranded commodities, cannot protect first-mover advantage in this way. Yet the success of brands such as Orville Redenbacher prove that a brand image can be a powerful resource in product categories once thought to be relatively homogeneous.

Brand Extension.   Brand images also allow firms to leverage customer franchises developed in one product market into another through brand extension

(Aaker, 1989; Aaker & Keller, 1990; Boush & Loken, 1991; Tauber, 1988). Brand extension strategies have become increasingly attractive as a way to reduce the tremendous cost of new product introduction. General Electric, for example, brands a remarkable range of products, from light bulbs to jet engines. Other brands have much more narrow brand images. For example, Coca Cola's extensions consist primarily of various colas. A question that recurs throughout this paper is whether brand images are stronger if narrow and simple or broad and complex.

Brand Alliances. One of the most popular new strategies for leveraging brand image is through a brand alliance. A brand alliance may best be described as the short-or-long term association or combination of tangible and intangible attributes associated with brand partners (Rao & Ruekert, 1994). One of the most popular types of brand alliances is a cobrand partnership. A cobrand is defined as the placement of two brand names on a single product or package (Lamb, Hair, & McDaniel, 1998; Shocker, 1995). Aaker (1996) identified two categories of cobranded products: ingredient and composite. An ingredient cobrand is characterized by the combination of tangible products associated with each partnering brand in the formation of a new product. Examples of ingredient cobrands presently in the marketplace include the Pillsbury Oreo Bars Baking Mix, Sugar-Free Kool Aid with Nutrasweet and Gateway computer with the Intel Pentium processor. A composite cobrand alliance involves the combination of less tangible brand image associations. An objective of composite cobranding is to suggest the enhancement of nonproduct-related attributes such as user and usage imagery (Keller, 1993) or experiential and symbolic benefits (Park, Jaworski, & MacInnis, 1986). Examples of composite cobrands presently in the marketplace include the Eddie Bauer edition of the Ford Explorer, Kellogg's Disney line of cereals and the L. L. Bean version of the Subaru Outback.

Source of Added Product Value

Virtually since Gardner and Levy (1955) first discussed brand image, marketers have recognized that the brand image not only summarizes consumer experience with the products of a brand, but can actually alter that experience. For example, consumers have been shown to perceive that their favorite brands of food or beverage taste better than those of competitors in unblinded as compared with blinded taste tests (Allison & Uhl, 1964). Brand image thus becomes a way to add value to a product by transforming product experience (Aaker & Stayman, 1992; Puto & Wells, 1984). One definition of brand equity is the added value with which a brand endows a product (Farquhar, 1989). Similarly Simon and Sullivan (1990) define brand equity as "the incremental cash flows which accrue to a branded product over and above the cash flows which would result from the sale of a product with no brand name" (p. 1).

Corporate Store of Value

The brand name is a store of value for the accumulated investments of advertising expenses and maintenance of product quality. Firms can use this store of value to convert a strategic marketing idea into a long-term competitive advantage. For example, the Hallmark brand image benefitted from a decision made during the 1950's to sponsor a few high-quality television specials each year. The emphasis in considering brand image as a store of value is its management as an asset over time. The central questions thus revolve around actions that increase or diminish brand store of value.

Channel Power

A strong brand name provides both an indicator and a source of power in a channel of distribution. Consequently brands are not only important for their effect horizontally, in outperforming their competitors, but vertically, in acquiring distribution and maintaining control of the terms of trade (Aaker, 1991; Porter, 1974). For example, Coca Cola's brand extension strategy arguably accomplishes three functions at once. Extension permits market entry at lower cost, inhibits competition by tying up shelf space, and may also provide leverage in negotiating terms of trade.

Brand image may also provide companies with unique distribution outlets. For example, *dual branding* is a term used to describe a brand alliance characterized by the association of two brands (Levin & Levin, 2000). Examples of this type of brand alliance include Kentucky Fried Chicken and A&W sharing a retail outlet and Federal Express shipping services inside a Kinko's copy center. Dual brand partnerships may allow companies to share expenses associated with the retail location (e.g., rent and equipment) and promotion.

THE INFORMATION-PROCESSING BASIS OF BRAND IMAGE FUNCTIONS

The accomplishment of all strategic functions depends on the way a brand image influences the information processing that underlies decisions made by consumers, competitors, and other channel members. The nature of these decisions is, of course, different for each type of stakeholder. This section describes the way brand memory, evaluation, and choice processes support strategic brand functions. Because virtually all the research on brand information processing has focused on the consumer, consumer memory, evaluation, and choice are described first. Then we discuss how brand-related information processing may influence decisions made by other channel members and competitors.

Memory Processes

Both recall and recognition may play a role in the process leading to brand choice, and the nature of their effects on choice depends on the circumstances of the choice decision. Consumers are sometimes faced with choices in which they must remember some or all of the alternatives (Lynch, Marmorstein, & Weigold, 1988). One recall mechanism that seems directly relevant to the function of brand image as a barrier to competitive entry involves the way attention to a given brand name inhibits recall of competing brands (Alba & Chattopadhyay, 1985). When a particular brand is brought to attention, either directly or because of contextual factors, it becomes more difficult to recall other brands in the same product category. If the probability of a brand being included in the choice set increases relative to its competitors, then the probability that the brand will be chosen increases (Nedungadi, 1990).

Alternatively, if the choice is made where a great deal of relevant and credible information about choice alternatives is available externally, then recognition may be used to make the choice (Bettman, 1979). However, brand recognition, defined as "the extent to which the buyer knows enough about the criteria for categorizing, but not for evaluating and distinguishing it from other brands in its product category" (Howard, 1989, p. 30), is more properly described as a precursor to the evaluation processes that are described next.

Evaluation Processes

A number of models in consumer research suppose that consumers form a positive attitude toward a product before purchasing it (Bettman, Capon, & Lutz, 1975). Following Fishbein and Ajzen (1975), attitude is defined as the location of the product on an affective dimension, such as liking. Evaluation processes are central to the accomplishment of strategic brand image functions to the extent that product evaluations are necessary prior to purchase and that brand image is evoked in product evaluations. Recent models of evaluation (Boush & Loken, 1991; Fiske & Pavelchak, 1986) suggest that people form attitudes toward products using two kinds of evaluation processes. One kind of process involves making inferences and combining individual attributes in some way; the other involves matching an object with a known category. For the former, there is extensive evidence suggesting that consumers actively construct and reconstruct brand associations in memory (Huber & McCann, 1982). One aspect of this constructive process is the way brand names can alter the context for thinking about product categories. For example, Schmitt and Dubé (1992) reported that a brand name (e.g., McDonald's) can modify a product category (e.g., amusement parks) to create original conceptual combinations (e.g., rides shaped like golden arches). Park, Jun, and Shocker (1996) examined brand alliances as composites of two names (Godiva cake mix by Slimfast and

Slimfast cake mix by Godiva) and found interesting effects based on the order each brand name was presented in the name of the product. In the latter process, attitude toward the known category transfers to the object being evaluated. For example, it is possible that consumers form an attitude toward Diet Coke by integrating beliefs about sweetness, tartness, and aftertaste; however, they may alternatively transfer some of their feelings about Coke Classic to Diet Coke.

Evaluation and Pioneering Advantage.   Research by Carpenter and Nakamoto (1989) describes a specific way that brand evaluation processes can maintain pioneering advantage. Based on earlier findings that pioneering advantages obtain even in mature markets where brands reposition and switching costs are minimal (Urban et al., 1986), they hypothesized that pioneering advantages occur as a result of the way consumers form brand preferences. They found that consumer preferences are shaped by the pioneering brand because, as the first entrant, it is the prototype against which later entrants in the product category are judged. The closer later entrants position themselves to the pioneer, the more distinct the pioneer becomes and the less distinct the competing brands become.

Evaluation and Brand Extension.   The two central issues relevant to evaluation and brand extension are the effect of the existing brand image on a potential extension and the reciprocal effect of the extension on the brand image. Evaluation of brand extensions repeatedly has been shown to depend on attitude toward the original brand and on a determination of match, or similarity fit, between the extension and the brand (Aaker & Keller, 1990; Boush et al., 1987). The processes involved in consumer evaluations of brand extensions depend on interproduct similarity judgments. Boush and Loken (1991) reported that extensions that were extremely similar to the existing products of a brand elicited category matching processes, whereas moderately similar extensions elicited slower inferential processes. For example, many attribute the failure of Coca-Cola's clothing line to the lack of similarity between the caffeinated beverage category and apparel. Park, Milberg, and Lawson (1991) found that evaluations of brand extensions may be based either on product attribute similarity or on a match to the overall brand concept. Negative evaluation of brand extensions can also hurt the original brand image by changing brand beliefs (Loken & John, 1993). However, "a single brand association may provide a persuasive connection between the brand and an otherwise dissimilar extension category" (Broniarczyk & Alba, 1994, p. 215). This view is consistent with a market structure belief that suggests consumers are interested in benefits more than products. In the context of this research, therefore, "a brand may fit into a product category regardless of the brand's category of origin, if the brand offers the benefits sought" (Broniarczyk & Alba, 1994, p. 215) in the new product category. Ahluwalia and Gürhan-Canli (2000) similarly viewed the brand name as a piece of information that will help a potential brand extension if it is accessible and diagnostic. Recent investigations into the interplay between brand names and brand attributes (Van Osselaer & Alba, 2003) demonstrate the importance for brand extension of contextual variables in the learning environment, such as information ambiguity.

Evaluation of Brand Alliances. Recent research has considered the evaluation of a variety of brand alliances. For example, Simonin and Ruth (1998) explored how the evaluation of a cobranded product influences subsequent evaluations of the partnering brands. The authors referred to the influence as a spill-over effect. Consumer attitudes toward the alliance were modeled as a function of the attitude toward the two participating brands prior to exposure to the alliance, the perceived fit between the two products, and the perceived fit between the images of the partnering brands. The results of the research indicate that attitudes toward the brand partnership have the potential to spill over to subsequent attitudes toward the parent brands (Simonin & Ruth, 1998).

Decision Processes

Consumers choose which brand to buy within a particular product category and usage situation. Consumers may choose a brand by forming summary evaluations of all competing brands, by comparing all brands on one or more product attributes, or by some combination of those processes (Bettman, 1979). However, in addition, consumers sometimes employ brand image more directly in the choice process by using a brand-based decision rule (Bettman, 1979; Hoyer, 1984). Consumers who regularly apply brand heuristics are termed *brand loyal*. However, brand loyalty is usually measured by a lack of brand switching, which may result from factors such as availability (Jacoby & Kyner, 1973; Kapferer & Laurent, 1989). A more useful construct may be *brand sensitivity*, which is the extent to which a consumer is influenced by brand image in the purchase decision. If brand choices are made by groups, rather than by individuals, they also may involve processes of negotiation and consensus formation (Corfman & Lehmann, 1987).

Information Processing By Competitors and Channel Members

Competitor Decisions. Decisions by competitors include whether to introduce new brands, how much to advertise to consumers, what incentives (including promotion and slotting fees) to give to the trade, and how aggressively to price. All these activities are likely to require costly defensive reaction from a brand wishing to maintain market share. The value of a strong brand thus goes beyond its ability to fend off competitors to its capacity to alter or preclude competitive action. Such competitive strategies may be viewed within the perspective of game theory (Moorthy, 1985), in which the brand image held by competitors consists of knowledge relevant to the difficulty it is likely to encounter in capturing market share from the established brand. Brand image therefore should affect the equilibrium between competitive strategies (Nash, 1950).

Channel Member Decisions.   Brand image is also likely to affect decisions by channel intermediaries, such as retailers. The most important brand-related choices for retailers are which brands to stock and how much shelf space to allocate to them. Other decisions may involve special advertising and sales promotion. Whether such decisions are made by an individual or by a buying group, brand image may be influential because of perceived prestige accruing to the retailer or inferences about the kind of customer that may be attracted to the store because of the brand.

Brand image may also play a role in selecting potential partners in the previously described dual branding scenario. For example, Levin and Levin (2000) considered the role of assimilation and contrast effects in the evaluation of a dual brand. The primary concern in studies considering contrast and assimilation effects is whether primed information regarding one partner (i.e., the context) serves as a comparison standard for contrast or as a frame for interpretation, thereby promoting assimilation of the second partner (i.e., the target). Key determinants in the assimilation process include the ambiguity of the description of the target restaurant and the number of shared features between the two brand images (Meyers-Levy & Sternthal, 1993).

Mediators of Consumer Evaluation and Decision Processes

A variety of factors have been shown to affect the decision processes consumers use. Although a complete review of such factors is beyond the scope of this chapter, some of the most important ones deserve mention. These factors include familiarity with the product class (Sujan, 1985), prior brand knowledge (Simonson, Huber, & Payne, 1988), brand loyalty (Tellis, 1988) and perception of fit between those products in the brand portfolio (Dacin & Smith, 1994). As it relates to the evaluation of brand alliances, perceived fit or complementarity between the images of the partnering brands may influence evaluations of the partnership (Simonin & Ruth, 1998). The mediating variables suggest that the information-processing effects that underlie the strategic functions of the brand are rooted in thoughts and feelings. The thoughts and feelings that comprise the brand image can be described in terms of both content and structure. Again, although past brand image research has been confined to consumer brand knowledge, the content and structure of competitor, alliance partner, and retailer brand images should be considered.

THE CONTENT OF BRAND IMAGE

Brand Name

Perhaps the content element most central to brand image is the brand name, because it ties all other aspects of the image together. As a consequence, the brand naming decision has received considerable attention. Although the brand name is often discussed as synonymous with the brand image (e.g., Gardner & Levy, 1955), consumers actually have distinguishable attitudes toward the brand name, the products of the brand, and the brand image as a whole (Zinkhan & Martin, 1987). Research into brand naming has been dominated by phonetic symbolism, whose essential tenet as applied to brand names is that the sound of a brand name conveys both connotative and denotative meaning (Dogana, 1967). Early work (Sapir, 1929) showed that even nonsense syllables conveyed fairly consistent meaning. For example, people who were told that mil and mal both referred to "stream" in some unknown language consistently judged mal to refer to a larger stream than mil. The importance of the connotative meaning conveyed by the sound of a brand name is especially important at first (i.e., before repeated associations with other brand image components have been made in a consumer's mind). As associations are made with the sound, the importance of the sound itself diminishes (Osgood, 1963). However, because new consumers enter even mature markets continually, some potential consumers will always be unfamiliar with a brand at any particular time. In addition to the symbolic meaning, the sounds used in brand names can offer advantages in memorability. Names beginning with plosives (i.e., sounds conveyed in English by the consonants B, C, D, G, K, P, and T) are more frequently recalled and recognized than others (Vanden Berg, Collins, Schultz, & Adler, 1984). It seems therefore more than coincidence that a disproportionate number of brand names begin with C, P, and K (Schloss, 1981). Research on brand names has shown that memory for brand names is improved if the names are meaningful and if they fit the products (Kanungo & Dutta, 1966). Consequently, additional research focused on ways to develop brand names with appropriate fit and meaning (Heaton, 1967). Peterson and Ross (1972) described a method of testing brand names based on how much the name reminded the participant of the product category. Mehrabian and de Wetter (1987) fit brand names to products based on minimizing the discrepancy between the emotional connotations of the name and the emotional state desired during product use. Although the issue is unexplored, it also seems plausible that brand names can improve the range of brand extension. For example, GE may accrue a competitive advantage from ownership of the sweeping range of meaning represented by the words *general* and *electric*.

Product Associations

Product Attributes and Benefits. Brand images convey both the attributes of branded products and the benefits consumers may expect. A recurring division in product attributes is that made between tangible and intangible attributes (Friedman, 1986; Lefkoff-Hagius & Mason, 1990). Tangible attributes are those that describe characteristics of the product that can be measured more or less objectively (e.g., the horsepower of a car), whereas intangible ones are more subjective (e.g., its level of excitement). Brand positioning strategies that emphasize tangible product attributes have been termed *functional brand concepts* (Park et al., 1986).

Product Quality.   One of the most important kinds of information that a brand can provide to consumers is the level of quality they can expect. From a marketer's perspective, associating a brand with high quality in consumers' minds has been described as a strategic goal (Jacobson & Aaker, 1987). It is not surprising then that a large body of empirical research has shown that brand image (as represented by the brand name) signals the level of expected product quality (Jacoby, Olson, & Haddock, 1971; Rao & Monroe, 1989). High quality brand associations both benefit existing products and improve the opportunity to leverage a brand into new product categories. Aaker and Keller (1990) demonstrated that a high-quality brand could extend its product line further than could a low-quality brand. The notion of brand image as a quality indicator also has been approached in the theoretical economics literature. For example, Wernerfelt (1988) presented a model in which a firm uses the reputation of an existing brand as a bond to ensure the quality of a brand extension. This and other research indicates that a branded product, even if the name is unfamiliar, should signal a level of quality greater than an unbranded product (Rao & Ruekert, 1994).

Source Associations

Products that share the same brand name share perceptions of origin. Perceived nationality of brand origin can affect consumer inferences (Erickson, Johansson, & Chao, 1984), principally, it seems, by associating a brand with national stereotypes. An interesting twist on perceptions of national origin was provided by LeClerc, Schmitt, and Dubé (1994), who showed that an English pronunciation of a brand name is preferred for utilitarian products and a French pronunciation of the same brand name is preferred for hedonistic products. One particularly interesting aspect of origin is its symbolic value, which sometimes is established through visual imagery. For example, cartoon images of fictitious places like the Valley of the Jolly Green Giant seem to have proven effective, despite the fact that consumers cannot literally believe such statements of origin. Keller and Aaker (1992) suggested that attributions about product source are particularly important for brand extensions. More specifically, they identify two aspects of producer credibility, expertise and trustworthiness, that are important in the evaluation of brand extensions.

Personality.   Brand images are frequently imbued with human personality dimensions, either explicitly (e.g., Betty Crocker, The Marlboro Cowboy) or implicitly by associating the brand with human characteristics such as friendliness, competence, or gender. Continuing characters (e.g., Mrs. Olson from Folger's Coffee, Mr. Whipple from Charmin) also associate personality with brands. The characters that represent brands need not be human but are frequently humanized (e.g., Tony the Tiger, the Michelin Man). Boulding (1956) theorized that such images satisfy a human desire to simplify complex stimuli. J. Aaker (1997) described five brand personality dimensions (i.e., sincerity, excitement, competence, sophistication, ruggedness) that map on to the "Big Five" personality traits. References to personality are common both in the development of brand image (Dobni & Zinkhan, 1990) and store image (Lindquist, 1974–1975; Martineau, 1958). In some cases a person, such as Martha Stewart, literally becomes the brand.

Buyer Associations

It has long been held that consumers buy certain products for purposes of self-expression and that brand image plays a role in that expression (Gardner & Levy, 1955). Sirgy (1982) noted that many self-concept investigators define product image as the stereotypic image of the generalized product user. Similarly, empirical evidence shows that brand image involves attributions about other people who buy the brand. Studies of car buyers, for example, showed that buyers of a particular brand have self-concepts similar to the self-concepts they attribute to others buying that brand (Grubb & Hupp, 1968). The result is a significant amount of brand congruence across individuals, depending on type of product and type of social relation (Reingen, Foster, Brown, & Seidman, 1984). The brand image can associate the buyer with others with whom he or she would like to associate, suggesting a kind of club whose membership derives from common brand preference or ownership such as MacIntosh computers or Harley-Davidson motorcycles (McAlexander, Schouten, & Koenig, 2002; Muniz & O'Guinn, 2000). Associations of a brand with consumers also may be important to retailers because attracting customers with desirable characteristics has advantages that extend beyond the sale of a particular branded product.

Brand positioning strategies that emphasize buyer associations fall into the category of symbolic brand concept-image strategies (Park et al., 1986). Three ideas may prove especially important in the management of symbolic concept images. First, different, more expressive attributes predict attitude toward the brand for symbolic, as opposed to functional, concept images (Mittal, Ratchford, & Prabhakar, 1990). Second, an individual may have many situational self-concepts that may be expressed (i.e., by different brands) in different situations (Schenk & Holman, 1980). Third, products communicate self-image differentially based on such characteristics as visibility in use, variability in use, and personalizability (Holman, 1981).

Attitude Toward the Brand

To this point the content of brand image has been confined to the thoughts consumers have about a brand. Sometimes these thoughts can generate positive feelings, as when a brand is judged to be of excellent quality. However, it is also useful to think of feelings (i.e., affect) toward a brand as separate from beliefs. These feelings, termed attitude toward the brand (e.g., Gardner, 1985; Mitchell, 1986), may be particularly strong if consumers associate the brand with a desirable or undesirable self-image. However, the notion of attitude toward the brand does not adequately capture the emotional response of loyal Coke drinkers to the reformulation of Coke. Strong emotional attachment to brands has been described by elevating the brand to the level of a close personal relationship (Fournier, 1998).

THE STRUCTURAL REPRESENTATION OF BRAND IMAGE

A variety of cognitive models have been suggested to describe the way brand image is represented in consumer memory. Although the empirical findings are consistent with virtually all these models, each illuminates a different aspect of brand image and suggests different questions.

Belief Hierarchies

Reynolds and Gutman (1984) proposed a means–end chain as the appropriate structure for describing brand image. A means–end chain is defined as the connection between product attributes, consumer consequences, and personal values (Gutman, 1982). The structural assumptions underlying the means–end chain are that attributes and beliefs are linked in a kind of network (Collins & Loftus, 1975) and that this network is organized according to levels of abstraction (Craik & Lockhart, 1972). Attributes, consequences, and values describe the content rather than the structure of the means-end chain. However, to appreciate the structure, the three content components must be described.

Attributes are divided into abstract and physical product characteristics, a distinction that closely parallels that described earlier between tangible and intangible product attributes. Examples of physical descriptions include "color" or "miles per gallon," and abstract characteristics include "smells nice" or "strong flavor." Consequences "accrue to people from consuming products or services" (Reynolds & Gutman, 1984, p. 29). If desirable, consequences are called benefits. Reynolds and Gutman divide consequences into psychosocial and functional categories. Midway between the more abstract values and the more concrete attributes, benefits seem to be at a useful level of abstraction for product or brand positioning. Respectively, functional and psychosocial consequences map easily on to the functional and symbolic brand concept-images described by Park, et al., (1986). For example, symbolic brands such as Chanel and Rolex seem to represent a rich variety of psychosocial consequences and few functional ones, whereas Xerox and Honda seem to represent the converse. Following Rokeach (1968), values are defined as important beliefs people hold about themselves and about their feelings concerning others' beliefs about them. Values have been shown to influence consumer behavior in powerful ways (e.g., Kahle, 1996). A clear strength of the means–end chain analysis is the way it links physical, tangible product attributes with the abstract personal values that make products meaningful to consumers.

Schemas

Representations of brand image, like other memory traces, are not completely stable or accurate; rather, they are frequently modified to fit into an existing framework (Bridges, 1990). This framework, or template, has been termed a *schema* (Bartlett, 1932). Schematic approaches to memory emphasize the extent to which memory is constructive. According to this perspective, brand image is flexibly built at the moment it is needed. There are, however, limits to the flexibility. Schemas specify the relevant attributes, supply default values for attributes (e.g. the default color of a sports car is red), supply constraint values to attributes (e.g., a Rolls Royce cannot be priced at $20,000), contain information about how variables are related (e.g., bigger greeting cards are higher priced), and include prototypes (e.g., the prototypical Campbell's product is soup; Crocker, 1984). A consumer may be viewed as having a product or brand schema that influences the selection, abstraction, interpretation, and integration of incoming product-relevant information (Alba & Hasher, 1983). A schematic view of brand image is supported by evidence that consumers go beyond the objective facts about a brand and draw inferences (Huber & McCann, 1982). However, research on categorization (Barsalou, 1985) has incorporated the notion of flexibility, and because it provides a more thorough consideration of similarity relationships, categorization theory has been more widely adopted as a framework for brand image.

Brand Categories

Brands are most commonly thought of as members of product categories (Carpenter & Nakamoto, 1989; Nedungadi & Hutchinson, 1985). For example, brands such as GE and Westinghouse can be described as competing within the home appliance category. However, a brand has also been considered to comprise a category (Boush, 1993a; Boush & Loken, 1991; Loken, Joiner, & Peck, 2002). In this context, a brand name such as GE is considered as the label of a category consisting of all GE products. The value of treating a brand as a category is that the categorization literature provides a rigorous consideration of the structure of attributes, objects, and concepts. Mervis and Rosch (1981) stated that "a category exists whenever two or more distinguishable objects are treated equivalently" (p. 89). However, the nonequivalence of category members, or *graded structure*, sets categories apart from unordered sets (Rosch, Simpson, & Miler, 1976; Smith, Shoben, & Rips, 1974). Graded structure and a second characteristic of category structure, brand breadth, are relevant for understanding how judgments of new brands are formed.

Graded Structure.   People perceive members of most naturally occurring categories as varying in the degree to which they are perceived as typical of those categories. For example, a cow is perceived as more typical of the mammal category than is a whale. Furthermore, even nonmembers differ in how good a nonmember they are of a category. For example, an unrelated object such as a shoe is a better nonmember of the mammal category than is a fish. This range in category representativeness from the most representative members of a category to the nonmembers that are least similar to the category is called graded structure (e.g., Barsalou, 1985; Mervis & Rosch, 1981) and has been demonstrated for a variety of consumer categories (Loken & Ward, 1990). Graded structure implies that some products are more representative of a brand category than are others.

Structure Bases.   A variety of models have been proposed as bases for category structure. Common to all is the notion that shared features provide a basis for similarity and typicality. However, some models disagree over the role of distinctive features. According to the contrast model (Tversky, 1977), the similarity between two objects, A and B, is a function of the number of features they have in common minus the distinctive features of both A and B. In other models distinctive features play no role (Rosch & Mervis, 1975). An interesting implication of this model is that similarity between products can be asymmetrical and can be influenced by the brand name (Boush, 1997). Barsalou (1985) proposed that some types of categories are flexibly constructed according to situational demands. Typicality for these goal-directed categories is based on values on a single critical attribute or dimension. The flexibility of brand and product meaning places particular importance on the context of brand decisions and usage (Ratneshwar & Shocker, 1991). It also suggests that it is vital to identify the elements of the brand image that are central to brand image structure.

Brand Breadth and Multiplexity.   Boush and Loken (1991) reported that evaluation of potential brand extensions was influenced by brand breadth, the variability among product types represented by a brand name. Dacin and Smith (1994) argued that the influence of fit within the brand portfolio (i.e., all the products utilizing a single brand name) is diminished when a brand has been successfully extended into multiple product categories. Brand breadth appears to be a result of the typicality of brand extensions. If brand managers consistently extend the brand by offering new products that are very similar to existing ones, then a narrow brand results. If brand extensions are very different from existing products, then a broad brand results. Similarly, Haugtvedt, Leavitt, and Schneier (1992) argued that brands can be usefully described as having either a *simplex* or *multiplex* structure. Simplex brands represent essentially one concept; multiplex brands represent two or more.

Nonverbal Images

Brands have associations with pictures and sounds as well as with words. There is some dispute over whether this kind of image is a stored representation or a mode of processing. Empirical findings are consistent with either view. Paivio (1969) proposed that nonverbal information is stored in memory in a separate code. MacInnis and Price (1987) treated imagery as a mode of processing, which they contrasted with discursive (i.e., language-like) processing. Regardless of which of these perspectives is taken, imagery has been shown to improve memory. For example, Lutz and Lutz (1977) demonstrated that interactive imagery facilitates the learning of brand–product associations. An interactive image integrates at least part of the brand name and the product in the same picture. For example, an interactive image for Rocket Messenger Service depicted a delivery man with a rocket strapped to his back. Robertson (1987) reported that high-imagery brand names were generally more memorable than low-imagery names. Many strong brands (e.g., CBS, Mercedes Benz) have logos that most readers can instantly visualize in their mind's eyes. Some brands have the additional nonverbal association of colors, such as Coca Cola red and IBM blue. The visual representation of brands through logos has received surprisingly little empirical attention.

HIGHER ORDER DESCRIPTORS OF BRAND IMAGE

Whichever model is used to describe the brand image, that image can be further described as having higher order structural properties. These are described as follows.

Consistency

Consistency has been called a key attribute of strong brand images (Farquhar, 1989; Ogilvy, 1983), but its definition is elusive. Ogilvy (1983) stated that "every advertisement should be thought of as a contribution to the brand image. It follows that your advertising should consistently project the same image year after year" (p.14). What Ogilvy referred to as consistency (i.e., the same image year after year) is treated here as having three dimensions: consistency, complexity, and stability. Consistency may be defined as the extent to which brand image attributes do not contradict each other. It seems intuitive that some brand attributes are essential to its image whereas others are not. A distinction between central and peripheral brand attributes mirrors the distinction in categorization theory between defining and accidental features (Smith et al., 1974). It follows then that inconsistencies in core brand attributes have a greater effect on brand image than do inconsistencies in peripheral attributes. Inconsistencies between the core attributes of the brand image and of a brand extension are likely to result in either failed extensions or seriously diluted brand equity.

Complexity

Brand image complexity may be defined as the number of different but consistent attribute associations in consumers' minds. Although inconsistency is unambiguously harmful to brand image, the effect of complexity is unclear. Boush and Loken (1991) reported results from an experiment that showed a brand with a wider variety of products to have an advantage in launching moderately similar brand extensions. Similarly, Keller and Aaker (1992) found that sequential brand extension can develop perceptions of greater manufacturer expertise. In general, complex knowledge structures reflect greater expertise (Sujan, 1985). Bahn (1986) reported that the structure underlying brand preferences of children became more complex (i.e., had more dimensions) as they progressed through cognitive stages.

Stability

Stability refers to the extent to which brand images change over time. Such changes may be superficial (e.g., a new logo) or may seriously alter what the brand means (e.g., a change in expertise). It may also be useful to distinguish between the amount of change that occurs in a brand image over time and the degree to which a brand image is resistant to change. Stability may affect content. For example, a brand image that has remained unchanged over a long period of time may be perceived as solid and dependable. A stable brand image may also be more accessible in a given decision or usage context or, conversely, less accessible in an unfamiliar context.

Distinctiveness

Brand image distinctiveness is the extent to which the brand is perceived to be different from its competitors. Recall that Carpenter and Nakamoto (1989) discussed distinctiveness as a characteristic possessed by the first brand to enter a product category as a consequence of its status as the prototype. Further, brands that are most typical of their product categories are the most easily recalled (Nedungadi & Hutchinson, 1985). From a categorization perspective, a distinctive brand is an informative cue because it differentiates a branded product from those of competitors in a way that informs choice.

MULTIPLE BRAND IMAGES OVER TIME

It is important to emphasize that brand image is neither static nor uniform across individuals. The most comprehensive treatment of brand image over time was offered by Park et al., (1986), who described brand image as being managed in three stages, termed introduction, elaboration, and fortification. Central to their model is the role of brand extensions in creating complexity in brand image (i.e., elaboration) and developing the brand image as a barrier to competitive entry (i.e., fortification). However, the notions of elaboration and fortification beg the question of when and how brand extension helps rather than hurts the brand image. Whereas Park et al. considered only the improvement in brand image wrought by brand extension, Ries and Trout (1981) considered only the negative implications of extension. Ries and Trout argued that brand extensions obscure the original meaning of the brand by stretching it too far. The actual effects of brand extension on brand image may be anticipated by considering the changes in brand image structure and content that are likely to occur because of changes in the sources of brand image and by explicitly considering that these brand images may differ by segment. Consider, for example, the implications of the model in Fig. 1.1 for the changes in the Jockey brand image that may accrue from extension into a product line for women. Jockey For Her seems likely to change both the content (i.e., less masculine) and the structure (i.e., more complex, less consistent, less stable) of the original Jockey image. However, looking at brand image by segment and considering the sources of brand image, those changes are mediated by the extent to which advertising and distribution can isolate the communication of brand image to each segment, the extent to which gender associations are salient in the Jockey image, and the extent to which the nesting brand "For Her" signals a new Jockey subcategory. Existing research has not addressed these mediating variables.

SUMMARY AND FUTURE RESEARCH DIRECTIONS

Effects of Brand Information Processing on Brand Strategic Functions

Past research substantiates an information-processing basis for establishing pioneering advantage and for extending the brand to new products. A number of recent studies (Boush & Loken, 1991; Carpenter & Nakamoto, 1989) take a categorization perspective, emphasizing the importance of typicality or prototypicality. It seems notable that much of this research has focused on evaluation processes rather than on memory or choice. Many interesting research issues involve extending the concept of brand image from consumers to alliance partners, competitors, and retailers.

Effects of Brand Image Content on Brand Information Processing

Previous work on cognitive and affective brand associations has been dominated by research on brand names. Brand image may be usefully considered to affect important retailer and competitor decisions. If, for example, retailers associate a brand with particular desirable customer characteristics, they may be inclined to carry it even if another brand is more profitable or to allocate more and better shelf space to it. Similarly, competitors' brand associations may influence their expectations about brand strategy. For example, competitors may expect a firm to defend vigorously against threats to an established or core brand. Such expectations are assumptions in models that forecast the impact of alternative marketing policies on market shares (e.g., Carpenter & Lehmann, 1985).

Relations Among Brand Image Content Elements

The association between a brand name and quality has been demonstrated repeatedly. Other associations with brand name include common product origin and national stereotypes. Again, future research may explore brand associations as perceived by alliance partners, retailers, and competitors. Retailers may logically associate brands with expected sales levels and promotional activity (e.g., discount brands). Competitors also associate brands with activities and more importantly, with competitive actions and reactions.

Effects of Brand Image Content on Brand Image Structure

Past research on the formation of brand image structure has looked at how distinctiveness is created (i.e., by becoming prototypical of a product category and by offering a unique selling proposition). Brand image complexity has been experimentally manipulated by creating brands with multiple products. Before future research tackles the effects of structural brand image components, there is substantial room for research on their operationalization. For example, Boush and Loken (1991), after operationalizing brand complexity (i.e., breadth) as a brand having multiple related products, noted that brand breadth could be characterized both by range (i.e., the difference between the two most dissimilar products) and by variability (i.e., a pairwise measure of interproduct differences squared and summed). Previously described categorization models, such as Tversky's (1977) contrast model, suggest alternative conceptualizations for other structural elements such as consistency and distinctiveness.

Effects of Brand Image Structure
on Brand Information Processing

Existing research on brand image structure in the perspective of the current model addresses consistency, complexity, and distinctiveness but not stability. Important questions for future research center on the effects of creating consistent brand images with varying degrees of structural complexity. The importance of nesting brands has been suggested (Aaker, 1991; Boush, 1993a) but remains largely unexplored. Corporate image is a useful area of inquiry in this context (e.g., Brown & Dacin, 1997).

Effects of Brand Image Structure on Brand Image Content

The proposition that brand image complexity leads to more moderate affect is an application of the complexity–extremity effect (Linville, 1982), which posits that the complexity of mental representations increases the probability of having features with offsetting affective associations. Other interesting propositions can be generated from the notion that consumers make inferences from brand image structure. For example, when brand images remain unchanged over long periods of time people may be more likely to generate positive associations such as dependability or negative ones such as dullness.

Effects of Brand Image Content on Brand Image Formation

Past research has shown that direct product experience, such as taste, can be influenced by expectations induced by brand associations. A more recent notion is that brand associations created through advertising can transform product experience. Future research may examine whether the notion of transforming experience can be extended to vicarious experience. For example, brand associations may influence consumers' perceptions of how much another person enjoys having or using a product. A related research idea is that retailers' perceptions of sales performance, in terms of either dollar sales or the ability of the brand to attract customers, may be subjectively influenced by brand image.

Effects of Brand Image Content and Structure on Strategic Functions

The present model predicts that effects of brand image on brand strategic functions are mediated by evaluation processes. However, it also may be reasonable to make assumptions about intervening processes and look for direct effects. For example, Smith and Park (1992) found that the strength of the parent brand was positively related to the market share of brand extensions, implicitly assuming (in the present model) that extensions of strong brands are more positively evaluated and more frequently chosen than those of weak brands. Their approach suggests that interesting hypotheses can be generated by looking at the direct effect of brand image characteristics, such as perceived origin or consistency, on profitability or market share.

CONCLUDING REMARKS

This chapter presents a model that both builds on and differs from previous conceptualizations. Like Aaker's (1991) model of brand equity, it describes strategic marketing functions; however, the current model makes strategic functions its focus. Enumerating the functions of brand image is useful as a basis for brand equity valuation because an incomplete inventory of strategic functions may undervalue a brand image. For example, defining brand equity as the added value with which a brand endows a product (Farquhar, 1989; Simon & Sullivan, 1990) does not place a value on such things as inhibiting competitors from certain actions aimed at capturing market share. Like the model discussed by Park et al., (1986), the present model explicitly considers the effects of knowledge change over time. However, the model presented here provides a basis for hypotheses concerning both fortification and erosion of brand image. The model both draws on earlier emphases on brand image structure (Haugtvedt et al., 1992) and separates brand image knowledge into structural and content components. This separation is important because it permits a discussion of the relations between structure and content. Further, the present model discriminates between different aspects of what has previously been called brand image consistency. Distinguishing among stability, consistency, and complexity is important because actions by brand managers may affect these components differently.

The present model is unique in its consideration of brand image from the standpoint not only of the consumer but of others who play roles critical to the strategic functions of a brand. It is also unique in the way it relates strategic marketing functions to their information-processing roots. This focus allows for a more complete consideration of the relations among the literatures on brand image, strategic marketing management, information processing, and advertising effects than has previously been possible. Much past brand image research has concentrated on only a few areas. Early brand image research was dominated by the study of brand associations such as quality, origin, and brand name connotations. More recently, the focus has shifted to brand extension, particularly the variables that influence the evaluation of brand extensions or of the original brand following brand extension (Barone & Miniard, 2002; Barone, Miniard, & Romeo, 2000; Loken & John, 1993).

Brand images are mental representations held not only by consumers but by other stakeholders such as competitors, alliance partners, and channel intermediaries. The linkages in the model presented here suggest a variety of interesting questions. Perhaps the most important question is, "What effect does the brand image have on these other stakeholders?"

REFERENCES

Aaker, D. A. (1989). Managing assets and skills: The key to a sustainable competitive advantage. *California Management Review, 3,* 91–106.

Aaker, D. A. (1991). *Managing brand equity: Capitalizing on the value of a brand name.* New York: The Free Press.

Aaker, D. A. (1996). *Building strong brands.* New York: The Free Press.

Aaker, D. A., & Keller, K. L. (1990). Consumer evaluations of brand extensions. *Journal of Marketing, 54,* 27–41.

Aaker, D. A., & Stayman, D. M. (1992). Implementing the concept of transformational advertising. *Psychology and Marketing, 9,* 237–253.

Aaker J. (1997). Dimensions of brand personality. *Journal of Marketing Research, 34,* 347–356.

Ahluwalia, R., & Gürhan-Canli, Z. (2000). The effects of extensions on the family brand name: An accessibility-diagnosticity perspective. *Journal of Consumer Research, 27,* 371–381.

Alba, J., & Chattopadhyay, A. (1985). Effects of context and part category cues on recall of competing brands. *Journal of Marketing Research, 22,* 340–349.

Alba, J.,& Hasher, L. (1983). Is memory schematic? *Psychological Bulletin, 93,* 203–231.

Allison, R., & Uhl, K. P., (1964). Effect of brand identification on perception of product quality. *Journal of Marketing Research, 1,* 36–39.

Bahn, K. D. (1986). How and when do brand perceptions and preferences first form? A cognitive developmental investigation. *Journal of Consumer Research, 13,* 394–404.

Bain, J. S. (1956). *Barriers to new competition.* Cambridge, MA: Harvard University Press.

Barone, M. J., & Miniard, P. W. (2002). Mood and brand extension judgments: Asymmetric effects for desirable versus undesirable brands. *Journal of Consumer Psychology, 12,* 283–290.

Barone, M. J., Miniard, P. W., & Romeo, J. B. (2000). The influence of positive mood on brand extension evaluations. *Journal of Consumer Research, 26,* 387–402.

Barsalou, L. W. (1985). Ideals, central tendency, and frequency of instantiation as determinants of graded structure in categories. *Journal of Experimental Psychology: Learning, Memory and Cognition, 11,* 629–648.

Bartlett, F. C. (1932). *Remembering: An experimental and social study.* Cambridge, England: Cambridge University Press.

Bettman, J. R. (1979). *An information processing theory of consumer choice.* Cambridge, MA: Addison–Wesley.

Bettman, J. R., Capon, N., & Lutz, R. J. (1975). Cognitive algebra in multiattribute attitude models. *Journal of Marketing Research, 12,* 151–164.

Boulding, K. E. (1956). *The image: Knowledge in life and society.* Ann Arbor, MI: University of Michigan Press.

Boush, D. M. (1993a). Brands as categories. In D. A. Aaker & A. L. Biel (Eds.), *Brand equity and advertising: Advertising's role in building strong brands,* (p.299–312). Hillsdale, NJ: Lawrence Erlbaum Associates.

Boush, D. M. (1993b). How advertising slogans can prime evaluations of brand extensions. *Psychology and Marketing, 10,* 67–78.

Boush, D. M. (1997). Brand name effects on inter–product similarity judgments. *Marketing Letters, 8,* 419–427.

Boush, D. M., & Loken, B. (1991). A process tracing study of brand extension evaluation. *Journal of Marketing Research, 28,* 16–28.

Boush, D., Shipp, S., Loken, B., Gencturk, E., Crockett, S., Kennedy, E., Minshall, B., Misurell, D., Rochford, L., & Strobel, J. (1987). Affect generalization to similar and dissimilar brand extensions. *Psychology and Marketing, 4,* 225–237.

Bridges, S. A. (1990). *A schema unification model of brand extensions.* Unpublished doctoral dissertation, Stanford University, Palo Alto, CA.

Broniarczyk, S. M., & Alba, J. W. (1994). The importance of the brand in brand extension. *Journal of Marketing Research, 31,* 214–228.

Brown, T. J., & Dacin, P. A. (1997). The company and the product: Corporate associations and consumer product response. *Journal of Marketing, 61,* 68–84.

Bullmore, J. (1984). The brand and its image revisited. *International Journal of Advertising, 3,* 235–238.

Carpenter, G. S., & Lehmann, D. R. (1985). A model of marketing mix, brand switching, and competition. *Journal of Marketing Research, 22,* 318–329.

Carpenter, G. S., & Nakamoto, K. (1989). Consumer preference formation and pioneering advantage. *Journal of Marketing Research, 26,* 285–298.

Collins, A. M. & Loftus, E. F. (1975). A spreading activation theory of semantic processing. *Psychological Review, 82,* 407–428.

Corfman, K. P. & Lehmann, D. R. (1987). Models of cooperative group decision-making and relative influence: An experimental investigation of family purchase decisions. *Journal of Consumer Research, 14,* 1–13.

Craik, F. I. M. & Lockhart, R. S. (1972). Levels of processing: A framework for memory research. *Journal of Verbal Learning and Verbal Behavior, 11,* 671–684.

Crocker, J. (1984). A schematic approach to changing consumer beliefs. In T. C. Kinnear (Ed.), *Advances in consumer research* (Vol. XI, pp. 472–477). Provo, UT: Association for Consumer Research.

Dacin, P., & Smith, D. C. (1994). The effect of brand portfolio characteristics on consumer evaluations of brand extensions. *Journal of Marketing Research, 31,* 229–242.

Day, G. S., & Wensley, R. (1988). Assessing advantage: A framework for diagnosing competitive superiority. *Journal of Marketing, 52,* 1–20.

Dobni, D., & Zinkhan, G. M. (1990). In search of brand image: A foundation analysis. In M. Goldberg, G. Gorn & R. Pollay (Eds.), *Advances in consumer research* (Vol. 17, pp. 110–119). Provo, UT: Association for Consumer Research.

Dogana, F. (1967). Psycholinguistic contributions to the problem of brand names. (Translated from the original Italian.) *European Marketing Research Review, 2,* 50–58.

Erickson, G. M., Johansson, J. K., & Chao, P. (1984). Image variables in multi-attribute product evaluations: Country of origin effects. *Journal of Consumer Research, 11,* 694–699.

Farquhar, P. H. (1989). Managing brand equity. *Marketing Research, 1,* 24–33.

Fishbein, M., & Ajzen, I. (1975). *Belief, attitude, intention and behavior.* Reading, MA: Addison-Wesley.

Fiske, S. T., & Pavelchak, M. A. (1986). Category-based versus piecemeal-based affective responses: Developments in schema triggered affect. In R. W. Sorrentino & E. T. Higgins (Eds.), *The handbook of motivation and cognition: Foundation of social behavior* (pp. 167–203). New York: Guilford.

Fournier, S. (1998). Consumers and their brands: Developing relationship theory in consumer research. *Journal of Consumer Research, 24,* 343–373.

Friedman, R. (1986). Psychological meaning of products: Identification and marketing applications. *Psychology and Marketing, 3,* 1–15.

Gardner, B. B., & Levy, S. J. (1955). The product and the brand. *Harvard Business Review, 33*(March/April), 33–39.

Gardner, M. P. (1985). Does attitude toward the ad affect brand attitude under a brand evaluation set? *Journal of Marketing Research, 22,* 192–198.

Grubb, E. L., & Hupp, G. (1968). Perception of self, stereotypes, and brand selection. *Journal of Marketing Research, 5,* 58–63.

Gutman, J. (1982). A means–end chain model based on consumer categorization processes. *Journal of Marketing, 46,* 60–72.

Haugtvedt, C. P., Leavitt, C., & Schneier, W. (1992). Cognitive strength of established brands: Memory, attitudinal, and structural approaches. In D. A. Aaker & A. L. Biel (Eds.), *Advertising and building strong brands*, (pp. 247–262). Hillsdale, NJ: Lawrence Erlbaum Associates.

Heaton, E. E., Jr. (1967). Testing a new corporate name. *Journal of Marketing Research, 4,* 279–285.

Holman, R. H. (1981). Product as communication: A fresh appraisal of a venerable topic. In B. M. Enis & K. J. Roering (Eds.), *Review of Marketing*, (pp. 106–119). Chicago: American Marketing Association.

Howard, J. (1989). *Consumer behavior in marketing strategy.* Englewood Cliffs, NJ: Prentice-Hall.

Hoyer, W. D. (1984). An examination of decision making for a common repeat purchase product. *Journal of Consumer Research, 11,* 822–829.

Huber, J., & McCann, J. (1982). The impact of inferential beliefs on product evaluations. *Journal of Marketing Research, 19,* 324–333.

Jacobson, R., & Aaker, D. A. (1987). The strategic role of product quality. *Journal of Marketing, 51,* 31–44.

Jacoby, J., & Kyner, D. B. (1973). Brand loyalty vs. repeat purchase behavior. *Journal of Marketing Research, 10,* 1–9.

Jacoby, J., Olson, J. C., & Haddock, R. A. (1971). Price, brand name, and product composition characteristics as determinants of perceived quality. *Journal of Applied Psychology, 55,* 570–579.

Kahle, L. R. (1996). Social values and consumer behavior: Research from the List of Values. In C. Seligman, J. M. Olson, & M. P. Zanna (Eds.), *The psychology of values: The Ontario Symposium* (Vol. 8, pp. 135–151). Mahwah, NJ: Lawrence Erlbaum Associates.

Kanungo, R. N., & Dutta, S. (1966). Brand awareness as a function of its meaningfulness, sequential position, and product utility. *Journal of Applied Psychology, 50,* 220–224.

Kapferer, J. N., & Laurent, G. (1989). Consumers' brand sensitivity: A new concept for brand management (working paper). Paris: Centre HEC ISA.

Keller, K. L. (1993). Conceptualizing, measuring, and managing customer-based brand equity. *Journal of Marketing, 57,* 1–22.

Keller, K. L., & Aaker, D. A. (1992). The effects of sequential introduction of brand extensions. *Journal of Marketing Research, 29,* 35–50.

Kotler, P. (1991). *Marketing management: Analysis, planning and control.* Englewood Cliffs, NJ: Prentice-Hall.

Lamb, C. W., Jr., Hair, J. F., & McDaniel, C. (1998). *Marketing* (4th ed.). Cincinnati, OH: South-Western College Publishing.

Leclerc, F., Schmitt, B. H., & Dubé, L. (1994). Foreign branding and its effects on product perceptions and attitudes. *Journal of Marketing Research, 31,* 263–270.

Lefkoff-Hagius, R., & Mason, C. H. (1990). The role of tangible and intangible attributes in similarity and preference judgments. In M. Goldberg, G. Gorn, & R. Pollay (Eds.), *Advances in Consumer Research, 17,* (135–143). Provo, UT: Association for Consumer Research.

Levin, I. P., & Levin, A. M. (2000). Modeling the role of brand alliances in the assimilation of product evaluations. *Journal of Consumer Psychology, 9,* 43–52.

Lindquist, J. D. (1974–1975). Meaning and image. *Journal of Retailing, 50*(Winter), 29–38.

Linville, P. W. (1982). The complexity–extremity effect and age-based stereotyping. *Journal of Personality and Social Psychology, 42,* 193–211.

Loken, B., & John, D. R. (1993). Diluting brand beliefs: When do brand extensions have a negative impact? *Journal of Marketing, 57,* 71–84.

Loken, B., Joiner, C., & Peck, J. (2002). Category attitude measures: Exemplars as inputs. *Journal of Consumer Psychology, 12,* 149–161.

Loken, B., & Ward, J. (1990). Alternative approaches to understanding the determinants of typicality. *Journal of Consumer Research, 17,* 111–126.

Lutz, K. A., &Lutz, R. J. (1977). Effects of interactive imagery on learning: Application to advertising. *Journal of Applied Psychology, 62,* 493–498.

Lynch, J. G., Marmorstein, H., & Weigold, M. F. (1988). Choices from sets including remembered brands: Use of recalled attributes and prior overall evaluations. *Journal of Consumer Research, 15,* 169–184.

MacInnis, D. J., & Price, L. L. (1987). The role of imagery in information processing: Review and extensions. *Journal of Consumer Research, 13,* 473–491.

Martineau, P. (1958). The personality of the retail store. *Harvard Business Review, 36.* 47–55.

McAlexander, J. H., Schouten, J. W., & Koenig, H. (2002), Building brand community. *Journal of Marketing, 66,* 38–54.

Mehrabian, A., & de Wetter, R. (1987). Experimental test of an emotion-based approach to fitting brand names to products. *Journal of Applied Psychology, 72,* 125–130.

Mervis, C. B., & Rosch, E. (1981). Categorization of natural objects. *Annual Review of Psychology, 32,* 89–115.

Meyers-Levy, J. & Sternthal, B. (1993). A two-factor explanation of assimilation and contrast effects. *Journal of Marketing Research, 30,* 359–368.

Mitchell, A. (1986). The effect of verbal and visual components of advertisements on brand attitudes and attitude toward the advertisement. *Journal of Consumer Research, 13,* 12–24.

Mittal, B., Ratchford, B., & Prabhakar, P. (1990). Functional and expressive attributes as determinants of brand attitude. *Research in Marketing, 10,* 135–55.

Moorthy, K. S. (1985). Using game theory to model competition. *Journal of Marketing Research, 22,* 262–282.

Muniz, A. M., & O'Guinn, T. C. (2000). Brand community. *Journal of Consumer Research, 27,* 412–432.

Nash, J. (1950). Equilibrium points in n-person games. *Proceedings of the National Academy of Sciences, 36,* 48–49.

Nedungadi, P. (1990). Recall and consumer consideration sets: Influencing choice without altering brand evaluations. *Journal of Consumer Research, 17,* 263–276.

Nedungadi, P., & Hutchinson, J. W. (1985). The prototypicality of brands: Relationships with brand awareness, preference, and usage. In E. C. Hirschman & M. B. Holbrook (Eds.), *Advances in consumer research* (Vol. 12, pp. 498–503.) Provo, UT: Association for Consumer Research.

Newman, J. W. (1957). New insight, new progress, for marketing. *Harvard Business Review,* 95–102.

Ogilvy, D. (1983). *Ogilvy on advertising,* New York: Crown.

Osgood, C. E. (1963). Psycholinguistics. In S. Koch (Ed.), *Psychology: A study of science* (Vol. 6) New York: McGraw-Hill.

Paivio, A. (1969). Mental imagery and associative learning and memory. *Psychological Review, 76,* 241–63.

Park, C. W., Jaworski, B. J., & MacInnis, D. J. (1986). Strategic brand concept–image management. *Journal of Marketing, 50,* 135–145.

Park, C. W., Jun, S. Y., & Shocker, A. D. (1996). Composite branding alliances: An investigation of extension and feedback effects. *Journal of Marketing Research, 33,* 453–466.

Park, C. W., Milberg, S., & Lawson, R. (1991). Evaluation of brand extensions: The role of product-feature similarity and concept consistency. *Journal of Consumer Research, 18,* 185–193.

Peterson, R. A., & Ross, I. (1972). How to name new brands. *Journal of Advertising Research, 12,* 29–34.

Porter, M. E. (1974). Consumer behavior, retailer power, and market performance in consumer good industries. *The Review of Economics and Statistics, 56,* 423–438.

Puto, C. P., & Wells, W. D. (1984). Informational and transformational advertising: The differential effects of time. In T. C. Kinnear (Ed.), *Proceedings of the Association for Consumer Research* (Vol. 11, pp. 638–643). Provo, UT: Association for Consumer Research.

Rao, A. R., & Monroe, K. B. (1989). The effect of price, brand name and store name on buyers' perceptions of product quality: An integrative review. *Journal of Marketing Research, 26,* 351–57.

Rao, A. R., & Ruekert, R. W. (1994). Brand alliances as signals of product quality. *Sloan Management Review, 36,* 87–98.

Ratneshwar, S., & Shocker, A. D. (1991). Substitution in use and the role of usage context in product category structures. *Journal of Marketing Research, 28,* 281–295.

Reingen, P. H., Foster, B. L., Brown, J. J., & Seidman, S. B. (1984). Brand congruence in interpersonal relations: A social network analysis. *Journal of Consumer Research, 11,* 771–783.

Reynolds, T. J., & Gutman, J. (1984). Advertising is image management. *Journal of Advertising Research, 24,* 27–38.

Ries, A., & Trout, J. (1981). *Positioning: The battle for your mind.* New York: McGraw-Hill.

Robertson, K. R. (1987). Recall and recognition effects of brand name imagery. *Psychology and Marketing, 4*(Spring), 3–15.

Rokeach, M. (1968). *Beliefs, attitudes, and values,* San Francisco: Jossey-Bass.

Rosch, E., & Mervis, C. B. (1975). Family resemblances: Studies in the internal structure of categories. *Cognitive Psychology, 7,* 573–605.

Rosch, E., Simpson, C., & Miller, R. S. (1976). Structure bases of typicality effects. *Journal of Experimental Psychology: Human Perception and Performance, 2,* 491–502.

Sapir, E. (1929). A study in phonetic symbolism. *Journal of Experimental Psychology, 12,* 225–239.

Schenk, C. T., & Holman, R. H. (1980). A sociological approach to brand choice: The concept of situational self-image. In J. Olson (Ed.), *Advances in Consumer Research,* Vol. VII, Ann Arbor, MI: Association for Consumer Research, 610–614.

Schloss, I. (1981). Chicken and pickles, choosing a brand name. *Journal of Advertising Research, 21,* 47–49.

Schmitt, B., & Dube, L. (1992). Contextualized representations of brand extensions: Are feature lists or frames the basic components of consumer cognition? *Marketing Letters, 3,* 115–126.

Shocker, A. D. (1995). Positive and negative effects of brand extension and co-branding. *Advances in Consumer Research, 22,* 432–434.

Simon, C. J., & Sullivan, M. W. (1990). *The measurement and determinants of brand equity: A financial approach.* Working paper, The University of Chicago.

Simonin, B. L., & Ruth, J. A. (1998). Is a company known by the company it keeps? Assessing the spillover effects of brand alliances on consumer brand attitudes. *Journal of Marketing Research, 35,* 30–43.

Simonson, I., Huber, J., & Payne, J. (1988). The relationship between prior brand knowledge and information acquisition order. *Journal of Consumer Research, 14,* 566–578.

Sirgy, J. M. (1982). Self-concept in consumer behavior: A critical review. *Journal of Consumer Research, 9,* 287–300.

Smith, D. C., & Park, C.W. (1992). The effects of brand extensions on market share and advertising efficiency. *Journal of Marketing Research, 29,* 296–313.

Smith, E. E., Shoben, E. J., & Rips, L. J. (1974). Structure and process in semantic memory: A featural model for semantic decisions. *Psychological Review, 81,* 214–241.

Sujan, M. (1985). Consumer knowledge: Effects on evaluation strategies mediating consumer judgments. *Journal of Consumer Research, 12,* 31–46.

Tauber, E. M. (1988). Brand leverage: Strategy for growth in a cost control world. *Journal of Advertising Research, 31,* 26–30.

Tellis, G. J. (1988). Advertising exposure, loyalty, and brand purchase: A two-stage model of choice. *Journal of Marketing Research, 25,* 134–144.

Tversky, A. (1977). Features of similarity. *Psychological Review, 84,* 327–350.

Urban, G. L., Carter, T. C., Gaskin, S., & Mucha, Z. (1986). Market share rewards to pioneering brands: An empirical analysis and strategic implications. *Management Science, 32,* 645–659.

Vanden Berg, B., Collins, J., Schultz, M., & Adler, K. (1984). Sound advice on brand names. *Journalism Quarterly, 61,* 835–840.

Van Osselaer, S. M. J., & Alba, J. W. (2003). Locus of equity and brand extension. *Journal of Consumer Research, 29,* 539–550.

Wernerfelt, B. (1988). Umbrella branding as a signal of new product quality: An example of signaling by posting a bond. *RAND Journal of Economics, 19,* 458–466.

Zinkhan, G. M., & Martin, C. R., Jr. (1987). New brand names and inferential beliefs: Some insights on naming new products. *Journal of Business Research, 15,* 157–172.

CHAPTER TWO

Measuring the Prototypicality of Product Categories and Exemplars: Implications of Schema Correspondence Theory

Laura A. Brannon
Kansas State University

Timothy C. Brock
The Ohio State University

To a great extent public image and public personality are coextensive. For example, the public image and public personality of Mother Teresa (or of Saddam Hussein) undoubtedly overlap. We here assume that products and particular brands of products have overlapping personalities and images, just as people do: "A brand's personality [or image] can be thought of as a gestalt of the brand schema—that is, a global or top-level description of the important and affect-laden features of the brand schema .... brand schemas largely determine how the consumer reacts to advertising and brand personalities describe the essence of brand schemas" (Sentis & Markus, 1986, p. 133). In other words, people have cognitive schemas representing all their beliefs and feelings about a brand of product, and the personality of a brand is a synthesis of the contents of the brand schema. The personality or image of a brand is important for advertising because "consumers will choose those products that match their self-perceptions" (Sentis & Markus, 1986, p. 134). Shavitt (1985, 1989) also argued that products have personalities that, in Shavitt's words, serve attitude-functions. Products should therefore be advertised using appeals that are congruent with the attitude-function, or personality type of the product. For example, an air conditioner serves a utilitarian attitude-function and would best be touted with utilitarian appeals.

People too, of course, have personalities, which may or may not conflict with the personality of the brand or product. Brock, Brannon, and Bridgwater (1990) reported experiments that demonstrated that gearing persuasive appeals to recipients' personality types significantly increased their effectiveness compared to nonmatching messages.

In which situations would matching messages to recipients' personalities increases message effectiveness more than matching messages to the personality type of the product, and vice versa? Of course, not all products have clearly defined personality types; in Shavitt's terms, some objects serve multiple attitude functions. As Shavitt (1989) stated:

> A situational induction should take into account the attitude functions that are typically engaged by attitude objects. That is, situational factors are unlikely to induce attitude functions for objects that rarely engage those functions. This suggests that attempts to induce new functions for attitudes would be more successful if they employed attitude objects that are unfamiliar to participants and capable of engaging a variety of attitude functions, rather than objects for which attitudes serving other functions already exist. Instead of attempting to overcome the functions of existing attitudes, the function(s) to be induced could guide the formation of attitudes toward an unfamiliar object. (pp. 329–330)

In sum, when matching message appeals to the personality type or attitude function of a product, the problem is that not all products have clearly defined personalities or images.

CONCEPTS AND EXEMPLARS

It may be apparent that the notion of some products as better exemplars of a particular personality type than others is directly related to the literature concerning concepts and prototypical-fuzzy sets (Smith, 1988). Concepts serve three primary functions: promoting cognitive economy, making inferences beyond the available perceptual information, and contributing to more complex thoughts and concepts (Smith, 1988). Although exemplars of a concept were once thought to have singly necessary and jointly sufficient properties, it is now acknowledged that not all exemplars are equally representative of a particular concept: Some exemplars are prototypical, in that they are "good" representatives of the concept, whereas other exemplars are fuzzy, in that they are rather "poor" representatives of the concept. One can also imagine, then, that some products or brands of products are more prototypical of a given personality type than others.

THE THEORY OF SCHEMA CORRESPONDENCE

Any persuasive situation can be thought of as consisting of three essential components: the recipient (and his or her personality type), the attitude object or topic (and its personality type), and the persuasive appeal. In a consumer setting, these components become the recipient, the product, and the advertisement and its appeals. The theory of schema correspondence states that advertising effectiveness is an increasing function of fit between the personalities of these three elements: the product (or brand), the appeal, and the recipient. The key question is, "When is it better to match the persuasive appeal to the recipient, versus the product?" For example, it seems clear that, if the recipient is a thrill seeker, and if motorcycles are seen as thrill seeking, then the best way to advertise a motorcycle to this particular person would be to use thrill-seeking appeals. However, what type of appeals should be used if the person is not a thrill seeker, but rather a reliable, family member? It has been suggested that products can vary in their degree of prototypicality for a given personality type. Perhaps the conflict between product–personality and recipient–personality matching can be resolved by examining the degree of prototypicality of the product. Product matching messages may be more persuasive than recipient-type matching messages in certain instances, such as when the product is prototypical. In most instances, however, when the type of product is fuzzy, gearing message appeals to recipients' personalities would probably be more persuasive. Brannon and Brock (1994) obtained some support for this latter hypothesis. They found that messages reflecting participants' needs and values were significantly more persuasive than product-type matching messages for a fuzzy product (as defined in the next section), whereas this difference disappeared for a prototypical product. Thus, it is possible to change people's perceptions of fuzzy products. For example, what was once seen as being a thrill-affording type of product may, through advertising, come to be seen as a reliable and dependable type of product.

PROTOTYPICALITY FORMULA

The key to testing the theory of schema correspondence is a metric for prototypicality—fuzziness. Two major approaches have been used for assessing category prototypicality, measures of between-participants disagreements and measures of within-participants disagreements (Mervis & Rosch, 1981). For the present purposes, it was decided that a measure of between-subject disagreement would best define prototypicality because, in an advertising situation, one wishes to persuade as many potential consumers as possible; one is interested in producing even small effects for as many people as possible, rather than producing somewhat larger effects on just a few individuals. It would be desirable to have a formula that would examine the nature of between-subject uncertainty and would consider the distribution of participants' ratings. A solution for an effective measure of prototypicality–fuzziness was found in a *Psychometrika* article by Shuford, Albert, and Massengill (1966). Shuford et al. were concerned with students' degree-of-belief probabilities about responses to test items. Briefly, Shuford et al. developed a scoring system in which students respond to multiple-choice test items by stating the probability that each possible response was correct: "the score is strictly determined by the probability assigned to the correct answer and the way in which the student's uncertainty is distributed over the other answers" (p. 134). The logic behind this formula can easily be modified to examine the degree of certainty a group of people has about an item representing a particular concept. Instead of using an individual's assigned probabilities for each concept, one could examine the probabilities of an entire group and use these probabilities in the formula. The final prototypicality formula was a modified version of that of Shuford et al. (with linear transformations performed to create a range of possible scores of 0 to 100, with 0 being totally fuzzy, and 100 being prototypical of a particular concept):

$$\text{Prototypicality} = \frac{[[1 + x_l^2 - (1 - x_l)^2 - (x_i^2 + \ldots + x_n^2)] - 1/n]}{1 - 1/n} * 100\%$$

where n = number of considered types or rating categories (here "colors," as described later), x_n is the proportion (from 0.00 to 1.00) of persons who rated the object as a given type, and x_l is the highest proportion that any type received. The object is assigned to the category to which most people assigned it (x_l) or, in the case of a tie, to both types (i.e., a matching message can match either type for the fuzzy object). The essential part of the formula is $[1 + x_l^2 - (1 - x_l)^2 -$ summation of $(x_i^2 + \ldots + x_n^2)$. Here is the linear transformation for the present case when $n = 4$:

$$\text{Prototypicality} = \frac{[[1 + x_l^2 - (1 - x_l)^2 - (x_i^2 + \ldots + x_n^2)] - .25]}{.75} * 100\%$$

This linear transformation can be changed for any n, if it is desired that 100% represent a totally prototypical exemplar and 0% represent a totally fuzzy exemplar.

The formula considers the distribution of ratings for an object, giving higher scores to objects for which there is a high degree of concept agreement and lower scores to items for which there is little agreement. Later in this chapter, the results of demonstrations dealing with the nature of prototypicality–fuzziness are discussed. In those demonstrations, participants were asked to pick which of four concepts a particular object exemplified. To demonstrate how the prototypicality formula functions, a few examples are now given. In this instance, n (i.e., the number of concepts under consideration) is equal to 4. The most prototypical exemplar is one for which 100% of the persons agree that the object is an exemplar of the same concept, x_l; in this case, the prototypicality formula yields a value of 100% ($x_1 = 100, x_2 = x_3 = x_4 = 0$). The most fuzzy exemplar is one for which there is virtually no consensus; 25% of the persons rate the object as being an exemplar of each of the four concepts ($x_1 = x_2 = x_3 = x_4 = 25$). In this case, the prototypicality formula yields a value of 0%. However, the logic behind the prototypicality formula is best demonstrated by examining objects that are neither totally fuzzy nor prototypical. An object that received 50% for two concepts (i.e., $x_1 = x_2 = 50, x_3 = x_4 = 0$) yields a prototypicality score of 33.3%. An object that received 50% ($x_j = 50$) for one concept and was fairly equally divided between the other three concepts ($x_2 = 17$, $x_3 = 17$, $x_4 = 16$) yields a prototypicality score of 55.6%. In the second mixed case, the concept for which the object is an exemplar is clear, whereas in the first mixed case, the concept that the object is an exemplar of is unclear. It is one of two concepts. Therefore, the first object is more fuzzy than the second and consequently yields a lower prototypicality score. Unlike other between-subject formulations of prototypicality (e.g., Cantor, Smith, French, & Mezzich, 1980; McCloskey & Glucksberg, 1978), the present prototypicality formula considers the distribution, as well as the degree of between-subject uncertainty. In the demonstrations that follow, the prototypicality formula is discussed in greater detail.

ASSUMPTIONS AND HYPOTHESES

It is assumed that products and their advertisements, as well as people, have personalities and that participants can categorize products and advertisements into their corresponding personality types. Akin to past research on prototypical–fuzzy sets, some products and advertisements should be easier to categorize than others because they are better exemplars (i.e., more prototypical) of a given personality type (i.e., concept). It is hypothesized that when the product itself is fuzzy, then specific brands, and perhaps even the product category, may be perceived differently (i.e., categorized differently) depending on the advertisement. Consequently, familiar brands of products may tend to be categorized differently than their corresponding product category (as a result of advertising and possibly use) or than unfamiliar brands. It is hypothesized that if a person has had no exposure to a particular brand of product, he or she will tend to perceive the unfamiliar brand as being similar to the generic category of product (because there is no other information on which to base categorization). It is also hypothesized that the prototypicality formula, by considering the distribution of between-subject uncertainty, will provide unique information above and beyond that given by participants' self-rated representativeness scores, which will be reflected in significant but not substantial correlations between self-rated representativeness and between-subject uncertainty (via the prototypicality formula).

DEMONSTRATION I

Method

Participants.   Seventy-one college freshmen participated for course credit.

Materials.   A card-ranking procedure was used to classify the products into their personality types (i.e., superordinate concepts). The aim was to enable participants to classify product categories, brands, and advertisements quickly and easily into one of four personality profiles (i.e., concepts). The profiles are not necessarily the ones that may emerge from psychometrically rigorous investigation (e.g. Mc-Crae & Costa, 1987). Instead, the profiles were adapted from a four-type scheme proposed by Keirsey and Bates (1978; see also Miscisin, 2001), a popular alternative to the 16-fold Myers-Briggs Type Indicator. The profiles, depicted on four cards, achieved their purpose, namely quick and easy classification by participants (Brannon & Brock, 1994). Participants received four cards printed in four colors (i.e., orange, brown, blue, and green), each containing four trait adjectives preceded by "I am ... ," a short descriptive paragraph that elaborated the adjectives, and a composite drawing of persons whose activities and costuming embodied the traits and descriptive paragraph. A distinct personality profile (i.e., concept) was depicted on each card: warm–communicative–compassionate (blue), adventuresome–skillful–competitive (orange), versatile–wise–conceptual (green), or responsible–dependable–helpful (brown). For example, the blue card displayed a man and woman holding hands; the top of the card listed the four adjectives, "I am warm–communicative–compassionate–feeling"; and the descriptive paragraph was as follows: "I need to search for the meaning and significance of life. I want to find ways to make my life count and matter, to become my own authentic self. Integrity, harmony and honesty are very important to me. I feel that I am highly idealistic and spiritual by nature."

Procedure.   Participants were given a consumer survey, which asked them to categorize (according to the four colored cards) 16 different familiar and unfamiliar brands of products and their corresponding product categories. One product category or brand was listed per page, and participants were asked to "Look at the four types on the four attached cards. A [category or brand] is what type of product (name the color)?" The items were chosen to represent a wide variety of consumer products.

Results

The prototypicality scores for the familiar and unfamiliar brands, and their corresponding categories are listed in the top panel of Table 2.1. People were able to categorize product categories and familiar and unfamiliar brands of those products rather easily. The prototypicality formula yielded a wide range of scores (ranging from 17.6% to 100%, across brands and categories); therefore, it appears that the formula is sensitive in detecting differences in perceived prototypicality. The formula effectively discriminates between prototypical and fuzzy products.

There was some support for the hypothesis that unfamiliar brands would be rated more similarly to their corresponding product category than familiar brands. The mean difference score between categories and their corresponding unfamiliar

TABLE 2.1

Prototypicality Scores for Product Categories, Brands (Unfamiliar and Familiar),
and Advertisements (Unfamiliar and Familiar)

	Demonstration 1 (N = 71)		
		Brand	
Product	Category	Unfamiliar	Familiar
Camera	[25.3 Gr]	41.5 Gr	[19.0 Br]
Cold remedy	[86.9 Br]	96.4 Br	95.5 Br
Computer	[94.5 Gr]	89.3 Gr	79.8 Gr
Credit card	[51.5 Br]	60.0 Br	67.6 Br
Florist	[97.0 Bl]	97.9 Bl	[97.1 Bl]
Hairspray	[51.9 Br]	46.0 Br	45.2 Br
Mouthwash	[88.5 Br]	82.3 Br	[97.5 Br]
Long distance phone	[58.0 Br]	66.3 Br	[65.0 Br]
Shampoo	[82.4 Br]	29.8 Br	71.9 Br
Department store	[54.5 Br]	59.4 Br	82.1 Br
Sweetener	[37.1 Bl]	26.4 Gr	17.6 Gr
Toothpaste	[91.5 Br]	84.1 Br	56.0 Br
Amusement park	99.6 Or	99.6 Or	96.9 Or
Greeting card	98.2 Bl	98.6 Bl	99.1 Bl
Scientific calculator	83.8 Gr	83.3 Gr	78.8 Gr
Motorcycle	100.0 Or	99.6 Or	99.4 Or
Overall mean	75.0	72.5	78.3

	Demonstration 2 (N = 120)				
		Brand		Advertisement	
Product	Category	Unfamiliar	Familiar	Unfamiliar	Familiar
Advertisements first (N = 74)					
Camera	82.5 Or	81.9 Or	71.7 Or	99.2 Or	54.8 Or
Cold remedy	87.2 Br	76.1 Br	90.7 Br	35.1 Bl	91.4 Br
Computer	67.0 Gr	75.8 Gr	76.8 Gr	21.5 Gr	86.0 Gr
Credit card	55.9 Or	52.1 Or	96.0 Or		
Florist	99.0 Bl	97.2 Bl	88.6 Bl		
Hairspray	31.5 Br	36.2 Or	65.5 Or		
Mouthwash	87.5 Br	81.1 Br	66.2 Br		
Long distance phone	34.7 Bl	43.0 Bl	50.1 Bl		
Shampoo	59.5 Br	54.0 Bl	97.6 Bl		
Department store	65.6 Br	66.0 Br	40.3 Br		
Artificial sweetener	54.9 Br	36.1 Gr	57.5 Gr		
Toothpaste	93.2 Br	93.2 Br	52.4 Br		
Mean	68.2	77.9	66.5	51.9	70.5
Advertisements last (N = 46)					
Camera	34.1 Or	39.9 Or	37.9 Or	98.4 Or	56.9 Or
Cold remedy	89.3 Br	95.1 Br	89.6 Br	41.1 Br	94.3 Br
Computer	65.5 Gr	79.5 Gr	73.4 Gr	46.9 Gr	69.6 Gr
Credit card	40.9 Or	31.6 Or	95.5 Or		

(continued)

TABLE 2.1 (*Continued*)

		Brand		Advertisement	
Product	Category	Unfamiliar	Familiar	Unfamiliar	Familiar
Florist	97.5 Bl	98.4 Bl	95.6 Bl		
Hairspray	49.4 Br	55.2 Br	31.3 Or		
Mouthwash	71.6 Br	81.5 Br	88.7 Br		
Long distance phone	58.6 Br	60.5 Br	69.8 Bl		
Shampoo	82.8 Br	80.4 Br	96.8 Bl		
Department store	46.7 Or	37.0 Or	18.2 Bl		
Artificial sweetener	25.9 Bl	22.9 Bl	30.9 Gr		
Toothpaste	92.9 Br	87.0 Br	94.1 Br		
Mean	69.9	71.5	63.0	62.1	70.1
Overall mean	69.1	74.7	64.7	57.0	70.3

Demonstration 2 (N = 120)

Note. See text for prototypicality formula. For Demonstration 1, products that have prototypicality scores in brackets are comparable to those in Demonstration 2. All other products or brands were different in Demonstrations 1 and 2. Letters appearing after prototypicality scores reflect the type of product (via card ranking). Bl = Blue = warm, compassionate, communicative; Or = Orange = adventuresome, skillful, competitive; Gr = Green = versatile, wise, conceptual; Br = Brown = responsible, dependable, helpful. See text for further description of types.

brand was 8.6%, whereas the corresponding difference between familiar brands and their product categories was 10.7%. An examination of the data revealed that, in most instances, unfamiliar brands received prototypicality scores closer to their product categories than did familiar brands. In fact, the only significant exception to this trend was for the unfamiliar brand of shampoo, which was rated significantly less prototypical than its corresponding category or familiar brand (29.8% versus 82.4% and 71.9%, respectively). Although the anomalous shampoo data should not be discounted, when it is not included in the analyses the mean prototypicality difference score and corresponding standard deviation between product category and unfamiliar brands drops significantly (i.e., mean difference changes from 8.6% to 5.7%; mean standard deviation changes from 12.6 to 4.7) relative to that of familiar brands versus categories (i.e., no mean difference change; standard deviation changes from 9.9 to 10.3). The removal of the shampoo data more clearly reveals that unfamiliar brands are closer in prototypicality to their corresponding categories than are familiar brands.

It appeared that brands of products sometimes were rated differently than their product category (perhaps as a result of advertising). This was especially the case for fuzzy products. The two fuzziest products, a camera and an artificial sweetener, were rated in at least one instance as being different types than their corresponding categories. Therefore, a second demonstration was designed to examine the impact of advertising on perceived prototypicality.

DEMONSTRATION 2

Method

Participants. One hundred twenty college freshmen participated for course credit.

Materials. The same card-ranking procedure used in Demonstration 1 was used to classify products and advertisements into their personality types. Participants were given a booklet of advertisements and three questionnaires, one referring to the advertisements, one to the brands of the products in the advertisements, and one to the category of the advertised products. Both familiar and unfamiliar brands and advertisements (where available) were used. Each page of the booklet contained a product category, brand, or advertisement, which the subject was asked to type. Depending on the object to be classified, the printed instructions on each page of the booklet were one of the following: "Look at the whole advertisement about a [type of product] in the accompanying booklet. Also, look at the four attached cards. The advertisement for the [name of product] is what type of advertisement (name the color)?" "Look at the four types on the attached cards. [Brand and product name] is what type of product (name the color)?" "Look at the four attached cards. A [category of product] is what type of product (name the color)?"

Procedure. Participants were given the booklet of advertisements and the three questionnaires. Participants filled out the questionnaires in one of two orders: advertisements–brands–categories, or categories–brands–advertisements (so that the impact of prior classifications on later classifications could be examined). In addition, the advertisements, brands, and categories in each booklet were randomly ordered. For each product category, brand, or advertisement, participants first classified the product as one of the four personality types and then filled out three 10-point scales concerning the product's representativeness of that type, their confidence in their classification, and the ease with which they classified the product. Participants were given as much time as they needed to fill out the questionnaires, with one exception: Participants were allowed to look at each advertisement for only one minute, after which time a tone sounded and participants were instructed to go on to the next advertisement. It was assumed that, under normal circumstances, people only look at an advertisement for about one minute, if that long.

Results. The primary results are shown in the bottom panel of Table 2.1, the prototypicality scores for product categories, brands, and advertisements. The table is divided into two sections: prototypicality scores for product categories, brands, and advertisements when the advertisement preceded the categories and brands; and prototypicality scores for product categories, brands, and advertisements when the advertisements were rated last, following the categories and brands. Due to space limitations, only selected findings are discussed here. People were able to rate advertisements as well as product categories and brands. Prototypicality scores were not significantly different for advertisements versus product categories versus brands: The overall mean prototypicality scores, collapsing across familiarity, ranged from 66.7% for brands to 69.1% for product categories. Also, as in Demonstration 1, the prototypicality formula yielded a wide range of scores, ranging from 18.2% to 99.2%, across categories and brands, and appeared to discriminate between fuzzy and prototypical products, brands, and advertisements. This wide range of prototypicality scores can be contrasted with that of the representativeness scores, which ranged from 51.80 to 86.30 (actually, the range was from 5.18 to 8.63 on 10-point scales; these scores were multiplied by 100 to make them comparable to those yielded by the prototypicality formula).

The prototypicality formula also yielded fairly reliable scores. The category ratings for Demonstration 1 can be compared to the category ratings of participants who rated the advertisements last in Demonstration 2 (the category data for those who first saw the advertisements might not be as pure as the data from those who saw the advertisements last). Also, participants rated some categories and brands in Demonstration 1 that were not rated in Demonstration 2. It should be noted that the specific brands of products used in Demonstration 2 were not necessarily those used in Demonstration 1. Only those products or brands that appear in brackets for Demonstration 1 corresponded to those in Demonstration 2 and are appropriate for comparison. The average difference between prototypicality scores of product categories for Demonstrations 1 and 2 was 7.7% (sd = 8.6), indicating a fairly high degree of reliability. Additionally, it appeared that products, brands, or categories that received prototypicality scores of 60 or higher did not, under any circumstances, change their rated personality types (i.e., categories). Therefore, from these limited data, it appears that objects that receive scores of 60% or higher may be considered to be prototypical, and those that receive scores lower than 60% may be considered to be fuzzy, with all the important cognitive implications of fuzziness.

Participants' responses to questions concerning the representativeness of the products or advertisements, their confidence in their categorizations, and the ease (Table 2.2) of categorizing the products were all highly correlated $(r > .98)$. These ratings were significantly, but not substantially, correlated with the prototypicality values (rs between .45 and .47, ps < .01), indicating that the prototypicality formula in fact added information beyond that of representativeness scores.

There was also some support for the hypothesis that rhetoric (or an advertisement) can change the way a fuzzy product is perceived. For example, participants who categorized the hairspray before the advertisement rated both the product category and the familiar brand as brown. However, participants who were first exposed to an orange advertisement for a hairspray subsequently classified that familiar brand of hairspray as being orange also, rather than brown. Similar tendencies for brands of products to be rated similarly to their corresponding advertise-

TABLE 2.2

Ease Scores (Demonstration 2)

Product	Category	Brand		Advertisement	
		Unfamiliar	Familiar	Unfamiliar	Familiar
Advertisement first (N = 74)					
Camera	6.81	6.05	6.74	8.94	6.89
Cold remedy	7.12	5.89	6.97	6.49	6.47
Computer	7.97	6.62	7.64	6.72	6.76
Credit card	7.49		8.16		8.11
Florist	8.15		7.95		7.04
Hairspray	6.59		6.70		6.33
Mouthwash	6.68		6.88		6.44
Long distance phone	7.15		7.22		6.64
Shampoo	6.46		7.26		7.95
Department store	6.18		6.03		5.78
Artificial sweetener	5.07		5.49		5.09
Toothpaste	6.85		6.88		6.18
Mean	6.88	6.19	6.99	7.38	6.64
Advertisement last (N = 46)					
Camera	5.24	4.72	6.63	8.26	6.43
Cold remedy	5.80	4.74	6.67	6.76	6.76
Computer	7.48	5.49	7.17	6.65	6.93
Credit card	6.43		6.61		7.55
Florist	6.82		7.59		7.41
Hairspray	4.32		4.98		6.22
Mouthwash	4.63		5.80		6.74
Long distance phone	5.45		6.59		6.69
Shampoo	5.09		5.61		7.13
Department store	5.50		5.33		5.78
Artificial sweetener	3.59		4.37		4.93
Toothpaste	4.40		6.04		6.37
Mean	5.40	4.98	6.12	7.22	6.58
Overall mean	6.14	5.59	6.56	7.30	6.61

ments were observed for the familiar long distance phone service, the familiar shampoo, and the familiar artificial sweetener. The data for the long distance phone service are particularly impressive: Not only did participants rate the familiar brand of phone service similarly to the advertisement, but they also rated the product category to correspond to the advertisement. This finding suggests one way of examining advertising effectiveness, namely, whether the advertisement is powerful enough to cause people to change not only their opinions of the particular brand of product but also their perceptions of the product category itself.

DEMONSTRATION 3

Purpose and Method

A follow-up demonstration was conducted to check assumptions about brand familiarity in Demonstration 2 and to assess the stability of product profiling and
prototypicality across time.

Participants.   Seventy-seven underclass men and women participated for
course credit.

Materials and Procedure.   The materials and procedure were similar to
Demonstrations 1 and 2 except that additional questions were included to measure
perceived category and exemplar familiarity. Participants were asked, "How easy
was it to color-type [names of category or product]," and "How familiar are you
with [name of product]?" No advertisements were considered in Demonstration 3.

Results.   Table 2.3 lists the brands used and their assumed familiarity. In general, it can be seen that our assumptions about familiarity versus unfamiliarity were
empirically well supported. For example, IBM (computer) was rated more familiar
than Entre (computer).

Table 2.4 shows prototypicality scores for categories and exemplars within categories. Participants' responses to questions concerning the representativeness of
the product or advertisement, their confidence in their categorizations, and the ease
of categorizing the products were all highly correlated ($rs > .96$). These ratings
were significantly, but not substantially, correlated with the prototypicality values
(rs between .54 and .62, $ps < .01$), again indicating that the prototypicality formula
added information beyond that of representativeness scores. Note that some brands

TABLE 2.3

Brand Familiarity Ratings (Demonstration 3)

	Assumed Unfamiliar	*Assumed Familiar*
Camera (Rollei vs. Polaroid)	1.2	9.2
Cold Remedy (Hismanal vs. Actifed)	1.3	3.8
Computer (Entre vs. IBM)	1.6	8.9
American Express		7.9
FTD		5.1
Final (hairspray)		2.6
Listerine		9.2
AT & T		9.1
Ivory (shampoo)		6.1
Marshalls (store)		6.5
Equal (sweetener)		7.7

Note. Familiarity ratings for brands in Demonstration 3. See text for explanation.

TABLE 2.4

Prototypicality Scores, Typing, Rating Ease, and Perceived Familiarity
for Categories and Brands in Demonstration 3

Product	Prototypicality	Color	Ease	Familiarity
Credit card category	55.08	Brown	5.98	—
Credit thrift credit card	62.05	Brown	4.93	1.93
MasterCard	69.79	Brown	7.46	8.42
Visa	75.41	Brown	7.68	8.68
American Express	67.27	Brown	7.20	7.43
Amusement park category	97.85	Orange	7.87	—
Lake Darien	93.62	Orange	5.96	1.96
Disney	76.21	Orange	8.10	8.50
King's Island	97.73	Orange	8.49	8.41
Deodorant category	31.58	Brown	5.44	—
CertainDri	33.51	Brown	4.62	2.38
Old Spice	31.27	Brown	6.93	7.69
Secret	77.30	Blue	6.84	7.20
Right Guard	49.22	Brown	6.67	6.74
Shampoo category	30.55	Blue	5.25	—
Abound	25.67	Blue	4.00	1.54
Herbal Essence	67.56	Blue	7.32	8.76
Suave	37.54	Blue	6.53	7.98
Pert	35.39	Green	6.57	7.25
Soap category	32.48	Brown	5.23	—
Caldrea	28.95	Blue	3.94	1.67
Caress	82.50	Blue	6.68	7.12
Dial	33.46	Brown	7.00	8.92
Lever 2000	12.58	Green	6.73	8.14
Zest	23.00	Blue	7.05	8.21
Safeguard	57.64	Brown	6.17	5.64
Oil of Olay	78.81	Blue	6.88	7.73
Toothpaste	43.95	Brown	5.03	—
Biotene	25.61	Green	4.36	1.57
Arm & Hammer	60.67	Brown	6.73	7.91
CloseUp	23.32	Blue	5.71	4.65

of products, like amusement parks, are always rated the same color as the category (orange). On the other hand, although all the amusement parks are orange, Disney is rated as being less prototypical. Evidently, advertising can influence strength of the color classification, even if it doesn't change the color.

All the other categories, except credit card, showed some product exemplars that were rated differently from the category. Secret was the only blue deodorant; Pert was the only green shampoo; the soaps and toothpastes could be brown, blue, or green. Again, there is evidence that advertising about image can change the image or personality of a brand of product from that of its category.

The category color types were similar to those found in previous demonstrations (i.e., amusement park is orange in all demonstrations; toothpaste is brown in all demonstrations). Credit card was orange in Demonstration 2 but brown in Demonstrations 1 and 3. Shampoo was brown in the previous demonstrations, whereas here it was fuzzy blue. For shampoo, even though there is a difference from the previous demonstrations, the change was not from one prototypical color to a different prototypical color: Shampoo changed from relatively prototypical brown, to fuzzy blue. Evidently categories can change their fundamental positionings over time (e.g., credit card). Given that the shampoo exemplars in our demonstration are largely blue, the blue advertising of specific brands (i.e., exemplars) of shampoos has led to a change in the way the category is perceived (cf. Loken, Joiner, & Peck, 2002).

GENERAL DISCUSSION

The prototypicality formula proposed in this chapter offers a new way of defining prototypicality–fuzziness. The prototypicality formula offers a reliable, quantified cutoff point for defining an object as prototypical (i.e., a score of 60% or higher), which is easier to implement than family resemblance analyses (Smith, 1988) and more sensitive than representativeness or ease of categorization scores. Three demonstrations showed that people represent consumer products, brands of those products, and advertisements as being fuzzy–prototypical exemplars of personality constructs.

Given that people can and do represent products and their advertising as fuzzy–prototypical exemplars of personality types, this chapter supported implications of the theory of schema correspondence, which states that advertising effectiveness is a function of the correspondence of three factors: an attitude object, a recipient, and a persuasive appeal. Certain formulations have suggested that persuasive messages, and consumer advertisements in particular, should reflect the personality of the product (i.e., Shavitt, 1989), whereas others have suggested recipient–personality type matching (Brock et al., 1990). The theory of schema correspondence suggests that gearing persuasive appeals to the type of product will be particularly successful for prototypical products. Otherwise, for fuzzy products, persuasive messages should reflect the recipient's needs and values. Although there has been some support for this hypothesis (Brannon & Brock, 1994), further research is necessary to examine exactly how prototypical a product must be for product–type matching to be particularly persuasive. Further research could also determine how prototypical a product or an attitude object must be before it cannot be modified through advertising or other persuasive appeals.

The implications for designing advertising messages are that if a product already has a clear (prototypical) image, attempting to adduce a new image may not be effective. However, if the image is fuzzy, by our definition its image is susceptible to change through advertising. An elaboration of this idea is that brand extensions must also respect prototypicality, whether of product or category. Extensions that stray from the central imagery are feasible provided that the focal original imagery is not highly prototypical (exceeding 60%, we propose). In this way, prototypicality offers boundary conditions on the extent to which the image of a product can be changed and on the kinds of extensions that can be effectively communicated.

A further implication is that certain (prototypical) products come with images that may precede any advertising (e.g., motorcycle may always be orange, even for respondents who have never seen a commercial for motorcycles); air conditioner may always be brown, and so forth. To the extent that the product has a preexisting, strong image (i.e., high prototypicality score) constraints are set on the ability to create new images for that product through advertising.

Much advertising, of course, is geared toward reinforcing the existing image of a product or brand and, indeed, the representation of a general category. The success of such reinforcement can be measured by the extent to which the images of familiar brands are rated similarly to the images of their corresponding categories.

Whereas the demonstrations presented here used clusters of values and lifestyle preferences as the superordinate concepts (i.e., the card-ranking procedure), neither the prototypicality formula nor the theory of schema correspondence is limited to this technique. This particular classification was used because it was meaningful to participants and facile to implement. Further research on the theory of schema correspondence could well use a more refined personality classification, one that better differentiated between unique characteristics of the products. Such research would likely find even stronger effects of product prototypicality. In addition, the prototypicality formula can easily be modified for any type of categorization, using any number of concepts and exemplars.

More research, using a wider variety of attitude objects and including more participants, is necessary to examine the precise cutoff point for defining objects as prototypical. In addition, further research could attempt to examine the extent of association between exemplar typicality measures (e.g., present method, or those of Loken et al. , 2002) and older measures (e.g., family resemblance scores or response latency measures). If these correlations are high, as one may expect, the prototypicality formula may be used instead of these other measures, which are more costly and time consuming to implement. The present formula offers a quick, precise, and efficient method of determining the degree of prototypicality of virtually any type of cognitive element.

REFERENCES

Brannon, L., & Brock, T. (1994). Test of schema correspondence theory: Effects of matching an appeal to actual, ideal, and product "selves." In E. M. Clark, T. C. Brock, & D. W. Stewart (Eds.), *Attention, attitude, and affect in response to advertising* (pp.169–188). Hillsdale, NJ: Lawrence Erlbaum Associates.

Brock, T. C., Brannon, L. A., & Bridgwater, C. (1990). Message effectiveness can be increased by matching appeals to recipient's self-schemas: Laboratory demonstrations and a national field experiment. In S. Agres, J. Edell, & T. Dubitsky (Eds.), *Emotion in advertising: Theoretical and practical explorations* (pp. 285–315). Westport, CT: Quorum Books.

Cantor, N., Smith, E. E., French, R., & Mezzich, J. (1980). Psychiatric diagnosis as prototype categorization. *Journal of Abnormal Psychology, 89,* 181–193.

Keirsey, D., & Bates, M. (1978). *Please understand me: Character and temperament types.* Del Mar, CA: Prometheus Nemesis Book Company.

Loken, B., Joiner, C., & Peck, J. (2002). Category attitude measures: Exemplars as inputs. *Journal of Consumer Psychology, 12,* 149–161.

McCloskey, M., & Glucksberg, S. (1978). Natural categories: Well defined or fuzzy sets? *Memory & Cognition, 6,* 462–472.

McCrae, R., & Costa, P. (1987). Validation of the five factor model of personality across instruments and observers. *Journal of Personality and Social Psychology, 52,* 81–90.

Mervis, C. B., & Rosch, E. (1981). Categorization of natural objects. *Annual Review of Psychology, 32,* 89–115.

Miscisin, M. (2001). *Showing our true colors.* Riverside, CA: True Colors.

Sentis, K., & Markus, H. (1986). Brand personality and the self. In J. Olson & K. Sentis (Eds.), *Advertising and consumer psychology* (Vol. 3, pp. 132–148). New York: Praeger.

Shavitt, S. (1985) Functional imperative theory of attitude formation and expression. Unpublished doctoral dissertation. Ohio State University, Columbus, OH.

Shavitt, S. (1989). Operationalizing functional theories of attitude. In A. R. Pratkanis, S. I. Breckler, & A. G. Greenwald (Eds.), *Attitude structure and function* (pp. 311–337). Hillsdale, NJ: Erlbaum Associates.

Shuford, E. H., Albert, A., & Massengill, H. E. (1966). Admissible probability measurement procedures. *Psychometrika, 31,* 125–145.

Smith, E. E. (1988). Concepts and thought. In R. Sternberg & E. E. Smith (Eds.), *The psychology of human thought* (pp. 19–49). Cambridge, England: Cambridge University Press.

CHAPTER THREE

Emergence and Change of Consumer Product Image in Social Constructionism Perspective

Junko Kimura
Hosei University, Tokyo

The purpose of this chapter is to explore what constitutes the belief or image of consumer behavior and products. The consumption patterns seem to become Westernized. Walking down the street in the Eastern countries, such as China, India, and Japan, we can find fast food restaurants such as McDonald's, KFC, and Starbucks and retail stores such as Wal-Mart and Carrefour. Not only the restaurants and retail stores but also various customs are imported from Europe and North America. McDonald's in Japan has the country-specific sandwiches like Tofu Burger, Teriyaki Burger, and so on. Some customs are differently understood and far from the original form. For example, a young woman confesses her love to a man by presenting chocolate on St. Valentine's Day in Japan. Watching the phenomena, some people may get upset or embarrassed, then they complain that Japanese consumers incorrectly assimilate Western culture without understanding the real meaning of the behavior or products in western countries.

Christmas consumption is the topic of research in this chapter. Christmas consumption refers to consumers' activities tied to the Christmas season, including the consumption of typically Christmas-related products, the copying of Christmas festivities, and the making of Christmas-season purchases.

For years, the Japanese have been active in Christmas consumption, even though there are not many Christians in Japan. A 1969 public opinion poll showed that 35.8% have no religious faith, and Christians (Protestant or Roman Catholic) represent only 1.5% of the population. Even so, in 1972, the poll showed that 63.9% of respondents participate in Christmas consumption, such as eating Christmas cake and having a party at home (82.8%), decorating a Christmas tree at home (29.5%), and exchanging gifts and cards (25.5%), followed by eating out with family or friends (8.4%), going out to a party (5.2%), going to church for Christmas service (5.2%), drinking and merrymaking (4.5%), going to the shopping district (3.8%), and listening to Christmas music (3.3%; Sankei Shinbun, December 23, 1972).

This chapter focuses on Christmas cake consumption. As the poll by Sankei Shinbun shows, cake, gifts, and tree are Three Sacred Treasures for Christmas consumption in Japan (Kuzuno, 1998; Suntory Limited and CDI, 1992). Japanese children are avid eaters of cake on Christmas Day. In the days leading up to Christmas, people place their orders for Christmas cake at convenience stores, hotel patisseries, department stores, and Western-style confectionery shops. The market for Christmas cake is quite large in Japan. Sales data reveal that approximately 15 billion Japanese yen (136 million U.S. dollars) is spent on Christmas cakes. The per capita monthly consumption of cake during December is 1,732 Japanese yen (U.S. $15.70). This is double the average expense on cake between January and November (PR House, 1989). According to research by Sanwa Bank Home Consultants (1993), the predominant way of celebrating Christmas is by eating cake. In fiscal 2002, the LOFT Department Store sold 350 million Japanese yen (3.18 million U.S. dollars) worth of baking tools and materials. During the three weeks leading up to Christmas, they sold 210 million yen (1.9 million U.S. dollars) worth of Christmas-related goods. During the Christmas season, LOFT's weekly sales average 35 million yen (U.S. $318,000).

For most Japanese, there is a specific type of Christmas cake. Figure 3.1 shows the Christmas cake image held by most Japanese—a round sponge cake, fancily decorated with red strawberries and a chocolate plate reading "Merry Christmas" with tiny candles on top. Because April and May are usually the harvest months for strawberries, the fruit sold during the Christmas season is greenhouse cultivated.

As a researcher, the author of this chapter has two frustrations. The first frustration is toward those who either laugh or are judgmental about Japanese Christmas cake, because this particular kind of cake cannot be found in any other Western country. Traditional Christmas cakes include brown fruitcakes or Christmas cookies in the United States, Christmas puddings in the United Kingdom, buche de Noel in France, Hexenhaus in Switzerland, speculaas in Holland, panettone in Italy, and stollen in Germany. Thus, seeing the Japanese Christmas cake, some may say it is not the right Christmas cake. They conclude that the Japanese try to import the Western ways of Christmas consumption and wrongly mimic them. But is the original product always right or proper?

The second frustration is toward those who criticize either sales promotions from companies or the mass media. These people believe Christmas should be religious and sacred and deplore its secularization by commercial activities. They also criticize the young people, who, without knowing the original meaning, spend much money on Christmas gifts and parties.

FIG. 3.1. Typical Christmas cake for the Japanese (Fujiya Christmas cake catalogue, 2000).

These two frustrations raise two questions. First, is there a proper consumer product for a certain occasion? Second, if a certain product is a very Christmas-related cake, what constitutes the image? Although consumption culture and Christmas cake are closely related, there are no answers for the questions. This relation was the focus of the empirical study reported here.

CONCEPTUAL FRAMEWORK

This study develops the framework for ethnomethodologically informed social constructionism, which proposes that the legitimacy of consumption and consumer products exists only when people believe its legitimacy and keep to established consumption practices. For the conceptual framework, I (a) discuss the perspective of ethnomethodology, (b) explain the essential concept of practical accomplishment, and (c) show some examples of practical accomplishment to help the reader understand the essence of this perspective.

This chapter develops a social constructionism perspective informed by ethnomethodology. The approach of ethnomethodology was indicated by H. Garfinkel (2002):

> Seek to treat practical activities, practical circumstances, and practical sociological reasoning as topics of empirical study, and by paying to the most commonplace activities of daily life the attention usually accorded extraordinary events, seek to learn about them as phenomena in their own right. (p. 1)

Coulon (1987/1995) explained what Garfinkel had argued. Garfinkel declared his interests to be mainly in practical activities, particularly in practical reasoning. Ethnomethodology analyzes commonsense beliefs and behaviors. It rejects the traditional perspective of the previous research on social reality. The traditional perspective makes the a priori assumption that a stable system of norms and significations is shared by the actors and governs any social system. In other words, the traditional perspective has a theoretical framework that presupposes the existence of an outside signifying world that exists independent of social interactions.

Whereas the traditional perspective sees research topics as models, things, givens and facts of life, ethnomethodology refers to continuous accomplishment of the actors and process. In the ethnomethodological perspective, social facts are the accomplishments of the members (Garfinkel & Sacks, 1970). Social reality is not preexisting but is constantly created by the actors (Coulon, 1987/1995).

Applying this viewpoint, ethnomethodologically informed social constructionism tries to uncover the methods with which the actors actualize the legitimacy of consumption. It is crucial to observe how the members build up a reasonable and legitimate world to be able to live in it. Legitimacy has to be considered as practical accomplishments. In other words, right consumption is not a stable object but is produced by the continual activities of people.

Let us here interpret the film *Miracle on 34th Street*, directed by Les Mayfield (1994), and originally written by Valentine Davis in 1947, using the ethnomethodologically informed social constructionism perspective. A man named Kris Kringle thinks of himself as Santa Claus. The crisis in the film comes when Kris must undergo a public hearing. Kris will be judged as either a psychopathic old man who declares himself to be Santa or the real Santa. Through the film, his and other people's practical accomplishments construct the social reality that Kris is Santa. For example, Kris himself keeps communicating to children that he is Santa. The district attorney tells his children that if they behave, Santa will come to give them Christmas gifts. A 5-year-old boy at the public hearing testifies that Kris is Santa. The Coles Department Store hires Kris to play Santa Claus through the holiday season in its main store on 34th Street in New York City.

Judge Harper, almost giving up on making a decision that Kris is Santa, finds how "Kris is Santa" could be the social reality when he sees a one dollar bill. He argues:

> It's a one-dollar bill. It is issued by the Treasury of the United States of America and it's backed by the Government and the people of the United States of America. Upon inspection of the article, you will see the words, In God we Trust. We are not here to prove that God exists. But we are here to prove that a being, just as invisible and yet just as present exists. The Federal Government puts its trust in God. It does so on faith alone. It's the will of the people guides the Government. And it is and was their collective faith in a greater being that gave cause to the inscription on this bill. If the Government of the United States can issue its currency bearing a declaration of trust in God without demanding physical evidence of the existence or non existence of a greater being, then the State of New York by a similar demonstration of the collective faith of its people, can accept and acknowledge that Santa Claus does exist and he exists in the person of Kris Kringle. (Mayfield, 1994)

In the decision, when the collective faith becomes describable, intelligible, reportable, and analyzable through practices, its subjective matter can turn into the objective reality. And all these features are revealed in the practical actions of the people (Coulon, 1987/1995).

Not only in the fictional film but also in our daily lives we can see the moments when subjective matter turns into the objective reality through practices. Let us take Santa Claus for example. A certain visual appearance of Santa Claus is relevant worldwide. Children draw him with a white beard and a fur-trimmed red outfit with boots and a large black belt. He carries numerous toys in his bag and has a ruddy laughing countenance (Belk, 1993). Even though the Santa image seems to have been relevant for years, this typical image was decided only 70 years ago, when Moore wrote a poem in 1822, Denslow drew his picture for his nephew in 1902, and Sundblom put a Coca-Cola red costume on Santa in 1931 (Belk, 1993; Kimura, 2001). Before reaching the particular appearance, Santa changed his images over time. As Levi-Strauss (1993) suggested, very old elements are thus shuffled and reshuffled, other are introduced, and original formulas perpetuate, transform, or revive old customs.

What we should notice here is that we share the certain and similar image of Santa, regardless of its arbitrariness. It is one object from previously scattered attributes of others: Christian Saint Nicholas, British Father Christmas, German Christkind, and Norway Julenisse. What then makes us share the similar Santa image? The ethnomethodologically informed social constructionism perspective explains that practices constitute the image.

Here are the examples of practices that turn the subjective matter into the objective reality. Virginia O'Hanlon, an 8-year-old girl in New York City, wrote to *The New York Sun* if there is a Santa Claus. Francis P. Church wrote the editorial to answer her question on September 21, 1897.

> Virginia, your little friends are wrong. They have been affected by the skepticism of a skeptical age. They do not believe except what they see. They think that nothing can be which is not comprehensible by their little minds. All minds, Virginia, whether they be men's or children's, are little ... Nobody sees Santa Claus, but that is no sign that there is no Santa Claus. The most real things in the world are those that neither children nor men can see. Did you ever see fairies dancing on the lawn? Of course not, but that's no proof that they are not there. Nobody can conceive or imagine all the wonders there are unseen and unseeable in the world ... (Church, 1897)

He explained by using social constructionism perspective. What he said was similar to what Judge Harper said in the film. Church said that no one sees Santa, but it does not mean he does not exist. If people trust his existence and act accordingly, they can create the reality with his existence. On the contrary, those who trust an existence only when they actually see the object, stand in the traditional perspective. They see the reality as models, things, givens, and facts of life as Coulon (1987/1995) suggested.

What we notice is not only the written contents of the editorial but also the practices of Church and the practices of *The New York Sun* as it continued to publish the article every year until it went out of business. The practices constitute the reality that Santa is playing an important role in Christmas consumption.

In England, a teacher told his pupils that Santa Claus does not exist. The parents criticized him for destroying the children's social reality.

> A head teacher has apologized to parents after the local vicar told 220 children: "There is no Father Christmas." The Rev Clive Evans, 41, Vicar of Long Buckby, near Northampton, gave out his news at an assembly where the children included his own eight-year-old son, Simon. The children are due to perform in their annual festive play, which is on the theme of Father Christmas. Mr. Evans, who has been in the parish for four years, was telling the story of the Wise Men, when he asked the children if they believed in Santa Claus. He then said: "If you don't want to hear what I am going to say, put your hands over your ears." His whispered revelation caused distress to some children, who told their parents.

Jeanette Goddard, the head teacher, sent out a letter to families apologizing for any distress caused, hoping it would not sour relationships. Mr. Evans said: "I did say, in a stage whisper, that there is no Father Christmas. The purpose was not to rubbish Santa Claus. I have children of my own. But I took the view that, in the context of an assembly which was not about Father Christmas, this kind of remark was not the kind of remark that would be offensive." "I still question those who say this has ruined their Christmas. But if this is so, I deeply regret it. The last thing I want to do is spoil a child's Christmas. But I do wonder where all this is coming from. I said it in good faith, bearing in mind the age of the children. We are not talking about toddlers here." Janet Best, whose eight-year-old twins, Danny and Billy, told her about their vicar's revelation, said: "I told them there is a Father Christmas and did not want their illusions shattered." (Times of London, December 15, 2000)

People can write a letter to Mr. Santa Claus at Santa Claus Post Office in Rovaniemi, Finland. In 1997, he received 700,000 messages and sent 160,000 replies to the senders all over the world (Kuzuno, 1998).

The examples here are practices by which the existence of Santa Claus is accomplished. Physical and objective existence does not matter for the members of the society. Regardless of the actual existence of Santa, the practices, such as writing the editorials, criticizing the teacher who denies Santa's existence, and writing a letter to Santa Claus, can construct the socially shared image of him.

As several researchers argued (Kuzuno, 1998; Sanwa Bank Home Consultants, 1993; Suntory Limited and CDI, 1992), in modern Japan, Christmas cake plays one of the most important roles in Christmas consumption. For Christmas cake in Japan, the practices are seen everywhere. The department stores, supermarkets and convenience stores compete with one another in creative products and services. For example, Mitsukoshi Department Store sells Christmas cake for dogs. Isetan Department Store sells preserved Christmas cake, which costs 25,000 yen (U.S. $227). Ito Yokado supermarket will deliver Christmas cake with refrigerated transportation to any place in the country (Nikkei Ryutsu Shinbun, December 3, 2002). In December 2002, Cuoca Planning, the retail store for baking materials and tools, sold twice as much as in any other month. The consumers also participate in practices. Mothers not only purchase but also bake Christmas cake by themselves. The poll in 1996 by Mitsukan, Co Ltd. shows that one third of the housewives bake Christmas cake at home (Mitsukan Co., Ltd., 1996). Mothers go to the retail stores, buy baking materials and tools, and bake Christmas cake with family members. Sometimes fathers join in baking cake for their children (Suntory Limited and CDI, 1992).

As shown in Fig. 3.1, certain kinds of cake are regarded as Christmas-related cake for the Japanese. In the remaining part of this chapter, I argue, using the ethnomethodologically informed social constructionism perspective, that people in Japan obtain legitimacy in the particular kind of cake. I draw on research on Christmas cake consumption in Japan throughout the 20th century (1900 to 2000) to establish the validity of this framework.

METHODOLOGY

Taking the ethnomethodologically informed social constructionism perspective, I used two research methods—discourse analysis and personal interviews with key personnel in manufacturing companies and consumers. In the discourse analysis, several data sources were used: (a) 448 magazine articles, (b) 926 newspaper articles, (c) 895 newspaper advertisements, (d) picturebooks and juvenile literature, and (e) academic papers and books. Data in detail were as follows:

> One hundred forty-four magazine articles collected in every 5-year period from 1955 to 1995. The author also purchased magazines published in 2000 that contain Christmas-related articles (304 articles in 110 magazines).
>
> Asahi Shinbun, daily newspaper issues, which carried Christmas-related articles in December of every 5 years from 1900 to 1995 and also 1999 (253 articles). In addition, using the NIKKEI Telecom searching system, the relevant articles in Nihon Keizai (Economics) Shinbun, Nikkei Ryutsu (Marketing) Shinbun, Nikkei Sangyo (Industrial) Shinbun, and Nikkei Kinyu (Financial) Shinbun were collected (673 articles).
>
> Christmas-related advertisements in newspapers in every 5-year period from 1900 to 1995 and also 1999 (895 advertisements). A sample is shown in Fig. 3.2. The data source, volume, page, and title of the article of all newspaper articles, magazine articles, and print advertisements are listed in a Microsoft Excel file in Japanese, and they can be reexamined at any time by interested researchers.
>
> Picturebooks and juvenile literature with Christmas-related stories (see Fig.3.3).
>
> Academic papers and books on Christmas.

In the personal interviews, interviewees and respondents were selected from various geographic areas in Japan. The interviewees were key company personnel at cake manufacturers, retail stores, and confectioneries and also consumers.

FIG. 3.2.   Newspaper advertisement of The Lion Dentifrice Co., Ltd. (the present Lion Corporation, Asahi Shinbun, December 11, 1910).

FIG. 3.3.   Christmas cake on picture book (Kiyono, 1972, p. 40).

DESCRIPTION OF A CHRISTMAS CAKE

In Japan, during the 20th century, there were five distinct phases of Christmas cake legitimacy. Each phase had different contexts of consumption, different kinds of consumers, and different meanings of cakes, even for the same kind of product.

To understand the characteristics of Christmas cake images in each phase, I focus on advertising strategies of two major cake manufacturers in Japan: Fujiya and Juchheim. Fujiya was founded in 1910. Its sales in 2002 were 942 million Japanese yen (8.6 million U.S. dollars). The company motto is "with love and sincerity, Fujiya will be loved by the customers." In 1921, the founder, Fujii, made a trip to the United States to observe the confectionary industry. He was impressed when he saw that the confections were sold in the best commercial districts. Fujiya's Christmas cake does not have any origins in any other countries. The company is tolerant of the fact that consumers freely put meanings on their products. In this sense, Fujiya is a consumer-conscious company. Figure 3.1 shows Fujiya's Christmas cake.

Juchheim was founded in 1921. Its sales in 2000 were 222 million Japanese yen (U.S. $2 million). Karl Juchheim, the German founder, was the first "meister" who baked "baumkuchen" in Japan. Juchheim's Christmas cake stollen strictly follows the traditional recipe of the German founder. The company is proud of its products for using natural ingredients, following the traditional recipe, and baking the products by certified artisans called "meister." In this sense, Juchheim is a more artisan-conscious company that emphasizes the quality to satisfy customers. Figure 3.4 shows the Juchheim's Christmas cake stollen.

Let us see how the advertising strategies of the companies differ and how they affect the reality construction of Christmas cake in Japan. Stage 1 (1900 to the start of World War II) is the period when Christmas cake was for foreigners living in Japan. In 1877, Fugetsudo, a manufacturer of Japanese and Western confections and

FIG. 3.4.   Juchheim's Christmas cake (Juchheim Christmas cake catalogue, 2000).

cakes founded in 1760, started manufacturing cakes for the first time in the country. Later, Fujiya sold Christmas cake in the market in 1910. It was intended not for the Japanese consumer but for the foreigners living in the Yokohama area near Tokyo. It was simple fruitcake with white boiled-down sugar, the British style of Christmas cake known as Irish Cake (see Fig. 3.5). Fujiya started manufacturing Christmas cake (i.e., sponge cake fancily decorated with butter cream) for the Japanese consumers and selling it in Ginza, the commercial district in Tokyo. Following this, the custom of eating cake on Christmas day began to spread among wealthy Japanese consumers. In 1921, Juchheim first sold the German Christmas cake called stollen. Initially, this cake was not popular.

The arrival of Stage 2 (the start of World War II to 1965), when drinking salary men enjoyed Christmas cake during cabaret shows, was marked by the introduction of mass production technology, making Christmas cakes affordable to many Japanese consumers (see Fig. 3.6).

The American occupation of Japan (1945–1950), following World War II, brought with it the uniquely American Christmas consumption culture. In addition, the sugar and flour rationing of wartime had been lifted. Fujiya began making decorative Christmas cakes in large quantities, and the custom of eating cake on Christ-

FIG. 3.5.   First Christmas cake in Japan (Fujiya Co., Ltd., 1990).

FIG. 3.6.   Mass manufacturing of Christmas cake (Asahi Shinbun, December 19, 1957).

FIG. 3.7.   Decorative Christmas cake (anonymous department store catalogue, 1952).

mas day took hold in Japan around 1955. Christmas cakes are the symbols of modernity, Westernization, and higher social status. They were much more decorative than cakes of today (see Figure 3.7). As Konagaya (2001) suggested, cakes represented a rise in the national standard of living. They implied a transformation into an affluent life in a new democratic society.

With their Christmas-season bonuses in their pockets, salary men would typically go out to a cabaret or bar after work and have a big party (see Fig. 3.8). They would often buy Christmas cake and even eat it on the spot, rather than bringing it home for the children. One popular type was a round, white cake with cream and strawberry decorations. On Christmas Eve in 1955, 1.2 million people went out to Ginza and 800,000 people went out to Sinjuku, the busy shopping and amusement districts in Tokyo.

Stage 3 (1965 to the mid 1980s) was marked by a growth in family parties, fueled by newspaper and magazine articles encouraging family gatherings on Christmas day. Christmas brought out feelings of togetherness and reinforced family ties.

FIG. 3.8.   Salary men with waitresses at Christmas party at a cabaret (Asahi Shinbun, December 24, 1955).

In other words, "in this urbanized context of postwar Japanese society, Christmas grew suitable as a festive occasion for the nuclear family" (Konagaya, 2001 pp. 130–131). Fujiya, in their advertisement, emphasized the Christmas family gatherings with their cakes (see Fig. 3.9).

During Stage 4 (mid 1980s to mid 1990s), the consumption culture shifted to a new consumer category, young couples in love. Popular TV dramas, songs, and fashion magazines featured young couples spending a romantic Christmas together. Yumi Matsutoya, the Japanese singer-songwriter, released "Koibito ga Santa Claus (My boyfriend is Santa Claus)" in 1980. Tokyo Disney Land (TDL) was opened in 1983. The young couples flooded the Tiffany jewelry boutiques in 1988. One of the Tiffany boutiques in Mitsukoshi Department Store in Ginza sold 20 million Japanese yen (180,000 U.S. dollars) in one day. The typical Christmas celebration for the young people was going out to a romantic place such as TDL, exchanging prestigious brand gifts, and eating Christmas cake together.

Thus, the size of cakes changed with the introduction in the Christmas cake market to the so-called "couple cake." Fujiya manufactures 12-cm in diameter (5") cakes for two people. This cultural shift also saw young couples enjoying various forms of Christmas cake, such as the French classic buche de Noel and the Italian

FIG. 3.9.　Christmas at home (advertisement of Fujiya Co., Ltd., 1959).

FIG. 3.10. Various kinds of Christmas cake (Fujiya Christmas cake catalogue, 2000).

dessert tiramisu. Even the German classic stollen by Juchheim was regarded as trendy and fashionable among the youth.

Characterizing the fifth and last stage (mid 1990s to 2000) was the emergence of a certain consumer refinement about Christmas cake. Wives no longer asked their husbands to buy the Christmas cake because men traditionally did not care much about the fine points of cake, whereas many female consumers had developed their own specific Christmas cake tastes. In response to this development, Fujiya offered 31 different kinds of Christmas cakes in the year 2000 (see Fig. 3.10).

FINDINGS

Three major findings are reached in this study. First, there is no a priori legitimacy in specific consumer products. Rather, it is practices, such as manufacturing, selling, buying, exchanging, giving, eating, and mentioning, that construct the legitimacy of the products. These practices are the means whereby members' subjective inner faith is transformed into objective and visible social reality. In this sense, the legitimacy exists, not in the cake as an object but in the process of practices. When members of a society stop practicing, the legitimacy disappears.

Second, this first finding helps us understand why the legitimacy changes over time. When the German Christmas cake stollen first came into the market in 1921, it was not regarded as typical Christmas cake. Years later in the mid 1990s, it became a more popular and relevant cake. Juchheim, the manufacturer, had not changed the product recipe or its form to make the cake meet the consumer's taste. Instead, stollen obtained its legitimacy as Christmas cake because the consumers had put meanings on it by themselves.

The third conclusion is that, even during the same period, there is more than one legitimacy. This means that, even for the same consumption phenomena and consumer products, a consumer has different ways of practical accomplishment and obtaining legitimacy. For example, some young couples have started purchasing and eating stollen. This is because they regard stollen as a more sophisticated and more fashionable Christmas cake than cakes fancily decorated with whipped cream. Others may purchase and eat stollen because they had lived in Germany and discovered that stollen is the traditional Christmas cake in that country.

CONCLUSION

The research presented here started with two questions: Is there a proper consumer product for a certain occasion? and If the certain product is a very Christmas-related cake to the members of a society, what constitutes the image?

The findings answer these questions. Moeran and Skov (1993) said, "Christmas in Japan seems to be made up of a vast unstructured accumulation of Western styles and Western commodities put together in a way that bears hardly any resemblance to Christmas in Europe and America" (p. 108). They seem to have made the assumption that the original products are right or proper and mimicked products are improper. The findings in this study show that there is no realistic properness in any consumer products. We cannot define the properness in specific terms. Thus, we cannot claim that the original way is always right. Moreover, companies cannot blame the consumers for failing to establish a Christmas image for their products that are associated with an episode related to Christmas. An episode or origin of the product, related to Christmas, does not guarantee the emergence of a Christmas-related image for the product.

What then constitutes the image? Companies seem to develop and constitute the image easily, just as Coca-Cola did with Santa Claus when it portrayed the jolly icon of Christmas wearing a Coca-Cola-red costume (Coca-Cola Company, 2000). Not only companies but also the consumers relate a certain product to an image of a certain occasion and change its image over time. Even when companies do not change their advertising messages for the products, the consumers put new meanings on the products and freely relate (or stop relating) the products with a Christmas image.

Relationships of the companies and the consumers should be understood as not having any hierarchical structures. Advertising is not an isolated entity but is always interrelated with the consumers. Consumers are capable of making sense of messages and products in the course of their daily lives (such as reasoning, understanding, and interpreting their actions).

Fujiya, the consumer-conscious company, flexibly adapted their products to the Christmas cake images that consumers created. Juchheim, the artisan-conscious company, tried to relate their products to Christmas cake images from the original country (i.e., Germany). For the Japanese, a round cake, decorated with strawberries and cream, became a typical Christmas cake.

Advertising strategy for a product may need to be changed. Instead of trying to communicate the "correct" consumption episodes of a product to consumers, marketers could give the product an open-ended status, thereby allowing consumers to create the image on their own and to decide the appropriateness of the product for a given need or consumption situation.

This argument does not mean that Fujiya has beaten Juchheim over the image of Christmas cake. It is true that Fujiya was a contributor to the construction of the social realities "We have to consume cake at Christmas" and "Christmas cake should be a round cake decorated with strawberries and cream." Unfortunately, the company could not construct the reality, "We have to consume Fujiya's cake at Christmas."

Moreover, the social reality is "continuous accomplishment of the actors," and "constantly created by the actors; it is not a preexisting entity" (Coulon, 1987/1995, p. 16). As the reality (i.e., Christmas cake image) is the process, there always remains the possibility of change. Fujiya was the initiator of the Christmas cake image. However, it does not guarantee a steady reality. Fujiya has to be involved in ongoing practices (such as efforts to attract the consumers). Thus, companies can change their product images through advertising, but they must relinquish the goal of communicating with consumers.

REFERENCES

Belk, R. W. (1993). Materialism and the making of the modern American Christmas. In Daniel Miller (Ed.), *Unwrapping Christmas* (pp. 75–104). Oxford, England: Clarendon.

Church, F. P. (1897, September 21). Is there a Santa Claus? *The New York Sun*.

Coca-Cola Company. (2000). Coca-Cola collectible Santas. Texas: Beckett Publications.

Coulon, A. (1995). L'ethnomethodologie (J. Coulon & J. Katz, Trans.). Newbury Park, CA: Sage. (Original work published 1987).

Fujiya Co., Ltd. (1990). *Company history of Fujiya Co., Ltd.*

Garfinkel, H. (2002). *Studies in ethnomethodology.* Cambridge, UK: Polity Press.

Garfinkel, H. & Sacks, H. (1970). On formal structures of practical action. In J. C. McKinney & E. A. Tiryakian (Eds.), *Theoretical sociology* (pp. 338–366). New York: Appleton-Century-Crofts.

Kimura, J. (2001). *Kochiku shugi no shohiron* (Consumer research in social constructionism perspective: Process analysis on Christmas consumption). Tokyo: Chikura Publishing Company.

Kiyono, S. (1972). *Non-Tan! Santakurosu dayo* (Non-Tan! It's Santa Claus). Tokyo: Kaiseisha.

Konagaya, H. (2001). The Christmas cake: A Japanese tradition of American prosperity. *Journal of Popular Culture, 34,* 121–136.

Kuzuno, H. (1998). *Santa Claus no dairyoko* (Big travel of Santa Claus). Tokyo: Iwanami.

Levi-Strauss, C. (1993). Father Christmas executed. In D. Miller (Ed.), Unwrapping Christmas (pp. 38–51). New York: Oxford University Press.

Mayfield, L. (Director). (1994). *Miracle on 34th Street* [Motion picture]. United States: Twentieth Century Fox.

Mitsukan Co., Ltd. (1996). *Wagaya no Kurisumasu* (Christmas at home). Unpublished manuscript.

Moeran, B. & Skov, L. (1993). Cinderella Christmas: Kitsch, consumerism and youth in Japan. In D. Miller (Ed.), *Unwrapping Christmas* (pp. 105–133). Oxford, England: Clarendon.

Nikkei Ryutsu Shinbun (Nikkei Ryutsu Newspaper). December 3, 2002.

PR House. (1989, December 20). Kurisumasu shobai dai hanjo (Big sales on Christmas business). *Spa!* pp. 80–87.

Sankei Shinbun (Sankei Newspaper). December 23, 1972.

Sanwa Bank Home Consultants. (1993). *Chosa report: Kurashi no gyoji wo furikaeru* (Research report: Looking back daily life events). Unpublished documents.

Suntory Limited. & CDI. (1992). *Gendai shakai no nenju gyoji* (Ritual ceremonies in contemporary families). Osaka: SUNTORY Limited.

Times of London. December 15, 2000.

CHAPTER FOUR

Understanding the Role
of Mental Imagery in Persuasion:
A Cognitive Resources Model Analysis

Philip J. Mazzocco and Timothy C. Brock
The Ohio State University

Consumer researchers have long been interested in the effects of imagery on attitude change, and recently interest has surged (see Scott & Batra, 2003). This interest is due, at least in part, to the surfeit of potential pathways through which mental imagery can affect attitude change. In this chapter, we first consider the various mechanisms involved in image-mediated attitude change and then briefly summarize and discuss some of the moderating factors of the effects of imagery on attitude change. We then focus on one particular moderating variable: attentional resources. We propose a new model of attentional resources in the processing of persuasive communications and compare and contrast this model with extant models. Finally, we discuss some of the implications of our model for research into the role of imagery in consumer attitudes.

IMAGERY EFFECTS ON ATTITUDE CHANGE: MECHANISMS

Early cognitive research established that imageable materials enjoy a memorial advantage (e.g., Bower, 1970) and, therefore, attitudes based on images may be more likely to persist. According to Paivio's (1986) dual coding theory, imageable materials can be encoded both analogically and symbolically, hence allowing a greater number of memorial associations; the abundance of associations created by mental images may confer increased embeddedness to image-based attitudes. Mental imagery may also confer reality status (Markham & Hynes, 1993) and thus lend credibility or urgency to arguments that are otherwise vague or unbelievable. In addition, imaginal processes are akin to sensation and may provide consumers with a more complete consumption experience (MacInnis & Price, 1987). It is also possible that mental images, as arguments, may be more difficult or unnatural to counterargue or attack than verbal statements. Thus, persuasive messages containing mental images should be more difficult to resist and, hence, enjoy increased effectiveness.

Mental imagery may affect attitude change through the mechanisms stipulated by the elaboration likelihood model (Petty, Cacioppo, & Schumann, 1983; Petty & Wegener, 1998). For example, imagery can act as a peripheral cue to argument strength. Although change based on peripheral processing would be predicted to be relatively weak (as compared to change based on central processing), if imagery remained a highly accessible and memorable cue, image-based persistence could be observed.

Imagery could also act as a processing cue, as suggested by Smith and Shaffer (2000). They created high and low imagery versions of written persuasive messages and orthogonally varied the argument strength of the messages (i.e., high vs. low). When the imagery was related to the themes of the message (i.e., central imagery) as opposed to being message irrelevant (i.e., peripheral imagery), participants differentiated more between strong and weak arguments in the high imagery condition—evidence for increased message processing (see Kisielius & Sternthal, 1986, for a similar perspective).

Hermans, de Houwer, and Eelen (1994) demonstrated automatic evaluation of extremely valenced pictures. Giner-Sorolla, Garciá, and Bargh (1999) replicated these findings using more moderately valenced pictures. Hence, persuasive communications that evoke representative mental images (via vivid language or pictures or imagery instructions) may be positively evaluated even when cognitive elaboration is exceedingly low. Finally, Scott (1994; Kenny & Scott, 2003) suggested that in some cases, images and pictures in advertisements can be read like metaphorical rhetoric.

Despite the numerous ways in which mental imagery can affect attitudes and attitude change, researchers have found that imagery sometimes enhances persuasion and sometimes interferes with it (e.g., Frey & Eagly, 1993; Keller & Block, 1997; Kisielius & Sternthal, 1984; Unnava & Burnkrant, 1991). For example, research on mental imagery has played a prominent role in the vividness effect literature (i.e., the idea that vivid information will be more influential than nonvivid information). An early review of this literature by Taylor and Thompson (1982) found little support for any consistent positive effects of vivid information on attitudes and judgments; instead, vivid information often did not influence attitudes and judgments or occasionally was even less influential than nonvivid information. Fortunately, researchers have begun to identify some of the key factors that determine the likelihood of finding imagery effects.

DETERMINANTS OF IMAGERY EFFECTS

Depending upon its specific usage in a persuasive communication, imagery may take on one of two nonexclusive functions. First, imagery may act as an argument itself, perhaps functioning to highlight or summarize a key persuasive theme (Kenny & Scott, 2003; Scott, 1994). Second, imagery, especially pictures, may draw attention to the communication, especially in a competitive informational environment (e.g., Frey & Eagly, 1993; Taylor & Thompson, 1982).

The effect of imagery may also be influenced by the extent to which imagery is central or peripheral to the main themes of the persuasive communication (Smith & Shaffer, 2000). For the purposes of attracting attention to the communication, either peripheral or central imagery may suffice; however, if peripheral images draw attention away from strong central message arguments, null or decreased attitude change may result (Frey & Eagly, 1993). It is also important to consider the idiosyncratic thoughts that an image brings to the mind of the receiver. If these thoughts are counter to the themes of the message or merely weaker than arguments presented in the message itself persuasion can be diminished (Kisielius & Sternthal, 1986).

Finally, it has been suggested that the effects of vivid mental images on persuasion are more likely to be detected by delayed measures of attitude change (Reyes, Thompson, & Bower, 1980). The rationale for this contention is that part of the persuasive power of vivid images may be their memorability. However, immediately after the initial reception of a persuasive communication, nonimaginal elements of a communication may be just as salient as imaginal elements. If, over time, the memory traces for the nonimaginal elements decay more rapidly than the traces of the imaginal elements, a delayed vividness effect of imagery may result.

Any or all of the factors discussed previously may influence the effects of imagery on attitude change. One additional factor that may be highly influential is attentional resources. Next we discuss a new model of attitude change, the cognitive resources model (CRM; Mazzocco, 2000), which incorporates notions of attentional resources.

THE COGNITIVE RESOURCES MODEL

Mental images can either be formed in a relatively automatic fashion (e.g., picture perception, image recall) or be constructed based on external stimuli (e.g., a vivid textual description, a vividly told story) or internal stimuli (e.g., imaginings, dreams). The typical consumer advertisement aims to evoke images via all three routes. For example, most TV ads contain both pictorial images as well as vivid narrations designed to evoke specific additional images. In addition, any ad may potentially evoke relevant idiosyncratic images in the mind of the consumer. For the present purposes, the key distinction between the many different information sources of mental image representations is that some automatically result in fully formed mental images, whereas others need to be effortfully processed into mental images (termed *imaginal elaboration*).

Further work requiring resources can be done to images after they have been formed. Consumers may attempt to understand the relation between the image and accompanying information or pre-existing information stores (i.e., argument elab-

TABLE 4.1

Processing of Pictorial and Nonpictorial Imagery in Persuasive Communications:
Resource Allocations

	Pictorial Perception	Nonpictorial Stimuli
Orienting response	x	x
Imaginal elaboration		x
Argument elaboration	x	x
Maintenance/manipulation	x	x

oration). The consumer may also attempt to maintain the image for some period of time, or perhaps even manipulate the image (e.g., picturing oneself interacting with the image). Table 4.1 summarizes the various common resource tapping processes as they relate to both the processing of preformed images and nonpictorial stimuli. The key difference between these two sources of mental representations is that the nonpictorial stimuli require imaginal elaboration.

Baddeley's (1999) working memory model offers a useful conceptualization of mental imagery and imaginal elaboration that can be used to derive predictions about when and how mental imagery will be most likely to influence attitudes. The working memory formulation consists of the central executive, the articulatory loop (which maintains and processes verbal and auditory information), and the visuospatial sketchpad (which stores and processes mental imagery and spatial information). The central executive is the main processing unit; it can be thought of as an attentional spotlight (Baddeley, 1996). The articulatory loop and the visuospatial sketchpad are two slave systems of the central executive in which information can be processed and temporarily stored. The central executive interacts with both of the slave systems, but in doing so a portion of its limited resources is consumed. Hence, when the central executive communicates with the visuospatial sketchpad to retrieve a waiting image (i.e., shines the spotlight on the sketchpad), fewer resources are available to interact with the articulatory loop, and vice versa.

To the extent that persuasive message processing involves more than one type of process, attentional resources must be taken into account. In response to persuasive communications that evoke mental images, both imaginal elaboration (i.e., the formation and maintenance of mental images) and argument elaboration (i.e., the scrutiny of message arguments) are likely to occur.

Research by Bruyer and Scailquin (1998) demonstrated that overloading the central executive via a random-number generation task interfered with the simultaneous formation of mental images (see Bolls & Lang, 2003, for converging evidence). This study suggested that the maintenance and formation of mental images in response to persuasive communications (i.e., imaginal elaboration) requires central executive (i.e., attentional) resources.

Given that argument elaboration undoubtedly requires attentional resources, it seems likely that argument elaboration may interfere with or inhibit the elaboration of mental imagery, and vice versa. The CRM (Mazzocco, 2000) predicts that imagery will have positive effects on persuasion only to the extent that sufficient attentional resources (i.e., central executive resources) are available. Specifically, when argument elaboration and the elaboration of mental imagery are concurrent, resource depletion should render both types of elaboration relatively less effective.

This prediction is based on the rationale behind the psychological refractory period (PRP: Pashler, 1994; Telford, 1931). The PRP refers to the phenomenon whereby engaging in one task slows or impairs performance on another task. As it relates to attitude change, dedicating resources to one type of processing reduces the effectiveness of other types of processing. In cases where both types of processing would tend to increase the persuasiveness of a communication, the PRP will generally reduce attitude change and attitude change persistence.

An empirical test of the CRM has been conducted in the domain of rhetorical persuasion (Mazzocco & Brock, 2005). Participants read a short message about the "horrors of veal-calf processing" that elicited either high or low mental imagery. Messages were also written in either the normal style of a rhetorical appeal or an off-putting, accusatory style. The consequence of the latter condition was to inhibit argument elaboration without causing participants to stop reading the message altogether. Furthermore, we measured participants' individual differences in the need for cognition (Cacioppo & Petty, 1982; Cacioppo, Petty, Feinstein, & Jarvis, 1996), a proxy for likelihood of engaging in argument elaboration. After reading the message, participants reported veal-related attitudes immediately and again two weeks later. We predicted that imagery would positively affect attitude change (and lead to increased attitudinal persistence) when argument elaboration could be assumed to be low (i.e., when argument elaboration was inhibited via the message style, or for participants with a low need for cognition).

The main results are shown in Fig. 4.1 (delayed attitude ratings on a 7-point scale). As predicted, imagery augmented persisting persuasion in the three cells wherein argument elaboration was expected to be low (i.e., high-response inhibition or low need for cognition). In the cell wherein argument elaboration was expected to be high (low-response inhibition and high need for cognition), imagery interfered with attitude change persistence. Manipulation checks and mediational analyses supported the CRM interpretation.

Accompanying this empirical test was a review of extant studies (Mazzocco & Brock, 2005) from the literature (22 within consumer, social, health, and cognitive psychology) for which assumptions could be made about both mental imagery and attentional resources. Nineteen of these studies produced principal findings that were consistent with the CRM. To take one example, Keller and Block (1997) designed experiments to manipulate vividness by pictures versus no pictures, imagery instructions versus careful instructions, and case history versus statistical information

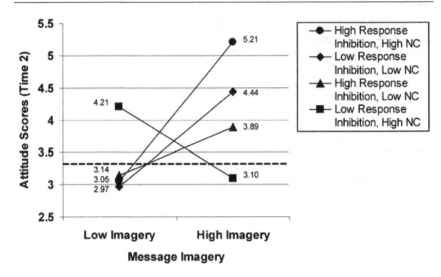

Note. NC = Need for Cognition (see text)

FIG 4.1.   Effects of message imagery, message tone, and need for cognition (NC; see text) on Time 2 attitude scores. Predicted values were computed using the following equation derived from regression analysis: Time 2 Attitude = 3.59*** + .18(imagery) – .49(message tone) + .05(NC) + 1.28(imagery × message tone) – .10(imagery × NC)* – .05(message tone × NC) + .15(imagery × message tone × NC)**. The dashed line represents the control baseline at time 2. *$p < .05$, **$p < .01$, ***$p < .001$.

(Studies 1–3, respectively). The topics were the dangers of skin cancer, smoking, and sexually transmitted diseases, respectively.

For each topic, perceived vulnerability to the topic problem was assessed as a measure of personal relevance and, hence, of resource allocation (i.e., higher resource allocation when personal relevance or vulnerability was high). For analytic purposes, participants were grouped into high, moderate, or low allocation groups, based on personal motivation to process the message. For nonvivid information, higher resource allocation led to increased persuasion. Vivid information, however, was found to be maximally effective under moderate resource allocation and less effective under very low or very high resource allocation. Hence, Studies 1–3 supported the CRM. Imagery was ineffective when people did not care about the message (i.e., very low perceived risk or low allocation). Imagery was also ineffective when resource allocation was very high (i.e., high perceived risk). It was only at a moderate level when people should not have been engaging in extensive argument elaboration that imagery should have been effective, as was found. For the nonvivid information, the CRM predicts that more argument elaboration is associated with increased attitude change, also as was found.

COGNITIVE RESOURCES IN PERSUASION: COMPARING
AND CONTRASTING THE CRM WITH RELATED MODELS

The importance of limited cognitive resources has always been recognized at some level in attitude change research. The learning model of Hovland and collaborators (e.g., Hovland, Janis, & Kelly, 1953; Hovland, Lumsdaine, & Sheffield, 1949), and the reception-yielding model of McGuire (e.g., 1969, 1985) both assume that message reception (i.e., attention, comprehension, retention) sets an upper limit on attitude change. Hence, if an individual is distracted while processing a persuasive message, less attitude change is predicted by the learning models (though distraction can lead to increased attitude change for other reasons; see Petty, Wells, & Brock, 1976).

From the mid 1960s to late 1970s the reception models of attitude change were all but swept away by cognitive response models (Brock, 1967; Greenwald, 1968). However, these models culminated in the delineation of the elaboration likelihood model (ELM; Petty et al., 1983; Petty & Wegener, 1998), which holds that the influence of cognitive elaboration is constrained, at least in part, by individual differences in the ability of an individual to processes a persuasive communication. Hence, distraction may constrain strong attitude change by lowering the ability of communication recipients to elaborate on the message arguments or cues. Furthermore, the ELM assumes that individuals who were motivated to elaborate on a persuasive communication will be likely to dedicate cognitive resources toward doing so. Examples are individuals high in the need for cognition (Cacioppo & Petty, 1982) or for whom a persuasive message is personally relevant (Petty & Cacioppo, 1984).

Nevertheless, in both the reception models and the ELM, the details of the interplay between cognitive resources, message processing, and persuasion are relatively vague. It is not made clear, for example, just what the nature of this store of limited cognitive resources is, nor how various factors interact to deplete this resource base.

Since the late 1980s, three major models involving cognitive resources have been proposed. In the communications literature, Lang (2000) offered a limited capacity model (LCM) of mediated message processing with two major assumptions that can be combined and summarized as follows: People are limited capacity information processors. Lang categorized the main tasks involved in information processing as encoding, storage, and retrieval. She further assumed that certain kinds of information would elicit orienting responses in individuals commanding attention and processing resources. Just what kinds of information elicit orienting responses can vary based on a number of factors, such as individual processing goals and characteristics of the information (e.g., vividness). Furthermore, orienting responses can result from automatic or controlled processes. The key to Lang's model is that resource depletion can occur within or between the three main levels of information processing. For example, at the encoding stage, vast amounts of information vie for scrutiny, but only some will actually be attended to. The process of encoding can be further impeded, however, by simultaneous attempts to retrieve information from long-term memory. A number of studies have provided evidence consistent with the LCM (e.g., Bolls, 2002; Bolls & Lang, 2003).

The applicability of the LCM to persuasive message processing is relatively straightforward. For example, imagine a written persuasive communication that induced argument elaboration. According to the LCM, the act of reading requires the dedication of cognitive resources to the encoding of the text, retrieval of context information to comprehend the text, and storage of relevant information for later use in comprehension. Similarly, argument elaboration requires resources to be dedicated to the retrieval of information from long-term memory. The LCM can, thus, predict resource interference at the level of retrieval because two processes were vying for retrieval-based resources. If resources were preferentially allocated to comprehension, the effectiveness of cognitive elaboration could be limited, and, hence, strong attitude change could be limited.

The second major model based on the notion of cognitive resources, and clearly the most popular in the consumer and marketing literature, is the resource matching model (RMM; Anand & Sternthal, 1989). The RMM is mainly concerned with the resources required and available (i.e., RR and RA, respectively) to process a persuasive communication. When RR exceeds RA, message processing will be limited. In this condition, receivers may either switch to a less resource intensive mode of processing, such as peripheral route processing (Petty & Wegener, 1998), or simply satisfice with an insufficiently processed message argument. In both cases, weak attitude change would be predicted. When RA exceeds RR, the RMM holds that one of two things is likely to happen (given a strong persuasive communication). It is possible that people will dedicate excess cognitive resources to counterarguing the message, hence reducing persuasion. It is also possible that people will engage in argument elaboration. In this case, the idiosyncratic argument elaborations are likely to be weaker than the actual message arguments and, given averaging, attitude change is again likely to be reduced. The key proposition of the RMM, then, is that persuasion is likely to be optimal when RA equals RR. This proposition has received an abundance of empirical attention and support (e.g., Keller & Block, 1997; Mantel & Kellaris, 2003; Peracchio & Meyers-Levy, 1997).

The CRM (Mazzocco, 2000; Mazzocco & Brock, 2005) is offered as a third model of cognitive resources. In practice, the CRM makes predictions about the relations among various persuasive processes and the three components of Baddeley's (1999) working memory model (i.e., the central executive, the visuospatial sketchpad, and the articulatory loop).

Other work has made use of the notion of resource competition. For example, Unnava, Agarwal, and Haugtvedt (1996) proposed that imaging in response to a persuasive message can interfere with similar types of processes due to resource competition (see also Unnava & Burnkrant, 1991). They tested this proposition by combining ads high in mental imagery with other visual tasks. In Study 2 (Unnava et al., 1996), for example, participants were exposed to advertisements that were high or low in imagery. Results indicated that in a condition in which the ads were presented visually, imagery had a detrimental effect on ad recall. It was only when ads were presented in an audio format that imagery augmented recall. Although no measures of persuasion were reported, the study has clear implications for attitude change. The predictions made by these authors were very similar to predictions that could be derived from the CRM (concerning only visuospatial sketchpad resources), however no attempt was made to delineate a full model of the interplay between cognitive resources and attitude change.

Raymond (2003) also offered theory and research relevant to attentional constraints to viewing sequential visual images. For example, one key finding of this research is that paying specific attention to a given perceptual stimulus will create memorial deficits for information presented immediately afterwards (i.e., the attentional blink; Raymond, Shapiro, & Arnell, 1992). This work deals with attention at a microlevel of analysis involving visual perception, whereas the CRM and related models make macrolevel predictions. It is not clear, for example, if the attentional blink and related phenomena would have any relevance to the generation of mental imagery from ad copy.

It is possible to compare and contrast the macromodels of attentional processing (CRM, ELM, LCM, and RMM) at a conceptual level (see Table 4.2 for a summary). All four models make predictions involving cognitive resources. In addition, all four models include the notion that cognitive resources can be overwhelmed or insufficient and that this can have implications for message processing and, by extension, persuasion. Only the RMM, however, makes the more fine-grained prediction that persuasion will be optimal when resources required equal resources available (as opposed to situations in which resources available exceed resources required). The LCM and the CRM are more specific than the RMM and the ELM when it comes to making predictions about interference between specific types of persuasive processes. For example, the CRM and the

TABLE 4.2

Comparison of Models That Make Cognitive Resources Predictions

	ELM	RMM	LCM	CRM
Cognitive resource predictions made	x	x	x	x
Distinguishes between RA < RR and RA > RR	x	x	x	x
Distinguishes between RA = RR and RA > RR	x	x		
Specific predictions about resource interference between multiple processes			x	x
Specific about the general levels at which resource competition occurs			x	x
Specific about the actual pool(s) of resources that are limited				x

Note. ELM = elaboration likelihood model; RMM = resource matching model; LCM = limited capacity model; CRM = cognitive resources model; RA = resources available; RR = resources required.

LCM can specifically model a situation in which mental imagery and argument elaboration are competing for a shared pool of limited resources. The ELM and the RMM can only make the general statement that resources (or ability) are not adequate. The CRM and the LCM can also make specific statements about the levels at which resource competition can occur. For example, both models predict that retrieval from long-term memory can interfere with message processing at the level of encoding or storage. It is only the CRM, however, that makes specific statements about the actual pools of resources that can become depleted and for which mental processes compete (i.e., Baddeley's 1999 working memory conceptualization), as opposed to a general and vague pool of "cognitive resources." Hence, all things considered, the CRM is the more comprehensive model of cognitive resources in the processing of persuasive communications.

The only comparison for which the CRM is the less complete model is with respect to predictions about situations in which resources available exceed resources required. In this situation the RMM predicts that persuasion will be constrained. This particular situation is not covered by the CRM because it is assumed that the ELM is already sufficiently delineated to handle that realm. To review, the RMM holds that persuasion will be nonoptimal when excess resources are present due to either increased counterargumentation or relatively weak argument elaborations. The general implication is that, in this situation, argument elaboration can only be detrimental to persuasion. According to the ELM, however, the effects of increased argument elaboration on message acceptance depend on a number of different factors. For example, given weak message arguments, decreased argument elaboration would lead to relatively more attitude change. The authors of the RMM hold that advertising communications are typically written with the strongest and most compelling arguments available. However, even granting generally strong arguments, increased argument elaboration could be put into the service of bolstering the message arguments. Also, the assumption of the RMM that relatively weak idiosyncratic argument elaborations will average with the actual message arguments is not intuitively obvious. It is plausible that the effects of argument elaborations and message arguments on persuasion could combine in an additive fashion. Due to these kinds of ambiguities, the CRM intentionally forgoes predictions about situations characterized by a glut of attentional resources.

IMPLICATIONS

That human beings are limited capacity information processors is obvious. Hence, there is a need for an articulated theory that takes into account the interplay among various persuasive processes and cognitive resources. We offer the CRM as such a model. The CRM suggests that in any persuasion context in which it can be reasonably assumed or demonstrated that recipients must rely on attentional processing, the resource capacity of the processing system (i.e., the central executive) must be considered. In many cases, the CRM predicts weak or nonexistent attitude change when two or more processes are concurrent in the processing of a persuasive message. The CRM can make these predictions in spite of the fact that any given subset of the total processes would, alone, enhance persuasion. Future work can attempt to examine CRM predictions for persuasive processes other than just imaginal and argument elaboration. For example, the use of music in commercials is often likely to cause recipients to dedicate cognitive resources to song itself. In these situations, the CRM predicts that other processes (such as imaginal elaboration or cognitive elaboration) may suffer from resource depletion.

At a theoretical level, the CRM has wide-ranging implications for the study of any variable thought to be related to attitude change. The ELM stipulates that variables can affect attitude change in multiple ways, depending on the motivation and ability of the recipient to elaborate on message arguments. As was previously discussed, the CRM offers a more fine-grained analysis of the ability component of the ELM, namely, how attentional resources relate to ability. Any variable that can affect persuasion can be characterized by its need for attentional resources (on a continuum from low to high). This means that variables will affect message processing not only in a variable-specific fashion but also with respect to the amount of attentional resources they command and, hence, "steal" from other processes. To study these kinds of attentional interactions between variables requires research paradigms that routinely explore multiple variables or processes within the same study. When processes are examined in isolation, it is likely that people can shift all their attention to the focal processes. However, in the real world, there will always be numerous stimuli competing for limited attentional resources. The CRM provides a framework for modeling the impact of variables on attitude change in naturalistic settings.

A major topic of interest is the extent to which different types of variables or processes will dominate persuasive communication processing in various contexts, for various products, or for different types of people. It is likely that with rhetorical communications, argument elaboration will be dominant over imaginal elaboration. This dominance is also likely to be the case for individuals who are high in the need for cognition or for products that are either expensive or important to the consumer and, thus, merit serious consideration. Under other common conditions, however, argument elaboration may not predominate. For example, it seems plausible that ads presented in a narrative format (i.e., story format), would be more likely to evoke imaginal elaboration (Green & Brock, 2000, 2002). In this case, argument elaboration may take a back seat and be much less demanding on attentional resources (e.g., Kopfman, Smith, Ah Yun, & Hodges, 1998).

A second topic of interest is how the operationalization of mental imagery will affect attentional resource demand and, hence, interactions with other attention-demanding variables. As summarized in Table 4.1, mental images that are the result of relatively effortless processing (e.g., pictures, recalled images) do not require imaginal elaboration. Imaginal elaboration is needed when perceivers must work on information (e.g., vivid textual descriptions) to create mental images. This does not necessarily mean, however, that vivid text descriptions will always tap more attentional resources than pictures. Pictures may, for example, tend to elicit more intense and longer lasting orienting responses than text descriptions. Additionally, both vivid text descriptions and pictures can elicit argument elaboration and attempts to maintain or manipulate the resulting mental images. Future research guided by the CRM can lend these kinds of issues empirical footing.

We do not contend that attention is everything in the prediction of the effects of mental imagery on attitude change. Some of the other determinants of imagery effects discussed previously (e.g., image centrality) will certainly be important in many contexts. In actual empirical investigations, there are a host of methodological factors that will also be influential (e.g., the exact wording of imagery instructions; Mani & MacInnis, 2003). However, given that images in advertisements are typically compelling (Babin & Burns, 1997), the level of attention that can be paid to them will very often moderate their effectiveness. Hence, in many cases, the CRM framework will help to account for significant variance in imagery effects. In general, it is hoped that the CRM will allow researchers to make increasingly precise predictions about attitude change that stems from imagery.

REFERENCES

Anand, J. W., & Sternthal, B. (1989). Strategies for designing persuasive messages: Deductions from the resource matching hypothesis. In P. Cafferata & A. Tybout (Eds.), *Cognitive and affective responses to advertising* (pp. 135–159). Lexington, MA: Lexington.

Babin, L. A., & Burns, A. C. (1997). Effects of print ad pictures and copy containing instructions to imagine mental imagery that mediates attitudes. *Journal of Advertising, 26,* 33–44.

Baddeley, A. D. (1996). Exploring the central executive. *The Quarterly Journal of Experimental Psychology, 49,* 5–28.

Baddeley, A. D. (1999). *Essentials of human memory.* East Sussex, UK: Psychology Press.

Bolls, P. D. (2002). I can hear you, but can I see you? The use of visual cognition during exposure to high-imagery radio advertisements. *Communication Research, 29,* 537–563.

Bolls, P. D., & Lang, A. (2003). I saw it on the radio: The allocation of attention to high-imagery radio advertisements. *Media Psychology, 5,* 33–55.

Bower, G. H. (1970). Imagery as a relational organizer in associative learning. *Journal of Verbal Learning and Verbal Behavior, 9,* 529–533.

Brock, T. C. (1967). Communication discrepancy and the intent to persuade as determinants of counterargument production. *Journal of Experimental Social Psychology, 3,* 269–309.

Bruyer, R., & Scailquin, J. C. (1998). The visuospatial sketchpad for mental images: Testing the multicomponent model of working memory. *Acta Psychologica, 98,* 17–36.

Cacioppo, J. T., & Petty, R. E. (1982). The need for cognition. *Journal of Personality and Social Psychology, 42,* 116–131.

Cacioppo, J. T., Petty, R. E., Feinstein, J., & Jarvis, B. (1996). Dispositional differences in cognitive motivation: The life and times of individuals varying in need for cognition. *Psychological Bulletin, 119,* 197–253.

Frey, K. P., & Eagly, A. H. (1993). Vividness can undermine the persuasiveness of messages. *Journal of Personality and Social Psychology, 65,* 32–44.

Giner-Sorolla, R., Garciá, M. T., & Bargh, J. A. (1999). The automatic evaluation of pictures. *Social Cognition, 17,* 76–96.

Green, M. C., & Brock, T. C. (2000). The role of transportation in the persuasiveness of public narratives. *Journal of Personality and Social Psychology, 79,* 701–721.

Green, M. C., & Brock, T. C. (2002). In the mind's eye: Transportation-imagery model of narrative persuasion. In M.C. Green, J.J. Strange, & T. C. Brock (Eds.), Narrative impact: Social and cognitive foundations (pp. 315–341). Mahwah, NJ: Lawrence Erlbaum Associates.

Greenwald, A. G. (1968). Cognitive learning, cognitive response to persuasion, and attitude change. In A. G. Greenwald, T. C. Brock, & T. M. Ostrom (Eds.), *Psychological foundations of attitudes* (pp. 147–169). New York: Academic Press.

Hermans, D., de Houwer, J., & Eelen, P. (1994). The affective priming effect: Automatic activation of evaluative information in memory. *Cognition and Emotion, 8,* 515–533.

Hovland, C. I., Janis, I. L., & Kelly, J. J. (1953). *Communication and persuasion.* New Haven: Yale University Press.

Hovland, C. I., Lumsdaine, A. A., & Sheffield, F. D. (1949). *Experiments in mass communication.* Princeton, NJ: Princeton University Press.

Keller, P. A., & Block, L. G. (1997). Vividness effect: A resource-matching perspective. *Journal of Consumer Research, 24,* 295–304.

Kenny, K., & Scott, L. M. (2003). A review of the visual rhetoric literature. In L. M. Scott & R. Batra (Eds.), *Persuasive imagery: A consumer response perspective* (pp. 17–56). Mahwah, NJ: Lawrence Erlbaum Associates.

Kisielius, J., & Sternthal, B. (1984). Detecting and explaining vividness effects in attitudinal judgments. *Journal of Marketing Research, 21,* 54–64.

Kisielius, J., & Sternthal, B. (1986). Examining the vividness controversy: An availability-valence interpretation. *Journal of Consumer Research, 12,* 418–431.

Kopfman, J. E., Smith, S. W., Ah Yun, J. K., & Hodges, A. (1998). Affective and cognitive reactions to narrative versus statistical evidence organ donation messages. *Journal of Applied Communication Research, 26,* 279–300.

Lang, A. (2000). The limited capacity model of mediated message processing. *Journal of Communication, 50,* 46–70.

MacInnis, D. J., & Price, L. L. (1987). The role of imagery in information processing: Review and extensions. *Journal of Consumer Research, 13,* 473–491.

Mani, G., & MacInnis, D. J. (2003). The role of imagery instructions in facilitating persuasion in a consumer context. In L. M. Scott & R. Batra (Eds.), *Persuasive imagery: A consumer response perspective* (pp. 175–187). Mahwah, NJ: Lawrence Erlbaum Associates.

Mantel, S. P., & Kellaris, J. J. (2003). Cognitive determinants of consumers' time perceptions: The impact of resources required and available. *Journal of Consumer Research, 29,* 531–538.

Markham, R., & Hynes, L. (1993). The effect of vividness of imagery on reality monitoring. *Journal of Mental Imagery, 17,* 159–170.

Mazzocco, P. J. (2000). *Mental imagery and the attitude change process.* Unpublished master's thesis, The Ohio State University, Columbus, OH.

Mazzocco, P. J., & Brock, T. C. (2005). *Delimiting the role of mental imagery in attitude change and persistence: A cognitive resources model.* Unpublished manuscript, The Ohio State University, Columbus, OH.

McGuire, W. J. (1969). Personality and susceptibility to social influence. In E. F. Borgatta & W. W. Lambert (Eds.), *Handbook of personality theory and research* (pp. 171–196). Chicago: Rand McNally.

McGuire, W. J. (1985). Attitudes and attitude change. In G. Lindzey & E. Aronson (Eds.), *Handbook of social psychology* (3rd ed., Vol. 2., pp. 233–346). New York: Random House.

Paivio, A. (1986). *Mental representations: A dual coding approach.* New York: Oxford University Press.

Pashler, H. (1994). Dual-task interference in simple tasks: Data and theory. *Psychological Bulletin, 116,* 220–244.

Peracchio, L. A., & Meyers-Levy, J. (1997). Evaluating persuasion-enhancing techniques from a resource-matching perspective. *Journal of Consumer Research, 24,* 178–191.

Petty, R. E., & Cacioppo, J. T. (1984). The effects of involvement on response to argument quantity and quality: Central and peripheral routes to persuasion. *Journal of Personality and Social Psychology, 46,* 69–81.

Petty, R. E., Cacioppo, J. T., & Schumann, D. (1983). Central and peripheral routes to advertising effectiveness: The moderating role of involvement. *Journal of Consumer Research, 10,* 135–144.

Petty, R. E., & Wegener, D. T. (1998). Attitude change: Multiple roles for persuasion variables. In D. T. Gilbert, S. T. Fiske, & G. Lindzey (Eds.) *The handbook of social psychology* (vol. 1, pp. 323–390). New York: McGraw-Hill.

Petty, R. E., Wells, G. L., & Brock, T. C. (1976). Distraction can enhance or reduce yielding to propaganda: Thought disruption versus effort justification. *Journal of Personality and Social Psychology, 34,* 874–884.

Raymond, J. E. (2003). When the mind blinks: Attentional limitations to the perception of sequential visual images. In L. M. Scott & R. Batra (Eds.), *Persuasive imagery: A consumer response perspective* (pp. 59–73). Mahwah, NJ: Lawrence Erlbaum Associates.

Raymond, J. E., Shapiro, K. L., & Arnell, K. M. (1992). Temporary suppression of visual processing in an RSVP task: An attentional blink? *Journal of Experimental Psychology: Human Perception and Performance, 18,* 849–860.

Reyes, R. M., Thompson, W. C., & Bower, G. H. (1980). Judgmental biases resulting from differing availabilities of arguments. *Journal of Personality and Social Psychology, 39,* 2–12.

Scott, L. M. (1994). Images in advertising: The need for a theory of visual rhetoric. *Journal of Consumer Research, 21,* 252–273.

Scott, L. M., & Batra, R. (2003). *Persuasive imagery: A consumer response perspective.* Mahwah, NJ: Lawrence Erlbaum Associates.

Smith, S. M., & Shaffer, D. R. (2000). Vividness can undermine or enhance message processing: The moderating role of vividness congruency. *Personality and Social Psychology Bulletin, 26,* 769–779.

Taylor, S. E., & Thompson, S. C. (1982). Stalking the "elusive" vividness effect. *Psychological Review, 89,* 155–181.

Telford, C. W. (1931). The refractory phase of voluntary and associative responses. *Journal of Experimental Psychology, 14,* 1–36.

Unnava, H. R., Agarwal, S., & Haugtvedt, C. P. (1996). Interactive effects of presentation modality and message-generated imagery on recall of advertising information. *Journal of Consumer Research, 23,* 81–88.

Unnava, H. R., & Burnkrant, R. E. (1991). An imagery-processing view of the role of pic-
. tures in print advertisements. *Journal of Marketing Research, 28,* 226–231.

CHAPTER FIVE

From Image to Experience

Bernd Schmitt
Columbia Business School

We know a lot about image and very little about experience.

Image is a key concept in our field. Image as a concept is an essential part of the mainstream model that we use in advertising and consumer psychology: information processing. There are theories about what images are like, how they are formed, and how they operate in memory. We distinguish types of images (i.e., visual and verbal) and have examined what happens when images are consistent or inconsistent with one another.

Experience is an equally important concept, but we have not treated it that way. We know very little about what experiences are like, how they work, and what types of experiences we should distinguish. Experiential appeals are used all over in advertising today, and in product design, packaging, and retail spaces. With our current models, we have a tough time describing and explaining these new communications. Think of Absolut Vodka. Absolut ads are not just image ads (e.g., "this is a great, cool drink"). They provide a great sensory experience (i.e., the way they are laid out, in terms of the color scheme as well as the relational messages, cf. the 'City Series'). Think of Fresh Samantha, Odwalla, and Naked fruit juices. The names and packaging of these products are not just images. They provide a sensory, emotional, and modern lifestyle experience. That's why they use Ginko Biloba, a very experiential ingredient: That ingredient is not in that bottle just to provide you with a functional benefit but to make you feel good. Think of the New Beetle (with the flower vase in the front of the car) and now the new Mini. Think of what Apple has done the last few years, and so on. Think of these examples— and experience! And realize that our research can grasp with most of these cases only in a superficial information-processing way that misses the essence of the communication.

79

WHAT IS AN EXPERIENCE?

Experiences involve the entire human being. Experiences involve the senses, the heart (i.e., the affective system), the mind (and there mostly the creative processes), and other body and motor systems. Because they involve the entire being, experiences are integrated. All the senses are involved, and thus we get synaesthetic experiences.

Experiences are triggered by context. All stimuli in a given context can trigger experiences (not just movies and jazz).

DO EXPERIENCES AFFECT CONSUMER BEHAVIOR?

The answer is yes. A field study with over 1,000 consumers shows that communications, web sites, and stores, measured on their degree of experience using a reliable and valid scale, the EX scale, result in people having better memory, more positive attitudes, and higher purchase intentions. Moreover, experiential ads at the same GRP level are more effective.

Finally, a choice study shows that experience (e.g., just putting a color or a smiley face on a floppy disk—sort of the 'Apple approach') can make up for functional product inferiority. When two products are functionally equivalent (a choice consumers often face today), the type of experiential appeal determines the choice.

IN CONCEPTUALIZING EXPERIENCES, ARE EXISTING RESEARCH PARADIGMS AND EXISTING RESEARCH MODELS USEFUL?

To a degree. Research on affect has expanded beyond the information processing paradigm. This research is useful for an experiential approach. However, most research on affect still views moods and feelings as information. The experiential approach goes beyond that: Affect is experiential; it is visceral.

Decision-making research has become behavioral and shows that many prior decision models made too many rational assumptions. Often, as the BDT work shows, consumers choose experiences (e.g., a free ticket for a spa) over money (e.g., the monetary value of a spa visit, although they could use that money also for something else). These findings are important for an experiential approach. The experiential approach then explains why this is so.

There are other areas where experiential ideas have popped up. Satisfaction is no longer just seen as expectations–performance comparisons. New models include a strong affective component. Brand associations can include remembered experiences with the product. In postmodernism, there are insightful case studies on product consumption.

MORE TO BE DONE, MORE TO BE RESEARCHED

Here is a start. Regarding structure, based on cognitive science and the modular theory of the mind (e.g., Pinker), I suggest we distinguish five mind modules that can create unique experiences with their own structures and processes. I have alluded to them earlier; simple words for them are sense, feel, think, and act. One could add relate to cover unique relationship experiences that an individual alone cannot have. Empirically, however, relate often loads on the same factor (in a factor analysis) as feel. Importantly, please note that, as with mind modules, experiences must be snapped together to create a holistic experience. The New Beetle I mentioned earlier is a good example.

Regarding process, I expect experiences to be: (a) holistic (rather than atomistic), (b) interactive (rather than step by step), and (c) adaptive (rather than fixed). In other words, they are quite different from the way we conceptualize processes in the information-processing paradigm.

In terms of experience determinants, I propose that any experience occurs through the interaction of three sources: the stimulus (e.g., colors and shapes trigger sense, a smiley face triggers feel, a complex text or visual triggers think, dynamic information triggers act, and people trigger relate), the experiencer (and there may be individual differences in sensitivity to sense, feel, think, act and relate), and finally, the context of that color and shape and smiley face and so on.

We need lots of research on the structure, process and determinants, of experiences.

A FEW WORDS ON APPLIED ISSUES

As experiential practitioners, we need to do advertising differently. First, in an experiential ad, the consumer must be there—explicitly or implicitly. The consumer—not the product—has the experience. The mere use of product shots and enumerating functional features and benefits is inconsistent with the experiential approach. We need to show the sensory experience and the feeling that the consumer is getting. We need to show—creatively—how the consumer is thinking about something and what that means to him or her. We need to show actions and relations with other consumers.

Applied marketing research needs to be conducted in consumers' natural environments, not in an antiseptic, controlled laboratory. Stimuli need to be multisensory (not just verbal), multimedia (not just print), and three dimensional, just like products in daily life. We need to move from marketing science to consumer insight.

Implementations of communications need to be designed and executed in an integrated fashion. The ad agency, PR firm, web designers, and retail consultants need to work jointly on the experience.

ISN'T IT FUNNY THAT THIS CHAPTER ORIGINATED FROM WORK IN KOREA?

Not just funny. Actually, quite appropriate. Korean and Asian culture share some of the key characteristics of the experiential approach. When you look at all the work on cross-cultural psychology and consumer behavior, you will find that Asian culture views people in terms of their entire beings (just think of medicine). Asian culture functions in an integrated way (i.e., community is of utmost importance). For Asian culture, context matters (think of all the politeness rules). Let's take the wisdom of Asian culture and use it for moving from image to experience and thus expand our models of advertising and consumer psychology.

Part II—Country Image

Globalization of markets and an increasing networked world have emphasized the need for the study of effective country image and cross-country implications for tourism and the attractiveness of products and people. This section contains discussions of various aspects of country image research, such as measurement and process of a country image, destination image and tourism implications, and evaluation of country products. Academic literature on recent country-image related findings (such as COO effects) are also discussed in detail in individual chapters. More important, the chapters cover new approaches to the conceptualization, processes, and measurement of country image and the impact on image-related consumer behavior.

CHAPTER SIX

Building a National Image With Words:
The Role of Word of Mouth
in Establishing Korea's International Image

WoonBong Na
Kyunghee University, Korea

Youngsoek Son
Hallym University, Korea

Chung-Hyun Kim
Sogang University, Korea

Roger Marshall
NTU, Singapore

The image of a country is vital to its health and well-being, in much the same way that one's image dominates the life of every individual. As an individual, the type of job you get depends on the appropriateness of your image in the eyes of your future employer; thus, your lifelong economic status is determined. Similarly, the type of person you marry depends largely upon the image perception your future potential partner has of you—hence your social and personal happiness also often largely depend upon the development and maintenance of a suitable personal image.

For a nation there is a parallel situation. For most countries, economic prosperity depends on selling services and products to people from other countries. The case of tourism (which is playing an increasingly important role in countries around the globe as travel and communication integration increases) is obvious and well researched, but many producers also rely on the images of their countries to shed enhancing halos over their national brands. Less obviously, even the social health of the people of a nation may be affected by image perception. The "ugly American" image, for instance, is very unkind and has harmed international relations for many an American traveler, yet was probably caused by a very few exchange-rich lower class American tourists in a few specific instances and has proven very hard to shake off.

The importance of national image is fully understood by most, and this understanding is reflected in the literatures of marketing, tourism and international business, as well as in the managerial energy that has been expended to try to establish, enhance, or change national images in some way. These efforts may largely be thwarted, however, unless greater attention is given to the processes by which the image of a nation is molded. It is our purpose to investigate and discuss the hitherto unheralded role of word of mouth (WOM) in this regard, comparing its power to that of the more conventional modes investigated elsewhere, such as advertising in the mass media.

Before describing the research to support the claims made about the power of WOM, we discuss the existing knowledge base concerning both country image and word of mouth studies, and then develop several hypotheses from that discussion. An international survey provides the database for the research, and regression is used to analyze the data. The chapter finishes with a few comments about where future research may be profitably undertaken.

COUNTRY IMAGE STUDIES

Country Image in Country-of-Origin Studies

It is both intuitively sensible and empirically demonstrable that the image of a country affects the sale of goods produced in that country. A simple, single-cue, country-of-origin (COO) study merely documents the extent to which COO data is used in the product/service evaluation process by a particular target audience, at a particular point in time, when purchasing particular goods that originated in the country of interest. This simple approach begs theory, though, and a stream of clarification studies over the years have gone some way to helping us understand and refine the nature of the COO construct. Bilkey and Nes (1982) conducted what has become a classic review of COO studies, and it is mainly since that time that the construct has been more rigorously investigated with a view to enhancing our theoretical understanding of country image and its role rather than merely documenting the empirical evidence.

Before discussing the stream of research in any depth, however, it seems sensible to leap forward a few decades to more recent discussion of the basic nature of the construct—that is, whether or not COO is a personal belief structure or some sort of universal cultural stereotype. Janda and Rao (1997) provided a good review of the investigation that started when Ericksen and his colleagues departed from the established practice of dealing with COO with a single-cue study and took the view that image affects both attitudes and beliefs (Ericksen, Johansson,& Chao, 1984). This multivariate, multiple-cue approach was vigorously pursued within the information-processing literature.

Included in the plethora of studies is a detailed experiment by Hong and Wyer (1989) that nicely illustrates the tenor of these enquiries. Hong and Wyer tested four hypotheses within an information-processing framework, all of which hold some relevance here. First, they were interested in the encoding process and the effect of a strong COO on the encoding of attribute information. There seemed two possibilities. The first is that the COO could act as a generalized halo, causing positive (or negative) emphasis to be placed on all attribute information, either good or bad. Alternatively, if the COO stereotype was seen to be unrelated to the attribute information, then greater emphasis would be placed on the positive or negative aspect itself, and the COO may merely make positive attributes seem more positive and negative more negative.

A second hypothesis is based on earlier cognitive information processing work by Bodenhausen and Lichetenstein (1987) and Bodenhausen and Wyer (1985). This hypothesis, simply stated, suggests that in the absence of strong attribute cues, the COO information will act as a heuristic and dominate the decision. Similarly, the third hypothesis (which is framed by a primacy–recency argument) suggests that COO information will or will not be used as attribute information, depending on whether or not the information is presented within an evaluative framework or is simply a preexisting heuristic framework into which more recent, specific, attribute information is included.

Finally, an interesting idea is tentatively put forward, that the existence of a strong country image may excite interest in the attribute information and thus generate more extensive cognitive elaboration. This elaborative idea would only work, we suggest, when the attribute information is received within a casual mode, rather than in a specific, evaluative condition.

Although some small positive results were found for all the hypotheses, it is reported that the strongest effect—against expectations—came from the fourth hypothesis. Thus, COO indeed acts as a stimulus to consider judgment criteria, especially when there is no awareness of a deliberate judgment situation being in place.

Although national image is the central topic of this paper, not COO, the COO literature contains some very relevant information. First, and most important, is that even in a cognitive information approach, country image is important. That is, there may well be specific, judgment-related criteria in evidence, but the holistic image of the source country still plays a role. Indeed, although unsupported by empirical evidence, Janda and Rao (1997) created a very interesting set of propositions about what may happen under conditions where the valence of COO attitude and specific attribute beliefs are contradictory. Second, this role varies considerably from situation to situation.

Variations in Importance of Country Image

We have already suggested that country image is more important as a judgment criteria when little is known of the judgment object (i.e., when the overriding COO heuristic is invoked) or when a less considered, more casual judgment is being made, as against a deliberate choice. There is also a great deal of empirical evidence about between-culture differences in identical COO cue strength and composition. To add to the confusion, COO stereotypes change over time. Being British used to be synonymous with being of high quality and was a proud boast attached to many British products. No more, according to recent research (Papadopoulos & Heslop, 1993), which explains that the Jaguar motorcar, which had become almost a British icon, now has to de-emphasize the "Britishness" of the vehicle and stress engineering excellence instead because of changing international attitudes toward the standard of British workmanship.

Can cultural variations in COO be usefully explained theoretically? Well, yes, to a point it seems that they can. The socialization process, which each individual experiences, seems to have certain similarities for individuals of a particular group. One role, or output, of this socialization is the formation of stereotypes, which are a form of cultural attitude encouraged by rewards and discouraged by punishment in the classical socialization process fashion. Janda and Rao (1997) explained that stereotypes can be used in several contexts and thus gather slightly different meanings. They used Ashmore and Del Boca's (1981) description of sociocultural, psychodynamic, and cognitive meanings of the word but claimed that the former is the most commonly understood usage and therefore adopted that frame, as we do. Clearly, the larger and more diverse the group, then the less specific a stereotype becomes and the less commonly it is held. For instance, new car buyers in New Zealand were shown to have strong stereotypical COO attitudes that were dominant in the purchase process (Lawrence, Marr, & Prendergast, 1992). This makes sense in that one would expect such a closely defined subset of a cultural group to hold similar views, but the results may have been far less clear if the total population of the country were to have been polled.

Nevertheless, there is strong evidence for the existence of images based on larger social structures, such as regional groupings of cultures. Thus, Schweiger and colleagues (Schweiger, Haubl, & Friederes, 1995) talked of a European quality image (as against a U.S. or Asian image) as being quite strong and well defined, and Marshall and his colleagues (Marshall, Tsee, & Lee, 1994) of a distinctive Asian image that, incidentally, poses some problem for marketers based in the Asian region.

Clearly, then, the socialization process, which tends to be similar within a culture group, need not be similar between cultural groups. Thus a stereotype held in one culture may be quite different to that in another. This is borne out, for instance, by evidence that more industrialized countries have different country stereotypes than nonindustrialized ones (Khachaturian & Morganosky, 1990). Similarly, and following on from the previous arguments, Hong and Yi (1992) told an interesting story about the views of Koreans and Americans concerning Chinese and Mexican stereotypes. That U.S. citizens evaluated products made in China and Mexico fairly positively—despite a generally negative country image—whereas Koreans evaluated the same products negatively is explained by the Koreans' general lack of experience with Chinese and Mexican products.

Kaynak and his co-authors (Kaynak, Kucukemiroglu, & Hyder, 2000) operationalized this national experience factor as a study classification they termed *environmental impact* (as against single-cue, multi-cue, and conjoint studies). Thus common national experiences, environments, and common cultural stereotypes influence the invocation, structure, and power of national or regional images during purchasing.

A final word here about the COO work comes from Janda and Rao (1997) who showed quite clearly that the extent of egalitarianism experienced in a culture seems to be a determinant of the power of cultural stereotyping in product purchasing decisions. This interesting research example illustrates nicely that there are many, many factors that may influence the power and nature of COO usage but that stereotypical national images play an important role in many purchase decisions.

Country Image

Thus far we have discussed the image of a country as part of a country-of-origin construct, but there is an emerging literature, which has developed in tourism, concerning the image of a destination. Although on first consideration, it seems a very different situation to the standard COO problem, it is actually very similar. For instance, if a potential tourist was forming a destination image of the city of Pusan, then there may well be an overriding halo effect caused by the individual's perception of South Korea as a country. Similarly, the tourist destination image of South Korea may well be tinted in some way by an overriding image of Asia held by a potential tourist. Again, the size and diversity of the nominated destination is critical—it is plainly more likely that a clear image of a single resort would emerge than of a complex, diverse city or, yet more, a whole country.

It is not surprisingly, then, that the literature of tourism echoes that of the country-of-origin literature in international business and psychology. Three papers from the tourism literature sufficiently illustrate the direction and maturity of this body of research. The first is a simple survey, whereas the other two are far more ambitious papers that attempt to model destination image formation.

The first paper is concerned with the survey to assess the image of Toronto as a destination. There is no attempt to measure or take into account any COO effect that may be caused by a halo image of Canada as a whole; instead, a list of product attributes is developed, from a series of interviews, into a single scale. Statistical analysis is performed on the responses to the resultant questionnaire-survey to establish differences in the overall destination image of people from different countries and on individual scale items. This pragmatic approach probably stems from the commonly adopted definition of image as a set of beliefs, ideas, and impressions that people have of a place or destination (Crompton, 1979; Kotler, Hamelin, Rein, & Haider, 1993).

The second illustrative work is entitled *Destination image: Towards a conceptual framework* and has been reported in the premium hospitality journal in the world (Gallarza, Saura, Garcia, 2001). The authors first provided a very useful meta-analysis of the scope of destination image studies in the tourism literature and a good summary of the methodologies that have been used, which, not surprisingly, are very similar to those found in the general marketing and international business literatures. The kernel of the paper is the development of a conceptual model of tourist destination image (TDI). The model is not supported by empirical research but is strongly grounded in the extent literature. The authors noted the complexity of the process by acknowledging cognitive, affective, and conative elements of the construct, the need for a multidisciplinary focus, and direct reference to collective images versus personal impressions—this is very much in line with the marketing literature. TDI is acknowledged both as a multiconstruct and as a Gestalt, and as having both static and dynamic elements in its structure. Finally, the relativistic nature of the construct is well noted, thus making allowances for between-culture, or between-group, differences. Although the model would be extremely hard to operationalize, it is conceptually sophisticated and provides a good summary of the thought on the topic to date.

The third paper, *A model of destination image formation*, is far more theoretically grounded and it takes a strong cognitive information approach (Baloglu & McLeary, 1999). The authors posit that overall destination image is a function of perceptual and cognitive evaluations and also affective evaluations is shown in Figure 6.1, which is taken directly from their work. The survey instrument is rigorously developed and the model variables consequently extracted from a factor analysis. Even though the sample was homogenous in terms of demographic char-

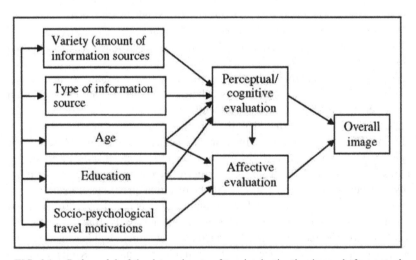

FIG. 6.1.   Path model of the determinants of tourist destination image before actual dissertation.

acteristics, the resultant path analysis provides quite impressive evidence for the intervening variables as hypothesized, with the effects of the conceptual and cognitive evaluations on effect proving stronger than the effects of travel motivations. Again, however, although three target countries were used in the research (i.e., Greece, Italy, and Egypt), there is no specific consideration or attempt to separate any halo effect from a generalized impression of the country—indeed, the responses gathered from all four surveys were pooled before analysis.

A minor, almost incidental finding of the path analysis is of importance to the work that follows. The type of information sources used by respondents in assembling their information was ascertained in the survey as one of the predictive variables. In the analysis of the model paths, it was revealed that only word of mouth had significant positive path coefficients with all three conceptual or cognitive variables, whereas advertisements were significant with only one, and two other information-source factors showed no significant path coefficients whatsoever. This effect leads very conveniently into the next section of this chapter, concerning the power of word of mouth as an information source for the construction of a country image.

WORD OF MOUTH

The General Research Background

The power of word of mouth (WOM) was realized in the very early days of modern marketing. The two most referenced studies in this context are those of Katz and Lazarfeld (1955) and Whyte (1954). The latter study relied on anecdotal evidence to determine the diffusion of air conditioners in a suburb of Philadelphia. Whyte identified a network of neighbors exchanging information about the air conditioners in informal situations, over the clothesline and across backyard fences. Katz and Lazarfeld conducted rather more rigorous research and came up with the startling and much quoted result that WOM is seven times more effective than newspapers and magazines, four times as effective as personal selling, and twice as effective as radio advertising in influencing consumers to switch brands. The type of research conducted by these authors is still being conducted today, although the bulk of the research on the topic was performed in the 1960s and early 1970s.

Early research was concerned most of all with positive word of mouth, which leads to brand or product adoption. Rogers (1962, 1983, 1995), in his diffusion of innovation work, asserted that although a buyer becomes aware of innovations mostly from the mass media, the word of mouth sources are mostly utilized by the buyer at the critical stage of evaluating the innovation. Along a similar vein, the plethora of work concerning opinion leadership—which has largely stemmed from the two-step flow of communication hypothesis of Katz (1957)—suggests that a small number of people in the community access information from mass media or technical sources and then pass this information on to a large number of people whose opinions are influenced by it. Later again the Bass diffusion model explicitly states that consumers are influenced by both media and WOM communications (Mahajan, Muller, & Bass, 1990).

Later research in WOM has proceeded in two general directions: first, with negative word of mouth within the context of dissatisfaction and repeat purchase behavior, and second, with refining our knowledge of the circumstances in which WOM is most utilized. Richens (1983, 1984) showed, not surprisingly, that as the severity of the problem associated with dissatisfaction increases, the tendency to engage in negative WOM increases. She also suggested that although for serious situations negative WOM will almost certainly occur no matter what action management takes, it is certainly worthwhile for management to try to stop negative WOM for minor or less important problem situations. Richins also suggested that negative WOM is more powerful than positive. Although this claim has sparked some surprise and controversy, there is strong evidence in psychology and marketing that negative information of any sort is, indeed, more persuasive than positive information (Maheswaran & Meyers-Levy, 1990; Martin & Marshall, 1998). However, the research material concerning the situations in which word of mouth is more or less important is of real interest here, as the major concern of this chapter is with WOM in conjunction with country image.

Factors That Influence the Power of WOM

Why is it word of mouth so powerful? There is some early evidence that interpersonal communication has a significant impact on consumer purchase behavior because of normative social influence (Stafford, 1966). However, recent research has pointed to the importance of the vividness of face-to-face personal communications, which are deemed to be trustworthy because the information gatherer has no vested or commercial interest in the persuasion process. There is a large literature concerning informational input to judgment processes, and it has been noted that almost everybody (including managers) preferred to act on vivid, personal information than on cold, hard data. This is probably not only because such vivid, personal data is readily accessible to the decision maker, but it is also diagnostic in nature (i.e., that people believe that they can accomplish their decision goals by using the information). This is referred to as the accessibility–diagnosticity model (Feldman & Lynch, 1998). This model would lead us to believe that the more vivid (and therefore accessible) the information, and the more diagnostic its nature, the more powerful WOM becomes.

It seems intuitive that more important situations or purchase decisions will lead to greater WOM. In spite of the early work by Sheth (1971), who showed that word of mouth pertains very strongly in low-risk innovations as well as high, later research has shown the intuitive thought to be correct and that severity of situation (Richens, 1983), or personal involvement in the WOM object or situation (Lau & Ng, 2001), is important.

Familiarity born of a personal experience is strongly related to risk reduction, and this relation led Sundaram and Webster (1999) to investigate brand familiarity as a moderating variable on the effect of WOM on brand evaluations. They found that the effect of negative word of mouth is reduced and positive word of mouth is exacerbated when the subject is familiar with the brand. Thus, the more important an object is, the more likely it is that WOM will occur, and the persuasive strength of the WOM will be enhanced in situations where the purchaser is unfamiliar with the purchase object or if the quality or utility of the purchase object is hard to change because of tangibility or technological reasons.

The corollary of the fact that high-risk innovations or purchases lead to greater WOM than lower is that individuals who are sensitive to risk are more likely to engage in WOM than those who are not. Recent research conducted within the banking sector has confirmed this effect (Ennew, Banergee, & Li, 2001). Similarly, Lau and Ng (2001) identified self-confidence, sociability, and social responsibility as personal factors having an impact on the extent of WOM behavior.

In marketing strategy it is often more valuable, though, to identify clusters of people who behave similarly rather than to identify individual differences, as aggregation can lead to profitability through the identification of market segments and by standardization of the marketing mix. The rather interesting list of individual differences pointed out by Ng and Lau point to the possibility that countries (or cultures, at least) may exhibit similarities in WOM behavior within their national borders and differences in WOM behavior to other countries. This transpires to be true both at a superficial level and in a more complex manner.

At a superficial level it is quite clear that some countries will be more or less familiar with certain objects, brands, or even other countries. Thus it would not surprise at all to find that word of mouth is more important as an information source in one country than another simply because of unfamiliarity. Similarly, education levels may play a part. That is, that even if people in two countries are equally familiar with a particular object, a lower education level in one country may increase the impact of WOM in that country as few people are able to understand the object and opinion leadership becomes more important.

At a deeper level there is both empirical evidence and a theoretical rationale for believing that WOM behavior varies from culture to culture. A sophisticated network analysis of word of mouth referral behavior in a natural environment was conducted in 1986 (Brown & Reingen, 1988). The major findings of this study are that strong and homophilious social ties are more likely to be activated for the flow of referral information and that strong ties are also more influential than weak ties and are thus more likely to be used as information sources. Given that many cultures are categorized by the strength of their within-group social ties, it seems to follow that WOM behavior is likely to be different in different societies. Some research work in the area ignores this fact and merely pools all the respondents regardless of their nationality or cultural origin (Baloglu & McLeary, 1999), but other work either incidentally or explicitly seeks between-culture WOM differences.

Lau and Ng (2001) investigated negative WOM and drew their sample from both Singapore and Canada. A high level of importance was found for the use and power of negative WOM in both countries, and a relation between negative word of mouth behavior and the likelihood of repurchase was established. There were also some significant differences reported between the two countries in terms of the personal characteristics of those most likely to be influenced by this information source. Money and his colleagues (Money, Gilly, & Graham, 1998) were specifically focused on exploring differences in WOM referral behavior in the purchase of industrial services between the United States and Japan. This interesting study established quite clearly that national culture indeed has a strong effect on the number of referral sources consulted, with the high context, highly collectivistic and risk-averse Japanese companies using more than comparable American companies.

DEVELOPMENT OF RESEARCH PROPOSITIONS

WOM is a powerful contributor to the image of any product, we know, but it is uncertain just how much more powerful WOM is than other sources of information in the specific case of the country image of the Republic of South Korea. Katz and Lazarfeld's (1955) statement that WOM is seven times more effective than newspapers and magazines, four times as affective as personal selling, and twice as effective as radio advertising in influencing consumers to switch brands was made a long time ago, used a homophilious American sample, and was concerned with consumer goods. A far more relevant guide is provided by Baloglu and McCleary (1999), although it must be noted that estimating the comparative strength of various information sources was not a central part of their work but was merely a small part of a destination image formation model validation exercise. Of professional advice from tour operators, travel agents, and airlines; word of mouth from friends, relatives, and social clubs; broadcast or print advertisements; and books, movies, and news, only WOM proved to be significant in the path analysis testing the tourist destination image model. This seems perfectly reasonable. For people who have never been to a country, it is very hard to envisage exactly what that country is like and, in the event that a judgment must be made (about the country itself, as a destination image, or as an attribute of some product or service made in the country), there is a large element of the unknown. In the face of risk and ambiguity it seems highly likely that WOM will become an important and influential source of information. Hence our first proposition:

P1: WOM will be more important than other communication modes to the development of a national image.

There is also clear evidence in the literature that negative word of mouth is more influential than positive. We see no reason why this should not be reflected in the case of country image formation, and this point is particularly pertinent for South Korea because of the close proximity of an unstable and unpredictable North Korea and the fact that most Americans in the country are attached to the military. Thus our second proposition:

> P2: WOM will be more important when negative rather than positive conditions exist.

In different cultural conditions the communication infrastructure will be at different levels of development, and the population will invest more or less trust in diffeels and the perceptions of the reliability of the various media channels. In addition, as discussed in the literature reviewed here, there are good theoretical reasons why we expect the power of WOM to vary across cultural borders. Thus we anticipate that although WOM will be universally important to the formation of the image of South Korea, this importance will vary in different cultures either for social reasons or because of the level of familiarity individuals have with South Korea.

> P3: The power of WOM will vary cross-culturally.

RESEARCH METHOD

After perusal of the relevant literature and analysis of a few exploratory interviews, a research instrument was designed and used to survey the opinions of a large international group about their sources of information about the Republic of South Korea. Analysis was conducted using multivariate methods (see Fig. 6.2).

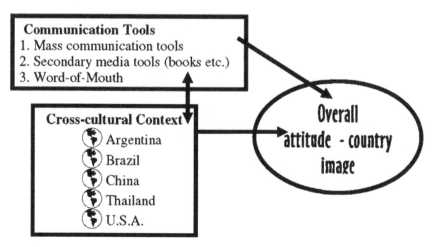

FIG. 6.2.   Overview of the research process.

Sample

To offer a satisfactory test of the research propositions, responses were sought from 1,534 urbanites on three continents; good responses were solicited from the United States (405), Brazil (206), Argentina (201), China (525) and Thailand (200). Although the sample is small, care was taken to collect quotas based on age, gender, and education level to provide some comparability between the different national sample groups.

Instrument

Overall country image was collected through the use of a 7-point Likert scale anchored by *agree strongly* and *disagree strongly*, measuring responses to the eight items. The items, drawn from several sources (Crawford & Lumpkin, 1993; Gastil, 1990; Han, 1990; Papadopoulos & Heslop, 1993) are history and tradition, democracy, cultural advancement, economic development, social stability, level of technology, trustworthiness of the people, and beauty of the countryside.

Media used to form opinions were indicated by multiple checks against a number of listed media: television or radio news, newspaper or magazine news articles, newspaper or magazine advertisements, reports and books, and WOM from acquaintances or friends who have visited Korea.

Procedure

The original questionnaire was written in English but was professionally translated into Spanish, Thai, and Chinese by the relevant branches of the Gallup organization. Fortunately, the questionnaire is very simple and back translation and pretesting revealed no problems. To relieve the social desirability and halo biases, in all countries except the United States, personal interviews were used. In the United States the research area is very large, but the telephone network is well developed, and the population is well used to telephone surveys. The professional Gallup field workers took some three days to collect the data. There was no attempt to attain a random selection of responses; quotas were filled merely on a convenience basis. Once again, the simplicity and the brevity of the research instrument, plus the fact the no sensitive information was sought, led to a largely trouble-free data collection process, although 150 responses (from all countries) were discarded as they had too much missing data.

RESULTS

Scales

The 8-item scale measuring perceived image of Korea has a Cronbach's alpha of 0.78, indicating reasonable reliability and yielding an overall image score for each

TABLE 6.1

Factor Loadings, Sources Used to Form Image

Source	Factor 1	Factor 2	Factor 3
Newspaper and magazine news articles	.830		
Television or radio news	.796		
Books		.765	
Movies and television shows		.750	
Word of mouth from a Korean friend/acquaintance			.828
Word of mouth from a Korean visitor			.820

TABLE 6.2

Results of Regression, Country Image by Source of Data

		Standardized	
	Beta value	t value	Significance
Mass communication	.15	5.8	< .001
Secondary sources	.06	2.1	.03
Word of mouth	.22	8.5	< .001

respondent. The data was submitted to principle component factor analysis, using a Varimax rotation. Three factors emerged, with eigenvalues of 1.99, 1.25 and 1.02, which together explain 61% of the variation in the data set. The factor loadings are shown in Table 6.1. The three factors are named as mass communications (MC), secondary media (SM) and word of mouth (WOM), and three new variables are formed from their means.

Proposition 1

The major proposition addressed by the research relates to the belief that WOM is more powerful than other modes. Regression analysis confirms the proposition (see Table 6.2). This is not a marginal result but a clear mandate for the power of WOM.

Proposition 2

WOM, we believe, will be more important where negative rather than positive conditions exist. As every respondents' image perception has been assessed, it is possible to sort the respondents into those with a negative and those with a positive impression of Korea. The first way this helps test the proposition is by allowing a check of the mean difference in attitude between positive and negative groups for each media type. ANOVA is used, and the results of the analysis are reported in Table 6.3.

This analysis is supportive in that it seems that the attitude difference is most significant for WOM as against either mass communications or secondary sources.

TABLE 6.3

Mean Differences Between Those Respondents With a Positive
or a Negative Attitude to South Korea

	Sum of squares	DF	Mean square	.F	Sig
Mass communication					
Between groups	4.80	1	4.80	5.82	.016
Within groups	1076.41	1306	.82		
Total	1081.22	1307			
Secondary sources					
Between groups	2.05	1	2.05	3.77	.052
Within groups	709.61	1306	.54		
Total	711.66	1307			
Word of mouth					
Between groups	13.36	1	13.36	22.88	<.001
Within groups	762.57	1306	.58		
Total	775.93	1307			

TABLE 6.4

Between-Country Differences in Extremes of Attitude Valency Toward Korea

	Argentina		Brazil		China		Thailand		United States	
	N	Mean	N	Mean	N	Mean	N	Mean	N	Mean
Mass Com.										
Unfavorable	38	2.02*	85	2.09	153	2.70*	81	2.01	145	1.96
Favorable	88	1.65*	72	1.91	323	2.48*	116	1.86	207	1.88
Secondary										
Unfavorable	38	1.76	85	0.47*	153	0.80	81	1.19	145	0.76
Favorable	88	0.55	72	0.76*	323	.091	116	1.16	208	0.83
Word of Mouth										
Unfavorable	38	0.39	85	0.75	153	0.71*	81	0.77*	145	0.87*
Favorable	88	0.29	72	0.59	323	0.54*	116	0.52	207	0.65*

Note. * = difference significant at .05.

More support is forthcoming when the ANOVA is repeated by country (see Table 6.4). Thus, it seems the contrast is strongest in the United States and Asia but not evident in South America, perhaps because communication integration is lower.

Proposition 3

All the evidence in the literature suggests that the power of WOM varies between cultures for economic infrastructural, educational, interest and social reasons. We expected to find the same pattern reflected in our data, and this proves to be the case, as can be seen from a perusal of Table 6.5.

TABLE 6.5

Regression Analysis Showing Relative Power of WOM by Country

	Argentina			Brazil			China			Thailand			United States		
	Std B	t	p	Std B	t	p	Std B	t	p	Std B	t	p	Std B	t	p
MC	.02	.31	ns	.00	.02	ns	.10	2.2	.03	.17	2.3	.02	.21	4.4	.00
SS	.03	.35	ns	.09	1.21	ns	.05	1.1	ns	.02	.21	ns	.08	1.6	ns
WOM	.36	4.7	.00	.07	.86	ns	.13	2.9	.01	.19	2.8	.01	6.3	6.3	.00

DISCUSSION

Summary

Thus far there have been a few surprises concerning the research reported here, which has offered strong support to many of the ideas already expressed in the literature. It has been confirmed that word of mouth is one of the most important sources of information, not only in the persuasive sense argued in the literature but also in the matter of the formation of a national image. Moreover, the existing, generally accepted knowledge that negative word of mouth is more powerful than positive within a persuasive context has also been confirmed within the national image framework.

Recommendations

With regard to harnessing the power of word of mouth communication to build an appropriate national image, there are two fundamental approaches. The country can stimulate positive word of mouth (and minimize negative), or it can simulate positive word of mouth. Bearing this in mind, the particular circumstance of South Korea can be considered and some recommendations can be made, based upon the understanding we have.

Stimulation. The impact of word of mouth is probably at its strongest when it originates from social contacts; they have greater perceived reliability and trustworthiness than commercial sources. However, this form of communication is usually outside the direct control of an organization or a nation no matter how desirable it is to harness this communication medium as a marketing tool. Nevertheless, there are several well-recognized methods to encourage this type of communication and, as far as the authors can tell, none of them are being widely utilized in image-building efforts of South Korea. The recommendations we can make at this juncture fall under the headings of quality control and the removal of post-experience dissonance.

For the relevant authorities in South Korea to take affirmative action to reduce the incidence of negative word of mouth, they need to understand exactly what is the image of South Korea at the present time and what type of incident has the highest impact (either for good or bad) on that image. This understanding can only be achieved through a comprehensive monitoring program. For instance, the tourism authority needs to monitor the image of both inbound and outbound tourists to ascertain what experiences made the most impression on tourists. Only when an extensive database has been gathered will the authority be able to isolate the situations or people who are having an impact and consequently to do something about it. Similarly, the relevant import–export authority needs to understand something of the country of origin and investment images of South Korea that are held in the minds of the prospective investors in the country. We also know that this image, and the strength of the media that affect the image, will vary from country to country; hence respondent nationality will have to be an important part of the database and different strategies devised for different national groups. We also know that this image will change over time; hence it is not enough simply to conduct a once-off research project. Monitoring research must be put into place and kept up to date.

In a more proactive vein, a great deal of evidence shows that negative and positive word of mouth can be directly affected with an intervention program to follow up on an experience and remove any dissonance that tourists or investors may have accumulated after a bad experience or to consolidate the good experiences. Extensive records are already kept of all those that come into and go out of South Korea, both as tourists and businesspeople. It really represents a very small effort indeed to select randomly a number of these people and send them personal messages to reinforce the positive parts of their experiences and seek out any negative. One of the authors has visited South Korea many times but never once has been contacted by either a private or a government organization to find out the likelihood of a further visit or to seek any response whatsoever toward the experience enjoyed (or otherwise!) in the country.

Simulation. The Republic of South Korea, like so many nation states, invests significant financial resource into advertising itself internationally. For instance, recently President Roh's help has been enlisted and film of him giving reassuring statements has been aired during prime time in Canada and the United States on CNN and CNN Headline News on some 160 occasions for 12 days from May, 2003. This is admirable, but this sort of advertising will not lead to WOM, according to both the discussion and the research reported here. What is required is vividness and opinion leadership.

Vivid experiences are those that are remembered and discussed and are most evocative to those who have been to a country. A Korean destination competitor, New Zealand, does an admirable job with this sort of thing, with their "100% pure" campaign that shows people having pure fun, pure adventure, enjoying pure air, and so on. The same country cashed in handsomely on the *Lord of the Rings* international epic film, painting the airplanes from its national carrier with images from the film and advertising holidays to "Middle Earth"! Korea has many such vividly dramatic opportunities, with the highest standing Buddha in the World, an ancient and well-preserved cultural heritage, a unique and exciting cuisine, many mountains, and a wonderful (and largely unspoiled) coastline. These are the images that capture the imagination, not a picture of a seated politician (even a very important one!) explaining that it is safe to travel in South Korea.

No matter how well intentioned he is, President Roh is also not an opinion leader to any tourist or investor and thus is unlikely to generate WOM. An opinion leader must be seen to be spontaneous, someone the target audience can relate to as well as trust. Pictures of an American tourist sitting on the floor enjoying kim chee soup, a Western family wandering among the ruins of an Emperor's palace, a successful-looking North American businessman having red tape cut for him by a friendly Korean bureaucrat—this is the stuff of opinion leader advertisements, which are the most likely to generate the sort of word of mouth Korea needs.

REFERENCES

Ashmore, R. D., and Del Boca, F. K. (1981). Conceptual approaches to stereotypes and stereotyping. In D. L. Hamilton (Ed.), *Cognitive processes in stereotyping and intergroup behavior* (pp. 1–35) Hillsdale, NJ: Lawrence Erlbaum Associates.

Baloglu, S., & McLeary, K. W. (1999). A model of destination image formation. *Annals of Tourism Research, 26,* 868–897.

Bilkey, W. J., & Nes, E. (1982). Country of origin effects on product evaluations. *Journal of International Business Studies, 13,* (Spring/Summer), 88–99.

Bodenhausen, G. V., & Lichetenstein. M. (1987). The impact of task complexity. *Journal of Personality and Social Psychology, 52,* 871–880.

Bodenhausen, G. V., & Wyer, R. S. (1985). Effects of stereotypes on decision making and information processing strategies. *Journal of Personality and Social Psychology, 48,* 267–282.

Brown, J. J., & Reingen, P. H. (1988). Social ties and word of mouth referral behavior. *Journal of Consumer Research, 14,* 350–362.

Crawford, J. C., & Lumpkin, J. R. (1993). Environmental influences on Country-of-origin bias. In N. Papadopoulos and L. Heslop (Eds.), *Product–country images: Impact and role in international marketing* (pp. 341–356) New York: The Haworth Press.

Crompton, J. L. (1979). Motivations for pleasure vacation. *Annals of Tourism Research, 6,* 408–424.

Ennew, C. T., Banergee, A. K., & Li, D. (2000). Managing word of mouth communication: Empirical evidence from India. *International Journal of Bank Marketing, 18,* 75–83.

Ericksen, G. M., Johansson, J. K., & Chao, P. (1984). Image variables in multi-attribute product evaluations: Country of origin effect. *Journal of Consumer Research, 11,* 694–699.

Feldman, J. S., & Lynch, J. G. (1998). Self-generated validity and other effects of measurement on belief, attitude, intention and behavior. *Journal of Applied Psychology, 73,* 421–435.

Gallarza, M. G, Saura, I. G., & Garcia, H. (2001). Destination image: Toward a conceptual framework. *Annals of Tourism Research, 29,* 56–78.

Gastil, R. D. (1990). The comparative survey of freedom: Experiences and suggestions. *Studies in Comparative International Development, 25,* 25–50.

Han, M. (1990). Testing the role of country image in consumer choice behaviour. *European Journal of Marketing, 14*, 24–40.

Hong, S., & Wyer, R. S. (1989). Effects of country of origin and product-attribute information on product evaluation: and information processing perspective. *Journal of Consumer Research, 16*, 175–87.

Hong, S., & Yi, Y. (1992). A cross-cultural comparison of country-of-origin effects on product evaluations. *Journal of International Consumer Marketing, 4*, 49–71.

Janda, S., & Rao, C. P. (1997). The effect of country of origin related stereotypes and personal beliefs on product evaluations. *Psychology & Marketing, 14*, 689–702.

Katz, E. (1957). The two-step flow of communication: An up-to-date report on an hypothesis. *Public Opinion Quarterly, 21*, 61–78.

Katz, E., & Lazarfeld, P. F. (1955). *Personal influence*. Glencoe, IL: Free Press.

Kaynak, E., Kucukemiroglu, O., & Hyder, A. S. (2000). Consumers' country of origin perceptions of imported products in a homogenous less-developed country. *European Journal of Marketing, 34*, 1221–1241.

Khachaturian, J. L., & Morganosky, M. A. (1990). Quality perceptions by country of origin. *International Journal of Retail and Distribution Management, 18*, 21–30.

Kotler, P., Hamelin, M., Rein, I., & Haider, D. (1993). *Marketing places: Attracting investment, industry and tourism to cities, states and nations*. New York: The Free Press.

Lau, G. T., & Ng, S. (2001). Individual and situational factors influencing negative word of mouth behaviour. *Canadian Journal of Administrative Sciences, 18*, 163–178.

Lawrence, C., Marr, N. E., & Prendergast, G. P. (1992). Country of origin stereotyping: A case in the New Zealand motor vehicle industry. *European Journal of Marketing, 26*, 37–51.

Mahajan, V., Muller, E., & Bass, F. M. (1990). New product differentiating models in marketing: A review and direction for research. *Journal of Marketing, 54*, 1–26.

Maheswaran, D., & Meyers-Levy, J. (1990). The influence of message framing and issue involvement. *Journal of Marketing Research, 27*, 361–367.

Marshall, R., Tsee, H., & Lee, C. K. L. (1994). Variations in the perception of "Country-of-origin" labels: An Asian perspective. *Asia-Pacific Advances in Consumer Research, 1*, 97–102.

Martin, B. & Marshall, R. (1998). The interaction of message framing and felt involvement in the context of cellphone commercials. *European Journal of Marketing, 33*, 206–218.

Money, B. R., Gilly, M. C., & Graham, J. L. (1998). Explorations of national culture and word of mouth referral behavior in the purchase of industrial services in the United States and Japan. *Journal of Marketing, 62*, 76–87.

Papadopoulos, N., & Heslop, L. (1993). What product and country images are and are not. In N. Papadopoulos & L. Heslop (Eds.), *Product and country images: Impact and role in international marketing* (pp. 39–76) New York: The Haworth Press.

Richens, M. L. (1983). Negative word of mouth by dissatisfied consumers: A pilot study. *Journal of Marketing, 47*, 68–78.

Richens, M L. (1984). Word of mouth communication as negative information. In T. C. Kinnear (Ed.), *Advances in Consumer Research* (pp. 697–702) (Vol. 11.) Ann Arbor, MI: Association for Consumer Research.

Rogers, E. (1962). *The Diffusion of Innovations*. New York: Free Press.

Rogers, E. (1983). *The Diffusion of Innovations* (3rd ed.). New York: Free Press.

Rogers, E. (1995). *The Diffusion of Innovations* (4th ed.). New York: Free Press.

Schweiger, G., Haubl, G., & Friederes, G. (1995). Consumers' evaluations of products labeled "Made in Europe'. *Marketing Research Today, 23*, 25–34.

Sheth, J. N. (1971). Word of mouth in low-risk innovations. *Journal of Advertising Research 11*, 15–18.

Stafford, J. E. (1966). Effect of group influence on consumer brand preference. *Journal of Marketing Research, 3,* 68–75.

Sundaram, D. S. & Webster, C. (1999). The role of brand familiarity on the impact of word of mouth communication on brand evaluations. *Advances in Consumer Research, 26,* 664–70.

Whyte, W. H. (1954 November). The web of word of mouth. *Fortune Magazine,* 140–43.

CHAPTER SEVEN

Measuring the National Image:
The Case of South Korea

Dong-Sung Cho
Seoul National University

Yong-Gu Suh
Sookmyung Women's University

The American Marketing Association defines a brand as a "name, term, symbol or design, or a combination of them which is intended to identify the goods or services of one seller or group of sellers and to differentiate them from those of competition" (Dictionary of Marketing Terms). It not only allows a product to be distinguished from its competitors but also enables it to maintain a competitive edge as a part of a differentiation strategy by signifying the product's unique characteristics. If we expand the concept of brand a little further, there can be national brands as well as regional brands for cities and provinces. Therefore, four brand types are possible: at the level of product, corporation, region, and country.

A regional brand refers to a brand created based on the characteristic images of a region. For example, when a specific industry is concentrated in a certain region like Silicon Valley or Hollywood, creating characteristic images of the region, it forms a regional brand. Taking it one step further, the national or country brand is a comprehensive image that encompasses various types of information about a country: its people, businesses, natural environment, government, political system, economic and cultural standards, and so on. In terms of marketing a country, a national brand can be defined as a "name, sign, symbol, design or combination of these, all of which are designed to distinguish a country from other countries, enabling people to identify a country, its products and services." If the name, color, and trademark of a product are parts of the product brand, then the national brand includes, for example, the country name, national flag, national flower, and country-of-origin labeling name.

It is important to know that various brand components, such as products, corporations, regions and countries, do not function separately but are closely related to one another, often creating synergies. For example, the well-known perfume, Chanel No. 5, creates value through the corporate brand Chanel. In other words, as Chanel No. 5, rather than simply No. 5, the product brand value depends on its corporate brand for added value. Chanel headquarters is based in Paris, which distinguishes the company culturally and lends recognition as a world-renowned brand. In addition, the image of France as an advanced country with a sophisticated culture adds the value of "Made in France." Thus, Chanel No. 5 can be perceived as world-renowned brand perfume. A substantial amount of literature indicates that the country of origin of the product has a significant effect on consumer behavior. Therefore, it is important to consider enhancing the value of brands, not just at the level of products and companies but also regionally and nationally. Ingeborg, Iversen, and Stensaker (2002) argued that marketers seek to activate specific associations from a country image, and to match these with important characteristics in the target market through marketing mix.

National image also plays an important role in foreign direct investment (FDI), and in tourist destination decisions. From the FDI perspective, countries will be products whose images may affect the choices of investors, as buyers, among alternative locations. In summary, national images are likely to influence people's decisions related to buying, investing, and changing residence and travel destinations, and therefore it requires urgent attention to manage and promote the national brand.

CONCEPT AND VALUE OF NATIONAL BRANDING

Aaker (1991) categorized factors of brand assets into brand loyalty, brand awareness, brand association, perceived quality, and other proprietary brand assets. From a corporate perspective, brand assets help consumers process and interpret massive amounts of information about products and brands and aid companies to attract new customers or re-attract previous customers. In particular, a well-known brand motivates consumers to purchase its products by increasing consumer loyalty to a brand. Furthermore, brand assets serve as the foundation for the further growth and expansion of the brand and to help increase the price of products. Kotler and Gertner (2002) examined how widely held national images affect attitudes toward the ability of the country to attract investment businesses and tourists and suggested strategic process to promote the image, attractiveness, and products of the country. Their study is notable to regard countries as brands, although it is only assessing the role of marketing.

There is a slight difference between the concept of corporate brand value, intangible assets, and the concept of a national brand value. National branding does not directly influence products but does so indirectly: National brands involve more complex and diverse brand players, including companies as well as people, government, and various agencies. Moreover, they are based on a more comprehensive

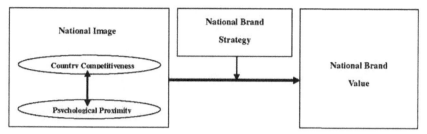

FIG. 7.1.   Creation of national brand value.

concept that involves not only economic factors but also social, cultural, and historical factors. Therefore, a national brand value refers to all the assets, including the people, companies, government, and products that form the basis of the image of a country and a national brand strategy. Given this definition, value can be created by the interaction of country images and national brand strategies as shown in Fig. 7.1. National image is built by the economic competitiveness and non economic factors of a nation, the so-called psychological proximity. In addition, national brand strategy is a strategic effort intended to enhance the brand value of a country. National, or country, brand value is considered in this chapter to include country images that involve recognition, reliability and loyalty, and strategic activities by people, government, nongovernmental organizations, and companies to build national brands.

EVALUATION OF NATIONAL BRAND VALUE: THE CASE OF SOUTH KOREA

Various types of research have been conducted on the subject of country image, and factors comprising national image have been suggested based on the parameters of each study (Lampert & Jaffe, 1998). Although some studies have taken a holistic approach toward all aspects of a country such as politics, economy, society, and culture, most of the studies have focused only on relations between products and consumers. This chapter approaches building national brand value in terms of national competitiveness, psychological proximity, and national brand strategy.

The identification and the relative importance of components in the determination of national brand value are analyzed by using the analytic hierarchy process (AHP).

National Competitiveness

As a source element driving the national brand, national competitiveness is further broken down, based on the 9-factor model, into material resources such as a) endowed resources, b) demand conditions, c) related and supporting industry, and d) business context; human resources such as a) workers, b) politicians & bureaucrats, c) entrepreneurs, and d) professionals; and last, the purely external factor of chance events.

TABLE 7.1

Factors of National Competitiveness

Factors	Subfactors
Material resources	
Endowed resources	Natural resources, capital resources foreign investment
Demand condition	Market size, demand quality
Infrastructure and related & supporting industry	Transportation, communications, banks and stock markets, education and science technology, living environment
Business context	Domestic conditions, international conditions
Human resources	
Workers	Labor quantity, labor quality
Politicians and bureaucrats	Systems, policies
Entrepreneurs	Social structure, individual competencies
Professional	Social infrastructure, individual competencies

Sub-factors under each factor are researched, based on national competitiveness ratings from The Institute of Industrial Policy Studies (IPS): natural resources, capital resources and foreign investment are endowed resources; market size and demand quality are demand conditions; transportation, communications, banks and stock markets, education and science technology, and living environment are related and supporting industries; domestic conditions and international conditions are business context; labor quantity and quality are workers; systems and policies are politicians and bureaucrats; social structure and individual competencies are entrepreneurs; and social infrastructure and individual competencies are professionals. See Table 7.1.

In terms of methodology, the IPS report first selected variables based on related theories, then directly collected hard data and survey data, published at home and abroad, from 64 countries around the world, in a uniform procedure through the 98 overseas trade offices of the Korea Trade-Investment Promotion Agency (KOTRA) 2002. KOTRA is a professional trade promotion organization (TPO) established in 1962.

Psychological Proximity

Psychological proximity is created by a person's knowledge, experience, beliefs and value system about a country. Higher psychological proximity results in higher preference, which in turn creates loyalty. In many studies on country of origin in the marketing area, political atmosphere, cultural development, education level, wealth, population density, and race, are suggested as base for belief. Contacts among countries, international events, and experience of products are suggested as aspects of direct experience.

Therefore, we first defined 10 factors—awareness, image, international exchange, information, experience, language, religion, distance, social system, and

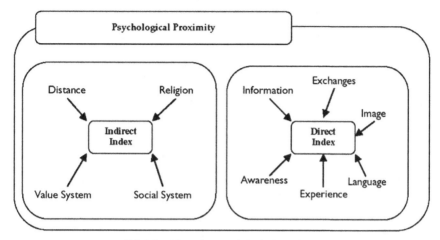

FIG. 7.2.   Measuring psychological proximity.

value systems—and set a hypothesis that they can be categorized as either indirect or direct. The five indirect factors include language, religion, distance, social system, and value system, and the five direct factors include awareness, image, international exchange, information, and experience. Then, a questionnaire was prepared to analyze the 10 factors by surveying 400 foreigners. The results supported the hypothesis, except for language, which was shown to be a direct, not an indirect, factor.

Regarding psychological proximity—and specifically, in terms of direct factors influencing the KOREA brand such as awareness, image, international exchange, information, experience, and language—information scored the highest, showing that in many cases foreigners get to know Korea through information, rather than through awareness and exchange. Compared to that, experience is scored low, showing that few foreigners get to know Korea through various experiences (see Fig. 7.2).

Among indirect factors in psychological proximity influencing the KOREA brand, such as distance, religion, social system, and value system, distance scored the highest, followed by value system, social system and religion.

National Brand Strategy

According to a study on how foreign nationals living in Korea viewed Korea (Suh & Park, 1997), the concept of one country in the integrated model for overseas promotion is explained as an interrelated organic body of companies, government, people, and other agencies.

Another approach to national brand strategy deals with activities such as image management and promotion efforts. However, seen from any perspective, the country brand is a result of complex and varied activities by various players at different

TABLE 7.2

National Brand Strategy

Factors	Index for measurement
National brand strategy	
Government (national CEO, bureaucrats, agencies)	1. International reputation reliability/recognition/image
Corporations	2. Social responsibility ethics/responsibility/contributions
Private organizations (press, non-governmental diplomatic organizations, international groups, etc.)	3. Competencies objective competency levels/ positive attitude in activities
People (private diplomats, celebrities, etc.)	

levels (Han & Terpstra, 1988), which is unlike corporate or product brand strategy (Suh & Kim, 2001). Thus, in evaluating the national brand, it is very important to measure not only economic and psychological proximity but also current status and value of the country brand based on country brand strategy.

Therefore, in this study, factors of country brands at the strategic level are broken down into government, corporations, nongovernmental organizations, and individuals. For the measurement index, public standing, recognition, and positive attitude are considered promotional aspects, whereas image and identity are seen as management aspects (see Table 7.2).

VALUATION OF KOREA AS A NATIONAL BRAND

Characteristics of the Study

Our study is differentiated from existing country image research in the following four ways.

First, this study aims to analyze and define the foundation underlying the country image. In dealing with the country image as a part of the national brand, it takes a comprehensive approach by addressing both economic and noneconomic factors, that is, national competitiveness and psychological proximity.

Second, this study addresses national brand in terms of outbound, (i.e., perspectives from other countries or people in other countries) and in-bound (i.e., perspectives from the country itself or foreign nationals staying in the country). Thus, by evaluating the national brand, as it is perceived both overseas and at home, a comprehensive evaluation is assured.

Third, this study introduces the concept of national brand strategy. Corporate brand value can be enhanced through corporate efforts. Attempting to improve national brand value merely through government efforts is more difficult because numerous biases interfere with the desired results. This study attempts to exclude those biases and defines the roles of individuals, companies, NGOs, and the government in enhancing the country brand. In this way, the current status of the country brand can be evaluated and a future strategy can be formulated.

Fourth, it aims to establish strategic measures to enhance the country brand. Until now, activities related to national image or country brand have been reactive. Promotion and PR have been focused on immediate requirements. However, such measures have simply produced short-term benefits, not necessarily long-term fundamental development or value improvement of country brand. Therefore, this study aims to present both short-term and long-term measures to develop country brand, and suggests an evaluation of the national brand in broader terms so as to directly enhance its value.

Scope

The purpose of this study is to devise strategies to enhance value of the (South) KOREA national brand through the process of survey, evaluation, and analysis. To that end, we first define the concept of national brand, thus laying the groundwork for the study. Next, we describe comprehensive surveys of outbound and inbound criteria. In terms of out-bound criteria, we evaluate the national brand values of 16 countries around the world to objectively measure KOREA brand values. For inbound criteria, we evaluate the opinions of foreign nationals in Korea. This group has been categorized as business travelers, tourists, investors, and long-term residents. The value of the KOREA brand is then measured, and afterwards, analysis is performed and strategies planned according to each group. For each aspect of the overall study, detailed research was conducted, including designing models for research, building methodology for the surveys, and analyzing results.

Methodology and Process

The purpose of evaluating national brand values was to measure the brand values of 16 nations, including Korea, and to quantify the values in dollar terms so that objective comparative studies could be made. Accordingly, countries were first selected and national brand indices measured, including national competitiveness, psychological proximity, and national brand strategy. Items to be converted into dollar terms were then measured to enable final determination of the values (see Table 7.3).

Selected Countries for Evaluation

Given that the model was applied for the first time in this study and considering the difficulties involved, the survey was confined to 16 countries (see Figure 7.3),

TABLE 7.3

Evaluation Process of Country Brand Values

1st phase	Select countries for evaluation
2nd phase	Measure country brand indices
3rd phase	Measure applied indicator
4th phase	Evaluate country brand values

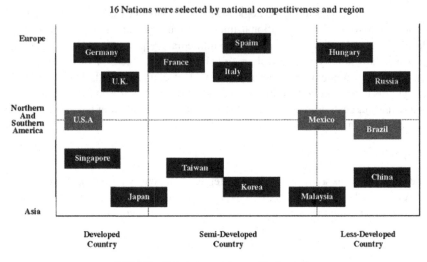

16 Nations were selected by national competitiveness and region

FIG. 7.3.   Selected countries used in the study.

based on various factors such as regional conditions and degree of national development. In addition, to examine the direction of national brand strategies in advanced countries, higher level of advancement was a priority.

Measurement of National Brand Index

National Brand Index refers to the quantitative results of measuring the values of country brand factors. In this chapter, the values were measured through secondary data and surveys on 3-dimensional factors, such as national competitiveness, psychological proximity, and country brand strategy.

In particular, the survey on the values of 16 countries was conducted through KOTRA. Based on information from a total of 630 respondents in 63 countries, the resulting indices were calculated according to {(national competitiveness + psychological proximity) x country brand strategy} to produce the final country brand index (See Table 7.4).

Measurement of Applied Indicator

Applied indicator refers to the potential revenues of a nation that are influenced by the national brand and are necessary for converting the country brand index to dollar terms. In this study, product export amount, service export amount, and tourism import amount are used. To obtain the values, the short-term government bond interest rates are applied to a) product export amounts, b) service export amounts, and c) tourism import amounts of each country for the past three years (Years 2000, 2001, and 2002). Then, the long-term government bond interest rates are also ap-

TABLE 7.4

National Brand Index

1. Come up with a national competitiveness index of each nation through IPS NCR 2002.
2. Conduct survey on the psychological proximity of 16 countries using 630 respondents in 63 countries. Analyze the survey results along with secondary data.
3. Conduct survey on brand strategies of the 16 countries, using 630 respondents in 63 countries.

National Brand Index = (national competitiveness + psychological proximity) × country brand strategy

TABLE 7.5

Measuring Applied Indicator

1. Values calculated by applying economic growth rates and short-term government bond interest rates to product export amount service export amount and tourism import amount for the past three years
2. Calculate national brand value projected for the next ten years
3. Come up with values to which national brand is to be applied

plied to these values to convert them into national brand values in the next 10 years (see Table 7.5). The reason is that brand value involves factors not only of the past but also of the future. In particular, projected values for the future are very important. It was therefore possible to finally get the national brand profit value, that is, values to which national brand index is to be applied.

RESULTS AND IMPLICATIONS

We have examined the value of 16 national brands. Based on the calculations presented, Korea ranked 8th among 16 nations, and its national brand value in dollar terms stood at $408.6 billion (see Table 7.6). The United States ranked 1st, with 7.1399 trillion dollars, and Germany ranked 2nd, with 2.8865 trillion dollars, followed by France, the United Kingdom, Japan, and Italy. Notably, in Asia, Korea was evaluated as having the 2nd highest national brand value, following Japan. Brazil and Hungary ranked the lowest, 15th and 16th respectively (note, however, that it is a relative evaluation only among 16 countries).

Of particular interest, Korea stood in the middle, not only in terms of ranking (8th) but also in analysis results, both in brand index and applied indicator as shown in Fig. 7.4. Also, in analysis of national brand factors, Korea ranked in the middle in all three factors of national competitiveness, psychological proximity, and national brand strategy, indicating that Korea needs to enhance all of these three factors.

A survey was conducted on the awareness of foreign nationals of the KOREA brand. Respondents were mostly foreigners visiting or staying in Korea and who had sufficient experience in the country. In the survey, foreign nationals were bro-

TABLE 7.6

Table of National Brand Values

Ranking	COUNTRY	National Brand Values (US$Million)	Applied Indicator (US$Million)	National Brand Index (1/10000)
1	United States	7,139,939	10,143,400	0.7039
2	Germany	2,886,539	6,123,332	0,4714
3	France	1,915,253	3,952,234	0.4846
4	U.K.	1,909,904	3,664,436	0.5212
5	Japan	1,023,730	4,539,821	0.2255
6	Italy	1,010,091	3,019,985	0.3348
7	Spain	545,657	1,818,856	0.3000
8	Korea	408,612	1,793,733	0.2278
9	China	243,347	2,810,006	0.0866
10	Singapore	160,539	1,471,486	0.1091
11	Taiwan	76,173	1,410,606	0.0540
12	Russia	71,123	1,099,271	0.0647
13	Malaysia	44,254	1,010,357	0.0438
14	Mexico	40,724	1,675,867	0.0243
15	Brazil	21,173	639,679	0.0331
16	Hungary	769	349,482	0.0022

ken down into four categories—investors, long-term residents of Korea, business travelers, and tourists—so that group differences of opinion about the KOREA brand could be noted. The investors group included foreign investors and foreigners working in Korea as employees of multinational companies. Long-term foreign residents in Korea included students, military personnel, consular representatives, and immigrant spouses of Korean nationals. Tourists included short-term visitors and business travelers engaged in trade or attending conferences, international events, and meetings. A total of 400 foreigner-respondents answered a 23-item questionnaire. As a result of the survey, foreigners with experience in Korea scored the KOREA brand 6.09 out of a possible 10 points. Specifically, tourists gave the highest score (6.87), followed by business travelers, those who had stayed long term, and finally, investors. In other words, short-term visitors gave the KOREA brand a higher score, whereas investors gave it a lower score.

Beyond the country image used thus far, our study makes it possible to build the concept of a national brand, establish elements comprising the country brand strategy, ensure substantial efforts to enhance the country brand, and conduct objective evaluation of the country brand by converting it from an intangible one into a national asset value. Unlike previous research on brand evaluation that was mostly focused on the micro level of national image, this study, designed to enhance the KOREA brand in the global market, is basically different in that it takes comprehensive, macro perspectives to evaluate the KOREA brand. Using a method we developed, this study makes it possible to calculate the real value of national brands and understand relative brand position of a country.

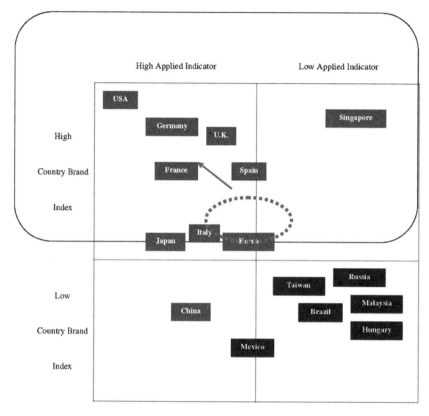

FIG. 7.4.   Position of 16 country brands.

In particular, one practical benefit of this research is that evaluation of the national brand has been conducted for each nation and group of observers. This will help the objective evaluation of KOREA brand images perceived by each preference group and lead to the appropriate strategies and differentiated policies for the Korean government to enhance the country brand value in a more strategic way. Sufficient levels of discussions and studies are needed in methodology, however, to develop a full-fledged country brand valuation model.

REFERENCES

Aaker, D. (1991). *Managing brand equity: Capitalizing on the value of a band name*. New York: The Free Press.

Han, C.M. & Terpstra, V. (1988). Country-of-origin effects for uni-national and bi-national products. *Journal of International Business Studies, 19,* 235–255.

Heslop, L. A., & Papadopoulos, N. (1993). But who knows where or when: Reflections on the images of countries and their products. In N. Papadopoulos & L. A. Heslop (Eds.), *Product-country images* (pp. 39–55). Binghamton, NY: International Business Press.

Ingeborg, A., Iversen, N. M., & Stensaker, I. G. (2002). Country images in marketing strategies: Conceptual issues and empirical Asian illustration. *The Journal of Brand Management, 10*(1), 61–75.

Lampert, I. S., & Jaffe, E. D. (1998). A dynamic approach to country-of-origin effects. *European Journal of Marketing, 32,* 145–155.

Philip, K., & Gertner, D. (2002). Country as brand, product and beyond: A place marketing and brand management perspectives. *The Journal of Brand Management, 9*(4), 249–262.

Suh, Y. & Kim, J. B. (2001). The role of country image in developing global brands. *Journal of Korea Trade, 5,* 45–64.

Suh, J. & Park, J. (1997). Image of Korea among foreign residents. *Yonsei University, Press Research Institute.*

CHAPTER EIGHT

The Social Construction of Destination Image: A New Zealand Film Example

Gretchen Larsen
University of Bradford, UK

Veronica George
University of Otago, NZ

Destination image has emerged as a crucial and widely studied concept within the tourism literature. The image of a destination is an important topic for tourism marketers, primarily because the research has illustrated that destination images and tourists' purchase decisions are positively correlated (e.g., Mayo, 1973; Mayo & Jarvis, 1981; Woodside & Lysonski, 1989). The importance of destination image has led to an increasingly large body of research on such topics as the images of particular places (e.g., Echtner & Ritchie, 1993; Gartner & Hunt, 1987; Mayo, 1973) and the communication of images (e.g., Bhattacharyya, 1997; Weightman, 1987). In his review of the literature, Pike (2002a) identified no less that 142 studies on this topic, published between 1973 and 2000.

Despite the importance of destination image and the amount of work undertaken in the area, "the concept of image has not been understood in a unified way" (Kim & Richardson, 2003, p. 218). The lack of a theoretically based conceptual framework underlying previous studies of destination image has been identified by a number of authors, particularly Echtner and Ritchie (1991); Fayeke and Crompton (1991), Gartner (1993), and Young (1999).

A new perspective has recently emerged in the literature, which views destination images as being socially constructed. Young (1999) proposed that "tourist places are socially constructed and negotiated phenomena...[and that] ordinary places become tourist places when they are attributed particular meanings and values which appeal to and attract tourists" (p. 373). This perspective has the potential to provide a conceptual basis for the unification of destination image research as it incorporates a holistic, systems-based view of the meaning of places.

117

This chapter contains a review of the current destination image literature to provide a background to the further development of the social construction perspective for destination image. This perspective is based on the processes of meaning production and consumption as described in literature such as McCracken's (1986) model of the movement of meaning.

A recent study on the impact of film on the destination image of New Zealand is then presented to provide some supporting evidence of the notions underlying the social construction perspective. This study examines the images of New Zealand tourists have, based on movies filmed in New Zealand and based on first-hand experience, to understand better how destination images can be constructed and influenced by various cultural processes.

PLACE BRANDING AND DESTINATION IMAGE

Brands are generally considered to be a marketer's main tool for creating product differentiation.

> Brands differentiate products and represent a promise of value. Brands incite beliefs, evoke emotions and prompt behavior. Marketers often extend successful brand names to new product launches, lending existing associations to them. As a result, they speed up consumer's information processing and learning. Brands have social and emotional value to users. They have personality and speak to the user. (Kotler & Gertner, 2002, p. 249)

Although it is widely accepted that products and corporations can be branded, the application of branding techniques and processes to places has often been questioned. For example, Girard (1999) insisted that only a corporation or product can be rebranded, not a state. However, Olins (2002) argued on the basis of historical evidence that this is simply not true and that it is the word brand that people object to, as opposed to the concept itself. Olins concluded that branding a place and branding a company involve many similar but not identical techniques.

A place (i.e., continent, country, region, city, attraction) differs from other products in that it is a composite product comprising a number of different brands and components of brands. Consequently, those involved in branding a place face a number of unique challenges as there are many diverse stakeholders, little control of the varying components, and more often than not an underdeveloped identity (Morgan, Pritchard, & Piggott, 2002). In an effort to understand the application of branding to places, a large volume of work has been published—over 750 major publications in 40 years (Papadopoulos & Heslop, 2002). However, these authors suggested that current understanding remains limited to the value of the idea rather than the specifics of the process.

Kotler and Gertner (2002) identified two main streams of place branding literature: (a) the impact of a place brand on consumers' attitudes towards products (e.g., country of origin effects and consumer ethnocentrism) and (b) the marketing of countries and the management of their brands. The first stream refers to the notion of a country serving as a brand component, whereas the second stream conceives of places as being products in themselves. "They [places] compete in the market for tourists, factories, businesses and talented people. Thus countries [places] must embark on more conscious country [place] branding" (p. 258).

Literature on tourism and destination marketing is located within the second stream of place branding literature. One of the key concepts in the tourism marketing literature on place branding is that of destination image. Pike (2002b) proposed that even if tourism marketers focus on the supply side, that is, the marketing mix components of product, price, promotion, and place, it is actually the demand side, perception, that is most important because for intending tourists, perception is reality. Consequently, tourism marketers keep returning to the concept of destination image.

The investigation of destination image in tourism research has indicated that it does influence tourist behavior (e.g., Hunt, 1975; Pearce, 1982). Essentially, people are more likely to choose to visit destinations that have strong and positive images (Woodside & Lysonski, 1989). This is primarily because the images that consumers have of destinations are based on their perceptions (Gallarza, Saura, & Garcia, 2002) and perceptions are closely related to attitudes, motivation, and consumption behavior (Ajzen, 2001; Bagozzi, 1988; Robertson, Zielinski, & Ward, 1984).

Although the term *destination image* is frequently used, a precise definition has not yet been adopted. "There are almost as many definitions of image as scholars devoted to its conceptualization" (Gallarza et al. 2002, p. 58). As illustrated in Table 8.1, these definitions range from vague descriptions of impressions of a place, to those that provide some indication of the components of image. However, a common theme can also be observed, which is that "most such literature describes a totality of impressions, beliefs, ideals, expectations and feelings accumulated towards a place over time" (Kim & Richardson, 2003, p. 218).

The conceptualization of destination image comprises one area of focus within the literature. Gallarza et al. (2002) identified five further topics of interest within the destination image literature. Each area is summarized briefly in the next section.

Destination Image Formation Process

Two approaches to the destination image formation process have been taken. The first is static in nature and investigates the relation between destination image and various aspects of tourist behavior such as destination choice (e.g., Hunt, 1975) and satisfaction (e.g., Chon, 1990). The second approach studies the structure and formation of destination image itself and therefore is dynamic in nature. Gallarza et al. (2002) suggested that Baloglu and McCleary's (1999) model of destination image formation is the most comprehensive of only a small number of successful studies in the area.

TABLE 8.1

Product, Place, and Destination Image Definitions

Hunt (1971) Impressions that a person or persons hold about a state in which they do not reside.

Marking (1974) Our own personalized internalized and conceptualizing understanding of what we know.

Lawson and Bond-Bovy (1977) An expression of knowledge impressions prejudice imaginations and emotional thoughts an individual has of a specific object or place.

Crompton (1979) and Kotler et al. (1994) An image may be defined as the sum of beliefs, ideas and impressions that a person has of a destination.

Dichter (1985) The concept of image can be applied to a political candidate, a product, and a country. It describes not individual traits or qualities but the total impression an entity makes on the minds of others.

Reynolds (1985) and Fayeke and Crompton (1991) An image is the mental construct developed by the consumer on the basis of a few selected impressions among the flood of total impressions. It comes into being through a creative process in which selected impressions are elaborated, embellished and ordered.

Embacher and Buttle (1989) Image is comprised of the ideas and conceptions held individually or collectively of the destination under investigation. Image may comprise both cognitive and evaluative components.

Echtner and Ritchie (1991) Destination image is not only the perceptions of individual destination attributes but also the holistic impression made by the destination. It consists of functional and psychological characteristics, and the images can be arranged on a continuum ranging from common to unique traits.

Gartner (1993, 1996) Destination images are developed by three hierarchically interrelated components; cognitive, affective and conative.

Santos Arrebola (1994) Image is a mental representation of attributes and benefits sought of a product.

Parenteau (1995) Destination image is an unfavorable or unfavorable prejudice that the audience and distributors have of the product or destination.

Note. Adapted from Gallarza et al., 2002. Reprinted with permission from Elsevier.

Assessment and Measurement of Destination Image

There is a substantial amount of literature that is dedicated to developing a measure of destination image. The most common type of study is an empirical paper that applies statistical instruments without developing an underlying theoretical body. However, a number of notable papers address methodological and measurement issues in addition to presenting empirical studies (e.g., Carmichael, 1992; Echtner & Ritchie, 1993; Reilly, 1990). In developing their measure of destination image, Echtner and Ritchie (1993) contributed greatly to the conceptualization of destination image. They proposed that three axes underlie the image of any destination: functional/psychological, common/unique, and holistic/attribute-based. To capture these dimensions accurately, Echtner and Ritchie's (1993) measure incorporates both structured (i.e., quantitative) and unstructured (i.e, qualitative) methodologies and is one of the first measures to do so.

Distance and Destination Image Change Over Time

The few studies that focus on distance concentrate mostly on comparing samples of respondents from different geographical origins (e.g., Crompton, 1979). Often the variable of time is also incorporated into the same studies in three different ways: (a) the influence of length of stay (e.g., Fayeke & Crompton, 1991), (b) repeated measures of the same destination image (e.g., Gartner & Hunt, 1987), and (c) the effect of previous visitation on destination image (e.g., Dann, 1996). However, Gallarza et al. (2002) implicitly suggested that none of these approaches are appropriate as "the correct way of assessing the influence of time on image formation should be not the comparisons of different sample, but longitudinal sampling studies" (p. 61).

Active and Passive Role of Residents in Image Studies

The role of residents in destination image takes two forms. Research that perceives the residents role as active compares residents' and tourists' images of the same place (e.g., Sternquist Witter, 1985). In addition, residents are thought to have a passive role when they themselves become part of the destination images (e.g., Echtner & Ritchie, 1991).

Destination Image Management Policies

In general, most empirical studies on destination image provide managerial implications in their conclusions. There are also a number of studies that utilize destination image as a management tool by, for example, linking it to positioning strategies (e.g., Haahti, 1986) or promotional strategies (e.g., Fesenmaier & MacKay, 1996).

A number of problems or issues within the destination image literature have been identified. First, the most fundamental problem about which there is general agreement is that there is a lack of conceptual framework underlying the current research (Echtner & Ritchie, 1991; Fayeke & Crompton, 1991; Gallarza et al., 2002; Gartner, 1993; Young, 1999).

Second, there is a preference for quantitative measurement techniques, a preference that is closely related to the proliferation of attribute-based definitions of destination image. Young (1999) identified a number of deficiencies related to using attribute-based measures of functional components of destination image. These are (a) that the psychological components of destination image have been ignored, (b) that research has tended to be goal oriented because it has been pragmatic and marketing based, (c) that there is a lack of understanding of the cultural context of image creation and the communication process, and (d) that what places mean to people and how those meanings have been constructed and consumed have been overlooked. Changes in measurement techniques, such as the inclusion of qualitative techniques in Echtner and Ritchie's (1993) measure of destination image indicate that the underlying conceptualizations are also changing. The move from a solely functionally based perspective to one that incorporates holistic and symbolic aspects and reflects philosophical shifts that are also occurring in the related field of consumer behavior (e.g., Holbrook, 1995).

CULTURAL MEANING AND THE SOCIAL CONSTRUCTION OF DESTINATION IMAGE

It is apparent that for destination image research to advance, an underlying conceptual framework must be developed and agreed upon. This framework would enable the full operationalization of the concept of destination image, which would in turn facilitate more meaningful and useful research to be undertaken.

Few studies attempt to address this issue: however, both Gallarza et al. (2002) and Young (1999) proposed and provided support for the development of a conceptual framework that incorporates the socially constructed nature of destination images. Further support for the adoption of this perspective can be gained from the changes in destination image measurement that have already occurred, which are based on the inclusion of both functional and symbolic aspects of image (e.g., Echtner & Ritchie, 1993).

Young (1999) studied the place meanings produced by tourist industry. A conceptual model of the tourism system of place construction was presented that argues that the success of a tourist place depends on the level of consensus on meanings negotiated between the systems of place production and place consumption. This model is, however, somewhat limited by its view of images as produced by marketing activities alone: thus, it does not fully incorporate the socially based meaning construction processes suggested by the approach. Cultural meaning or symbols, which form part of the image of a destination (Echtner & Ritchie, 1991, 1993), is the subjective meaning that is attached to the destination by individuals and can be described in terms of the cultural categories and cultural principles to which it refers (McCracken, 1986). The source of this meaning is not limited to marketing strategies but can also arise from other cultural activities (e.g., music, film, art, consumption), all of which should be included in a social constructionist framework (e.g., Arnholt, 2002).

The theoretical model presented by Gallarza et al. (2002) represents destination image in a manner that is congruent with a social construction perspective. The model was developed on the basis of the previous literature on the conceptualization of destination image and a taxonomy of methodologies employed for its measurement. Four features of destination image emerged from this review, and these form the basis of the model (see Table 8.2). "Every feature found underlies a useful Dimension of the concept of image for strategic management of destinations: 'complexity' underlies an analytical Dimension, 'multiplicity' provides an action Dimension, 'relativistic' character translates [destination image] as a strategic tool,

TABLE 8.2

Gallarza et al.'s (2002) Conceptual Model of Destination Image

Destination Image Nature	Literature Review	Taxonomies
Complex: DI has an analytical dimension	Cognitive, affective, and/or conative elements Collective images vs. personal impressions Selective images vs. additive images	Need of considering three different variables Combination of complex statistical techniques
Multiple: DI has an action dimension	Need of a multidisciplinary focus on DI Image as a multi-item construct or/and as a gestalt Static and dynamic structure of DI	Multiple attributes (functional and psychological) Use of bidimensional and multidimensional techniques
Relativistic: DI is a strategic tool	DI varies across people (segmentation) DI involves comparisons among objects (positioning)	Comparisons of different destinations for different subjects Different techniques chosen for different strategic purposes
Dynamic: DI is a tactical variable	Time affects DI Distance affects DI	Comparison tests between different samples

Note. Adapted from Gallarza et al., 2002, p. 69.

and 'dynamic' character allows for tactical decisions based on [destination image]" (Gallarza et al., 2002, p. 68). Thus the conceptualization of destination image presented in this model is similar to the nature of cultural meaning that is described in other social construction models such as that of McCracken's (1986) model of the movement of meaning.

Although Gallarza et al.'s (2002) conceptual model of destination image is based on existing literature, the authors themselves call for more empirical evidence to support the underlying notions and structure of the model. The following study provides some evidence to support the complex, multiple, and relativistic features of destination image.

AN ILLUSTRATIVE EXAMPLE—FILM
AND THE DESTINATION IMAGE OF NEW ZEALAND

This exploratory study was designed to help explain the nature of destination images with regard to a certain cultural process—film or motion pictures—by examining the images tourists have of New Zealand based on movies filmed in New Zealand and those images based on first-hand experience. A secondary objective was to begin to evaluate the appropriateness of tourism marketing strategies that are based on the association with motion pictures filmed in that destination. The underlying reason is that New Zealand has recently received much media attention and promotion as the filming location of a number of award winning films, such as *The Lord of the Rings* trilogy, *Once Were Warriors*, and *The Piano*. Destination image literature suggests that films that are recognized as made in a particular destination may contribute to the overall image of that destination. However, these perceptions may be different from the reality of that destination and could result in dissatisfaction and cognitive dissonance upon arrival in the destination (MacKay & Fesenmaier, 1997).

Methodology

A self-completion questionnaire was administered to international backpacking tourists in Queenstown and Dunedin, New Zealand, in August 2002. The questionnaire was based on a survey, designed by Echtner and Ritchie (1993), that measured the perceptions of individual attributes as well as the more holistic impressions of a destination. The measure was adapted to account for images that could be obtained from film and then was used to determine tourists' overall image of New Zealand from first-hand experience and from any New Zealand-made films that they had seen. The respondents could choose a maximum of three New Zealand-made films. Both measures were taken at the same time; thus, the images gained from film made in New Zealand were retrospective. The questionnaire was administered to 240 tourists, from whom 120 (50%) usable surveys were collected.

The quantitative element of the survey, that is, the Likert scale, was analyzed using SPSS, first by factor analysis and then by multidimensional scaling techniques. Factor analysis was used to reduce the number of items that could then be used to describe the main images of New Zealand that tourists have. The factor scores were extracted using the maximum likelihood method. Varimax rotation with Kaiser normalization was used so that orthogonal factors were produced. A six-factor solution, which explains 58.5% of total variance, was selected. Multidimensional scaling was then used so that the images of New Zealand based on experience could be compared to the images of New Zealand based on films. The factor scores calculated for the tourists' overall images of New Zealand were used to weight each respondent's destination image based on the New Zealand films. Thus, a new variable was calculated for each film so that the factor scores of New Zealand and the four movies could be compared accurately. The New Zealand movies used for analysis were reduced to four movies: *The Lord of the Rings: The Fellowship of the Ring*, *Once Were Warriors*, *The Piano*, and *Vertical Limits*, as these were respectively the most common movies filmed in New Zealand to have been seen by respondents.

The qualitative measure was analyzed by determining the frequency of certain responses. Along with the most common responses recorded, some individual remarks were incorporated into the analysis, thus producing an overall account of the qualitative responses.

The Sample

The sample was divided equally between genders but was predominantly younger, with 60% of the respondents between 16 and 24 years of age. There were no respondents over the age of 44, which is primarily a consequence of the sampling frame of backpackers. The majority of respondents had a university qualification (50%) and were from England (51.7%). The remaining respondents were from Scotland, Canada, Ireland, The Netherlands, Germany, France, United States, and Sweden. The nature of the sample is fairly representative of the backpacker market from which the sample was obtained.

Unstructured Image of New Zealand—Experience

The main image that respondents tended to have of New Zealand is that it is a country with beautiful scenery, particularly the mountains and the lakes (see Table 8.3). New Zealand is also perceived to be quite a green country with much wilderness and many wide open spaces as well as fiords and rugged coastlines. It is also thought that New Zealand has many adventure activities and extreme sports, such as skydiving, bungee jumping, skiing, snowboarding, white water rafting, surfing, sailing, and trekking. Further images that come to mind when respondents think about New Zealand are that it is quite a peaceful country and that not many people live in New Zealand but those who do are generally friendly. Many respondents believe there to be a large number of sheep in New Zealand; some even say there are more sheep than people. Maori culture and the All Blacks are two further images associated with New Zealand by tourists. Also, when describing their images of New Zealand, a number of people stated the scenery to be very "Lord of the Rings-like."

TABLE 8.3

Unstructured Image of New Zealand—Experience

Image	n	Atmosphere	n	Distinctive Attractions	n
Scenery	168	Relaxed	86	Adventure/extreme sports	120
Adventure activities	108	Friendly	80	Scenery	88
Sheep	50	Adventurous	10	Milford Sound	40
Friendly locals	20	Enjoy life	10	Rotorua	30
Peaceful and quiet	20	Peaceful	5	Queenstown	26
Sparse population	14	Proud	5	Sea life	18
'All Blacks'	14	Wonderful	4	Franz Josef Glacier	14
Maori culture	12			Bay of Islands	8
				National Parks and walks	8
				Glow worm caves	6
				Hot springs	6
				Zorbing	6

The atmosphere or mood of New Zealand was largely described as being friendly and relaxed whereby the locals are perceived to be helpful, trusting, open, cheerful, proud, and hospitable. New Zealand is also thought to be slightly old fashioned, and the locals are perceived to live quite a slow paced lifestyle where they emphasize enjoying life and having a good time. New Zealand is considered to be a rather peaceful country, although it has an adventurous side to it. As one participant said of the atmosphere is that it is a "cruisy, laidback kind of country."

The most distinctive attractions of New Zealand are its adventure activities and scenery. The specific adventure activities and extreme sports that were mentioned are body-boarding, surfing, skiing, snowboarding, skydiving, hang gliding, jet boating, rafting, bungee jumping, and tramping. The aspects of the scenery most commonly mentioned were the mountains, lakes, beaches, glaciers, and fiords. The volcanic nature of the landscape was also considered to be a distinct New Zealand attraction, along with the image that the New Zealand landscape is very varied in form. The abundance of flora and fauna is also unique, along with, according to one respondent, the "pancake rocks." Specific places that appear to stand out are Milford Sound, Rotorua, Queenstown, Franz Josef Glacier, Mt. Cook, and the Bay of Islands. Some other specific attractions are the glow-worm caves in Te Anau and the Waitomo caves, the hot springs, the Sky Tower in Auckland, the national parks and bushwalks (particularly the Abel Tasman National Park), zorbing, and watching penguins, seals, whales, and dolphins. The Maori culture is also considered to be a unique tourist attraction.

Unstructured Image of New Zealand—The Lord of the Rings: Fellowship of the Ring

The main image of New Zealand that comes to mind when thinking of *The Lord of the Rings* is the scenery (see Table 8.4). A number of respondents stated it to be "amazing and beautiful" and "unlike other parts of the world." The variety of landscape and the undisturbed nature are characteristics of New Zealand that are portrayed in *The Lord of the Rings: Fellowship of the Ring*. One respondent said, "it has made tourists interested in entering the country to see the diverse scenery." The wilderness, greenness, and mountains are the main characteristics of the scenery. New Zealand is considered to be very picturesque and *The Lord of the Rings* portrays it

TABLE 8.4

Unstructured Image of New Zealand—The Lord of the Rings

Image	n	Atmosphere	n	Distinctive Attractions	n
Scenery	180	Beauty of landscape	40	Scenery	88
Undisturbed nature	20	Magical and mystical	30	Milford Sound	14
Magical and mystical	10	Calm and peaceful	24	Adventure activities	10
Remote/sparse population	8	Adventurous and interesting	24	Filming locations	4

as being a magical and mystical country—the "land of make believe" according to one respondent. A number of people stated that they had no idea what New Zealand would look like before they saw *The Lord of the Rings: Fellowship of the Ring* and after seeing the movie they perceived New Zealand to be a beautiful country to visit, which made them want to visit.

The Lord of the Rings: Fellowship of the Ring seemed to generate a magical and mystical atmosphere of New Zealand. It made New Zealand appear interesting and intriguing and slightly undiscovered—almost "a world untouched by man." The film also portrays an atmosphere of tranquility and peacefulness, with a beautiful, pristine landscape.

The main distinctive attraction that *The Lord of the Rings: Fellowship of the Ring* conveyed about New Zealand was scenery, particularly the mountains. The wilderness, rivers, lakes, fiords, and glaciers were all aspects of the New Zealand landscape that were portrayed in *The Lord of the Rings: Fellowship of the Ring*. Many respondents likened the scenery in the movie to that of the Milford Sound. Tramping through the forests was also perceived to be a distinctive attraction in New Zealand. It was even stated by one respondent, "the whole film was a sales pitch for NZ."

Unstructured Image of New Zealand—Once Were Warriors

Once Were Warriors tended to portray images of violence, urban poverty and gender inequality amongst the Maori people of New Zealand (see Table 8.5). A sense of national pride was also portrayed alongside an insight into some aspects of Maori culture. It was perceived that there were social problems with regard to Maori people adapting to European life and that urban life was tough for modern Maori. One respondent felt that the movie portrayed a "marginalization of indigenous cultures." Another respondent suggested that the "urban environment is at odds with the usual perceptions of New Zealand."

Once Were Warriors tended to portray a violent and dark atmosphere in New Zealand. It showed despair and poverty amongst a country steeped in culture. One respondent stated that the "negative aspects of modern life that exist in New Zealand for many" were conveyed, as was the "dark under side of the pretty pictures" that are normally associated with images of New Zealand. The general atmosphere

TABLE 8.5

Unstructured Image of New Zealand—Once Were Warriors

Image	n	Atmosphere	n	Distinctive Attractions	n
Violence	20	Violent	18	Maori culture	8
Social problems	12	Despair	10	Maori culture	6
Maori culture	12	Darki	8	Rotorua	2
Poverty	10	Proud interesting people	6		
National pride	8				

or mood of New Zealand, as perceived through *Once Were Warriors*, is one of hardship and gloom.

The most distinctive attraction of New Zealand portrayed in *Once Were Warriors* was that of the Maori culture. Related to this, the Maori marae was mentioned as being a distinctive attraction. A number of respondents stated that the movie portrayed aspects of South Auckland and that it deterred them from visiting that particular region of New Zealand.

Unstructured Image of New Zealand—The Piano

The images associated with the movie, *The Piano*, are mainly that of the various aspects of the scenery (see Table 8.6). The scenery was considered to be "stark, wild and beautiful" by a number of the respondents. Further respondents stated that the scenery was "not seen anywhere else on earth." One respondent said it is a "virginal territory, untouched by man, a real wild frontier place." The beaches and forests in particular are the main aspects of scenery that are noticed in the movie. New Zealand is also perceived to be rather desolate, with a sparse population and a primitive style of living. It is also perceived as a relaxing place that is quiet and tranquil, with one respondent stating that "harmony is found in nature." In contrast to this *The Piano* also portrays images of sadness and loneliness in a country where it often rains, painting a rather "bleak picture of the lifestyle," according to a number of respondents.

The atmosphere of New Zealand, as conveyed through *The Piano*, is rather mixed. First, New Zealand is thought of as a quiet, calm, gentle, and peaceful place where the landscape is exotic and inviting. This is, however, in comparison to images of a dark, cold landscape, rain, scariness, and weirdness. On the one hand, this movie creates an atmosphere of love and thoughtfulness, whereas on the other hand the mood is seen to be one of despair.

The coastlines and the beaches, as well as the wilderness, are considered to be the most distinctive attractions portrayed through the movie. The scenery is likened to Dunedin, the West Coast, Milford Sound, and the Bay of Islands. The image of a

TABLE 8.6

Unstructured Image of New Zealand—*The Piano*

Image	n	Atmosphere	n	Distinctive Attractions	n
Scenery	32	Calm and peaceful	20	Beaches	24
Beaches	24	Depressing	14	Scenery	18
Sparse population	10	Isolation	10	West Coast	4
A depressing place	8	Scary/wild	6	Islands	2
Quiet, tranquil, relaxed	6			Rest and relaxation	2
Rain	6				
Primitive living	6				

TABLE 8.7

Unstructured Image of New Zealand—*Vertical Limits*

Image	n	Atmosphere	n	Distinctive Attractions	n
Extreme sports	50	Exciting, adventure	46	Adventure Activities	24
Scenery	40	Powerful mountains	14	Mountains	16
Cold and snowy	20			Glacier hikes	48

restful and relaxing place, as seen in *The Piano*, is also an attraction that is distinctive to New Zealand.

Unstructured Image of New Zealand—Vertical Limits

The main image of New Zealand portrayed through *Vertical Limits* is the snowy mountains (see Table 8.7). The scenery is considered to be stunning and amazing, as are the ice caves, glaciers, and ski fields. It also appears to convey images of adventurous and exciting activities such as skiing, snowboarding, and ice climbing, that is, anything that has an adrenalin rush.

There is an exciting atmosphere associated with New Zealand through *Vertical Limits*, along with danger and adrenalin rush-related activities. The mountains are perceived to be both powerful and beautiful, creating a mood of both fear and enjoyment.

The distinctive attractions in New Zealand conveyed through *Vertical Limits* are outdoor adventure activities such as glacier hikes, skiing, snowboarding, heli-skiing, skydiving, and climbing. The scenic mountains are a unique attraction, and the specific places that were mentioned were Queenstown, the Southern Alps, Mount Cook, and the South Island in general.

Summary of Unstructured Results

The image of New Zealand the respondents have from experience is that it is a country with beautiful scenery and many adventure activities. They also perceive New Zealand to have a friendly and relaxed atmosphere. *The Lord of the Rings: Fellowship of the Ring* also appears to portray New Zealand as having beautiful scenery. This is an interesting result as there are many scenes in *The Lord of the Rings: Fellowship of the Ring* where the scenery looks quite dark and uninviting, yet the respondents seem to notice only the more appealing aspects of the scenery that are conveyed in the film.

The image of New Zealand tourists have based on *Once Were Warriors* contrasts with the image they have of New Zealand from experience, with the latter image being more positive. With regard to *The Piano*, the main image of New Zealand respondents have is that it has beautiful scenery and a relaxed atmosphere. This is therefore similar to the image of New Zealand respondents have from experience.

The image of New Zealand obtained from *Vertical Limits* once again includes beautiful scenery; however, it also includes images of adventure activities. These two perceptions are both similar to tourists' images of New Zealand from experience.

Overall, *The Lord of the Rings: Fellowship of the Ring*, *The Piano*, and *Vertical Limits* convey images of the scenery that are similar to the scenery found in New Zealand. The image of New Zealand based on *The Piano* is also similar to the image of New Zealand from experience in terms of a relaxed atmosphere. *Vertical Limits* conveys images of New Zealand as having adventurous activities, images that are retained once experience is gained. The image of New Zealand based on *Once Were Warriors* contrasts with the image of New Zealand that is based on experience.

Structured Results—Factor Analysis

A factor analysis reduced the variables to six factors that describe the main images of New Zealand respondents have from experience. The factor solution explains 58.5% of total variance. The six factors are as follows:

1. Adventurous, different, and fascinating (20.0% of variance explained). The items that load on to this factor are 'a holiday in NZ is an adventure' (0.343) and 'NZ is different and fascinating' (0.405).
2. Environmentally friendly, clean, and green (11.1% of variance explained). The items that load on to this factor are 'NZ is environmentally friendly' (0.281), 'NZ is a clean country' (0.654), and 'NZ is a green country' (0.128).
3. Environmentally friendly, good beaches, high quality of service (8.9% of variance explained). The items that load onto this factor are 'NZ is environmentally friendly' (0.200), 'the beaches in NZ are good' (0.388), and 'the quality of service in NZ is generally good' (0.242).
4. Not environmentally friendly but clean (7.4% of variance explained). The items that load on to this factor are 'NZ is environmentally friendly' (−0.354) and 'NZ is a clean country' (0.379).
5. No problems of overcrowding (5.9% of variance explained). The item that loads on to this factor is 'NZ has no crowdedness problems' (0.108).
6. Friendly locals (5.1% of variance explained). The item that loads on to this factor is 'the local people are friendly' (0.199).

The overall image that tourists have of New Zealand can therefore be described by these five factors. Multidimensional scale plots were produced by comparing each of the factors with the factorized scores for each of the four movies. Please note NZ refers to the images respondents have of New Zealand based on experience. The titles of the films are coded on the bi-plot as TLOTR = *The Lord of the Rings: Fellowship of the Ring*; OWW = *Once Were Warriors*; PIANO = *The Piano*, and VL = *Vertical Limits*.

Object Points

Common Space

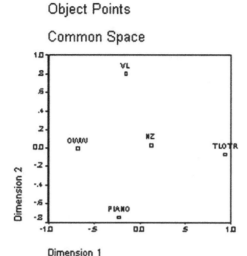

Dimension 1

FIG. 8.1.   Factor 1: Adventurous, different, and fascinating.

Vertical Limits is positioned the closest to NZ on Dimension 1 (see Fig. 8.1); however, it is positioned more negatively than NZ. The images of New Zealand as an adventurous, different and fascinating place conveyed in *Vertical Limits* are therefore the most similar to the images of New Zealand respondents have from being in there. However, New Zealand is perceived more positively post-experience.

The film image positioned the closest to New Zealand on Dimension 2 is *Once Were Warriors*; however, this is a negative position whereas the image respondents have of New Zealand as a result of experience is positive. They are positioned close enough to suggest that the images are quite similar. The images of New Zealand obtained from *The Piano* are not at all similar to NZ.

Once Were Warriors and *The Lord of the Rings* appear to be similar on Dimension 2, whereas *Vertical Limits* and *The Piano* appear to be similar on Dimension 1. This may therefore mean that Dimension 1 may be described as the different and fascinating aspects of the New Zealand scenery and Dimension 2 may be described as the different and fascinating aspects of the New Zealand lifestyle. The images of New Zealand from the *Lord of the Rings: Fellowship of the Ring* may therefore portray the most positive aspects of the New Zealand scenery. The New Zealand lifestyle may be considered to be quite adventurous due to all the adventure activities available; thus, the images of the adventurous aspect of New Zealand portrayed in *Vertical Limits* may be why this movie is positioned the most closely to NZ on Dimension 1.

On Dimension 1 (see Fig. 8.2), the images of the environmental friendliness, cleanliness, and greenness of New Zealand portrayed in *The Piano* are the most similar to NZ. On this Dimension, *The Lord of the Rings: Fellowship of the Ring* and *Once*

Object Points

Common Space

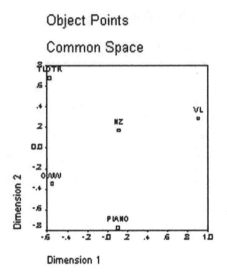

Dimension 1

FIG. 8.2.   Factor 2: Environmentally friendly, clean, and green.

Were Warriors are very similar to each other, but they are both positioned negatively, implying that they portray quite different images to NZ. On Dimension 2, *Vertical Limits* is most similar to NZ. On this Dimension, the image of New Zealand obtained from *Once Were Warriors* and *The Piano* are the most dissimilar to NZ.

The Piano is positioned close enough to NZ on Dimension 1 and *Vertical Limits* is positioned close enough to NZ on Dimension 2 to imply that the images of NZ portrayed in these two movies are quite similar to the images of New Zealand based on experience. The images of New Zealand based on *The Lord of the Rings* and *Once Were Warriors* however, are quite different on both dimensions to NZ.

A possible reason why *The Piano* is very similar to NZ on Dimension 1 and not on Dimension 2 could be that *The Piano* portrays images of both peace and beauty as well as images of despair and darkness. Thus Dimension 1 may incorporate the more positive aspects of this factor, whereas Dimension 2 may represent the more negative aspects.

The Lord of the Rings: Fellowship of the Ring is the most similar to NZ, on Dimension 1 (see Fig. 8.3), and they are positioned close enough together to imply that these images are rather similar. On Dimension 2 *The Piano* is the most similar to NZ; however, it is positioned more negatively.

On Dimension 1 the image of New Zealand respondents have based on *The Piano* is the least similar to their image of New Zealand from experience, and on Dimension 2 *Once Were Warriors* is positioned the furthest from NZ. The image of New Zealand based on these two movies is quite different than the image of New Zealand post-experience, as these movies are both positioned negatively, whereas NZ is positioned positively.

Object Points

Common Space

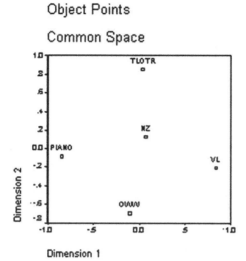

FIG. 8.3.   Factor 3: Environmentally friendly, good beaches, and service.

Dimension 1 may be linked to the quality of service in New Zealand, and Dimension 2 may be linked to aspects of the New Zealand scenery. On Dimension 1, *Vertical Limits* is positioned the most positively and *The Piano* the most negatively. These positions could be related to the fact that in *Vertical Limits* many rescue operations take place and in *The Piano* there is not much evidence of civilized society; thus, a high quality of service is not evident. *Once Were Warriors* and *Vertical Limits* are positioned in between these two movies, with the former being positioned slightly negatively and the latter more positively. This could be because the violence associated with *Once Were Warriors* also indicates a low quality of service but the mystique associated with *The Lord of the Rings* links to overall positive feelings about New Zealand, including a high quality of service.

Dimension 2 may therefore be based more on the scenery aspects of New Zealand, as *The Piano* and *Vertical Limits* are quite similar to NZ and *The Lord of the Rings: Fellowship of the Ring* is the most positively positioned movie on this dimension, with *Once Were Warriors* the most negatively positioned movie. This may be because many positive aspects of the New Zealand scenery are portrayed in *The Lord of the Rings: Fellowship of the Ring* but not in *Once Were Warriors*. The images of New Zealand in *The Piano* and *Vertical Limits* are still relatively similar to NZ even though they are positioned slightly more negatively that NZ.

Overall, the images of the environmental friendliness, cleanliness, and greenness of New Zealand that respondents have from experience are similar to their images of New Zealand based on *The Lord of the Rings: Fellowship of the Ring* on Dimension 1.

Object Points

Common Space

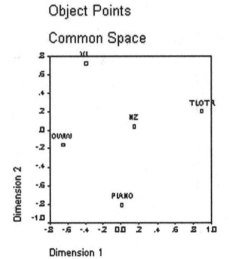

Dimension 1

FIG. 8.4.   Factor 4: Not environmentally friendly, clean.

On Dimension 1 (see Fig. 8.4) *The Piano* is positioned close enough to NZ to suggest that these two images of New Zealand are quite similar; however, on Dimension 2 it is positioned the furthest from NZ. *Once Were Warriors* is positioned the furthest from NZ on Dimension 1 and on Dimension 2 *The Lord of the Rings: Fellowship of the Ring* is the most similar to NZ. *Vertical Limits* is the closest to *The Piano* on Dimension 1 but the furthest from it on Dimension 2. Also on Dimension 1 *The Piano* is positioned more positively than *Vertical Limits*.

Once Were Warriors and *The Piano* are both positioned negatively on Dimension 2 which may suggest that the dark atmosphere in these two movies, such as depression and despair may form the basis of this dimension. *Vertical Limits* and *The Lord of the Rings* are positioned positively on this dimension, and they generally do not have such a dark atmosphere associated with them. Dimension 1 may therefore be linked to the level of environmental friendliness of New Zealand, as *The Piano* and *The Lord of the Rings* may convey more positive images of New Zealand through a lack of human impact on nature. *Vertical Limits* and *Once Were Warriors*, however, may convey images of human impact on the environment.

On Dimension 1 (Fig. 8.5), *Vertical Limits* is the most similar to NZ in relation to overcrowding in NZ. *The Lord of the Rings: Fellowship of the Ring* is the most similar to NZ on Dimension 2. Although this movie is positioned closer to NZ than the other three movies on this Dimension, it is not positioned closely enough to suggest that the two images are in fact similar. Therefore, on Dimension 2, the images based on films that respondents have are quite different than their image of New Zealand post-experience. On Dimension 1, on the other hand, *Vertical Limits* is positioned quite close to NZ. *Vertical Limits* is therefore the only movie where the images are

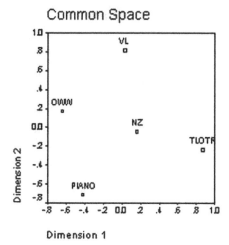

FIG. 8.5.   Factor 5: No overcrowding.

similar. *The Lord of the Rings: Fellowship of the Ring, Once Were Warriors,* and *The Piano* portray quite different images of the population than the experience-based image.

Vertical Limits is positioned positively on both Dimensions 1 and 2, but *The Lord of the Rings: Fellowship of the Ring* is positioned positively only on Dimension 1. This difference may suggest that the differentiating aspect could be that Dimension 1 is based on the perception of overcrowding in relation to the wilderness and Dimension 2 includes all aspects of New Zealand, such as the wilderness and the suburban areas.

The image of the friendliness of New Zealand locals appears to be quite similar between *Once Were Warriors* and *The Piano* on Dimension 1 (see Fig. 8.6). These movies portray a fairly negative image of local people. However, they are positioned quite far from the experience-based images of New Zealand, implying that the images of the locals are in fact quite different. *The Piano* is however perceived to be the most similar to NZ on Dimension 2, although they are not positioned close enough to imply that these two images are actually similar, just that they are the most similar on that dimension.

On Dimension 1 the image of the friendliness of New Zealand locals from experience is the most similar to the image of New Zealand respondents have from the movie *The Lord of the Rings: Fellowship of the Ring.* These are positioned closely enough together to suggest that these two images are in fact quite similar. This is rather unexpected, as New Zealanders are not portrayed in this movie. However, an explanation could be that the images of New Zealand based on *The Lord of the*

Object Points

Common Space

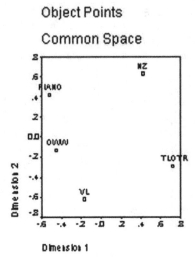

FIG. 8.6.   Factor 6: Friendly locals.

Rings: Fellowship of the Ring are not based solely on the movie but on related media exposure of New Zealand, which could involve New Zealanders.

Summary of Quantitative Results

Overall, the images of New Zealand based on films appear to be quite different than respondents' experience-based images. On only a few occasions are some of the movies positioned close enough to NZ to suggest some congruency between the images. For each factor there was no more than one movie positioned close to NZ on each dimension, and in some cases all the movies were positioned quite far from NZ.

The majority of movies are therefore positioned far enough apart from NZ that it can be concluded that the images of New Zealand based on New Zealand-made films are not similar to the overall images respondents have based on experience. Similarities exist only on some aspects and Dimensions. Quite often, *The Lord of the Rings: Fellowship of the Ring* and *Once Were Warriors* were positioned opposite each other, as were *The Piano* and *Vertical Limits*. This may be because *The Lord of the Rings: Fellowship of the Ring* tends to portray a positive atmosphere, whereas *Once Were Warriors* is more negative. *Vertical Limits* may portray images of excitement, contrasting with the images of peacefulness conveyed in *The Piano*.

Overall, the images that New Zealand films tend to generate about New Zealand are quite different than the experience-based images of New Zealand. Thus, the expectations of their time in New Zealand that tourists have may be quite different than the reality of their experiences in New Zealand. In addition to the implications these results hold for tourism marketers for New Zealand, they are also important in developing our understanding of how destination images are formed.

DISCUSSION AND CONCLUSION

The New Zealand film example illustrates three of the four features included in Gallarza et al.'s (2002) model. First, the destination image of New Zealand is complex. Both cognitive and affective elements of the destination image were found, as were collective and personal impressions. This is, in part, due to the selection of the measurement instrument, which uses both unstructured and structured methodologies to capture three Dimensions: functional/psychological, common/unique, and holistic/attribute based. Because images of New Zealand based on different sources were measured, both selective and additive elements were apparent. The image of New Zealand that was based on experience incorporated some of the same elements as the images gained from films made in New Zealand (additive, but not all; selective). Much like current conceptualizations of possible selves (Markus & Nurius, 1986), it is likely that all these elements are part of the total destination image, but only some are relevant in any particular situation.

The idea of possible and situational destination images that is implied by the comparison to possible selves also supports Gallarza et al.'s (2002) second feature—destination image is multiple. There are multiple sources of images, and the destination image was perceived in both a multidimensional and a gestalt manner. This was illustrated through the use of both multi-item attribute scales and holistic measures that produced related but different images of New Zealand. In addition, the image of New Zealand is both static, in that respondents had selected New Zealand as their destination based on their images of it, and dynamic, as the structure of formation of destination image is manifest differently.

The third and final of Gallarza et al.'s (2002) features to be supported by the New Zealand film example is the relativistic nature of destination image. The images of New Zealand differed substantially depending on the source of that image. Thus, certain films are more or less appropriate to utilize in a promotional campaign. For example, *Once Were Warriors* is not appropriate for developing an image of New Zealand based on beautiful scenery and friendly people.

In conclusion, further research based on hypothesis testing is required to provide full empirical support for the model. However, the exploratory study of the impact of New Zealand-made films on the destination image of New Zealand provides some supporting evidence for Gallarza et al.'s (2002) conceptual model of destination image and for a social construction perspective in general.

REFERENCES

Ajzen, I. (2001). Nature and operation of attitudes. *Annual Review of Psychology, 52,* 27–58.
Arnholt, S. (2002). Foreword. *Brand Management, 9,* 229–239.

Bagozzi, R. (1988). The rebirth of attitude research in marketing. *Journal of the Market Research Society, 30*(2), 163–195.

Baloglu, S., & McCleary, K. W. (1999). A model of destination image formation. *Annals of Tourism Research, 26,* 868–897.

Bhattacharyya, D. (1997). Mediating India: An analysis of a guidebook. *Annals of Tourism Research, 24,* 371–389.

Carmichael, B. (1992). Using conjoint modeling to measure tourist image and analyze ski resort choice. In P. Johnson & B. Thomas (Eds.), *Choice and demand in tourism* (pp.93–106). Mansell: London.

Chon, K-S. (1990). The role of destination image in tourism: A review and discussion. *Revue du Tourism, 2,* 2–9.

Crompton, J. L. (1979). An assessment of the image of Mexico as a vacation destination and the influence of geographical location upon the image. *Journal of Travel Research, 18*(4), 18–23.

Dann, G. M. S. (1996). Tourists images of a destination: An alternative analysis. *Journal of Travel and Tourism Marketing, 5*(½), 41–55.

Echtner, C. M., & Ritchie, J. R. (1991). The meaning and measurement of destination image. *The Journal of Tourism Studies, 2*(2), 2–12.

Echtner, C. M. & Ritchie J. R. (1993). The measurement of destination image: An empirical assessment. *Journal of Travel Research, 31*(4), 3–13.

Fayeke, P., & Crompton, J. (1991). Image differences between prospective, first-time and repeat visitors to the lower Rio Grande Valley. *Journal of Travel Research, 30*(2), 10–16.

Fesenmaier, D., & MacKay, K. (1996). Deconstructing destination image construction. *Revue du Tourisme, 51*(2), 37–43.

Gallarza, M. G., Saura, I. G., & Garcia, H. C. (2002). Destination image: towards a conceptual framework. *Annals of Tourism Research, 29*(1), 56–78.

Gartner, W. C. (1993). Image formation process. *Journal of Travel and Tourism Marketing, 2,* 191–216.

Gartner, W. C., & Hunt, J. D. (1987). An analysis of state image change over a twelve year period (1971–1983). *Journal of Travel Research, 16*(Fall), 15–19.

Girard, M. (1999). *States, diplomacy and image making: What is new? Reflections on current British and French experiences.* Paper presented at the Image, State and International Relations Conference, London School of Economics.

Haahti, A. J. (1986). Finland's competitive position as a destination. *Annals of Tourism Research, 13,* 11–35.

Holbrook, M. (1995). *Consumer research: Introspective essays on the study of consumption.* Thousand Oaks: Sage.

Hunt, J. D. (1975). Image as a factor in tourism development. *Journal of Travel Research, 13* (Winter), 1–7.

Kim, H., & Richardson, S. L. (2003). Motion picture impacts on destination images. *Annals of Tourism Research, 30*(1), 216–237.

Kotler, P., & Gertner, D. (2002). Country as brand, product and beyond: A place marketing and brand management perspective. *Journal of Brand Management, 9*(4/5), 249–262.

Mackay, K. J., & Fesenmaier, D. K. (1997). Pictorial element of destination in image formation. *Annals of Tourism Research, 24*(3), 537–565.

Markus, H. & Nurius, P. (1986). Possible selves. *American Psychologist, 41*(9), 954–969.

Mayo, E. J. (1973 August 12–15). Regional images and regional travel behavior. Proceedings of *The Travel Research Association* (pp. 211–218). Sun Valley, ID.

Mayo, E. J., & Jarvis, L. P. (1981). *The psychology of leisure travel.* Boston: CBI Publishing.

McCracken, G. (1986). Culture and consumption: A theoretical account of the structure and movement of the cultural meaning of consumer goods. *Journal of Consumer Research, 13*(June), 71–84.

Morgan, N., Pritchard, A., & Piggott, R., (2002). New Zealand, 100% pure. The creation of a powerful niche destination brand. *Journal of Brand Management, 9*(4/5), 335–355.

Olins, W. (2002). Branding the nation—the historical context. *Journal of Brand Management, 9*(4/5), 241–248.

Papadopoulos, N., & Heslop, L. (2002). Country equity and country branding: Problems and prospects. *Journal of Brand Management, 9*(4/5), 294–315.

Pearce, P. (1982). Perceived changes in holiday destinations. *Annals of Tourism Research, 9*, 145–164.

Pike, S. (2002a). Destination image analysis—A review of 142 papers from 1973 to 2000. *Tourism Management, 23*, 541–549.

Pike, S. (2002b). Destination image evaluation: Part 1. *Eclipse, 9*, 1–11.

Reilly, M. D. (1990). Free elicitation of descriptive adjectives for tourism image assessment. *Journal of Travel Research, 28*(4), 21–26.

Robertson, T. S., Zielinski, J., & Ward, S. (1984). *Consumer behavior.* Glenview: Scott, Foresman.

Sternquist Witter, B. (1985). Attitudes about resort areas: A comparison of tourists and local retailers. *Journal of Travel Research, 24*(1), 14–19.

Weightman, B. (1987). Third world tour landscapes. *Annals of Tourism Research, 14*, 227–239.

Woodside, A.G., & Lysonski, S. (1989). A general model of traveler destination choice. *Journal of Travel Research, 27*(4), 8–14.

Young, M. (1999). The social construction of tourist places. *Australian Geographer, 30*(3), 373–389.

CHAPTER NINE

Chinese Consumers' Evaluation of Hybrid Country of Origin Products: Effects of Decomposed Elements of Country of Origin, Brand Name, and Consumers' Ethnocentrism

Kwon Jung
KDI School of Public Policy & Management

Ah-Keng Kau
National University of Singapore

Since Dichter's (1962) mention and Schooler's (1965) empirical observation of country-of-origin effect, country-of-origin effect has been examined in numerous consumer studies across many countries. Many reviews and meta-analysis on country of origin research found generalizable supporting evidence for the effect of country of origin on product evaluations (Bilkey & Nes, 1982; Perterson & Jolibert, 1995; Verlegh & Steenkamp, 1999). It has been found that consumers display a preference toward the products from developed countries more than those from developing countries. However, with the recent increased offshore manufacturing and global sourcing, product–country association is no longer just a single-country phenomenon. It is becoming common for firms to source products or components from different parts of the world. It is achieved by assigning firms in various countries to different specialized tasks in the production process, such as key component production, product marketing, product design, and final assembly. For example, a Sony television set carrying a Japanese brand name but manufactured in Malaysia and equipped with a China-made picture tube is an example of a hybrid product. Consumers cannot tell with certainty which specific country the television is tied to. Considering this situation, some researchers argued that previous findings that are largely based on uninational origin could not be applicable to many products to-day, which are more likely to be hybrids that involve binational or multinational production (Ahmed & d'Astous, 1996; Chao, 1993, 2001; Cordell, 1993; Han & Terpstra, 1988; Tse & Lee, 1993).

In addition to the uninational origin of past studies, some research also questioned the validity of previous findings that were derived mostly from single-cue models (Bilkey & Nes, 1982). In single-cue studies, country of origin was the only cue available to the respondents for product evaluation (Bilkey & Nes, 1982). In fact, some multiple-cue studies showed either no significant or only minor effects due to country image (Ettenson, Wagner, & Gaeth, 1988; Johansson, Douglas, & Nonaka, 1985). Indeed the absolute magnitude of country effects is less useful than the magnitude of country effects relative to other information cues, such as price or brand name on the evaluation of products. Besides, single-cue studies provide no insights as to how consumers combine country image information with information on other easily available cues such as brand name.

One of the most important and still unresolved issues in the multiple-cue origin study is the relative salience of brand name versus country image in product evaluations. Some studies found country image as a more enduring cue than brand name (Ahmed & d'Astous, 1995, 1996; Han & Terpstra, 1988; Tse & Gorn, 1993). Other studies suggested that brand name can overcome country image on product judgment (Ahmed, d'Astous, & Zouiten, 1993; Tse & Lee, 1993). So far, the issue of whether country image is still an important factor for product evaluations in the presence of brand name remains unclear. Given that hybrid products are linked to several country images, whether brand name can outweigh all or just one aspect of country image is an important issue to be investigated. Thus, one main objective of this study is to examine the influence of decomposed aspects of country image on product evaluation in the presence of brand name.

In evaluating products with foreign origin, nationalism plays a major role in determining consumers' acceptance and preference of foreign brands (Dichter, 1962). Consumer ethnocentrism (Shimp & Sharma, 1987) has been suggested as one key factor that explains consumers' preference for domestic products over foreign products (Pecotich & Rosenthal, 2001). In examining country-of-origin effect under a situation that includes both foreign and domestic country-of-origin information, it is necessary to examine the interactive effect of consumer ethnocentrism and country-of-origin information on product evaluations.

Although some past studies have examined the influence of decomposed country-of-origin aspects on product evaluations (e.g., Chao, 2001; Tse & Gorn, 1993; Tse & Lee, 1993), most of the studies have focused on consumers from developed countries rather than from developing countries. With the increased market size of developing countries, it is necessary to examine consumers' responses to hybrid products from the perspective of consumers from developing countries. It is especially interesting to examine their responses to a hybrid product that has either assembly or key component origin in their home country. Therefore, this study aims to examine the effects of decomposed elements of country of origin (i.e., assembly origin and key component origin) and brand name, together with the effect of ethnocentrism on the evaluation of hybrid products by consumers from a developing country (i.e., China).

CONCEPTUAL BACKGROUND

Multidimensional Concepts of Country of Origin Image

Although researchers have made considerable progress in studying the country-of-origin effect, few of them clarify what the term *country of origin* means to a consumer. Country of origin (COO) denotes the home country with which a firm is associated. Most of the time, COO is the home country of brands. For example, IBM and Sony imply U. S. and Japanese origins respectively (Samiee, 1994). With the rapid development of global technology and communication, the need to seek new market opportunities, access to cheaper labor, and raw materials, and favorable strategic alliance, firms would be able to create global brand reputations while manufacturing in or sourcing from different parts of the world. As a result, products are more likely to be hybrid, associated with several countries. Hybrid refers to a product branded in one country with components manufactured in another country and final product assembly in the third country. For hybrid products, country of origin can be understood as representing a composite of the "made in" image—country-of-brand-origin image, country-of-manufacture image, and key-component-made-in image—each having a different impact on consumer evaluation of a product. *Country of manufacture (COM))* denotes the location of manufacture or assembly of a product. Although many products include parts and components from several countries, COM refers to the final point of manufacture or assembly, which can be the same as country of origin (Samiee, 1994). On the other hand, *Country of manufacture of the key component (CMKC)* denotes the final location in which key components are manufactured or assembled, although its parts may come from other places.

Effects of Country of Manufacture (COM). Research interest in consumer evaluation of hybrid products began with binational product studies that involved country of origin and country of manufacture. In a seminal analysis, Johansson and Nebenzahl (1986) examined the effects of manufacturing location on perceptions of the quality and image of passenger cars. From a multidimensional scaling of many attributes, including reliability, durability, price, performance, workmanship, service quality, and style, they concluded that West Germany was the best country in which to manufacture cars. The label, "made in West Germany," improved the image of all brands under study. On the other hand, moving production to a low-image country resulted in a loss of brand prestige. Using Sony stereo equipment, Tse and Gorn (1993) asked the subjects to evaluate the products when they were made in Japan and when they were made in Indonesia respectively. They found that higher ratings were indicated for Sony from Japan than from Indonesia. Using television and automobile as the target products, Han and Terpstra (1988) examined the evaluation of those products manufactured in the United States, Japan, Germany, and South Korea. They reported that Japan was rated to have the most favorable image to manufacture both the televisions and cars, followed by the United States, Germany, and Korea. Iyer and Kalita (1997) investigated the impact of country-of-origin and country-of-manufacture cues on consumers perception of quality, value, and willingness to buy. Using the brand origin instead of the specific brand name, they found that in the presence of country-of-origin information cues and the absence of known and real brand names, a strong effect of country of manufacture information was observed on all product categories (e.g., sneakers, jeans, stereos, watches). In particular, products manufactured in the United States were perceived significantly better than those manufactured in Korea or China. Chao (1993) partitioned the country of origin cue into country of design (COD) and country of assembly (COA[1]) cues for television sets produced by a Taiwanese company. Using a within-subjects experimental design, he found that country perceptions independently influenced quality perceptions and that, in the case of hybrid products, country-of-origin effects could be strategically partitioned to obtain favorable quality perceptions among consumers.

The literature cited suggests that manufacturing in a developed country contributes to a more favorable product evaluation than manufacturing in a developing country. Moreover, perceived risk and purchase intention would also be affected by the country-of-manufacture factor as they are related to product evaluation. Therefore, the following hypothesis is suggested.

H1:   Chinese consumers will have (a) higher product quality evaluation, (b) lower perceived risk, and (c) higher purchase intention for a product manufactured in a developed country than in a developing country.

Effect of Country of Manufacture of the Key Component (CMKC). Samiee, Shimp, and Snyder (1990) pointed out that the majority of respondents were aware of the global sourcing in multinational production. Component sourcing becomes rather common in international business. Khanna (1986) was the first to identify the component origin effect. He reported Indian consumers would open the back of televisions to make certain that their subassemblies were imported from Japan and Germany but not from South Korea. In the market, Indian consumers were willing to pay premium prices for color televisions assembled from Japanese and German kits but not for those from South Korean kits. Tse and Lee (1993) examined the effects of decomposing country image into component and assembly origins on product quality evaluations and performance expectations. The effects of component

---

[1]COA equals to country of manufacture (COM).

and assembly origins were found to be significant but less than those obtained from earlier country-of-origin studies. Therefore, similar to the country-of-manufacture effect, it is hypothesized that a key component sourced from a developed country would contribute to higher evaluation of products than when it is sourced from a developing country.

> H2: Chinese consumers will have (a) higher product quality evaluation, (b) lower perceived risk and, (c) higher purchase intention for a product with a key component manufactured in a developed country than in a developing country.

Because the key component is a major part of a product, it is expected that it will play a significant role in consumer evaluations, together with the place of manufacture. Chao (2001) speculated that a country schema may be invoked first by country-of-assembly information, which in turn influences the way other informational cues, such as country of manufacture of component, are used in product evaluations. Although we do not know yet the relative importance of COM and CMKC, we are more interested whether the favorable country image of key component can compensate for the negative COM effect. Thus, the following interaction effect between COM and CMKC is hypothesized:

> H3$_1$: When a product has a key component manufactured in a developed country, there will be no significant difference in (a) product quality evaluation, (b) perceived risk, and (c) purchase intention, whether the product is manufactured in a developed country or a developing country.

> H3$_2$: When a product has a key component manufactured in a developing country, there will be (a) higher product quality evaluation, (b) lower perceived risk, and (c) higher purchasing intention for the product manufactured in a developed country than for the product manufactured in a developing country.

Country Image and Brand Name

Brand name is an extrinsic cue that has been used by consumers as a surrogate to infer product quality (Jacoby, Szybillo, & Busato-Schach, 1977). Literature in consumer behavior has long established the importance of brand name in product evaluation (Jacoby, Olson, & Haddock, 1971). One basic component in designing an effective global marketing strategy is the strength of a company's brand in the international marketplace (Porter, 1980). Brand name provides a customer with readily recognizable information about a firm's products (Aaker, 1991; Chao, 1993; Johansson, 1989). It contributes significantly to the success or failure of new products (Aaker & Keller, 1990). Brand equity can add value to the firm, the trade, and the consumer (Chay, 1991). A well-known brand is a major asset for a firm. It provides the firm with a distinctive image that can translate into an important sustainable competitive advantage. Hence we hypothesize that:

H4:   Chinese consumers will have (a) higher product quality evaluation, (b) lower perceived risk and, (c) higher purchase intention for a product with a well-known brand than with an unknown brand.

Under the multiple cue model, the previous research findings on whether an established strong brand name can remove a negative country image effect are mixed, although there is strong evidence that producers' name (Johansson & Nebenzahl, 1986) and retailer's name (Chao, 1989a, 1989b) enhance sales of products from less favorable countries. Gaedeke (1973) found that consumers' rankings of established brand names did not change when country of manufacture was present. More recent studies also suggest that brand name is a more enduring cue than country of manufacture. Actually, country of manufacture has either no impact at all or only a very weak impact on consumer product evaluations (Cordell, 1992; Johansson et al., 1985). Cordell (1993) showed that the derogation associated with products manufactured in developing countries could be mitigated when products were bearing a famous brand. It may be explained that the strong brand name can provide the insurance needed to accept developing country—a Sony television manufactured in China is still backed by the Sony warranty. Ahmed et al. (1993) asked 90 Canadian students to evaluate the automobiles from Japan, Canada, and Philippines on the purchase appropriateness. They found that brand was the most important factor in consumers' purchasing decisions. After decomposing the country image into component and assembly origin, Tse and Lee (1993) suggested that influences of component and assembly origins were attribute specific and that strong brand name and favorable product experience could override any negative "made-in" images. The findings suggest that a well-known brand name can compensate for the negative effect of country image.

On the other hand, some studies found greater significance of country image to brand name (Cattin, Jolibert, & Lohnes, 1982; Wall, Liefeld, & Heslop, 1991). Nes (1981) reported that the negative evaluation of products manufactured in developing countries was not overcome by a well-known brand name. Han and Terpstra (1988) suggested that country of manufacture had a more powerful effect than brand name on consumer evaluation of binational products. Given the cues as country of design, country of assembly, brand, price, and warranty, Ahmed and d'Astous (1996) asked Canadian males to rate automobiles, VCRs and shoes from various countries on their overall quality and purchase value. They found country of assembly and country of design to have stronger influence than brand name, and the magnitude of country effects became smaller in multiple-cue situations. Other studies also support the greater importance of country of manufacture relative to brand name (Ettenson, 1994; Okechuku, 1994; Tse & Gorn, 1993). Nes and Bilkey (1993) showed that although a well-known brand name may enhance the quality perceptions despite its manufacturing location, brand name does not completely compensate for the negative country-of-manufacture bias.

Although the results of past studies seem to be conflicting, an interesting interaction effects between country-of-origin information and brand name can be predicted from the combined results: Although effect of country image may be stronger than brand name, a strong brand name reputation may eliminate the negative impacts of country image. Therefore, the following interaction effects between the decomposed country of origin information and brand name are proposed:

$H5_1$: For a well-known brand, there will be no significant difference between products manufactured in developed and developing countries with respect to (a) product quality evaluation, (b) perceived risk, and (c) purchase intention.

$H5_2$: For an unknown brand, there will be significantly (a) higher product quality evaluation, (b) lower perceived risk, and (c) higher purchase intention if it is manufactured in a developed country versus in a developing country.

$H6_1$: For a well-known brand, there will be no significant difference on (a) product quality evaluation, (b) perceived risk, and (c) purchase intention whether its key component is manufactured in a developed country or in a developing country.

$H6_2$: For an unknown brand, there will be significantly (a) higher product quality evaluation, (b) lower perceived risk, and (c) higher purchase intention if its key component is manufactured in a developed country rather than in a developing country.

Ethnocentrism

Although the psychological aspects of consumers, such as nationalism and patriotism, may influence their responses to foreign and domestic products (Dichter, 1962), relatively few country-of-origin studies have explicitly examined this aspect. One of the indirect findings from a meta-analysis is a preference for domestic products (Perterson & Jolibert, 1995). If the country of origin of the stimulus product is the same as the respondent's country, the effect size for the quality perceptions is larger than if the product comes from a country other than that of the respondent.

Recently, the issue has been addressed by a few studies that explicitly consider consumer ethnocentrism in examining country-of-origin effect (Moon & Jain, 2001; Pecotich & Rosenthal, 2001). Consumer ethnocentrism refers to the beliefs held by local consumers about the appropriateness, indeed morality, of purchasing foreign-made product (Shimp & Sharma, 1987). Ethnocentric consumers tend to believe that the purchase of imported goods is wrong because it is unpatriotic and results in damage to the domestic economy. On the other hand, nonethnocentric consumers consider foreign goods as objects to be evaluated on their own merit, and the country of origin of the product is not relevant for evaluation (Pecotich & Rosenthal, 2001). Therefore, it is hypothesized that:

$H7_1$: Chinese consumers with high ethnocentrism, will show significantly (a) higher product quality evaluation, (b) lower perceived risk, and (c) higher purchase intention for a product manufactured in the home country rather than in a foreign country.

$H7_2$: Chinese consumers with low ethnocentrism show no significant difference on (a) product quality evaluation, (b) perceived risk, and (c) purchase intention for a product whether it is manufactured in the home country or a foreign country.

$H8_1$: Chinese consumers with high ethnocentrism will show significantly (a) higher product quality evaluation, (b) lower perceived risk, and (c) higher purchase intention for a product whose key component is from the home country rather than from a foreign country.

$H8_2$: Chinese consumers with low ethnocentrism will show no significant difference on (a) product quality evaluation, (b) perceived risk, and (c) purchase intention for a product whether its key component is from the home country or from a foreign country.

METHODOLOGY

Experimental Design

A 3 (country of manufacture: developed country, less developed country, home country) x 3 (country of manufacture of key component: developed country, less developed country, home country) x 2 (brand: well-known and unknown) x 2 (ethnocentrism: high and low) full factorial mixed design is used in this study. Brand, country of manufacture of the key component, and ethnocentrism are manipulated as between-subjects factors, and the country of manufacture is manipulated as a within-subjects factor.

Participants

A total of 267 Chinese consumers participated in the study. They were recruited from two major cities in Southern China (i.e., Fuzhou and Shenzhen). Because these two cities are the first to benefit from China's open door policy, consumers in these two cities have relatively high income and have been exposed to various foreign products. The participants were from a range of factories, institutions, and government offices. The majority of respondents (71%) were between 20 and 40 years old. Men represented 54.5% and women 45.5%. Sixty-four percent of the total participant group had college educations. Eighty percent of the respondents had a monthly household income under $600. Ninety-seven percent had color televisions, whereas 63% had foreign brand televisions.

Experimental Stimuli and Manipulation of Independent Variables

Professional copies of print ads were used as the experimental stimuli. A picture of color a television set was included in the ad with the following features: 25", double front speakers, TV/video remote control, picture in picture, Chinese/English menu. Brand name, country of manufacture, country of manufacture of the picture tube, and the manufacturer were presented in a natural way. Picture tube was selected as the key component to be manipulated because it is directly related to the picture quality of television sets.

The choice of a color television was made based on the following considerations. First, a majority of Chinese consumers are very familiar with it. Television lies in the center of modern Chinese family life. On an average, 86% of urban families possessed color televisions in 1995, whereas 62% of rural households owned black and white television sets (Li & Gallup, 1995). Second, color television is a high-cost and high-involvement item. Both men and women, young and old, are likely to be involved in such a purchase. Third, because televisions are well known to consumers, it is logical to expect them to have the knowledge of or to be familiar with the key component—the picture tube. Fourth, color televisions are relatively complex products. They are often multinational or hybrid in nature. Moreover, a color television has been the most often used product in previous country image studies (Ahmed & d'Astous, 1996; Ettenson, 1994; Han & Terpstra, 1988).

Selection of Country. Countries to represent the three levels of country of manufacture and country of manufacture of key component respectively were chosen based on the following criteria. First, the selected countries had to be active producers and sourcing locations for hybrid products. Second, the country images between developed and developing countries were expected to differ considerably. Last, the selected countries were relatively well known to Chinese consumers. Based on the criteria, Japan, Malaysia, and China were selected to represent the developed country, the developing country, and the home country. A pretest ($n = 21$) was conducted to check country image difference on product quality perceptions on the color television set and the picture tube on a 7-point scale. For both television set and picture tube quality perceptions, Japan received higher ratings than China (5.70 vs. 3.74, $t = 6.67$, $p < .01$, for television set; 6.23 vs. 4.00, $t = 5.64$, $p < .01$ for picture tube) and Malaysia (5.70 vs. 3.22, $t = 8.75$, $p < .01$ for television set; 6.23 vs. 3.57, $t = 7.83$, $p < .01$).

Selection of Brand Name.   A high-quality, well-known brand and an unknown fictitious brand were selected based on the pretest. A fictitious brand was used for the unknown brand to remove any confounding effect of its already exposed image (Tse & Gorn, 1993). To avoid another confounding effect of brand name with country of origin information[2] (Hui & Zhou, 2002), known and fictitious brands originated from the same country, so that the results would not be affected by different images of country of origin. Because Japanese televisions have enjoyed the reputation for high quality as well as high popularity, the positive well-known brand should be a Japanese brand that is familiar to most consumers. A pretest was conducted to find out appropriate names for both well-known and fictitious Japanese brands for color television set. Among several established Japanese brands, Sony was selected as the well-known brand because it produced the highest ratings on quality perception ($M = 6.14$ on a 7-point scale) and familiarity ($M = 6.23$ on a 7-point scale). Several fictitious Japanese brand names were also generated and tested for appropriateness as a Japanese television brand name. Takai received the highest rating ($M = 5.57$); thus, it was chosen as the name of the unknown brand.

Ethnocentrism.   Ethnocentrism is measured using the scales developed by Shimp and Sharma (1987). Due to the length of questionnaire, a shorter version of the scale was used in this study (Herche, 1992). The 7-item scale produced a decent level of reliability (alpha = .79). The scale was averaged, and the high and low ethnocentric groups were divided through the mean split method.

Dependent Measures

Product quality evaluation, perceived risk, and purchase intention are three dependent variables measured in this study. Product quality evaluation is measured on eleven 7-point semantic differential scales (i.e., unreliable–reliable, cheap–expensive, bad workmanship–good workmanship, bad picture quality–good picture quality, backward technology–advanced technology, bad performance–good performance, not durable–durable, likely to break down–unlikely to break down, bad service–good service, more for lower class–more for higher class, not proud to own– proud to own), which are adopted from Nagashima (1970, 1977), Johansson

---

[2]In most of the past country-of-origin studies that examine brand effects together with country-of-origin effects, the selection of brand names is made in such a way that the strong brand is chosen from developed countries and the weak brand is chosen from developing or underdeveloped countries. When this happens, the brand name can be used as a proxy of country-of-origin information; thus, there is a possibility of the confounding effect of brand name with country of origin information (Hui & Zhou, 2002). This confound could be one reason why we still have inconclusive findings on the relative impact of country image as against the brand name on product evaluations.

and Nebenzahl (1986), and Han and Terpstra (1988). The scale showed a high level of reliability (ranged between .92 and .93), and exploratory factor analyses produced single factor solutions for all three within-subject factor conditions. Thus, average values of the 11 scales were calculated and used in hypothesis testing. Perceived risk (low–high) and purchase intention (unlikely to purchase it–likely to purchase it) were measured on a single 7-point semantic differential scale.

RESULTS

To test the hypotheses, MANOVA was first conducted using SPSS for Windows 11.0. The results of the multivariate analysis are summarized in Table 9.1. First, MANOVA results show significant main effects of country of manufacture (COM) and brand and a significant 2-way interaction effect between country of manufacture and brand, providing supporting evidence for H1, H4, and H5 at a multivariate level. The effect of country of manufacture of key component (CMKC) was not found to be significant. Its interaction effects with COM and brand were not found to be significant either. Therefore, H2, H3, and H6 were not supported at the multivariate level. Although the main effect of ethnocentrism and its 2-way interaction effects with COM and CMKC were not found to be significant, thus failing to support H7 and H8, a significant 3-way interaction effect among COM, CMKC,

TABLE 9.1

MANOVA Results

Source	Pillai's Trace	Wilks' Lamda	Hotelling's Trace
Main Effects			
COM	.535**	.465**	1.151**
CMKC	.039	.961	.040
Brand	.056**	.944**	.059**
Ethnocentrism	.016	.984	.040
2-way Interactions			
COM x CMKC	.069	.932	.071
COM x Brand	.065**	.935**	.070**
COM x Ethnocentrism	.048	.952	.050
CMKC x Brand	.019	.981	.019
CMKC x Ethnocentrism	.035	.965	.036
Brand x Ethnocentrism	.017	.983	.017
3-way Interactions			
COM x CMKC x Brand	.060	.941	.062
COM x CMKC x Ethnocentrism	.083*	.918*	.089*
COM x Brand x Ethnocentrism	.037	.963	.039
CMKC x Brand x Ethnocentrism	.030	.970	.031
4-way Interaction			
COM x CMKC x Brand x Ethnocentrism	.065	.936	.067

Note. *p < .05, **p < .01.

and ethnocentrism was observed at the multivariate level. This finding suggests that the effect of ethnocentrism is rather more complex than predicted.

The effects found to be significant at multivariate level were further investigated using univariate analysis. Table 9.2 summarizes the univariate ANOVA results for all three dependent variables. First, the COM main effects were significant on all dependent variables as predicted ($F_{2, 266} = 159.29$, $p < .01$ for quality perception; $F_{2, 266} = 30.57$, $p < .01$ for perceived risk; $F_{2, 266} = 61.34$, $p < .01$ for purchase intention). Pairwise t tests revealed that the mean value of product quality evaluation was significantly higher when the color TV was manufactured in Japan than when it was manufactured in China (4.93 vs. 4.16, $t_{1, 266} = 12.31$, $p < .01$) or Malaysia (4.93 vs. 3.88, $t_{1, 266} = 16.48$, $p < .01$). The mean value of perceived risk was significantly lower when the TV was manufactured in Japan than when it is manufactured in China (3.41 vs. 3.97, $t_{1, 266} = 4.84$, $p < .01$) or Malaysia (3.41 vs. 4.23, $t_{1, 266} = 7.57$, $p < .01$). Purchase intention was higher when the color TV was manufactured in Japan than when it was manufactured in China (4.14 vs. 3.52, $t_{1, 266} = 5.59$, $p < .01$) or Malaysia (4.14 vs. 2.96, $t_{1, 266} = 11.19$, $p < .01$). All differences were significant at the .05 level. Thus, H1a, H1b, and H1c were supported.

Second, main effects of brand were also found to be significant on all dependent variables, as predicted. Compared to Takai (i.e., unknown brand), Sony (i.e., well

TABLE 9.2

Univariate ANOVA Results

| | | F value | | |
| | | Product | Perceived | Purchase |
Source	df	Evaluation	Risk	Intention
Main Effects				
COM	2	159.29**	30.57**	61.34**
CMKC	2	2.88	.49	.19
Brand	1	10.83**	7.62**	8.97**
Ethnocentrism	1	.02	.01	2.43
2-way Interactions				
COM x CMKC	4	2.31	1.10	2.25
COM x Brand	2	5.76**	.50	4.43*
COM x Ethnocentrism	2	2.63	3.12*	1.22
CMKC x Brand	2	.05	1.95	.02
CMKC x Ethnocentrism	2	1.22	.47	1.52
Brand x Ethnocentrism	1	.15	1.55	.80
3-way Interactions				
COM x CMKC x Brand	4	.72	.61	2.10
COM x CMKC x Ethnocentrism	4	.13	1.37	2.77*
COM x Brand x Ethnocentrism	2	.26	2.33	1.35
CMKC x Brand x Ethnocentrism	2	2.82	.20	3.26*
4-way Interaction				
COM x CMKC x Brand x Ethnocentrism	4	1.13	.64	1.65

Note. *$p < .05$, **$p < .01$.

known brand) received higher ratings on product quality evaluation (4.48 vs. 4.15, $t_{1,265} = 3.04, p < .01$), lower ratings on perceived risk (3.68 vs. 4.08, $t_{1,265} = -2.76, p < .01$), and higher ratings on purchase intention (3.76 vs. 3.31, $t_{1,265} = 2.80, p < .01$). Thus, H4a, H4b, and H4c were supported.

Third, significant COM by brand interaction effects were found on product quality evaluation and purchase intention but not on perceived risk. The nature of COM by brand interaction effects is shown in Figs. 9.1 and 9.2. Although there were significant interaction effects between COM and brand, the pattern of the interaction was not consistent with the prediction suggested in H5. For the unknown brand situation (i.e., Takai), we observed significantly higher ratings on perceived quality evaluation when the color TV was manufactured in Japan rather than in China (4.86 vs. 3.89, $t_{1,266} = 10.08, p < .01$) or Malaysia (4.86 vs. 3.71, $t_{1,266} = 12.34, p < .01$). The same pattern was observed on purchase intention (4.01 (Japan) vs. 3.11 (China), $t_{1,266} = 5.70, p < .01$; 4.01 (Japan) vs. 2.82 (Malaysia), $t_{1,266} = 7.50, p < .01$). Thus, $H5_{2a}$ and $H5_{2c}$ are supported. Although no difference in quality evaluation and purchase intention is suggested for the known strong brand (i.e., Sony) in $H5_{1a}$ and $H5_{1c}$, we observe significant COM effects on perceived quality (4.99 for Japan vs. 4.42 for China, $t_{1,266} = 7.49, p < .01$; 4.99 for Japan vs. 4.04 for Malaysia, $t_{1,266} = 11.01, p < .01$) and purchase intention (4.27 for Japan vs. 3.91 for China, $t_{1,266} = 2.32, p < .05$; 4.27 for Japan vs. 3.09 for Malaysia, $t_{1,266} = 8.34, p < .01$). Thus, $H5_{2a}$ and $H5_{2c}$ are not supported. The interaction effect rather occurs when the COM is from Japan. The difference between the strong and the weak brands becomes insignificant when the color TV is manufactured in Japan (4.99 (Sony) vs. 4.86 (Takai), $t_{1,266} = .26, p > .10$ for product evaluation; 4.27 (Sony) vs. 4.01 (Takai), $t_{1,266} = .31, p > .10$ for purchase intention). Rather than the strong brand overcomes the negative COM effect as predicted in the hypothesis, COM seems to compensate for the negative effect of weak brand.

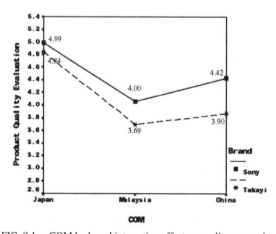

FIG. 9.1.   COM by brand interaction effect on quality perception.

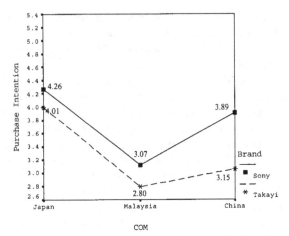

FIG. 9.2.   COM by brand interaction effect on purchase intention.

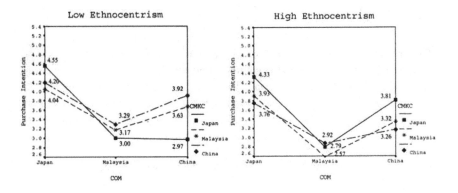

FIG. 9.3.   COM by CMKC by ethnocentrism interaction effect on purchase intention.

Last, the moderating effect of ethnocentrism is observed as a three-way interaction among COM, CMKC and ethnocentrism in the purchase intention measure. The nature the three-way interaction is shown in Fig. 9.3. The detailed explanation of this relation follows in the discussion section.

DISCUSSION

This study examines how Chinese consumers evaluate a hybrid country-of-origin product that has multiple country origins with regard to its key component and manufacture site. Effect of brand name is examined as well. Several interesting findings are observed. First, country of origin of key component (CMKC) does not significantly influence product quality evaluation, perceived risk, or purchasing intention, whereas country of manufacture (COM) and brand do. This finding suggests the assembly location of the final product is more important than the location of its key component when a product has multiple countries of origin.

Second, regarding the relative influence between COM and brand name, the effect of COM is found to be more salient than that of brand. This is evidenced by two factors: difference in the magnitude of the effects (i.e., Eta square) and the pattern of the significant interaction effect between COM and brand name. The Eta square of the COM main effect was .54, whereas the Eta square of brand main effect was .06. This finding indicates that more than half the total variance (54%) is explained by the COM main effect. The pattern of the COM by brand interaction also confirms a stronger effect of COM over brand. Although it mitigates the COM effect to some extent, the effect of well-known brand name cannot overcome the negative COM effect. On the other hand, the negative effect of weak brand name seems to be compensated for by the strong positive COM effect.

Third, the comparisons between the China COM condition and the Malaysia COM condition confirm the general tendency of preference for domestic products over foreign products (Bileky & Nes, 1982). Product quality evaluation and purchase intention of the product manufactured from China were higher than those from Malaysia (4.16 vs. 3.88, $t_{1, 266} = 5.17$, $p < .01$ for product quality evaluation; 3.52 vs. 2.96, $t_{1, 266} = 5.26$, $p < .01$ for purchase intention), whereas the perceived risk was lower (3.97 vs. 4.24, $t_{1, 266} = 2.75$, $p < .01$). In general, however, this tendency of preference for domestic products was not strong enough to overcome the COM effect (i.e., overcoming the negative COM effect of home country against the developed country).

The moderating effect of ethnocentrism is evidenced in the three-way interaction among COM, CMKC, and ethnocentrism in the purchase intention measure. Although the ethnocentrism could not overcome COM effect between developed and developing domestic countries, it could influence purchase intention between products from similar developing countries, depending on CMKC conditions. This study found that when the CMKC was Japan, there was no difference in purchase intention between the China COM and the Malaysia COM conditions for the low-ethnocentric consumer group (2.97 vs. 3.00, $t_{1, 37} = .71$, $p = .94$), whereas the purchase intention of the China COM condition was higher than that of the Malaysia condition for the high-ethnocentric consumer group (3.81 vs. 2.79, $t_{1, 51} = 4.49$, $p < .01$). However, when CMKC was from developing countries including home country, the general tendency of preference for domestic product was observed from Chinese consumers. From this finding, it could be inferred that Chinese consumers' ethnocentrism is only triggered when CMKC is from developed countries. Because the country-of-origin concept is inherently related to nationalism and patriotism (Dichter, 1962), consumers may tend to prefer the domestic product by default. The effect of ethnocentrism kicks in when the country-of-origin concept becomes complex, as in the case of hybrid COO products, and when the additional country-of-origin information provided by the hybrid product is important and relevant. When the key component is from developed countries, it may be regarded as important and relevant information. Therefore, it may be processed deeply and may trigger the ethnocentric tendency of Chinese consumers. On the other hand, when it is from other developing countries, it may not be regarded as important; thus, it may not be processed deeply and may not trigger the ethnocentric tendency of Chinese consumers. To validate this speculation, however, a more elaborated study on this aspect is needed in the future.

Although we found interesting results, this study has several limitations. The sample of this study was not a representation of the Chinese population. China is a big country with a 1.2 billion population. The sample of this study was drawn only from southern China. The results may be different with more samples from all parts of China. Because the findings are likely to be product specific, a greater variety of products should be included in future studies.

Research suggests product involvement had a significant influence on the use of country label (Ettenson et al., 1988; Wall et al., 1990). A color television is a high-involvement and high-priced product. Products that are of low involvement are not examined and may not yield similar results. There are other product classes that may mediate the respondents' perceptions and thus need to be studied to verify the generalization of these findings.

Also, this study included only three countries, which may not provide a complete picture of country of manufacture. More countries should be examined. In addition, the brands used in this study originated from developed countries, which may result in a biased finding. Brands that originated from developing countries may not yield the same findings. Future study can add other dimensions of country variables, such as country of engineering, into the research. More information cues should be included on product evaluation in future study.

ACKNOWLEDGMENT

The authors thank Hu Xiaohong for her valuable assistance in the development of this study and data collection.

REFERENCES

Aaker, D. A. (1991). *Managing brand equity.* New York: The Free Press.
Aaker, D. A., & Keller, K. L. (1990). Consumer evaluations of brand extensions. *Journal of Marketing, 54,* 27–41.
Ahmed, S. A., & d'Astous, A. (1995). Comparison of country-of-origin effects on household and organizational buyers' product perceptions. *European Journal of Marketing, 29,* 35–51.
Ahmed, S. A., & d'Astous, A. (1996). Country of origin and brand effects: A multi-dimensional and multi-attribute study. *Journal of International Consumer Marketing, 9,* 93–115.
Ahmed, S. A., d'Astous, A., & Zouiten, S. (1993). Personality variables and the made-in concept. In N. Papadopoulos & L. A. Heslop (Eds.), *Product–country images: Impact*

and role in international marketing (pp. 197–222). New York: International Business Press.

Bilkey, W. J., & Nes, E. (1982). Country-of-origin effects on product evaluations. *Journal of International Business Studies, 13,* 89–95.

Cattin, P., Jolibert, A., & Lohnes, C. (1982). A cross-cultural study of "made in" concepts. *Journal of International Business Studies, 13,* 131–141.

Chao, P. (1989a). Export and reverse investment: Strategic implications for newly industrialized countries. *Journal of International Business Studies, 20,* 75–91.

Chao, P. (1989b). The impact of country affiliation on the credibility of product attribute claims. *Journal of Advertising Research, April/May,* 35–41.

Chao, P. (1993). Partitioning country of origin effects: Consumer evaluations of a hybrid product. *Journal of International Business Studies, 2,* 291–306.

Chao, P. (2001). The moderating effects of country of assembly, country of parts, and country of design on hybrid product evaluations. *Journal of Advertising, 30,* 67–81.

Chay, R.F. (1991). How marketing researches can harness the power of brand equity, *Marketing Research, 9,* 30–37.

Cordell, V. V. (1992). Effects of consumer preferences for foreign sourced products. *Journal of International Business Studies, 23,* 251–270.

Cordell, V. V. (1993). Interaction effects of country of origin with branding, price, and perceived performance risk. *Journal of International Consumer Marketing, 5,* 5–20.

Dichter, E. (1962). The world customer. *Harvard Business Review, 40,* 113–122.

Ettenson, R. (1994). Brand name and country of origin effects in the emerging market economies of Russia, Poland and Hungary. *International Marketing Review, 10,* 14–36.

Ettenson, R., Wagner, R. J., & Gaeth, G. (1988). Evaluating the effects of country of origin and the "made in the USA" campaign: A conjoint approach. *Journal of Retailing, 64,* 85–100.

Han, C. M., & Terpstra, V. (1988). Country-of-origin effects for uni-national and bi-national products. *Journal of International Business Studies, 19,* 235–256.

Herche, J. (1992). A note on the predictive validity of the CETSCALE. *Journal of Academy of Marketing Science, 20,* 261–264.

Hui, M. K., & Zhou, L. (2002). Linking product evaluations and purchase intentions for country-of-origin effects. *Journal of Global Marketing, 15,* 95–116.

Iyer, G. R., & Kalita, J. K. (1997). The impact of country of origin and country of manufacture cues on consumer perceptions of quality and value. *Journal of Global Marketing, 11,* 7–28.

Jacoby, J., Olson, J., & Haddock, R. (1971). Price, brand name and product composition characteristics as determinants of perceived quality. *Journal of Applied Psychology, 55,* 470–479.

Jacoby, J., Szybillo, G., & Busato-Schach, J. (1977). Information acquisition behavior in brand choice situations. *Journal of Consumer Research, 3,* 209–216.

Johansson, J. K. (1989). Determinants and effects of the use of "made-in" labels. *International Marketing Review, 6,* 27–41.

Johansson, J. K., Douglas, S. P., & Nonaka, I. (1985). Assessing the impact of country of origin on product evaluations: A new methodological perspective. *Journal of Marketing Research, 22,* 388–396.

Johansson, J. K., & Nebenzahl, I. D. (1986). Multinational production: Effect on brand value. *Journal of International Business Studies, 17,* 101–126.

Khanna, S. R. (1986). Asian companies and the country stereotype paradox: An empirical study. *Columbia Journal of World Business, 21,* 29–38.

Li, D., & Gallup, A. M. (1995). In search of the Chinese consumer. *The China Business Review, 22,* 19–22.

Moon, B. J., & Jain, S. C. (2001). Consumer processing of international advertising: The roles of country of origin and consumer ethnocentrism. *Journal of International Consumer Marketing, 14,* 89–109.

Nagashima, A. (1970). A comparison of Japanese and U.S. attitudes toward foreign products. *Journal of Marketing, 34,* 68–74.

Nagashima, A. (1977). A comparative 'made in' product–images survey among Japanese businessmen. *Journal of Marketing, 41,* 95–100.

Nes, E. B. (1981). *Consumer perceptions of product risk and quality for goods manufactured in developing versus industrialized nations.* Unpublished doctoral dissertation. University of Wisconsin, Madison.

Nes, E., & Bilkey, W. J. (1993). A multi-cue test of country of origin theory. In N. Papadopoulos & L. A. Heslop (Eds.), *Product-country images: Impact and role in international marketing* (pp. 179–196). New York: International Business Press.

Okechuku, C. (1994). The importance of product country of origin: A conjoint analysis of the United States, Canada, Germany and the Netherlands. *European Journal of Marketing, 28,* 5–19.

Pecotich, A., & Rosenthal, M. (2001). Country of origin, quality, brand and consumer ethnocentrism. *Journal of Global Marketing, 15,* 31–60.

Perterson, R.A., & Jolibert, A. J. P. (1995). A meta-analysis of country-of-origin effects. *Journal of International Business Studies, 26,* 883–900.

Porter, M. (1980). *Competitive strategy.* New York: The Free Press.

Samiee, S. (1994). Customer evaluation of products in a global market. *Journal of International Business Studies, 25,* 579–604.

Samiee, S., Shimp, T., and Snyder, D. (1990). Consumers' cognitive structures for countries and their products. In W. Bearden, R. Despande, T. J. Madden, P. R. Varadarajan, A. Parasuram, V. S. Folkes, D. W. Stewart, and W. L. Wilke (Eds.), *Enhancing knowledge development in marketing* (43). Chicago: American Marketing Association.

Schooler, R. D. (1965). Product bias in the Central American common market. *Journal of Marketing Research, 2,* 394–397.

Shimp, T., & Sharma, S. (1987). Consumer ethnocentrism: Construction and validation of the CETSCALE. *Journal of Marketing Research, 24,* 280–289.

Tse, D. K., & Gorn, G. J. (1993). An experiment on the salience of country of origin in the era of global brands. *Journal of International Marketing, 1,* 57–76.

Tse, D. K., & Lee, W. (1993). Removing negative country images: Effects of decomposition, branding, and product experience. *Journal of International Marketing, 1,* 25–48.

Verlegh, P., & Steenkamp, E. M. (1999). A review and meta-analysis of country-of-origin research. *Journal of Economic Psychology, 20,* 521–546.

Wall, M., Liefeld, J., & Heslop, L. A. (1991). Impact of country of origin cues on consumer judgments in multi-cue situations: A covariance analysis. *Journal of the Academy of Marketing Science, 19,* 105–113.

Part III—Individual and Celebrity Source Image

Cornwell (1995) described sponsorship marketing as the " ... orchestration and implementation of marketing activities for the purpose of building and communicating an association (link) to a sponsorship" (p. 15). In the last two or three decades, the practice of commercial sponsorship by companies for marketing programs has increased at an exponential rate. In accordance with the growth in interest, research into the area of commercial sponsorship has surged. By leveraging on a successful celebrity brand and establishing a good fit between product and brand (i.e., "the celebrity"), marketers can improve the brand image and appeal of their products or services. This section includes the leveraging of individuals (i.e., celebrities, models, etc.) to endorse products for advertising purposes. Also, celebrity source image (i.e., the process and implications of endorsements for the celebrity and endorser), cross-cultural studies on advertisements and individuals, and individual source expertise are discussed.

CHAPTER TEN

Managing Celebrities as Brands: Impact of Endorsements on Celebrity Image

Ajit Arun Parulekar and Preety Raheja
Goa Institute of Management, India

The use of celebrities in advertisements is gaining popularity due to the belief of marketers that endorsement messages delivered by the celebrity will result in greater consumer attention and subsequently better recall, a higher degree of appeal, reinforce the image of the brand and increase the likelihood of purchase of the endorsed brand (Atkin & Block, 1983; Burnett & Menon, 1993). It is estimated that more than 15% of all television advertising include celebrity endorsements (Bradley, 1996; Sherman, 1985). In the endorsement process, celebrities may be used in four possible ways. First, in a testimonial, the celebrity has personally used the brand and attests to its quality. Second are endorsements wherein celebrities only lend their names to the brands. The celebrity can also be used as an actor, in which case the celebrity enacts a character rather than a personal testimonial or endorsement, as in the case of Pierce Brosnan who enacts James Bond in the endorsements for Omega watches, Reid and Taylor suitings, and Ericsson mobile phones. Finally, the celebrity can be a spokesperson or brand ambassador, in which case the celebrity represents a brand over an extended period of time (Schiffman & Kanuk, 2000).

Considerable amount of research has examined the benefits a brand stands to gain by associating with endorsers, more specifically with celebrity endorsers, because the endorsement fees for high profile celebrities like golfer Tiger Woods, cricketer Sachin Tendulkar, singer Geri Halliwell (Ginger Spice), and other similar celebrities run into millions of dollars (Carvalho, 2001; Pappas, 1999). Are these phenomenally larger sums paid to celebrity endorsers over noncelebrity endorsers worth the premium?

The use of celebrity endorsers was found more appropriate than noncelebrity endorsers for products where the major risk involved for the consumer was social or psychological risk, involving elements like self-image and presence or lack of good taste (Friedman & Friedman, 1979).

Gail et al. (1992) compared the effectiveness of celebrity spokespersons versus created spokespersons, like Betty Crocker of General Mills and Joe Isuzu of Isuzu Motors. Although celebrity endorsers were unparalleled in their ability to get consumer attention to advertisements and thereby to the endorsed brand, created spokespersons were more effective in establishing a link to the product owing to their singular association with a specific product over a long period of time. Celebrities, lured by generous compensation offered by marketers, opt to advocate several products, resulting in overexposure, reduced credibility, and a muddied image (Klebba & Unger, 1983; Tripp, Jenson, & Carlson, 1994). Additionally, a marketer can control the development of created spokespersons by endowing them with characteristics that are desired by and effective with the target consumers of the endorsed product.

Baker and Churchill (1977) evaluated the impact of sex and attractiveness of the celebrity on the endorsed brand. Their findings suggest that sex and attractiveness of the celebrity are important in the attention-getting value of the advertisement but are ineffective in influencing beliefs of the consumers about the endorsed brand.

Although a lot of research has evaluated the effect of celebrity endorsers on products, very little research has focused on the impact of the endorsed brand on the image of the celebrity. The only study that has examined the influence of an endorsed product on the image of the celebrity endorser (Till, 2001) is a 2 X 2 X 2 factorial design that examined the influence that the type of product—differentiated as a positively evaluated product, orange juice, and a negatively evaluated product, chewing tobacco—has on the image of two types of celebrities; a volleyball player (i.e., athlete) and a fashion model (i.e., nonathlete). The findings pointed out that the product a celebrity endorses affects the evaluation of the celebrity. In this study, associating the celebrity with chewing tobacco (i.e., a negatively evaluated product) lowered the evaluation of the celebrity endorser more than associating the endorser with orange juice (i.e., positively evaluated product).

As an endorsement results in a relationship between a celebrity and a brand, it is equally valid to evaluate the impact that the endorsed brand has on the celebrity. After all, the celebrity is a brand in his or her own right (Carvalho, 2001). Celebrities have become astute in managing their own brand images to enhance their brand equity and then attaching it to a saleable product or service for a price (Pappas, 1999). Celebrities employ professional celebrity managers like Worldtel and Mark McCormack's IMG to actively manage their "brands." Celebrities such as Tiger Woods limit the number of brands they endorse and choose to endorse only those brands that will best fit and complement their own images (Carvalho, 2001).

Various frameworks, models, and theories have been propounded to understand how celebrities add value to brands through endorsements, the criteria for choosing the most appropriate celebrity for a brand, and the impact of changes in the image of the celebrity on the image of the endorsed brand. However, there is very little evidence of the impact of endorsed brands on the celebrity endorsers' images.

RESEARCH OBJECTIVE

The purpose of this conceptual study is to determine the effect of the endorsed brand on the image of the celebrity by first examining the applicability of the models developed to understand the effect of the celebrity on the endorsed brand for studying the impact that the endorsed brand has on the celebrity. Also, a goal is to develop a basis for determining the right fit between a celebrity brand and the endorsed product or service brand.

EFFECTIVENESS OF CELEBRITIES AS BRAND ENDORSERS

Source Models

The source credibility and source attractiveness models were the first models that attempted to explain the effectiveness of celebrity endorsers. The source credibility model contends that the effectiveness of a celebrity depends on the degree of expertise and trustworthiness of the source (Ohanian, 1991; Sternthal, Dholakia, & Leavitt, 1978). The source attractiveness model asserts that effectiveness of an endorsement depends upon the familiarity, likeability, and similarity of a celebrity endorser (Baker & Churchill, 1977; Joseph, 1982). Research has shown that the type of celebrity—in terms of attractiveness and sex of the celebrity (Baker & Churchill, 1977) and even the sport of the athlete celebrity—influences the effectiveness of the endorsement (Martin, 1996). The source models focus only on the celebrity and ignore the product. They do not allow marketers to understand the appeal of the celebrity or to discriminate among various types of celebrities in terms of their unique qualities and appeal (Klebba & Unger, 1983).

Match-Up Hypothesis

Effectiveness of celebrity endorsements is more than just the expertise, trustworthiness, attractiveness, and sex of the celebrity. Otherwise, the same celebrity would have been effective for a whole range of products. Bill Cosby was successful as an endorser for Kodak and Coca Cola; however, he failed as an endorser for E. F. Hutton (McCracken, 1989).The effectiveness depends on a synergistic association or match-up of the brand to be endorsed and the celebrity endorser (Kamins, 1990). The physical attractiveness of a celebrity (e.g., Tom Selleck) was found to improve the respondents' evaluations of the product and advertisements only for an attractiveness-related product (i.e., a luxury car) and had no effect on the attractiveness-unrelated product (i.e., a computer). The findings suggest a need for congruence between the image of the celebrity and that of the endorsed product or brand. Conversely, an endorsement will enhance the image of the celebrity to the extent that the salient characteristics in the image of the endorsed brand match with the characteristics of the celebrity endorser. For instance, people perceived Winston Churchill as appropriate to endorse cigars, whiskey, and books (Levy, 1959), owing to the image consumers perceive of Winston Churchill. Celebrities own their meanings because they have created them through their careers and also by carefully managing their public lives (McCracken, 1989). Association of a celebrity with a brand by way of an endorsement will either dampen or strengthen the celebrity's brand value, depending upon the extent of match between the celebrity image and the product brand image.

Cultural Meaning Transfer

The meanings contained in a celebrity are numerous and include age, gender, status, personality, and lifestyle. Even stereotyped celebrities such as Hollywood actor Clint Eastwood (i.e., cowboy, western movies) represent not a single meaning but a set of related meanings. Celebrities build these meanings through their performances in their careers, their public lives, and associations with objects, people, and events. Association with various objects, people, and events leads to the development of the cultural meanings that reside in a celebrity. An endorsement involves the transfer of the cultural meanings of the celebrity onto the endorsed brand. The advertiser, depending on the meanings and associations desired for the brand, chooses a celebrity who is endowed with these desired cultural meanings (McCracken, 1989). Brands, too, are endowed with a multitude of associations and meanings, such as physical characteristics, personality, culture, and a self-image (Kapferer, 2000). Just as meanings get transferred from the celebrity to the brand via an endorsement, association of celebrities with brands via an endorsement changes the meanings contained in the personas of the celebrity endorsers. Celebrities have been known to exploit this effect by carefully choosing their endorsements so as to enhance their own brand images.

The extent to which the brand image and the celebrity image are influenced by the endorsement process, in terms of transfer of cultural meanings from their association, depends upon how well defined each of these two brands are. A brand that lacks a well-defined image will be influenced to a larger extent by association with a brand that has a stronger and well-defined brand image (Walker, Langmeyer, & Langmeyer, 1992). The transfer of cultural meanings will happen for positive as well as negative information about the brand and the celebrity (Till & Shimp, 1998).

Schema Congruity Theory and Associative Learning

The schema congruity theory offers further insight beyond the match hypothesis and cultural meanings transfer model. A schema is an organized web of associations and expectations that a consumer has for a celebrity, product, or any other object. The schematic memory of a brand or celebrity is what the consumer thinks of and feels when the name of the brand or celebrity is mentioned (Hawkins, Best, & Coney, 2002). In the long-term memory of consumers, every brand (i.e., product, service, or celebrity) that the consumer is aware of represents a node that in turn is associated with other objects, people, contexts, and concepts. These interconnected nodes represent the association set or schema that the consumer has for the brand and for the celebrity (Till & Nowak, 2000). The number of associations that a brand possesses in the mind of a consumer forms the brand's or celebrity's association set. It is the collection of associations and affiliations that a consumer attaches to a brand.

These association sets are consumer specific. For example, a consumers association set for Nike may consist of the swoosh, athletes such as Michael Jordan and Tiger Woods who endorse Nike, Seattle as the corporate headquarters of Nike, Air Jordan and the pair of Nikes he owns (Till & Nowak, 2000). Another individual may not even be aware of Nike and hence will have formed a very small and probably vague association set for the brand.

Brands having a high number of positive associations have stronger brand equity (Aaker, 1991). If the association sets of the celebrity and the endorsed brand are a complete match, then the endorsement gets a positive response from the consumer. When the two association sets are a mismatch, the endorsement will not be accepted by the consumer. For example, if the association set for a consumer for Michael Jordan consists of Chicago Bulls, Nike, the University of North Carolina, the Dream Team, basketball, baseball, and Gatorade, then the degree of overlap of the association sets the consumers has for Michael Jordan and Nike will facilitate the development of a positive associative link between the brand and the celebrity and will consequently enhance the association sets and brand equity of both Nike and Michael Jordan (McSweeney & Bierley, 1984).

CELEBRITIES AS BRANDS

"The celebrity is known to the public for his accomplishments in areas unrelated to the product class endorsed" (Page 22 Friedman, Termini, & Washington, 1976). Celebrities including movie stars, sportspersons, models, rock stars, and televisions anchors derive a large chunk of their incomes from endorsements. These celebrities can be considered as brands (Till, 2001; Carvalho, 2001). Factors such as their personality, personal behavior on and off their careers, and their professional competency contribute to their marketability and overall brand image.

Celebrities need to be sensitive to the need to manage their brand image by assessing the impact of every action they take on their brand equity. Their careers and public lives are like large ads. Continually the celebrity comes into contact with objects, people ,and contexts that transfer meanings and build associations for the celebrity (McCracken, 1989). The celebrity has to be astute in choosing the objects, activities, and people to ensure that desirable associations and meanings are added to the celebrity brand, similar to the manner in which product, service, and corporate brands strengthen their images and equity by way of intense focus on associations that are synergistic with and strengthen their own positioning (Aaker, 1991). The variety of meanings contained in a celebrity includes distinctions of status, age, gender, class, personality, and lifestyle. If a brand wants to acquire some of these associations, the advertiser associates the brand with the celebrity who owns the particular desired association.

Interestingly, celebrities are relatively unaware of the impact of this meaning transfer process on their image, positioning, and marketability. This is evident when actors say they dislike being cast in a similar role repeatedly, claiming that this casting restricts their career and creativity options (McCracken, 1989). It is, however, precisely typecasting that makes brands, including celebrities, create and occupy a distinct and firm position in the minds of the consumers. Without typecasting or focus, celebrities bring ambiguous meanings to their own brands and undermine their own brand images and marketability.

Many celebrity endorsers represent not themselves but their stage personas in their endorsements. For example, Pierce Brosnan represents James Bond in most of his endorsements. In such a case, what will be the impact of the endorsement on the stage persona and on the celebrity himself or herself? In this case, the association set of the stage persona, the celebrity, and the endorsed brand should have a match. They should complement one another for all three brands to benefit from the endorsement.

The stage persona of a celebrity is the brand image, whereas the celebrity himself or herself forms the brand identity. If the brand image is not congruent with the brand identity of the celebrity, consumers will form a ambiguous image of the celebrity, resulting in depreciation of brand equity of the celebrity and the stage persona (Kapferer, 2000).

BRAND PERSONALITY OF CELEBRITIES

The perception that an individual has of the personality of another living human being is based on that human being's behavior, physical appearance, attitudes and beliefs, and demographic profile (Park, 1986). However, the perception that an individual forms about the personality of a brand (i.e., product, service, or corporate) is based on the product attributes, product class, brand name, symbol and logo, advertising style, user imagery, corporate associations, and event sponsorships (Aaker, 1996). Direct and indirect contact of the consumer with the brand is responsible for formation of these perceptions of the personality of a brand (Plummer, 2000).

How do consumers form the perception about the personality of celebrities? Is it formed like human personalities or like brand personalities? Celebrities are living human brands, which share some similarities and some differences with product and service brands. Consumers perceive these celebrity brands based on the direct and indirect exposure that they have to them. Consumers infer the physical characteristics, demographics, and especially attitudes and beliefs of a celebrity based on the performance of the celebrity in his or her professional career, the roles played in public and private life (i.e., consumers often get a peek into private lives of celebrities due to the press coverage of incidents in the private lives of celebrities), and the people, objects, and events (such as social causes) the celebrity is associated with.

The brands that celebrities endorse have a very large bearing on the way their personality perceptions are formed by consumers. This is due to the high exposure consumers get to these associations, owing to the astute media selection and planning by the advertiser of these brands.

Personal miscues (e.g., by Michael Jackson, Mike Tyson, O. J. Simpson), which are transformed into public reputations by the press, special interest groups, and public investigations, are another source of influence on the perception of brand personality of celebrities, against which celebrities have to guard themselves. Miscues can significantly reduce their credibility, likeability, and appeal as endorsers (Klebba & Unger, 1983; Till & Shimp, 1998).

CONCLUSIONS AND FUTURE RESEARCH

Most research on endorsement has focused on the impact that the endorser has on the endorsed brand. In the past, celebrities have managed their personal brands with a short-term perspective, choosing brand endorsements mainly based on the endorsement fees, without evaluating the effects on their brand images. This process has undermined the longevity of the celebrity as a brand, resulting in most celebrities diminishing their potential as endorsers and celebrities. This charge has been a major contributing factor behind celebrities losing their endorsement potential when they reach the end of their professional careers. Celebrities too have the potential of becoming immortal brands as product, service, and corporate brands. Hence, this study has focused on celebrities as brands and has attempted to evaluate the effect an endorsed brand has on the image and brand equity of a celebrity. Celebrities are becoming increasingly conscious of themselves as brands, and a trend of employing professional celebrity managers to manage celebrities' personal brands has emerged.

Many frameworks are available for product and service brands that cannot be applied in their existing form to celebrity brands. Future research can be aimed at developing a framework to diagnose and manage a celebrity as a brand.

REFERENCES

Aaker, D. A. (1991). *Managing brand equity: Capitalizing on the value of a brand name.* New York: The Free Press.
Aaker, D. A. (1996). *Building strong brands.* New York: The Free Press.

Atkin, C., & Block, M. (1983). Effectiveness of celebrity endorsers. *Journal of Advertising Research, 23*(1), 57–61.

Baker, M. J., & Churchill, G. A. (1977). The impact of physically attractive models on advertising evaluations. *Journal of Marketing Research, 14,* 538–555.

Bradley, S. (1996, February 26). Marketers are always looking for good pitchers. *Brandweek,* 36–37.

Burnett, J., & Menon, A. (1993). Sports marketing: A new Ball game with new rules. *Journal of Advertising Research, 33*(5), 21–35.

Carvalho, B. (2001, June 21). Sachin Tendulkar: Celebrity or Brand? Business *Today, 10*(11), 58–61.

Friedman, H. H., & Friedman, L. (1979). Endorser effectiveness by product type. *Journal of Advertising Research, 19*(5), 63–71.

Friedman, H. H., Termini, S., & Washington, R. (1976). Effectiveness of advertisements utilizing four types of endorsers. *Journal of Advertising, 5*(3), 22–24.

Gail, T., Clark, R., Elmer, L., Grech, E., Masetti, J. Jr., & Harmona, S. (1992). The use of created versus celebrity spokespersons in advertisements. *Journal of Consumer Marketing, 9*(4), 45–51.

Hawkins, D. I., Best, R. J., & Coney, K. A. (2002). *Consumer behavior: Building marketing strategy* (8th ed.). New Delhi: Tata McGraw-Hill.

Joseph, B. W. (1982). The credibility of physically attractive communicators: A review. *Journal of Advertising, 11*(3), 15–24.

Kamins, M. A. (1990). An investigation into the 'match-up' hypothesis in celebrity advertising: When beauty may be only skin deep. *Journal of Advertising, 19*(1), 4–13.

Kapferer, J. N. (2000). *Strategic brand management: Creating and sustaining brand equity long term* (2nd ed.). New Delhi: Kogan Page.

Klebba, J. M., & Unger, L. S. (1983). The impact of negative and positive information on source credibility in a field setting. In R. P. Bagozzi & A. M. Tybout (10th Ed.), *Advances in consumer research* (pp. 11–16). Ann Arbor, MI: Association for Consumer Research.

Levy, S. J. (1959). Symbols for sale. *Harvard Business Review, 37*(4), 117–134.

Martin, J. H. (1996). Is the athlete's sport important when picking an athlete to endorse a non-sport product. *Journal of Consumer Marketing, 13*(6), 28–43.

McCracken, G. (1989). Who is the celebrity endorser? Cultural foundations of the endorsement process. *Journal of Consumer Research, 16*(3), 310–321.

McSweeney, F. K., & Bierley, C. (1984). Recent developments in classical conditioning. *Journal of Consumer Research, 11*(2), 619–631.

Ohanian, R. (1991). The impact of celebrity spokespersons' perceived image on consumers' intention to purchase. *Journal of Advertising Research, 31*(1), 46–55.

Pappas, B. (1999). Star power, star brands. *Forbes Magazine Online,* Vol. 6.

Park, B. (1986). A method for studying the development of impressions of real people. *Journal of Personality and Social Psychology, 51,* 907–917.

Plummer, J. T. (2000). How personality makes a difference. *Journal of Advertising Research, 40*(6), 79–83.

Schiffman, L. G., & Kanuk, L. L. (2000). *Consumer behavior* (6th ed.). New Delhi: Prentice-Hall.

Sherman, S. P. (1985, August 18). When you wish upon a star. *Fortune,* 66–71.

Sternthal, B., Dholakia, R. R., & Leavitt, C. (1978). The persuasive effect of source credibility: Tests of cognitive response. *Journal of Consumer Research, 4*(4), 252–260.

Till, B. D. (2001). Managing athlete endorser image: The effect of endorsed product. *Sport Marketing Quarterly, 10*(1), 35–42.

Till, B. D., & Nowak, L. I. (2000). Toward effective use of cause-related marketing alliances. *Journal of Product and Brand Management, 9*(7), 472–484.

Till, B. D., & Shimp, T. A. (1998). Endorsers in advertising: The case of negative celebrity information. *Journal of Advertising, 27*(1), 67–82.

Tripp, C., Jensen, T. D., & Carlson, L. (1994). The effects of multiple product endorsements by celebrities on consumers. *Journal of Consumer Research, 20*(4), 535–547.

Walker, M., Langmeyer, L., & Langmeyer, D. (1992). Celebrity endorsers: Do you get what you pay for? *The Journal of Services Marketing, 6,* 35–42.

CHAPTER ELEVEN

A Cultural Third-Person Effect: Actual and Expected Effects of Source Expertise Among Individualists and Collectivists

Sukki Yoon
Cleveland State University

Patrick T. Vargas
University of Illinois at Urbana-Champaign

Imagine someone asking the following question: "Would you describe yourself as unique or harmonious?" Regardless of which part of the globe the reader is from, the most likely answer to this question would probably be, "I am neither that unique nor that harmonious." Or one may respond, "I am kind of a harmonious (or unique) person." This propensity to view oneself as a mixture of both unique and harmonious, regardless of one's cultural background, may be somewhat surprising to a casual reader of cross-cultural psychology. Previous research provides extensive evidence of Eastern–Western cultural differences. For example, East Asians tend to value harmony, which is a core concept of collectivism, and North Americans tend to value uniqueness, a core concept of individualism (e.g., Kim & Markus, 1999).

A vast body of literature in cross-cultural psychology suggests that Eastern society emphasizes an interdependent perspective of the self, whereas Western society emphasizes an independent perspective of the self (e.g., Triandis, 1995). Accordingly, the ideal member of a society is also likely to be defined differently depending on the culture to which he or she belongs. East Asians are taught to be in tune with group norms (Chao, 1994); in contrast, the most important Western cultural values include freedom and individual rights. As Kim and Markus (1999) noted, uniqueness in the United States may be considered deviance in East Asia; and harmony in East Asia may be considered conformity in the United States. Although literature in psychology indicates the existence of cross-national differences,

171

sometimes people, when directly asked, do not seem to express these differences in an obvious way (Heine, Lehman, Peng, & Greenholtz, 2002).

Now consider another question: "Compared to yourself, do you view other members in your society as more unique or more harmonious?" In this chapter, we propose that most East Asians' answer to the latter question would be "more harmonious." Certain cultural values are likely to be overemphasized in East Asian societies, so it may be the case that a person living in a collectivistic country views others in the same nation as relatively more collectivistic than they actually are. This idea leads to the main thesis of this chapter: Among East Asians, there will be a perceived difference between oneself and others in the degree of conformity to one's own cultural values.

Previous research indicates that differences in cultural orientation influence patterns of emotions and behavior. For example, individualism is positively correlated with the perception of negative emotions (Matsumoto, 1989), and collectivism is associated with child rearing patterns that emphasize conformity, obedience, and reliability (Triandis, 1989). Evidence suggests differences between Eastern and Western cultures in the manner in which individuals respond to persuasive messages. According to Aaker and Maheswaran (1997), certain heuristic cues may be use more frequently in collectivist cultures than in individualist cultures. In most studies that have examined cross-cultural differences in persuasion, participants were asked directly to report their own attitudes toward certain objects (e.g., I like brand X), but little has been done to examine cross-cultural differences in how others are perceived (e.g., I think people will like brand X) or how self and others are perceived differently (e.g., I like brand X, but most people will not like it). With this in mind, we try to build on the previous work in this area by addressing the issue of cross-cultural differences in terms of the self–other discrepancy in perceiving persuasive arguments endorsed by expert versus nonexpert sources in advertising.

A large amount of research in social psychology indicates that people often hold biased views of themselves and others (e.g., Alicke, Klotz, Breitenbecher, Yurak, & Vredenburg, 1995). One such bias that seems most relevant to advertising is the third-person effect. This effect occurs when people perceive that the influence of media will be greater on others than on themselves (Davison, 1983). Although many studies have yielded robust support for the third-person effect (e.g., Lasorsa, 1992), researchers have failed to agree on why and how this perceived self–other discrepancy takes place. Although a variety of psychological theories have been used to explain the third-person effect (e.g., attribution theory, self-serving bias, etc.), research has yet to provide a definitive single explanation of how or why individuals perceive themselves as less resistant or others as more susceptible to media messages. However, it is clear that people are prone either to overestimate media impact on others or to underestimate media impact on the self (Price, Huang, & Tewksbury, 1997). Meta-analyses suggest that the third-person effect becomes more salient when the nature of the message is persuasive (Paul, Salwen, & Dupagne, 2000). In this regard, many studies examining the third-person effect were conducted in an advertising context (Henriksen & Flora, 1999; Prabu, Morrison, Johnson, & Ross, 2002; Shah, Faber, & Young, 1999; Youn & Faber, 2000). This chapter considers a cross-cultural version of the third-person effect in the context of advertising. More specifically, we contend that others are perceived to be more influenced by their own cultures than oneself in the context of source-expertise effects in persuasion.

The remainder of this chapter is organized as follows. First, we discuss more fully what is meant by the cultural-third-person effect. We then briefly review previous work in source expertise from the perspective of cross-cultural psychology. Next, we provide some evidence of the cultural-third person effect that emerges between nations and discuss the role of an individual's culture in the context of source expertise perception. Finally, we discuss implications of this perspective for researchers and practitioners in advertising.

CULTURAL DIFFERENCES AMONG NATIONS AND INDIVIDUALS

Nearly 25 years ago, on the basis of a large-scale value survey, Hofstede (1980) proposed four dimensions of cultural variation: power distance, uncertainty avoidance, individualism and collectivism, and masculinity. Among these, individualism and collectivism is one dimension that has generated a great deal of new research over the past 20 years. Most cross-cultural studies have been conducted by contrasting European American and East Asian cultures (e.g., Chan, 1994; Kitayama, Markus, Matsumoto, & Norasakkunkit, 1997; Yamaguchi, 1994). In Hofstede's (1980) study, most European and North American countries emerged as high on individualism, whereas most Latin American and Asian countries emerged as low on individualism. In a recent meta-analysis, Oyserman, Coon, and Kemmelmeier (2002) reviewed over 80 studies and concluded that Americans differ in individualism and collectivism from people in other countries and that individualism and collectivism influence basic psychological processes such as self-concept, well-being, and attribution style. Also, a variety of measurement scales that directly and indirectly assess the construct of individualism and collectivism have been developed (e.g., Triandis, Bontempo, Villareal, Asai, & Lucca, 1993).

Although controversy remains over whether the two dimensions of culture (i.e., individualism and collectivism) are independent constructs or a single construct conceptualizing individualism as the opposite of collectivism, researchers have often, but not always, agreed on the latter because in most situations the construct of individualism and collectivism is believed to reflect contrasting world views. Consistent with this view, it has traditionally been assumed that individualism and collectivism form a single continuum, with low individualism isomorphic with high collectivism (e.g., Hofstede, 1980). This bipolar single dimension approach is popular among researchers studying psychological implications of individualism and

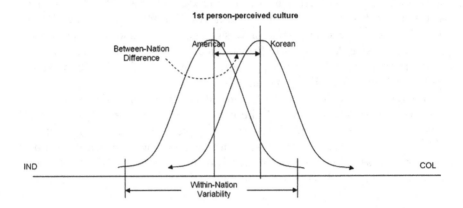

FIG. 11.1.   First-person between- and within-nation cultural variability. Adapted from Yoon et al. (2005).

collectivism (see Oyserman et al., 2002). In the studies presented in this chapter, we follow this conventional assumption of unidimensionality of the construct.

The focus of the majority of the past studies has been on cultural values at the aggregate level (e.g., nations), emphasizing intercultural units (Oyserman et al., 2002). However, it is important to note that the development of measures for individualism and collectivism is based on a model of individual-differences assessment. It is presumed that there is variation among individuals' tendencies toward different cultural orientations. Thus, even within the same national boundary, some may behave in a more collectivistic manner whereas others behave more individualistically. For example, a cultural difference between Korea and the United States simply refers to a mean difference between two nations in the cultural scores measured with a given cultural measurement scale. In other words, it is not that collectivists do not exist in the United States, nor that individualists do not exist in Korea, but both cultures exist, normally distributed, in each nation. A national difference between two populations (i.e., mean difference) and within-nation variation reflecting cultural differences among individuals within each nation is shown in Fig. 11.1.

PERCEIVED VERSUS ACTUAL INFLUENCE OF COLLECTIVISTIC CULTURE AMONG KOREANS

We suggest that Koreans are likely to overestimate the influence of their own culture on others within their nation (viz., a cultural third-person effect). Precisely, we believe that Koreans view other Koreans to be more collectivistic than they actually are. For example, Koreans will perceive others to be more willing to rely on the voice of an expert source in a persuasion situation.

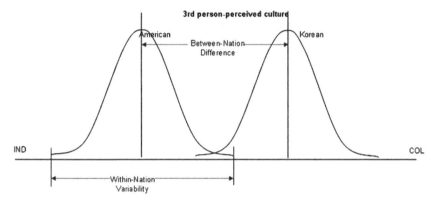

FIG. 11.2.   Third-person between- and within-nation cultural variability.

As can be seen by comparing Fig. 11.1 and Fig. 11.2, the cultural third-person effect can be represented by a larger mean difference between two nations when a person takes the third-person position rather than the first-person position (Yoon, Vargas, & Han, 2005). For example, on a given scale ranging from 1 to 10, in which higher values represent a more collectivistic orientation, imagine that the average score in the first-person position for the Korean population is 7 (see the normal curve on the right in Fig. 11.1). However, if asked to evaluate the overall collectiveness of the general public (e.g., "How collectivistic do you think other Koreans are, in general?"), on average, each individual living in Korea would say 9 (see the bell curve on the right in Fig. 11.2), reflecting a collectivistically biased view of others. This perceived difference between oneself and others is what we label a cultural-third person effect. In other words, the distance between the mean of Americans and that of Koreans in Fig. 11.1 (first person) will be smaller than the one in Fig. 11.2 (third person).

There are a number of possible reasons why a cultural third-person effect may emerge. Several studies suggest that East Asians' expectations about others are likely to be biased in the direction of collectivist cultural norms. For example, collectivist cultural norms emphasize the context of actions, whereas individualists focus primarily on the actions of themselves and of others. Consistent with these cultural norms, it has been found that, compared to North Americans, East Asians are more likely to make more external and less dispositional attributions for the behavior of others (e.g., Morris & Peng, 1994). Accordingly, the perceived discrepancy between the impact of culture on one's self and others in perceiving source expertise may be greater among East Asians than among North Americans. Because East Asians would expect others to behave according to collectivist cultural norms, and this expectation about others is likely to be greater than any expectation they hold about themselves, we believe that source expertise would be perceived as more influential in persuading others than themselves in East Asian countries.

Another possible reason for the cultural third-person effect may be the Westernization of East Asia. It seems that many Koreans hold ambivalent attitudes toward Westernization or Americanization. Although sometimes, especially in public, being Westernized may have a negative connotation and therefore is undesirable, at other times, mostly in private and among the younger generations, East Asians seem to see being independent as a positive thing. This mixed feeling about Westernization is well reflected in the following articles. *The New York Times* (French, 2002) recently reported that "Korea is a group-oriented society, where socializing in bunches is the preferred form of interaction, and Western-style individualism is frowned upon" (p. 8). On the other hand, *Joonang Ilbo* ("Generation 2030," 2002) reported that "Those in their 20s and 30s, the first Internet generation in Korea, give priority to their own time and space, rejecting all invasions of privacy. They are also changing the culture of collectivism to one of individualism" (p. C3). Koreans' conflicting feelings about the Westernization may be, to some extent, expressed in the cultural third-person effect. Although being Westernized may not be socially desirable, it may be the case that being individualistic helps Koreans preserve a positive sense of the private self (i.e., how I see myself). Considered in this framework, the observed cultural third-person effect may be considered as a form a self-serving bias, as we argue in this chapter.

We would like to make it clear that we do not have any directional hypotheses for an American sample. Americans may perceive others to be either more or less independent than themselves. If third-person effects are based on self-serving biases or actor-observer type effects, Americans may perceive themselves to be more independent than other Americans. It is also possible that Americans perceive themselves to be less independent than other Americans.

On the other hand, we also point out that the within-nation variance (i.e., within-nation individual differences) should remain unchanged in both the first- and third-person perception, although the score distribution and the mean value of Koreans are likely to move to the right on the horizontal axis in the third-person perception (see Fig. 11.1 and Fig. 11.2).

In sum, our discussion has two important implications: a) Koreans' perceptions of others may often be biased toward their own national cultural orientations (i.e., collectivism), and b) cultural differences indeed exist among individuals, regardless of one's nationality. There may be numerous conditions under which this cross- and within-national phenomenon can be manifested. One such situation where we may observe the cultural third-person effect is the differential use of heuristic cues in persuasion, such as source expertise in advertising.

SOURCE EXPERTISE AND CULTURES

Expertise, as defined by Hovland and colleagues, is the extent to which a communicator is perceived to be a source of valid assertions (Hovland, Janis, & Kelly, 1953). Source expertise tends to be operationalized by presenting a communicator who is both knowledgeable and trustworthy (DeBono & Harnish, 1988). Thus, for example, highly respected and well-published medical doctors and physicists should be expert sources for persuasive communications related to their respective professions (Ohanian, 1991).

The research on source credibility has shown that in most situations a highly expert source is more effective than a low-expert source (Hass, 1981; McGuire, 1969; Sternthal, Phillips, & Dholaki, 1978). Highly credible sources have been found to produce more positive attitude change toward the position advocated and to induce more behavioral change than have less credible sources (Craig & McCann, 1978; Woodside & Davenport, 1974). Furthermore, Whittaker and Meade (1968) suggested, based on their study investigating both Western and Eastern nations, that the effect of source credibility in persuasive communication is a universal phenomenon across cultures. Thus, regardless of cultural background, individuals will have more favorable attitudes toward the advertised brand when an expert rather than a nonexpert endorses the brand. However, the level of favoritism toward the brand may vary depending on the viewers' cultural background because collectivists seem to put more emphasis on source expertise than do individualists (Pornpitakpan & Francis, 2001). Therefore, Koreans are more likely to be susceptible to an ad endorsed by an expert source than Americans are.

Why should collectivists perceive expert sources to be more persuasive than individualists? Several theoretical explanations for this phenomenon can be derived from previous work. First, this differential impact of source expertise may be explained by cross-national differences between Korea and the United States in terms of Hofstede's (1980) power distance dimension. According to Hofstede's analysis of 53 countries, Korea ranks high in the power distance dimension and low in the individualism dimension, whereas the United States ranks low in power distance but high in individualism. Hofstede discussed power distance in terms of the amount of respect and deference between those in superior and those in subordinate positions. Within the culture high in power distance, individuals are more likely to expect and accept that power is unequally distributed. As Hofstede (1991) further argued, in high power distance societies, those people in positions of influence hold power over what is right and good. This argument suggests that in persuasive communication such as advertising endorsed by an expert, the expert's impact on the degree of message acceptance will be greater in a collectivistic culture than in an individualistic culture. Consistent with this, Pornpitakpan and Francis (2001) found that Eastern Asians tend to exhibit a greater reliance on source expertise cues than North Americans.

A second explanation can be drawn based on a theory of analytic versus holistic cognition, a distinction made by Nisbett, Peng, Choi, and Norenzayan (2001). Nisbett et al. found that Asians tend to be holistic, attending to the entire field, whereas Westerners are more analytical, paying attention primarily to the object. In a similar vein, Gudykunst (1983) and Triandis (1994) argued that members of collectivistic cultures pay more attention to contextual cues, whereas those of individualistic culture focus more on content-related thoughts. Shavitt, Nelson, and Yuan (1997) also found that Americans are more persuaded by product-related information in the ads, whereas Taiwanese people focused more on ad-related claims. All these findings suggest that East Asians are more likely to be responsive to the context of ads, such as source expertise, whereas Americans pay more attention to the content of ads, such as product information.

Lastly, Aaker and Maheswaran (1997) showed that cross-cultural variation in perceived diagnosticity of heuristic cues exists, although the dual process models of persuasion—the elaboration likelihood model (Petty & Cacioppo, 1979) and the heuristic systematic model (Chaiken, 1980)—are generally robust across cultures. Cue diagnosticity refers to the extent to which consumers perceive that inferences based on the information alone would be adequate to achieve their objectives (Feldman & Lynch, 1988; Lynch, Marmorstein, & Weigold, 1988). Aaker and Maheswaran (1997) view consensus cues (i.e., the opinions of others) as highly diagnostic in collectivist cultures but relatively low in individualist cultures. Likewise, as Pornpitakpan and Francis' (2001) findings suggest, source expertise may be viewed as a heuristic cue that is highly diagnoistic in collectivist cultures. Thus, source expertise should play a more important role among Koreans than Americans in processing persuasive arguments. Dual process models suggest that heuristic cues are considered to be less important than attribute information and therefore tend to be discounted when they conflict with attribute information (Maheswaran & Chaiken, 1991). However, Aaker and Maheswaran (1997) found that consensus information (i.e., a heuristic cue) influences message evaluations regardless of the level of elaboration likelihood for members of collectivistic cultures but not individualistic cultures. Aaker and Maheswaran's (1997) findings support the view that perceptual differences in cue diagnosticity account for systematic differences in persuasive effects across cultures.

However, because most past studies that examined differential usages of heuristic cues (e.g., source expertise) in cross-cultural contexts have used direct measures by asking participants to report their own attitudes and behaviors, the results reflect only first-person cultural differences. To date we lack data on third-person perceived cultural differences manifested as susceptibility to source expertise as a variable influencing persuasion. In the following, we present two related studies: a) an experiment examining the hypothesis that other Koreans are perceived to conform more than oneself to one's national culture and how this perceived discrepancy and source expertise jointly influence persuasion, and b) another experiment examining the effects of within-nation cultural variability and source expertise on persuasion.

THE ROLE OF NATIONAL CULTURE IN PERCEIVING SOURCE EXPERTISE

Although we claim that source expertise is perceived to be more influential in persuading others than oneself in East Asian countries, we do not intend to repudiate any of the previous findings regarding the cross-cultural differences that have been found by examining respondents' own attitudes (i.e., first-person point of view). That is, we simply suggest that this differential source effect (i.e., more persuasiveness of expert sources in collectivistic countries than individualistic countries) will be more pronounced when a perceiver takes the third-person viewpoint. Therefore, we hypothesized that, compared to Americans, Koreans would perceive an expert source to have a greater impact on the general public than on themselves (Yoon et al., 2005).

To illustrate, our cultural third person effect predicts that, among Koreans, the influence of national culture will be greater on what one thinks will be the case than on what is actually the case (see Fig. 11.3). We designed an experiment to test this idea of a discrepancy between perceived cultural differences (i.e., third-person perception) and actual cultural differences (i.e., first-person perception). We expected a greater perceived impact of expert sources (third person) compared to the actual impact of expert sources (first person) in a collectivistic culture.

To test this hypothesis, we developed a series of mock advertisements featuring either expert or nonexpert spokespeople for American and Korean subjects. Source expertise was manipulated by presenting different occupations for the spokespeople (e.g., doctors vs. sales clerks). After viewing the advertisement, sub-

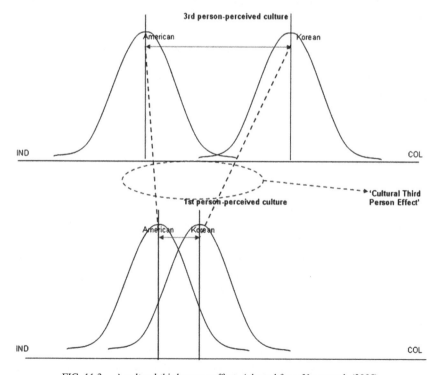

FIG. 11.3.   A cultural third-person effect. Adapted from Yoon et al. (2005).

jects were instructed to fill out a questionnaire in their own language. The question-naire asked about the efficacy of the ad for both first and third person.

The data were analyzed using a 2 (Koreans, Americans) × 2 (expert source, nonexpert source) × 2 (first person, third person point of view) mixed design. The first two factors were between-subjects factors, whereas the third-person effect was within subjects.

Two main effects were significant out of the three factors: source expertise, $F(1, 360) = 7.57, p < .01$, and point of view, $F(1, 360) = 29.05, p < .001$. As expected, people generally perceived expert spokespeople to be more persuasive than nonexperts ($Ms = 4.78$ and 4.44, respectively). This main effect is consistent with previous findings (Hass, 1981; McGuire, 1969; Sternthal et al., 1978) asserting that expert sources induce more positive attitudes toward the advertised product than nonexpert sources. Participants responded in a more positive way when the first-person position was taken than when the third-person position was taken ($Ms = 4.81$ and 4.42, respectively). Although unexpected, this main effect is understandable considering that the product subjects evaluated in the experiment was nonfat milk, which is commonly believed to be healthy and good. If the third-person effect is driven by a self-serving bias, people should be willing to acknowledge the first-person effects for communications that are regarded as socially desirable, healthy, or otherwise good for them (Perloff, 2002). That is, they should believe that they would respond more favorably than others to positive persuasive communications but more negatively than others to manipulative persuasive communications.

There were significant two-way and three-way interactions: source expertise × point of view, $F(1, 360) = 4.03, p < .05.$; source expertise × point of view × nation: $F(1, 360) = 3.89, p < .05$. The two-way interaction suggested that perceived effectiveness of expert-endorsed ads was greater when responding in the third-person perspective than in the first-person perspective. Participants seemed to believe that other participants were less susceptible than themselves to an ad message when it was endorsed by a nonexpert.

To clarify the nature of the three-way interaction, we analyzed the data for each population in two separate two-way ANOVAs. The left panel of Fig. 11.4 shows a significant two-way (source expertise × point of view, $F(1, 175) = 7.82, p < .01$) interaction in the Korean sample. Korean participants rated expert-endorsed ads as more effective than non-expert-endorsed ads only when responding in the third-person perspective. Koreans seemed to believe that other Koreans were less susceptible than themselves to an ad message when it was endorsed by a nonexpert. This can be explained as a self-serving bias.

Being aware that accepting the ad message would lead to a desirable outcome (i.e., drinking milk is good for one's health), participants were willing to accept the message whether it was endorsed by expert or nonexpert spokespeople. On the other hand, the need to maintain or enhance self-esteem may have triggered the downward comparison of others, resulting in participants perceiving others as less swayed by nonexpert sources although the message of the ad is certainly beneficial.

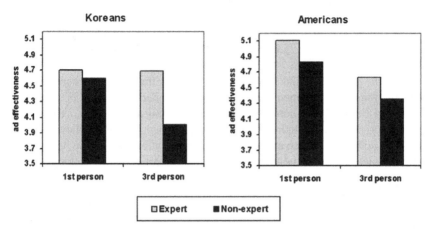

FIG. 11.4. Effects of source expertise, respondent nation, and respondent point of view on perceived ad effectiveness.

However, this was not the case among Americans. No such interaction occurred among the American respondents, meaning that expert sources were perceived to be more persuasive than nonexperts equally in both the first- and third-person positions.

This result reflects Koreans' tendencies to overestimate the degree to which other Koreans conform to collectivistic cultural values (i.e., being influenced by expert opinion). As demonstrated in previous studies we discussed (i.e., Aaker & Maheswaran, 1997; Pornpitakpan & Francis, 2001; Shavitt et al., 1997), collectivists may place a greater emphasis on certain heuristic cues such as source expertise, but in the study reported here this effect emerged only when respondents were estimating others' responses to the advertisement.

In this regard, our study provides additional insights into Aaker and Maheswaran's (1997) findings by revealing the tendency for members of a collectivistic society to perceive some heuristic cues (e.g., source expertise) to be seen as more diagnostic by others than by themselves. What adds to Aaker and Maheswaran's (1997) findings is that, although it may well be the case that an expert source is more influential among Koreans, our findings indicate that Koreans seem to believe that other Koreans perceive an expert source to be more persuasive than it actually is.

There seem to be two things at work for a cultural third-person effect to take place: the presence of culturally congruent heuristic cues and self-serving biases. Source expertise can be viewed as the context of an ad, and therefore culturally congruent among Koreans, but at the same time, susceptibility to an expert-endorsed ad message may be tantamount to acknowledging gullibility or that one possesses undesirable traits. Assuming that the self is less vulnerable to expert-endorsed argument whereas others are naïvely susceptible seems to preserve a positive sense of self. Therefore, our finding of a cultural third-person effect among Koreans fits well with previous findings in cross-cultural psychology as well as third-person effects; Koreans' greater sensitivity to source expertise and self-serving biases may have jointly resulted in the greater perceived discrepancy between themselves and others.

It may be possible to find a cultural third-person effect among Americans with manipulation of those elements frequently used in American culture. For example, as Han and Shavitt (1994) demonstrated that advertising appeals vary in their effectiveness across cultures, studies employing collectivistic versus individualistic appeal with collectivistic versus individualistic populations may allow us to see a more complete picture of the cultural third-person effect, revealing both sides of the cultural third-person effect.

In addition, an interaction effect between nation and source expertise in the first-person perception did not emerge in this study. In a sense, the absence of a first-person effect in our study, along with the presence of the third-person effect, enhances our belief that in terms of individualism and collectivism, the cultural difference between the United States and Korea may be smaller than we perceive it to be.

THE ROLE OF INDIVIDUAL CULTURE IN PERCEIVING SOURCE EXPERTISE

Thus far we have discussed a perceived role of national culture in viewing source expertise. In this section, we shift our attention from national cultural differences to individual cultural differences.

The importance of individual-level cultural differences has been recognized by many. For example, Oyserman et al. (2002) reported a startling amount of cross-national convergence, suggesting that individualism and collectivism can be assessed at an individual level. Recent work by Cialdini, Wosinska, Barrett, Butner, and Gornik-Durose (1999) provides a good example of an individual cultural difference as a critical factor that moderates national cultural difference. Compared with Polish undergraduate students, American students were more likely to be persuaded to participate in a survey if their own past cooperation was made salient than if their group's cooperation was made salient (Cialdini et al., 1999). More interestingly, however, assessed levels of individualism and collectivism moderated this effect: Both American and Polish students high in individualism were more persuaded by individualist appeals to their own past cooperation, whereas students high in collectivism were more persuaded by collectivistic appeals to their group. The importance of these sorts of individual differences directed us to investigate a within-nation variation shown in Figs. 11.1 and 11.2. For the initial stage, we chose to look into an American sample rather than at Koreans because, in addition to other practical reasons, the American population is more diverse than that of Korea. We believe that this diversity of population in the United States may result in a greater within-nation cultural variation, which may enable us to see more clearly the impact of individual differences and perceived source expertise on persuasion.

As can be seen in Fig. 11.5, the range of the distribution of Americans in the first-person perspective is equal to the one in the third-person perspective, although the positions of the bell curves on the horizontal axes differ from each other. In other words, the distance between the minimum and the maximum scores among Americans in the first-person perception should be equal to the one in the third-person perception. If the shape of the bell curve is flat enough (i.e., divergent individual cultural differences exist within the United States), a significant interaction between an individual's culture and source expertise should emerge, not only in the third-person but also in the first-person perception. This is what we found in Study 2 (Yoon et al., 2005).

Study 2 was a conceptual replication of Study 1, except that the national culture variable in Study 1 was replaced with an individual culture variable, measured with Triandis et al.'s (1993) INDCOL scale. Because we intended to examine the clear influence of individual differences within a homogenous group, only White Americans were included in this study, removing the potential effects of ethnic background as a confounding variable.

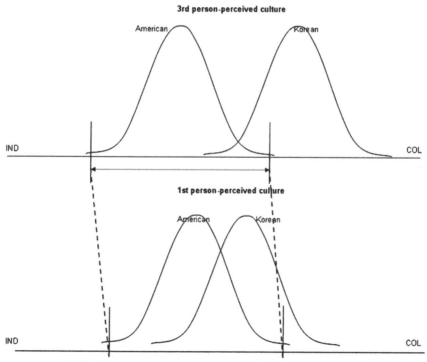

FIG. 11.5.   First- and third-person within-nation cultural variability.

To assess individuals' tendencies to a certain cultural orientation, we used a direct measurement scale. Likert-type ratings of values and attitudes are known to be the most prevalent method used to assess individualism and collectivism (Oyserman et al., 2002). Finding an appropriate scale was not an easy task because there is no single standard or most common measure for individualism and collectivism, although some items are common across many scales; moreover, at least 27 distinct scales have been identified that are related to the construct of individualism and collectivism (Oyserman et al., 2002). Use of Triandis et al.'s (1993) scale allowed us to examine both specific and broad aspects of the construct because the scale has three specific subdimensions: self-reliance with competition, concern for in-group, and distance from in-groups.

We first analyzed the data with a composite score of individualism and collectivism to look at a broad aspect of culture. Regression analyses revealed that main effects of source expertise were significant for both the first- ($b = -1.50$, $p < .005$) and third-person perspective ($b = -1.53$, $p < .005$). Participants generally perceived expert spokespeople to be more persuasive than nonexperts. Consistent with our prediction, interactions between expertise and culture were significant for both the first- ($b = -1.46$, $p < .005$) and third-person perception ($b = -1.44$, $p < .005$), suggesting that source expertise influences collectivists more than individualists, regardless of the viewer's point of view (see Fig. 11.6). That is, collectivistic participants rated expert-endorsed ads as more effective than nonexpert-endorsed

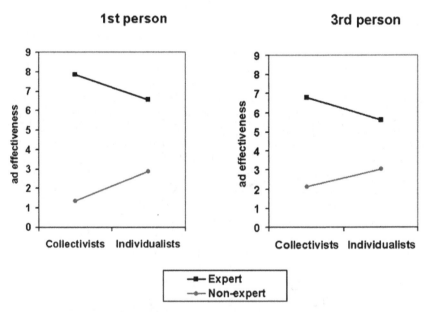

FIG. 11.6.   Effects of source expertise, respondent level of individualism/collectivism, and respondent point of view on perceived ad effectiveness.

ads both when responding in the third-person perspective and when responding in the first-person perspective. Collectivists seemed to believe that both they and other Americans were more susceptible to an ad message when it was endorsed by an expert rather than by a nonexpert.

In Study 1, the same pattern of an interaction emerged only among Korean respondents in the third-person perception but not in the first-person perception. The findings of Study 2 show that individual cultural differences are equally influential in how source expertise is perceived in both first- and third-person perceptions. It turns out that, as predicted, in both the first- and third-person point of view, collectivists responded more positively when the expert source, rather than the nonexpert, endorsed the product.

To gain a better understanding of how specific aspects of individual culture influence source expertise perception, we also analyzed the data with the three subdimensions of the scale (i.e., self-reliance with competition, concern for in-group, and distance from in-group). We found a significant interaction between source expertise and the distance from the in-group dimension in both the first- and third-person perceived perception but found no significant interactions between source expertise and the other two dimensions. This finding is reminiscent of Oyserman et al.'s (2002) suggestion that the most basic way of defining and assessing collectivism is the extent to which duty to in-group is valued; duty to in-group in Oyserman's terms is conceptually similar to distance from in-group in the Triandis' scale we used in this study. From an operational standpoint at least, the distance

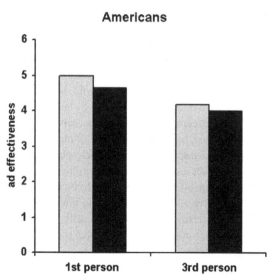

FIG. 11.7.   Effects of source expertise and respondent point of view on perceived ad effectiveness.

from the in-group dimension seems best to capture the contrast between individualism and collectivism in perceiving source expertise.

In addition, as can be seen in Fig. 11.7, the absence of an interaction between expertise and point of view (first vs. third) partly confirms the findings in Study 1. Expert spokespeople are more influential than nonexpert spokespeople to an equal degree whether one takes the first- or third-person position.

DISCUSSION

The results of these experiments provide evidence that, although individual cultural differences clearly exist (Study 2), people sometimes misperceive the degree of the influence of national culture (Study 1). As implied in the introduction of this chapter, what we termed as a cultural third person effect may be an inconsistency between what an individual is supposed to do within a certain culture and what one actually does.

In this chapter, we examined source expertise as a way in which a cultural third-person effect can be manifested. A similar phenomenon may be observed in other conditions under which those heuristic cues that are regarded as more meaningful in a collectivist society are present. For example, among East Asians, an ad copy that emphasizes family values may be perceived to be more effective than it really is. Or, for a similar reason, the effect of word of mouth by an in-group member or opinion leader (e.g., a father) may be overestimated in a collectivistic society.

However, as discussed previously, whether a heuristic cue is consistent with a given collectivistic cultural norm alone should not bring about a cultural third-person effect. As discussed, the major driving force of the cultural third-person effect is believed to be self-serving biases, so to observe a cultural third-person effect, a persuasive argument may require, along with the presence of culturally salient heuristic cues, a motivational or cognitive element that can serve as a trigger for self-enhancement. In this regard, source expertise as a heuristic cue in our studies seems to satisfy these two conditions: a) an expert's opinion should be respected according to collectivistic cultural norms, b) but being persuaded by an expert may not be a desirable outcome for one's self-esteem. In other words, merely agreeing with an expert's opinion is culturally acceptable, but at the same time, it may be perceived as an unintelligent reaction to a persuasive argument. Under such specified conditions (i.e., culturally congruent heuristic cues and self-enhancing motivation), one may be able to observe a cultural third-person effect, which seems to be a psychological process to resolve the contradiction between an individual and the group one belongs to—it seems that people in a collectivistic culture strive to achieve the benefits of both the group and the individual, which conflict with each other more often than they do in an individualistic culture.

The implicit assumption we made in Study 2, in which culture was directly measured at the individual level, was that individuals differ in the extent to which individualism and collectivism are chronically accessible. Another stream of cross-cultural research may shed light on this phenomenon of the cultural-third person effect from a different perspective. In priming research (e.g., Gardner, Gabriel, & Lee, 1999), individualism and collectivism are made salient through the manipulation of situational cues. According to this dynamic perspective of culture, an individualistic or collectivistic frame can be switched back and forth depending on what kinds of situational cues are available at the time of one's judgment. The cultural-third person effect may be influenced in this manner, too. For example, manipulating the independent (or interdependent) self may induce a greater (or smaller) cultural third-person effect among East Asians because the temporarily accessible independent self may be attentive to differences between oneself and others and therefore widen self–other discrepancy at the moment, whereas the interdependent self may exaggerate self–other similarity.

The demographic characteristics of nations may moderate the size of the cultural third-person effect. For example, the fact that Korea, like Japan, is among the most ethnically homogeneous nations in the world may be related to the degree of the cultural third- person effect manifested. Population homogeneity is known to be correlated with collectivism (Triandis, 1995). Is there then a systematic relation between the degree of homogeneity and the degree of the cultural third-person effect? Two plausible but opposite hypotheses may be derived. First, it seems intuitively reasonable to assume that a culturally homogenous population may incur a smaller cultural third-person effect because of its relatively limited diversity and therefore fewer perceived differences exist among members. It seems also plausible that homogeneity may result in an exaggerated cultural third-person effect because individuals living in such nations are more likely to have vivid and clear exemplars of others, which can be directly compared to the viewer himself or herself. Furthermore, this highly tangible image of others may allow for less variability of different images of others held by each individual within those nations, and this small variability will lead to a statistically greater overall mean difference.

IMPLICATIONS

By nature, the concept of culture may be restricted to what things mean to a group of people. For example, Rohner (1984) saw culture as an organized system of shared meanings. Perhaps for this reason, culture has traditionally been the subject of study as the characteristics of a nation or group, with a focus on differences between nations. Embracing the inclusiveness of Herskovits' (1948) widely cited definition of culture—"man-made part of the environment"— (p. 17) most cross-cultural studies seem to focus on differences among diverse nations, emphasizing commonality among individuals within a given nation or group. However, as many have argued (e.g., Fiske, 2002; Smith & Bond, 1999), nations are nothing but political units, none of which coincide exactly with cultural units and very few of which correspond at all. Nations may be comprised of many diverse cultures (e.g., Chinese), so a tendency to equate nation with culture must be avoided.

Our findings cast some doubt on a widespread belief among advertising practitioners. International marketers often describe their target market as Chinese, or Mexican, or Asian, or Latin American. However, the studies presented in this chapter leave the clear message that national differences are sometimes exaggerated and what really matters are individual differences. The practical implications of our study are clear: If the target audiences are clearly identified collectivistic individuals, the use of an expert spokesperson will increase advertising effectiveness, but if the target audiences are broadly defined collectivistic nations such as "Koreans" or "Chinese," more careful consideration may be needed because the use of an expert source may not be as effective as one expects.

REFERENCES

Aaker, J. L., & Maheswaran, D. (1997). The effect of cultural orientation on persuasion. *Journal of Consumer Research, 24,* 315–328.

Alicke, M. D., Klotz, M. L., Breitenbecher, D. L., Yurak, T. J., & Vredenburg, D. S. (1995). Personal contact, individuation, and the better-than average effect. *Journal of Personality and Social Psychology, 68,* 804–825.

Chaiken, S. (1980). Heuristic versus systematic information processing and use of source versus attribute cues in persuasion. *Journal of Personality and Social Psychology, 53,* 30–40.

Chan, D. K. (1994). COLINDEX: A refinement of three collectivism measures. In U. Kim, H. C. Triandis, C. Kagitcibasi, S. Choi, & G. Yoon (Eds.), Individualism and collectivism: *Theory, method, and applications* (pp. 200–210). Thousand Oaks, CA: Sage.

Chao, R. K. (1994). Beyond parental control and authoritarian parenting style: Understanding Chinese parenting through the cultural notion of training. *Child Development, 65,* 1111–1119.

Cialdini, R. B., Wosinska, W., Barrett, D. W., Butner, J., & Gornik-Durose, M. (1999). Compliance with a request in two cultures: The differential influence of social proof and commitment/consistency on collectivists and individualists. *Personality and Social Psychology Bulletin, 25,* 1242–1253.

Craig, S. C., & McCann, J. M. (1978). Assessing communication effects of energy conservation. *Journal of Consumer Research, 3,* 82–88.

Davison, W. P. (1983). The third-person effect in communication. *Public Opinion Quarterly, 47,* 1–15.

DeBono, K., & Harnish, R. J. (1988). Source expertise, source attractiveness, and the processing of persuasive information: A functional approach. *Journal of Personality and Social Psychology, 55,* 541–546.

Feldman, J., & Lynch, J., Jr. (1988). Self-generated validity and other effects of measurements on belief, attitude, intention, and behavior. *Journal of Applied Psychology, 73,* 421–425.

Fiske, A. P. (2002). Using individualism and collectivism to compare cultures—A critique of the validity and measurement of the constructs: Comment on Oyserman et al. (2002). *Psychological Bulletin, 128,* 78–88.

French, H. W. (2002, October 9). Korea's real rage for virtual games. *The New York Times,* p. 8.

Gardner, W., Gabriel, S., & Lee, A., L. (1999). "I" value freedom, but "We" value relationships: Self-construal priming mirrors cultural differences in judgment. *Psychological Science, 10,* 321–326.

Generation 2030 went from apathy to passion. (2002, December 22). *Joongang Ilbo English Edition*, p. C3.

Gudykunst, W. B. (Ed.). (1983). *Intercultural communication theory*, Beverly Hills, CA: Sage.

Han, S., & Shavitt, S. (1994). Persuasion and culture: Advertising appeals in individualistic and collectivistic societies. *Journal of Experimental Social Psychology, 30*, 326–350.

Hass, R. G. (1981). Effects of source characteristics on cognitive responses and persuasion. In R. Petty, T. Ostrom, & T. Brock (Eds.), *Cognitive responses in persuasion* (pp. 141–172). Hillsdale, NJ: Lawrence Erlbaum Associates.

Heine, S. J., Lehman, D. R., Peng, K., & Greenholtz, J. (2002). What's wrong with cross-cultural comparisons of subjective Likert scales? The reference-group problem. *Journal of Personality and Social Psychology, 82*, 903–918.

Henriksen, L., & Flora, J. A. (1999). Third-person perception and children. *Communication Research, 26*, 643–665.

Herskovits, M. J. (1948). Man and his works: *The science of cultural anthropology*. New York: Knopf.

Hofstede, G. (1980). Culture's consequences: *International differences in work-related values*. Beverly Hills, CA: Sage.

Hofstede, G. (1991). *Cultures and organizations: Software of the mind*. London: McGraw-Hill.

Hovland, C. I., Janis, I. L., & Kelley, H. H. (1953). *Communication and persuasion*. New Haven, CT: Yale University Press.

Kim, H., & Markus, H. R. (1999). Deviance or uniqueness, harmony or conformity? A cultural analysis. *Journal of Personality and Social Psychology, 77*, 785–800.

Kitayama, S., Markus, H. R., Matsumoto, H., & Norasakkunkit, V. (1997). Individual and collective process in the construction of the self: Self-enhancement in the United States and self-criticism in Japan. *Journal of Personality and Social Psychology, 72*, 1245–1267.

Lasorsa, D. L. (1992). Policymakers and the third-person effect. In J. D. Kennamer (Eds.), *Public opinion, the press, and public policy* (pp. 163–175). Westport, CT: Praeger.

Lynch, J. G., Marmorstein, H., & Weigold, M. F. (1988). Choices from sets including remembered brands: Use of recalled attributes and prior overall evaluations. *Journal of Consumer Research, 15*, 169–184.

Maheswaran, D., & Chaiken, S. (1991). Promoting systematic processing in low-motivation settings: Effect of incongruent information on processing and judgment. *Journal of Personality and Social Psychology, 61*, 13–25.

Matsumoto, D. (1989). Cultural influences on the perception of emotion. *Journal of Cross-Cultural Psychology, 61*, 13–25.

McGuire, W. J. (1969). Attitudes and attitude change. In G. Lindzey & E. Aronson (Eds.), *Handbook of social psychology, Vol. 3* (pp. 233–346) Reading, MA: Addison-Wesley.

Morris, M. W., & Peng, K. P. (1994). Culture and cause: American and Chinese attributions for social and physical events. *Journal of Personality and Social Psychology, 67*, 949–971.

Nisbett, R. E., Peng, K., Choi, I., & Norenzayan, A. (2001). Culture and systems of thought: Holistic versus analytic cognition. *Psychological Review, 108*, 291–310.

Ohanian, R. (1991). The impact of celebrity spokespersons' perceived image on consumers' intent to purchase. *Journal of Advertising Research, 20*, 46–54.

Oyserman, D., Coon, H. M., & Kemmelmeier, M. (2002). Rethinking individualism and collectivism: Evaluation of theoretical assumptions and meta-analyses. *Psychological Bulletin, 128*, 3–72

Paul, B., Salwen, M. B., & Dupagne, M. (2000). The third-person effect: A meta-analysis of the perceptual hypothesis. *Mass Communication & Society, 3*, 57–85.

Petty, R. E., & Cacioppo, J. T. (1979). Issue-involvement can increase or decrease persuasion by enhancing attribute-relevant cognitive responses. *Journal of Personality and Social Psychology, 37,* 1915–1926.

Perloff, R. M. (2002). The third-person effect. In J. Bryant & D. Zillmann (Eds.), *Media effects: Advances in theory and research* (2nd ed., pp. 489–506). Mahwah, NJ: Lawrence Erlbaum Associates.

Pornpitakpan, C., & Francis, J. N (2001). The effect of cultural differences, source expertise, and argument strength on persuasion: An experiment with Canadians and Thais. *Journal of International Consumer Marketing, 13,* 77–101.

Prabu, D., Morrison, G., Johnson, M. A., & Ross, F. (2002). Body image, race and fashion models: Social distance and social identification in third-person effects. *Communication Research, 29,* 270–294.

Price, V., Huang, L., & Tewksbury, D. (1997). The third-person effect of news coverage: Orientations toward media. *Journalism & Mass Communication Quarterly, 74,* 525–540.

Rohner, R. (1984). Toward a conception of culture for cross-cultural psychology. *Journal of Cross-Cultural Psychology, 15,* 111–138.

Shah, D. V., Faber, R. J., & Youn, S. (1999). Susceptibility and severity: Perceptual dimensions underlying the third-person effect. *Communication Research, 26,* 240–267.

Shavitt, S., Nelson, M. R., & Yuan, R. M. L., (1997). Exploring cross-cultural differences in cognitive responding to ads. *Advances in Consumer Research, 24,* 245–250.

Smith, P. B., & Bond, M. H., (1999). *Social psychology across cultures.* Needham Heights, MA: Allyn & Bacon.

Sternthal, L., Philips, L. W., & Dholakia, R. (1978). The persuasive effect of source credibility: A situation analysis. *Public Opinion Quarterly, 3,* 285–314.

Triandis, H. C. (1989). The self and behavior in differing cultural contexts. *Psychological Review, 96,* 506–552.

Triandis, H. C. (1994). *Culture and social behavior.* New York: McGraw-Hill.

Triandis, H. C. (1995). *Individualism and collectivism.* Boulder, CO: Westview.

Triandis, H. C., Bontempo, R., Villareal, M. J., Asai, M., & Lucca, N. (1993). Individualism and collectivism: Cross-cultural perspectives on self-ingroup relationships. *Journal of Personality and Social Psychology, 54,* 323–338.

Whittaker, J. O., & Meade, R. D. (1968). Retention of opinion change as a function of differential source credibility: A cross-cultural study. *International Journal of Psychology, 3,* 103–108.

Woodside, A. G., & Davenport, J. W., Jr. (1974). The effect of salesman similarity and expertise on consumer purchasing behavior. *Journal of Marketing Research, 11,* 198–202.

Yamaguchi, S. (1994). Collectivism among the Japanese: A perspective from the self. In U. Kim, H. C. Triandis, C. Kagitcibasi, S. Choi, & G. Yoon (Eds.), *Individualism and collectivism: Theory, method, and applications* (pp. 175–188). Thousand Oaks, CA: Sage.

Yoon, S., Vargas, P. T., & Han, S. (2005). "I" versus "they" and "East" versus "West": Cross-cultural differences in perceived impact of source expertise. *Advances in Consumer Research, 32.*

Youn, S., & Faber, R. J. (2000). Restricting gambling advertising and the third-person effect. *Psychology & Marketing, 17,* 633–649.

CHAPTER TWELVE

Sports Celebrities' Image: A Critical Evaluation of the Utility of Q Scores

Kevin E. Kahle and Lynn R. Kahle
University of Oregon

People are eager to purchase a pair of shoes endorsed by Michael Jordan or a candy bar endorsed by Shaq. Firms dish out millions of dollars to athletes each year to lure them to appear in commercials for products and services. These days, athletes are paid by firms to endorse a wide variety of products, but how do the firms know to which athletes consumers will respond? Oftentimes, companies base the decision of which athlete to hire on Q-ratings. Q-ratings are meant to inform firms about the celebrities that groups of people identify with the most, but is this the best way to determine who should endorse a specific product? How and to what extent are Q-ratings an effective way of predicting marketing success among professional athlete endorsers? What other factors could possibly be incorporated in the decision related to determining the perfect athlete endorser? The thesis of this chapter is that, although Q-ratings are a reliable method of determining an athlete's general popularity, they ignore many important aspects of successful endorsers. This chapter examines the method by which Q-ratings are calculated as well as important attributes of successful endorsers.

Q-RATINGS

A Q-rating, or quotient rating, is essentially a numerical value associated with celebrities involved in advertising. The purpose of the number is to represent potential celebrity success in marketing products. Theoretically, the higher the number assigned to the celebrity, the more success he or she will have in advertising. A New York-based firm called Marketing Evaluations/TvQ collects data to calculate and

The authors gratefully acknowledge comments on an earlier draft from Robert Madrigal.

publish the Q-ratings commercially (Shimp, 2003). The company evaluates approximately 1,500 celebrities (over 400 of whom are athletes) by sending out surveys to a representative sample of people each year. The sample group ranges in age from 12 to 65, and exactly 2,000 completed surveys count toward the final Q-ratings. For the data to count towards athletes' Q-ratings, the person completing the survey must indicate that he or she has a general interest in sports.

In spite of the fact that Q-ratings are the industry standard in advertising, only a mere two factors go into the calculation of the ratings. Let's pretend members of the panel were evaluating Celebrity A. They would rate the celebrity on two criteria, familiarity (f) and popularity (p). First, to measure familiarity, they would be asked if they had heard of Celebrity A. Second, they would have to rate Celebrity A as poor, fair, good, very good, or one of my favorites (Shimp, 2003). These options are a measure of popularity. The quotient rating of Celebrity A is determined by the percentage of panel members who select Celebrity A as one of their favorites, divided by the percentage of panel members who specified that they have heard of Celebrity A. The mathematical formula for determining Celebrity A's Q-Rating is p% / f%.

Bill Cosby's Q-rating in 2000, for example, was 47. This number was determined because 95% of the members on the panel said they had heard of him and 45% stated that Cosby was one of their favorites. The nearest whole number value to 45/95 is 47; thus, Cosby received a Q-rating of 47 in 2000.

Among professional athletes in 2003, Michael Jordan took the top spot with a SportsQ of 51. This figure is down from the 58 he received in 2002. In second place for Q-ratings among athletes in 2003 was Tiger Woods, with a 44. Nolan Ryan took the third spot with a 40, followed by Joe Montana (39), Cal Ripken, Jr. (38), Jerry Rice (37), and John Madden (36). Wayne Gretzky and Jackie Joyner-Kersee shared a 35, and Arnold Palmer and Howie Long shared a 33. Magic Johnson took the tenth position in 2003 with a 32 (Stone, Joseph, & Jones, 2003).

One of the biggest flaws in the Q-rating system is the way in which popularity is calculated. The only time that the factor goes into the final value is if the panel member selects the celebrity as one of his or her favorites. The other levels of popularity have no impact on the final rating. Therefore, if Celebrity A received a ranking of poor or very good from a panel member, it would have an equal influence on the data. Clearly, these levels of popularity are not equal; however, they are recorded as such.

The fact that only two factors go into the ratings calculating Q-ratings presents a gap in the accuracy of the ratings because many important factors go unevaluated. There is an incongruity between Q-ratings and many endorsement contracts, especially in the realm of athlete endorsements. In the following section we examine other attributes that successful endorsers possess.

SOURCE

Two major factors in the effectiveness of marketing communication are the sender and the receiver (Belch & Belch, 1998). The receiver is simply the audience who observes and absorbs the message of the advertisement. The sender, or source, is the individual or group of people who communicates the message to the receiver. In this context, the source would be an athlete or group of athletes paid to communicate the message of a company to the target market (i.e., receiver). It is important for marketers to pay attention to many aspects of the source because the way in which the receiver perceives the source affects his or her opinion of the brand and the product being sold.

For the message from the company to get across to the receiver, the sender's and the receiver's fields of experience must cross. Marketers must select words, symbols, and pictures to go along with the source in the advertisement that corresponds to the image message they would like to send. This process is called encoding. Encoding along with certain qualities of the source determines how effective an advertisement is. Let's look into the essential source qualities needed that are widely agreed upon by most marketers.

One of the most important factors that contributes to a successful athlete source is the image of being a winner (Jones, Bee, Burton, & Kahle, 2004). Products have to differentiate themselves from the competition. In our capitalist society where competition is viewed as good, we reward brands that seem to be winners through the image of athletes. For instance, Budweiser chose the message "King of beers" as its slogan. To live up to this image as the best in the field, it needs a source with a winning image.

Source credibility or believability is also important. The sender is much more persuasive if the receiver believes the source has expertise relating to the product (Belch & Belch, 1998). For example, famous race-car driver Jeff Gordon endorsing Pennzoil motor oil is a believable endorsement. The audience identifies that Jeff Gordon has knowledge about the product. The receivers make the connection that Jeff Gordon uses Pennzoil to help him win auto races, and they believe that it could help them, too. If the source has knowledge about the product, it may not matter how likeable the source is (Kahle & Homer, 1985). If John McEnroe endorsed a tennis racket, it would be believable that he actually uses this racket to help him win. Even if the receivers do not like his on-court antics, they could still agree that he has credibility in the field of tennis. In turn, this credibility and believability could persuade the receiver to purchase the advertised product. Other intangible attributes such as being hard working, tough, or classy, which are represented in the athlete's personality, are also likely to rub off on the receiver.

Trustworthiness is also an important trait of a successful athlete endorser. For the most part, an honest and ethical source has more success in advertising. The receiver wants to see sincerity in the sender. Trustworthiness plays a role in source credibility. If the source is not trustworthy and honest, the source is not as believable. Wayne Gretzky is a perfect example of a trustworthy athlete. He has an image of morality and on top of that he was one of the biggest hockey stars of all time. He's on the list of nice guys, whom marketers have determined as stars both on and off the field. Along with Gretzky in the nice guy class of 1996 were Pete Sampras, Michael Chang, Steve Young, Cal Ripken, Jr., Shaquille O'Neal, and Tiger Woods

(Belch & Belch, 1998). There are times, however, that endorsers of dubious morality can actually be more effective in advertising (more on that later), but as a general rule they are less effective because they lose an element of trustworthiness.

Likeability is a factor that goes into trustworthiness. A source is likeable if the receiver admires the source's appearance, skill, behavior, or other personal traits. More than 20% of all TV advertisements feature celebrities or athletes for this reason. Celebrities are likeable and admired. On top of that, they have the fame to convey their message to many different types of people effectively. If the receiver does not like the source, this opinion leads to source derogations (Belch & Belch, 1998). Source derogations are essentially negative opinions about the source, company, and product being sold. Conversely, if the receiver likes the source, this liking leads to source bolsters. Source bolsters are positive opinions about the source, company, and product being sold. This factor illustrates how important source likeability is. It is often valuable for the target receiver to find the source to be likeable, or else the message may not be interpreted correctly or accepted (Krugman, Reid, Dunn, & Barban, 1994). But likeability is not the only relevant trait.

Source charisma and charm in the advertisement are important attributes of endorsers. The sender needs to have acting skill if the advertisement is on TV. The receiver wants an interesting personality, someone who is articulate in delivering the message. After Michael Jordan retired from basketball, Nike tried to replace him with Penny Hardaway as the new front of Nike basketball. In spite of the fact that Hardaway was credible, likeable, trustworthy, and a winner, Nike's sales in basketball apparel plummeted because Hardaway just was not as charismatic as Jordan. Also, the way in which the advertisement is presented can take away from the articulateness and persuasiveness of the message. Any distraction from the message in the advertisement is referred to as noise. If the advertisement is full of noise, it won't matter how charismatic the source is. A good message, however, finds a way to reduce noise and to utilize a charismatic source. In this way the message will be more direct and easier for the receiver to decode.

Physical attractiveness can play a role in persuading the receiver by including the ideas of similarity, familiarity, and likeability. This type of persuasion, through attractiveness, is known as identification (Belch & Belch, 1998; Kahle & Homer, 1985; Kahle, Kambara, & Rose, 1996). The receiver admires or identifies with the sender's physical attractiveness. The receiver either desires the identity of attractiveness or feels similar to the source due to attractiveness (Krugman, Dunn, Reid, & Barbin, 1994). A study examining the attractiveness effect showed a higher purchase intent if receivers believed the source was attractive, in contrast to less attractive sources (Till & Busler, 2000). Consumers follow this trend both for products designed to enhance their appearance and for products virtually unrelated to appearance. The best recent example of physical attractiveness playing a dominant role in endorsements is Ana Kournikova. At a time when she ranked around 19th in the women's professional tennis tour, she made more money from endorsements than any other female tennis player. She has never even won a singles Grand Slam title, yet her website is one of the top five most-visited websites for athletes in any sport in the world. In spite of her lackluster performance on the tennis court, she is still the most successful female tennis endorser. The main explanation for her success is her attractiveness, because the receiver certainly is not identifying with her image of winning.

Power is another possible attribute of a successful endorser. The source must have the power to persuade the receiver into believing the message. Perceived control, perceived concern, and perceived scrutiny are all aspects of an endorser's power. Perceived control refers to whether the source can dole out both positive and negative responses from the receiver (Belch & Belch, 1998). Perceived concern refers to whether the receiver believes that the source cares about the receiver hearing and conforming to the message. Perceived scrutiny refers to whether the receiver can effectively analyze the source's message (i.e., decoding). Compliance is the term used to analyze source power. Compliance is the influence a powerful source has on the receiver. If the receiver is persuaded by the source's message, this concept is known as compliance through power.

Uniqueness is yet another important factor. Consider Yao Ming. As a 7-foot 6-inch Chinese basketball player in the NBA, Yao Ming is a perfect example of a unique athlete in America. Along with his distinctiveness, he also brings charisma and a winning mentality to the game. He has already been featured in advertisements for Apple Computers, Gatorade, and many other companies. As the first high profile Chinese basketball player in the NBA, he also brings a whole new NBA fan base along with him.

MATCH HYPOTHESIS

The match hypothesis states that, for the message to be sent clearly, there needs to be a match between the product or service being advertised and the source (Jones & Schumann, 2004; Kahle & Homer, 1985). There needs to be a similarity between either the product and the source or the consumer and the source. The classic example of the match working to perfection came a few years back when Hertz rent-a-car service hired professional football player O.J. Simpson to pitch its service. O. J. Simpson was famous for having speed on the football field, and Hertz used this trait to match and convey the message that Hertz rent-a-car service was also speedy. Consumers made the connection between the speed of the source and the speed of the service. Hertz saw increased sales after this advertisement campaign. Simpson served as their spokesperson for 20 years, until he was accused of murder and Hertz Corp. was forced to drop him because the match took on added dimensions of complexity (Belch & Belch, 1998).

Successful companies and products are positioned; they stand for something. Matching qualities about their products with qualities of the source they choose allows them to be positioned in the minds of consumers. When advertising is done with celebrities, the celebrity may draw attention to an ad, thereby increasing its effectiveness. However, the image of the celebrity can be part of the message. If the celebrity's personality conveys something about a product, the effectiveness of the ad is increased.

According to Till and Busler (2000), it is statistically defensible to assert that advertisements are more effective if there is an obvious fit between the endorser and the endorsed product. Another example of the match hypothesis working to perfection is when John McEnroe, a controversial tennis star, endorsed Bic razors (Kahle & Homer, 1985). McEnroe was known for being abrasive, for his on-court tantrums and heated arguments. This personality trait provided the perfect match to the edginess of the razors. He also projected an image of physical attractiveness, a goal related to shaving for many consumers. The campaign was a huge success. McEnroe, incidentally, illustrates how a celebrity, as with a product, can be repositioned; today he has a much more charming image and even jokes about his earlier temper. This anecdote provides the perfect transition into the next topic, source edginess. Edginess can be beneficial in endorsements if there is a match between source and product (and if the source generally stays out of trouble with the law).

EDGINESS

One factor that helps sales that you will usually not find in marketing textbooks is the trait of edginess. According to Rick Burton, Commissioner of the National Basketball League in Australia and New Zealand, although an athlete with a negative public reputation can be a risky investment for endorsement contractors, this investment can also generate large sales in today's markets (Burton, personal communication). A primary example of this theory is Allan Iverson. He has repeatedly been in trouble with the law and with the NBA, and he makes inappropriate public statements. In spite of this behavior, the amount of money he gets paid in endorsement contracts is almost comparable to the figures Michael Jordan earned in his prime. Bruce O'Neal, President of the American Basketball Academy, believes that as a rule, moral players do better in endorsement contracts; however, there are exceptions to this rule (O'Neal, personal communication). Allan Iverson is one of these exceptions. The reasoning behind this idea is that using an athlete with a negative public reputation in advertising is something different. A company viewed as different attracts attention to itself and its products. Certain consumers either look up to or identify with the rebels of society. This type of consumer is more likely to purchase products endorsed by Iverson and similar athletes. Essentially, Iverson's likeability reaches some people but not others.

An article by Laurence Chalip (1997) entitled "Celebrity or Hero?" supports this idea. In his article, he argues that our society does not idolize heroes any more and that celebrities have replaced heroes. Allan Iverson's case illustrates this argument. He may not be a hero off the court, but he shows up in the news for negative things, which makes him a celebrity. This celebrity contributes to his success as an endorser. When he was in the news for one recent scandal, his endorsed-shoe sales skyrocketed. Is it a coincidence that profits improved tremendously as his public reputation disintegrated, or is getting negative press a wise decision for athletes hoping to boost sales?

The hype surrounding LeBron James could explode into a battle for public relations. An issue of USA Today (4/23/03) projected that his endorsement contract for shoes would be worth approximately $50 million, but he signed with Nike for $90 million over 10 years (Graves, 2003). As far as the general public knows, LeBron James does not have a negative reputation. He has never been in jail or in trouble with the law; however, Nike knows that edgy basketball players often have superior sales. They know that negative attention is still attention. On top of the $90 million to sign him, it will cost Nike another $300 million to market him effectively. According to Bruce O'Neal (personal communication), one of the reasons Nike is putting up so much money is that it sees high sales potential in the inner-city markets. The major obstacle for Nike is how to market him. How the public responds to this marketing will depend on how they encode LeBron's message.

A NEW SYSTEM

An alternative method for evaluating athlete celebrities would begin, as with all successful marketing plans, with a careful assessment of current marketplace perceptions of the product or service in question. Research should develop current image maps of the marketplace position of the product or service and its relevant competitors. Based on principles of marketing strategy, the company should decide what positioning image the product or service should have. Next the company should brainstorm about any appropriate athlete celebrity whose image corresponds or matches with the desired product or service image. Ideally a list of 20 or so candidates will be developed. Then the athlete celebrities should face the same kind of image positioning map used to evaluate the product or service and its competitors in the minds of members of the target market. Among celebrities with sufficient fame, the one with the best match with the desired product or service image should be approached regarding the endorsement opportunity. Thus, celebrity attributes much more central to effective image positioning than just likeability will play a central role in celebrity choice. The communication using that celebrity will likely be much more effective than with a celebrity picked merely because of Q-score.

In the hierarchy of effects, the traditional use of celebrities has emphasized the attention-grabbing virtue of use of celebrities or the generating of sports talk (Kahle, Elton, & Kambara, 1997). The approach described here expands the role of celebrities to include communication effects as well, such as helping consumers to understand the positioning of the product. Using celebrities for double duty will increase their effectiveness (Kamins & Gupta, 1994; Misra & Beatty, 1990).

CONCLUSION

Jordan was the ultimate athlete endorser. He was a star on the court, usually stayed out of trouble, and had charisma and cleverness in nearly every interview. In spite of his retirement, he still tops the athlete Q-ratings. He is still America's favorite sports icon; thus, he earned over $40 million in 2002, mostly from endorsements. Tiger Woods is another example of the ideal endorser. He is a likeable person and a great golfer. He is the highest paid athlete with respect to endorsements, and he has virtually no negative public reputation. He is also interesting, articulate, and trust-worthy. It is no surprise that these two athletes have the highest Q-ratings of profes-sional athletes today. Most people with any interest in sports could determine Jordan and Woods as the top athlete endorsers of today without any system at all. Yet they are not the ideal endorsers for every product.

One major flaw in the Q-rating system is picking the endorsers of the future. How can Nike be sure that LeBron James is worth the $90 million contract and the $300 million it will cost to promote his endorsed products? Selecting the correct athletes to endorse the products for a company is becoming more important as ath-letes sign at younger ages and for larger amounts of money. A 13-year-old soccer player recently signed a multimillion-dollar deal.

The point is that times are changing quickly in the realm of athletic endorsement contracts, yet the system by which these athletes are rated is not keeping up with the pace at which times are changing. In fact, the Q-rating system is not changing at all, and it will undoubtedly become more and more obsolete. It certainly ignores some recent scholarly research.

Ignoring important traits in endorsers is a major flaw in the whole quotient rat-ing system. Traits other than likeability and fame, which are described in this chap-ter, can play a critical communication role in endorsements. Most new marketing textbooks describe and support the importance of the majority of these traits with hard evidence. It is ironic that the industry standard for rating endorsers ignores this marketing communication research.

On the positive side, Q-ratings have been around for decades; thus, this older rat-ings system serves as a benchmark against which current celebrities are judged. Another positive aspect of Q-ratings is that they're easy to collect and understand. Any change is the system would have to acknowledge these benefits. Creating a second system that takes the factors discussed in this chapter into account is advis-able. This new system would aid endorsement companies in the decision of whom to sign and how much to pay. Basing multimillion-dollar contracts on a system that looks at only two factors is absurd. A second system would take away much of this absurdity, and it could also give athletes feedback about where improvement is needed. There will always be a risk involved in signing athletes to multimillion dol-lar endorsement contracts; however, much of that risk could be alleviated though an improved evaluation system.

REFERENCES

Belch, G. A., & Belch, M. A. (1998). *Advertising and promotion* (4th Ed.). New York: Irvin/McGraw-Hill.

Chalip, L. (1997). Celebrity or hero? Toward a conceptual framework for athlete promotion. *Advancing Management of Australia and New Zealand Sport.* Melbourne, Australia: SMAANZ.

Graves, G. (2003, April 25). James must pick shoes for NBA leap. *USA Today* p. 13c.

Jones, M. J., & Schumann, D. W. (2004). The strategic use of celebrity athlete endorsers in print media: A historic perspective. In L. R. Kahle & C. Riley (Eds.), *Sports marketing and the psychology of marketing communication* (pp. 107–131). Mahwah, NJ: Lawrence Erlbaum Associates.

Jones, S., Bee, C., Burton, R., & Kahle, L. R. (2004). Marketing through sports entertainment: A functional approach. In L. J. Shrum (Ed.), *The psychology of entertainment media: Blurring the lines between entertainment and persuasion* (pp. 309–322). Mahwah, NJ: Lawrence Erlbaum Associates.

Kahle, L. R., Elton, M. P., & Kambara, K. M. (1997). Sports talk and the development of marketing relationships. *Sport Marketing Quarterly, 6*(2), 35–40.

Kahle, L. R., & Homer, P. M. (1985). Physical attractiveness of the celebrity endorser: A social adaptation perspective. *Journal of Consumer Research, 11,* 954–961.

Kahle, L. R., Kambara, K. M., & Rose, G. M. (1996). A functional model of fan attendance motivations for college football. *Sport Marketing Quarterly, 5,* 51–60.

Kamins, M. A., & Gupta, K. (1994). Congruence between spokesperson and product type: A match-up hypothesis perspective. *Psychology & Marketing, 11,* 569–586.

Krugman, D., Reid, L., Dunn, S., & Barban, A. (1994). *Advertising: Its role in modern marketing.* Philadelphia: Dryden.

Misra, S., & Beatty, S. E. (1990). Celebrity spokesperson and brand congruence. *Journal of Business Research, 231*(2), 159–173.

Shimp, T. A. (2003). *Advertising, promotion, and supplemental aspects of integrated marketing communication.* Mason, OH: South-Western.

Stone, G., Joeseph, M., & Jones, M. A. (2003). An exploratory study on the use of sports celebrities in advertising: A content analysis. *Sports Marketing Quarterly, 12,* 94–102.

Till, B., & Busler, M. (2000). The match-up hypothesis. *The Journal of Advertising, 29*(3), 1–13.

CHAPTER THIRTEEN

A Range of Female Beauties: A Cross-Cultural Analysis of Cosmetics TV Commercials

Kyoo-Hoon Han
University of Georgia

Federico de Gregorio
University of Alabama

In 1987, the American Society of Plastic Surgeons announced that 591,000 aesthetic, noncorrective plastic surgery operations had been performed in the previous year (Synnott, 1989); that number had risen to 6.9 million by 2002 ("Stats speak," 2002). The Miss Universe beauty pageant has been an annual event since 1952 and regularly draws a worldwide television audience of more than 600 million (Banet-Weiser, 1999). The top five brands of hair coloring totaled more than $600 million in sales in 2002 (Bittar, 2003).

Consumers' fascination with and pursuit of physical beauty has not gone unnoticed by advertisers. Downs and Harrison (1985) noted in their content analysis of 4,294 network television commercials that one of every 3.8 messages was related to the desirability of attractiveness. Beautiful models can be seen in advertisements for a vast range of products. Surprisingly, however, little attention has been paid the conceptualization of beauty itself as found in advertising.

BACKGROUND

Explorations of Beauty in Advertising Research

Advertising researchers have commonly examined the construct of beauty from two main perspectives. The first adopts a communication effectiveness point of view, which has generated a body of research examining the tactical and

201

executional usefulness of using physically attractive models in advertisements. Taken as a whole, this stream of research has revealed conflicting findings. A number of studies support the assumption that a physically attractive model will facilitate recognition, recall, or attitude toward both brands advertised and the advertisements themselves (e.g., Baker & Churchill, 1977; Caballero & Pride, 1984; Chestnut, LaChance, & Lubitz, 1977; DeBono & Telesca, 1990; Kahle & Homer, 1985; Reid & Soley, 1981). However, other studies found that physical attractiveness of the source does not always enhance these effects and in fact may potentially lead to negative evaluations (e.g., Bower, 2001; Bower & Landreth, 2001; Caballero, Lumpkin, & Madden, 1989; Caballero & Solomon, 1984; for in-depth reviews of findings in this literature, see Joseph, 1982, and Wolin, 2003).

The second major approach to studying beauty in advertising research is the adoption of a social effects orientation. This stream of research primarily has examined the negative impact of exposure to idealized images of physical attractiveness in advertisements on consumers' self-esteem, body satisfaction, feelings of guilt, and level of comparison with others. Commonly using Festinger's (1954) social comparison theory, research in this area has found that women consumers experience decreased self-esteem, increased feelings of guilt, and greater levels of dissatisfaction with their own bodies as a consequence of the proliferation of such difficult-to-imitate standards of physical attractiveness (Martin & Gentry, 1997; Martin & Kennedy, 1993; Richins, 1991). Although investigations of the communicative and social effects of using attractive models have been a steady stream of advertising research, a focus on the beauty image itself as used in advertisements has been lacking. The use of beautiful models resulting in certain positive or negative communicative effects, as well as often detrimental social effects through comparison, is well documented—but little is known about what kinds of beauty have been encoded in advertising content, which physical features are associated with being beautiful in advertisements, and cross-cultural differences in both these areas.

Origins of Beauty Notions

Eagly, Ashmore, Makhijani, and Longo (1991) proposed two primary sources from which commonly held notions of beauty (both definitions and perceived benefits) are derived: direct observation of positive and negative reinforcement in response to people of certain appearances in one's social environment and exposure to cultural representations of attractive and unattractive people. Through direct observation, people notice that better looking people receive more favorable reactions from others; for example, attractive people are more popular with peers and receive preferential treatment (see Feingold, 1990, and Patzer, 1985, for reviews).

Regarding cultural messages about physical appearance, although rarely explicitly stated, advertising is often considered a powerful source of idealized imagery against which people can evaluate and compare themselves (Martin & Kennedy, 1993; Richins, 1991). The strength of the influence of advertising as a source of cultural meaning regarding beauty is inherent in the criticisms of its social effects (Lakoff & Scherr, 1984; Pollay, 1986; Striegel-Moore, Silberstein, & Rodin, 1986). After all, there would be little need for criticism if people were not using advertising as a barometer for beauty. Advertisements tend to imitate the association of beauty with good things and ugliness with bad. For example, attractive models commonly appear in positive settings and with valuable possessions, whereas unattractive or average-looking models are depicted as lacking something or looking for a change in their lives (Eagly et al., 1991).

CONCEPTUAL FOUNDATION

Gatekeeping

The importance of the gatekeeping function has been well-established in the communication literature. Gatekeeping is generally defined as "all forms of information control that may arise in decisions about message encoding, such as selection, shaping, display, timing, withholding, or repetition of entire messages or message components" (Donohue, Tichenor, & Olien, 1972, p. 53). Schramm (1949) noted that "there is no aspect of communication as impressive as the enormous number of choices and discards which have to be made between the formation of the symbol in the mind of the communicator, and the appearance of a related symbol in the mind of the receiver" (p. 176). Although the gatekeeping notion is usually associated with the field of journalism, the original conceptualization by Lewin (1947) focused more broadly on how social change may be induced in communities (Shoemaker, 1991). In fact, Lewin's illustrative example involved a depth analysis of how food consumption trends were changing as a result of passing through several influential "gates" before reaching consumers. In a journalistic context, gatekeeping discussions primarily center on the range of subject matter, issues, and information that appear in the news media. Although advertising certainly has an informational function, it also serves as a source of reflections and reinforcements of cultural meanings (Frith & Mueller, 2003). Given gatekeepers' potential to mold people's social reality (Shoemaker, 1991), it is easy to see how advertising creators can be considered a type of "cultural gatekeeper" (Solomon, Ashmore, & Longo, 1992, p. 24) and how their works can be examined based on the range of cultural and social messages and associations they present in their attempts to persuade.

Advertisements are not created in a casual or random fashion. From the choice of scenery and background color to the size and nuance of copy, meticulous attention is paid to the executional elements to be included in promotional imagery (Solomon & Greenberg, 1993). Among the many choices that advertisers, creative directors, copywriters, art designers, production directors, and many others involved in advertising production (in this study, "advertising creators" refers to this group of people collectively) must make are who to utilize as models and how to represent them in the advertisements they are asked to create. Thus, those involved in the creation of an advertisement play a critical role in defining, reinforcing, and sanctioning receivers' perceptions and definitions of beauty through their advertising production decisions, including casting, wardrobe and props, make-up, motions, dialogue, and so on (Solomon et al., 1992). By virtue of their occupations and experience, those advertising creators are considered experts, whose tacit knowledge regarding the types of female beauty images most suitable for a particular advertisement governs their selection and decoration of models (Englis, Solomon, & Ashmore, 1994; Solomon et al., 1992). As it were, the particular beauty types chosen by advertising creators reflect the creators' implicit understanding of the elements that constitute physical attractiveness as well as their beliefs about the types of beauty that appeal to specific audiences.

However, advertising creators' notions of beauty do not suddenly arise fully formed out of nothing, nor are they solely a result of occupational experience. Rather, through observation of reactions, people's notions of attractiveness begin to form from birth (Samuels & Ewy, 1985) and continue throughout their lives. Hence, although these cultural gatekeepers' conceptualizations of beauty are certainly influenced by their work, they are formed from "a common Zeitgeist" (Englis et al., 1994, p. 51) of beauty notions that are a part of the citizens of a society. Consequently, their preconceived and implicit notions of what constitutes beauty limits the range of beauty types to be found in advertising material.

A Typology of Beauty Types

To illustrate the notion of cultural gatekeepers in advertising and their influence over the variety of beauty conceptualizations to which consumers are exposed, Englis et al., (1994) conducted two content analyses. Their studies revealed that all female models appearing in advertisements across five fashion magazines and all females featured in 267 MTV music videos (in essence, 3–4 minute commercials for specific music products) could be categorized into eight somewhat overlapping beauty types: classic beauty, feminine, sensual, exotic, cute, girl-next-door, sex kitten, and trendy (the typology itself was developed in an earlier study by Solomon et al., 1992). However, this categorization of attractiveness has not yet been utilized to examine the range of beauty types prevalent in advertisements outside the United States; that is, it is not a reflection of the cross-cultural gatekeeping effects of non-U.S. advertising creators. Because this typology was created in a generally Western (and specifically American) environment, cross-cultural applications are necessary to discover whether these beauty types can be applied universally or if refinements are needed to make the typology as comprehensive as possible.

Although some critical analyses of the societal definitions and importance of feminine beauty have supported the commonly held notions of cultural differences in perception and evaluation (e.g., Liggett, 1974; Wolf, 1991), a stream of social psychological research has revealed contradicting results. That is, evaluations of physical beauty, although exhibiting slight differences at a micro-level, often hold stable at a larger level, even across cultures. Consistencies in evaluations of cross-cultural facial attractiveness have been demonstrated by Chinese, Indian, and English women judging the facial attractiveness of Greek men (Thakerar & Iwawaki, 1979); Cruzans and Americans rating White men and women (Maret & Harling, 1985); and Whites, African Americans, and Chinese evaluating White and Chinese men and women (Bernstein, Lin, & McClellan, 1982).

The gap in cross-cultural applications of Solomon et al.'s (1992) typology of female beauty types, and the conflicting findings regarding the definitions of attractiveness across cultures, suggest the first research question addressed in this study:

RQ1. How do the distributions of female beauty types (using the typology proposed by Solomon, Ashmore and Longo) portrayed in beauty product advertising differ by culture?

Physical Characteristics of Female Beauty

Although the typology refined by Solomon et al. (1992) incorporates several physical dimensions as components of its eight beauty types, a large part of the categorization revolves around aesthetic judgments (e.g., one criterion for being considered cute is a combination of awkwardness and naturalness). Research has shown that perceived beauty is also a function of more objective predictors such as age. For example, a generally negative relation between age and physical female beauty has been found (Bassili & Reil, 1981; Henss, 1991; Perlini, Bertolissi, & Lind, 1999), indicating that youthfulness is a prime criterion in the use of beautiful models in advertisements.

Attractiveness-focused research has also demonstrated that body size (e.g., slim, obese) is an important predictor of and tends to be negatively correlated with positive evaluations of attractiveness. For example, mid-size and large women are perceived as less attractive than thin women (Pederson, Markee, & Salusso, 1994; Singh & Young, 1995; Tassinary & Hansen, 1998). However, research on the impact of body images has been somewhat inconclusive when applied cross-culturally, with some demonstrating deviations from this pattern (e.g., Furnham & Alibhai, 1983; Furnham & Baguma, 1994) and others not (e.g., Singh, 1994; Singh & Luis, 1995).

Other work on the construction and judgment of female beauty has found that hair features (e.g., color, length, style) play significant roles in positive ratings on attractiveness (McCracken, 1996; Rich & Cash, 1993; Synnott, 1987). For instance, Rich and Cash (1993) found that in *Playboy* magazine, a publication assumed to be a barometer of the notions of sensual beauty in a society, blonde hair color was overly represented (42%) in comparison to its estimated base rate in the

U.S. population (26%). Although these studies have not focused specifically on advertising, applicability to the current study is high.

The types and distributions of physical features found among the female models selected for beauty product advertisements reflect cultural gatekeepers' implicit understandings of the elements that constitute feminine beauty. Based upon the body of literature on physical attractiveness components, the following second research question is derived:

RQ2. How do the physical characteristics of female models in beauty product advertising differ by culture?

Female Model–Product Interaction as a Function of Gender Role

The gatekeeping function of advertising creators does not end with the selection of beauty types and attendant physical features to incorporate into their advertisements. Once a female model is selected, these cultural gatekeepers must then decide how to depict the model in their advertisement. Thus, the gatekeepers' decisions regarding the manner in which female models are portrayed reflect their tacit gender role beliefs. Although several content analyses have found evidence of increasing female stereotyping (e.g., Belkaoui & Belkaoui, 1976; Ferguson, Kreshel, & Tinkham, 1990; Soley & Kurzbard, 1986), others suggest that such portrayals, although clearly still existent, are decreasing over time (e.g., Bartsch, Burnett, Diller, & Rankin-Williams, 2000; Busby & Leichty, 1993).

Although gender roles are multidimensional, due to the particular nature of beauty product advertisements (e.g., commercials for cosmetics products tend to feature sole female models in limited social contexts), the study presented here examines the role of female beauty models in terms of their interactions with the advertised product, such as brand claims and demonstrations. Several studies have found that women in Western advertisements tend to be portrayed as active product users or demonstrators and used as voice-over narrators (e.g., Gilly, 1988; Michell & Taylor, 1990) to a greater extent than women in Eastern advertisements (e.g., Ford, Kramer, Honeycutt, & Casey, 1998; Moon, 2002). Thus, the final research question is posed as follows:

RQ3. How do the levels of female models' interaction with the product in beauty product advertising differ by culture?

METHOD

This study employed content analysis to investigate the types, distributions, physical characteristics, and level of product interaction of female models as portrayed in beauty product advertising across different cultures. An evaluation of the beauty images proliferated by advertising gatekeepers has been conducted by means of a survey or interviews with advertising agency or production personnel. However, such approaches run the risk of tapping into and relying on respondents' ideals, biases, and memories rather than the specific characteristics of the finished advertisements themselves (Yale & Gilly, 1988). The use of content analysis for such content-focused studies goes a long way toward resolving some of these issues. In essence, content analysis is a highly effective technique by which the cultural definitions of female beauty may be validly evaluated, due to its objective, systematic, nonreactive, and quantitative nature (Kassarjian, 1977; Kolbe & Burnett, 1991; Wimmer & Dominick, 2003).

Sampling

South Korea and the United States were selected as sample countries for the current content analysis. Both countries are assumed to have strikingly different cultural values based on the established cultural frameworks (Hall, 1981; Hofstede, 1997). As an illustration, according to the results of Hofstede's two cross-national surveys reported in 1980 and 1991, South Korea was ranked as collectivistic, feminine, more uncertainty-avoiding, and long-term oriented, whereas the United States was ranked as individualistic, masculine, less uncertainty-avoiding, and short-term oriented.

The selected product category was cosmetics. Cosmetics advertisements were considered as the appropriate unit of analysis because they provide the context that reflects beauty definitions resulting from the cultural gatekeeping functions of advertising creators. Another reason for the selection of cosmetics advertisements was an assumption that most female models appearing therein are supposed to be beautiful by definition (i.e., they must have been selected for the advertisement by virtue of their embodiment of a particular type of beauty).

This study sampled television commercials. Whereas most beauty-focused studies have analyzed print advertisements, little effort has been made to examine how beauty images are incorporated and characterized within a dynamic communication context such as television. Television commercials were obtained from the archive of a major South Korean advertising agency. All commercials in the cosmetics category were prescreened to ensure that only commercials for women's cosmetics were selected (i.e., commercials for men's cosmetics products were excluded from the sample). Thus, a total of 182 unduplicated cosmetics advertisements consisting of 95 South Korean and 87 U.S. commercials were chosen for the study. All commercials had aired in either South Korea or the United States throughout 2002 and were estimated to represent at least 70% of all the women's cosmetics commercials televised in both countries in that year. The selected pool of cosmetics commercials included such items as facial make-up, skin care, hair care, and fragrances. Typical lengths of the sampled commercials were 15, 20, and 30 seconds.

Coding Scheme

The analyses of overall beauty image, physical characteristics, and female model–product interaction were conducted only on the central female model in each commercial. Centrality was operationalized as prominence and duration on screen. Major categories in the coding scheme include the central female model's (a) overall beauty type (based on the typology developed by Englis et al., 1994, and Solomon et al., 1992; see Table 13.1); (b) physical characteristics (i.e., perceived age, race, body size, hair color, hair length, hair style, skin exposure, main color of costume); and (c) interaction with the product (i.e., role played for the product, brand name call, brand claim, the model's vocal presence in any product-focused messages).

In establishing the coding frame, the researchers referred to previous content analyses and created some new coding items considering the purpose of the current study. The eight categories of beauty, suggested by Englis et al., (1994) and Solomon et al., (1992) were slightly modified by combining the feminine type with the class of classic beauty and collapsing the attributes of girl next-door as outdoorsy. These modifications were to minimize the raters' possible confusions in their coding of beauty types because, as found by Solomon et al., (1992), the types of classic beauty and feminine would be closely associated with each other in expert's implicit theories of beauty, and the main characteristics of the girl next-door type (e.g., casualness and activeness) could be better incorporated into the outdoorsy feature. Thus, the following seven beauty categories were utilized and operationalized for the current content analysis: classic beauty, sensual, exotic, cute, outdoorsy, sex kitten, and trendy. Because those categories of female beauty are not mutually exclusive by definition (e.g., a model may be both sensual and exotic), the coders were allowed to mark on more than one category of this measure. The upper part in Table 13.1 exhibits the descriptions and coding criteria for each type of beauty used for this analysis.

It is also important to note that, although all seven beauty types were subject to the same characteristics for both countries, the researchers considered some probable variations in specific physical features associated with each type of beauty, perhaps resulting from the racial differences between the two countries. As an example, whereas the classic beauty was characterized as having blonde hair and Nordic features in Englis et al.'s (1994) content analysis study, the rating criteria focused on such Western classic beauty images were converted in coding the South Korean sample, considering some typical appearances of Korean women (e.g., black hair, yellowish skin). A similar kind of adaptation was also applied in deciding coding criteria for the exotic beauty type. In addition, despite a general view of age and race as demographic variables, both factors—perceived age and race—were included in the coding items for physical characteristics because they could be visually identified by the female models' overall physical appearance anyway.

TABLE 13.1

Coding Scheme for the Content Analysis

Variables	Selection Items
Country	(1) South Korea (2) United States
Product type	(1) Face make-up (2) Eye make-up (3) Lip make-up (4) Skin care (5) Hair care (6) Fragrance (7) General brand (8) Other (9) Unsure
Overall beauty image (Englis et al., 1994; Solomon et al., 1992)	
Model's image*	(1) Classic beauty (2) Sensual (3) Exotic (4) Cute (5) Outdoorsy (6) Sex kitten (7) Trendy (8) Unsure
	Classic beauty: soft image, feminine apparel, typically blonde or brown hair for a U.S. model, black hair for a Korean model
	Sensual: sexually attractive in a classy way, more skin exposure, deep make-up
	Exotic: ethnic looking, typically non-Caucasian model for the U.S. sample, non-Asian model for the Korean sample
	Cute: youthful appearance, casual attire, combination of innocence and naturalness
	Outdoorsy: casual, active, or athletic image, light make-up
	Sex kitten: sexy and modern attire, unintelligent and unnatural looking, youthful appearance
	Trendy: modern and faddish attire, hairstyle, and accessories
Physical Characteristics	
Perceived age	(1) Teen (2) 20–29 (3) 30–39 (4) 40 or older (5) Unsure
Race	(1) Caucasian (2) Korean (3) Non-Korean Asian (4) African-American (5) Hispanic (6) Other (7) Unsure
Body type	(1) Slim (2) Medium size (3) Plus size (4) Unsure
Skin exposure*	(1) Shoulder (2) Upper chest (3) Breast (4) Stomach (5) Upper leg (6) Lower leg (7) Foot (8) Arm (9) Back (10) Buttocks (11) Head only
Hair color	(1) Black (2) Brown (3) Blonde (4) Other (5) Unsure
Hair style	(1) Deep curl (2) Light curl (3) Straight (4) Other (5) Unsure
Hair length	(1) Long (2) Medium (3) Short (4) Unsure
Main color of costume	(1) Black (2) White (3) Blue (4) Red (5) Yellow (6) Green (7) Brown (8) Pink (9) Black & White (10) Skin only (11) Other
Interaction with the product	
Role played for the product	(1) Mere beauty symbol (2) Spokesperson (3) Heroine in drama (4) Demonstrator (5) Testimonial speaker (6) Other (7) Unsure
Brand name call	(1) Yes (2) No
Brand claim	(1) Yes (2) No
Speaking (lip-sync)	(1) Yes (2) No
Voice-over narration	(1) Yes (2) No (3) Unsure

Note. * indicates that multiple choices are allowed in coding.

210 HAN AND DE GREGORIO

Coders and Intercoder Reliability

Two bilingual coders fluent in both Korean and English were recruited to code the selected commercials. After individual training sessions and pretesting with a small sample of cosmetics commercials not included in the main pool, the first coder independently viewed and coded all the commercials. Subsequently, the second coder analyzed approximately 50% of the sample to calculate intercoder reliability. The overall percentages of agreement between the two coders were determined to be 89.2% for the South Korean sample and 85.8% for the U.S. sample. Based upon Kassarjian's (1977) recommendations regarding the satisfactory levels of intercoder reliability, both reliability scores were considered to be sufficient for the content analysis study.

RESULTS

For the statistical analyses of the female models' beauty image characteristics and product interaction level in the selected cosmetics commercials, a series of chi-square tests were conducted, comparing the South Korean and U.S. content. First, an analysis using the female beauty categories proposed by Solomon et al. (1992) was conducted to compare the female models' overall beauty images as portrayed in the two countries' commercials. As shown in Table 13.2, the classic beauty image was most frequently depicted in both nations (Korea, 48.4%; United States, 59.8%), followed by cute (Korea, 30.5%; United States, 23.0%). Comparatively, the U.S. commercials featured more classic beauty and sensual images than did the South Korean commercials, whereas the South Korean commercials used more exotic, cute, sex kitten, and trendy beauty types than did the U.S. sample. However, the proportional differences indicated in Table 13.2 may not be significant because of the small number of cases belonging to several beauty categories, such as sensual, exotic, outdoorsy, sex kitten, and trendy.

The next set of coding items concerned specific physical characteristics of the central female models, who were theoretically cast to represent an idealized beauty image or intentionally selected (considering the product and target audience) by advertising gatekeepers in different cultures. First, the differences in perceived age and race between South Korean and U.S. commercials were statistically significant. That is, whereas the age group of 20–29 was dominant in both the South Korean and U.S. samples, South Korean advertising creators appeared to hire more female models in that age range (89.5%) than their U.S. counterparts (64.4%; $\chi^2(5)$ = 138.2, $p < .05$) to be in cosmetics commercials. The distribution of female model races indicates that the most frequently depicted racial group in both countries is consistent with the majority race of each nation. That is, the South Korean sample used mostly Korean women (85.3%), whereas the U.S. sample usually utilized - Caucasian women (81.6%) as central model, ($\chi^2(3)$ = 17.1, $p < .05$). Noticeably, Caucasian models appeared relatively often in South Korean commercials (12.6%),

TABLE 13.2

Summary of Major Findings

Variables	South Korea		U.S.		Chi-square
Overall beauty image					
Model's image	Classic beauty:	48.4%	Classic beauty:	59.8%	NA
	Sensual:	5.3%	Sensual:	10.3%	
	Exotic:	7.4%	Exotic:	2.3%	
	Cute:	30.5%	Cute:	23.0%	
	Outdoorsy:	3.2%	Outdoorsy:	4.6%	
	Sex kitten:	9.5%	Sex kitten:	3.4%	
	Trendy:	8.4%	Trendy:	4.6%	
	Unsure:	3.2%	Unsure:	9.2%	
Physical characteristics					
Perceived age	20–29:	89.5%	20–29:	64.4%	$\chi2(5) = 138.2, p < .05$
	30–39:	8.4%	30–39:	28.7%	
Race	Korean:	85.3%	Caucasian:	81.6%	$\chi2(3) = 17.1, p < .05$
	Caucasian:	12.6%	Hispanic:	5.7%	
	Other:	2.1%	African-American:	4.6%	
Body type	Slim:	98.9%	Slim:	79.3%	$\chi2(2) = 18.7, p < .05$
	Medium size:	1.1%	Medium size:	19.5%	
Skin exposure	Head only:	21.1%	Head only:	31.0%	NA
	Other parts:	78.9%	Other parts:	69.0%	
Hair color	Black:	54.7%	Brown:	43.7%	$\chi2(2) = 18.7, p < .05$
	Brown:	41.1%	Blonde:	36.8%	
	Blonde:	2.1%	Black:	19.5%	
Hair style	Light curl:	61.1%	Light curl:	70.1%	$\chi2(2) = 46.0, p < .05$
	Straight:	35.8%	Straight:	19.5%	
	Deep curl:	1.1%	Deep curl:	10.3%	
Hair length	Long:	44.2%	Long:	65.5%	$\chi2(2) = 8.4, p < .05$
	Medium:	29.5%	Medium:	19.5%	
	Short:	26.3%	Short:	14.9%	
Main color of costume	White:	36.8%	White:	25.3%	$\chi2(10) = 16.5,$ n.s.
	Black:	26.3%	Black:	19.5%	
	Blue:	7.4%	Blue:	14.9%	
	Red:	4.2%	Red:	13.8%	
Interaction with the product					
Role played for the product	Beauty symbol:	64.2%	Beauty symbol:	34.5%	$\chi2(7) = 34.8, p < .05$
	Spokesperson:	10.5%	Spokesperson:	31.0%	
	Heroine in drama:	9.5%	Heroine in drama:		
	Demonstrator:	4.2%		10.3%	
			Demonstrator:	8.0%	
Brand name call	Yes:	21.1%	Yes:	17.2%	$c2(1) = .4,$ n.s.
	No:	78.9%	No:	82.8%	
Brand claim	Yes:	43.2%	Yes:	52.9%	$\chi2(1) = 1.7,$ n.s.
	No:	56.8%	No:	47.1%	
Speaking (lip-sync)	Yes:	42.1%	Yes:	50.6%	$\chi2(1) = 1.3,$ n.s.
	No:	57.9%	No:	49.4%	
Voice-over narration	Yes:	11.3%	Yes:	20.7%	$\chi2(2) = 15.5, p < .05$
	No:	84.5%	No:	67.8%	
	Unsure:	4.2%	Unsure:	11.5%	

but minority racial groups in the United States, such as African Americans and Hispanics, were seldom used as central female models in the selected commercials.

Further analyses of the female models' physical characteristics were conducted, revealing both similarities and dissimilarities between the South Korean and U.S. samples. As indicated in Table 13.2, the use of slim models was predominant for both countries, but the tendency was more prevalent for South Korean cosmetics commercials (98.9%) than U.S. ones (79.3%; $\chi^2(2) = 18.7, p < .05$). Concerning the level of skin exposure, more South Korean commercials presented female models' body skin (not including the head, 78.9%) than did U.S. commercials (69.0%). However, when a commercial exposed more parts of the female model's skin, the U.S. sample showed a greater variety of body parts than did the Korean sample. The proportions for each body part in terms of skin exposure are: arm (69.5%), shoulder (63.2%), upper chest (26.3%), lower leg (24.2%), foot (11.6%), upper leg (9.5%), back (2.1%), and no exposure of the breast, stomach, and buttocks areas in the South Korean sample; and arm (66.7%), shoulder (65.5%), upper chest (31.0%), lower leg (20.7%), back (17.2%), upper leg (14.9%), foot (11.5%), breast (4.6%), buttocks (3.4%), stomach (2.3%) in the U.S. sample.

Differences in the presentation of female models' hair were compared in terms of three characteristics: color, style, and length. Regarding hair color, brown was very frequently used in both countries' commercials (Korea, 41.1%; United States, 43.7%). Likely serving as a function of the natural racial features of each country, black hair (54.7%) in the Korean sample and blonde (36.8%) in the U.S. sample were also prevalent, and this tendency yielded a statistically significant difference between the two countries, $\chi^2(2) = 18.7, p < .05$. On the other hand, light curl is the most frequently used hairstyle in both samples (Korea, 61.1%; United States, 70.1%), followed by straight (Korea, 35.8%; United States, 19.5%; $\chi^2(2) = 46.0, p < .05$). In terms of hair length, long hair was the majority in both countries (Korea, 44.2%; United States, 65.5%), despite a statistically significant difference caused by proportional distinction, $\chi^2(2) = 8.4, p < .05$. In particular, the U.S. sample depicted female models with long hair much more frequently than those with medium (19.5%) or short hair (14.9%).

The analysis of the main color of costume that female models were wearing was designed to find out which colors in an external visual stimulus, like costume, were most employed to assist or enhance the models' physical attractiveness in advertising content. The result yielded a similarity between the two countries: white was most frequently used (Korea, 36.8%; United States, 25.3%), followed by black (Korea, 26.3%; United States, 19.5%), in both countries.

The analysis of the central female models' role portrayals focused on the level of product interaction, that is, the extent to which a female model plays a role for the advertised product or brand beyond being visually presented as a mere beauty icon. The results indicate that the majority of female models in the South Korean sample functioned as mere beauty symbols (64.2%) without further product interaction (e.g., speaking about product benefits or use experience), whereas female models in the U.S. sample often acted as spokespersons (31.3%), heroines in a dramatized storyline (10.3%), or product demonstrators (8.0%). In addition, although some differences from the results are not statistically significant, female models in the U.S. commercials were more often utilized to endorse the product verbally (brand claim, 52.9%; speaking with lip-sync, 50.6%; voice-over narration, 20.1%), compared to female models in the South Korean commercials (brand claim, 43.2%; speaking with lip-sync, 42.1%; voice-over narration 8.4%).

To evaluate the cross-cultural differences in the female models' level of product interaction more accurately, the researchers combined all the individual measures and calculated a composite score of product interaction per sample unit, which ranges from 0 to 5. Subsequently, an independent-samples t test yielded a statistically significant difference in the level of female models' product interaction between the two nations, $t = -2.709$, $p < .05$, confirming that female models in the U.S. sample had a higher level of product interaction than those in the South Korean sample ($M_{Korea} = 1.57$, $M_{US} = 2.28$).

DISCUSSION

The findings of this exploratory content analysis revealed the concomitant similarities and dissimilarities in the definitions of female beauty resulting from the gatekeeping actions of advertising creators in different cultures. Despite the selected two countries—South Korea and the United States—being considered highly different on multiple cultural dimensions (Hall, 1976; Hofstede, 1997) and a stream of literature supporting the great variability of beauty definitions across cultures (e.g., Liggett, 1974; Wolf, 1991), in the aggregate the two countries evinced similar patterns in their characterizations of female beauty as reflected in the sample of cosmetics commercials.

Summarizing our major results, samples of commercials from both countries disclosed: (a) dominant proliferation of the classic beauty and cute beauty types; (b) strong associations of youthfulness, slim body size, long hair length, and light curly hair style with female beauty; and (c) a majority of the female models utilized only as beauty symbols, although a relative minority served as active endorsers for the advertised brand (this tendency was particularly prominent in the South Korean sample). These overall findings provide managerial implications to global marketers with regard to the 40-year ongoing debate over the comparative effectiveness of standardization versus localization strategies (see Agrawal, 1995, for a longitudinal review). On the surface, the results suggest that, at least in the choice of female models for beauty product advertisements, the utilization of dominant beauty types will be of equivalent effectiveness cross-culturally.

However, one must not lose sight of the fact that although overall (i.e., macro-level) patterns are similar, the samples of commercials also showed micro-level differences on the measured items, indicating that cultural values influence definitions of female beauty and thus ignoring local values is often a mistake.

As an illustration, there was an interesting contrast in the prevalence of the sex kitten beauty type (9.5% for the South Korean sample, 3.4% for the U.S. sample). Lee (2002) argued that South Korea has long been and largely continues to be a patriarchal society whose notions of female sexuality are conservative in comparison with the United States. However, the greater instances of the sex kitten image in the South Korean sample than in the U.S. sample hint at an undercurrent of increased acceptance for more overtly sexualized depictions of female beauty, a trend that marketers who automatically adopt a standardized tactic of using either of the top two beauty types may overlook and not use to their advantage.

Another implication of this study has to do with the gatekeeping function of non-U.S. advertising creators. Few discussions of gatekeeping theory apply it to cross-cultural contexts. Our results indicate that the cultural gatekeeping in female model selections that advertising creators of all cultures make by virtue of their occupations may result in a similar range of beauty types appearing in commercials. Although there are micro-level differences in prevalence, the specific types of beauty and their macro-level distributions were rather similar. This finding implies that although the specific beauty types may be slightly different in their incidence, the range of types is similarly limited across both cultures. Thus, it seems that the cultural gatekeeping function of advertising creators results in a narrowing of the kinds of representations that the public is exposed to.

In addition, the levels of female model–product interaction have implications regarding the ability of cultural dimensions such as Hofstede's (1997) masculine–feminine continuum to predict gender role portrayals in advertising. The commonly posited notion is that countries rated as being more masculine in orientation tend to exhibit greater degrees of gender-stereotyped portrayals in their advertisements (Milner & Collins, 2000; Moon, 2002). Although some studies have supported this proposition (e.g., Gilly, 1988; Milner & Collins, 2000), our results hint at an opposite relation. South Korean culture is considered significantly less masculine than U.S. culture, according to Hofstede's (1997) masculinity index scores (South Korea, 39; United States, 62). In our analysis, however, the South Korean sample was found to use female models as mere beauty symbols to a notably greater extent than the U.S. sample (64.2% vs. 34.5%). This finding indicates that female models in the South Korean commercials were portrayed as relatively feminine and passive; in contrast, those in the U.S. commercials appeared to be relatively independent and performance oriented, corresponding to more masculine attributes. Accordingly, it is interpreted that female role stereotypes were more prevalent in the South Korean sample than in the U.S. sample. This inconsistency between our results and the implications of Hofstede's feminine–masculine dimension suggests that cross-cultural stereotypes of gender roles reflected in the advertising context may not currently be the same as those found in Hofstede's work-related values more than two decades ago. Therefore, replication studies on this issue are encouraged, in that any resulting theoretical modifications will enable us to understand better the relation between gender role portrayals in media content and the "gender of countries" (Milner & Collins, 2000, p. 68).

As a marginal implication from our findings, it is interesting to notice that 3.2% and 9.2% of models in the South Korean and U.S. samples respectively could not be categorized into any of the seven beauty types based on the typology by Solomon et al. (1992). Initially this categorization was considered to be an artifact of coder uncertainty as to which type a particular model belonged to, but subsequent discussions with coders indicated that it may point to the existence of beauty types not covered by Solomon, Ashmore, and Longo's typology. Although not specifically noted in their article, it would seem that Englis et al.'s (1994) coding of magazine advertisements and MTV videos did not allow for unsure or other categories, an indicant that there may be additional beauty types that in such cases were forced into a category. On a related note, during discussions it was revealed that in the midst of coding, coders found themselves automatically adapting the seven beauty types to the beauty norms of South Korea (both coders were familiar with the cultures of both South Korea and the United States). This phenomenon suggests that Solomon et al.'s (1992) beauty typology may need some adaptation if it is to be utilized successfully to evaluate the attractiveness of non-Western models. Although acceptable intercoder reliabilities were achieved, this may be due to the fact that both coders' intimate knowledge of the two cultures resulted in their mentally adapting the beauty types in the same way. It would be interesting to see if coding by those not familiar with the culture of a country would also yield acceptable intercoder reliability.

Limitations and Future Research

Although this content analysis of cross-cultural beauty types and several attendant physical features in cosmetics commercials has revealed some significant trends, the generalizability of our findings is limited in several ways. First, because the selected sample of commercials spanned only a one-year period, the findings are somewhat confined to that time range. One of the underlying premises of this study was that longitudinal changes in perceptions and preferences of female beauty may occur superficially but that the physical features and aesthetic characteristics considered beautiful likely do not change very much. However, the one-year period utilized in this study does not allow for this tenet to be either verified or disproved. So that longitudinal trends in the relation between beauty types and the physical and aesthetic features associated with them can be made, future research needs to utilize a longer or different range of time for its analysis.

A second inhibitor of generalizability is the number of countries selected for this study. As stated earlier, South Korea and the United States were regarded as appropriate sample countries for analysis because of their extremely different cultural values, as suggested by many cross-cultural researchers. However, even if they are considered to be near opposites (e.g., an Eastern culture versus a Western culture), two countries cannot serve wholly to represent the diverse cultures of the world. Therefore, it is recommended that future cross-cultural research on the current issue include a wider variety of countries to assess more reliably the influence of cultural values on beauty image portrayals in advertising.

The fact that only commercials for cosmetics products were analyzed in this study suggests another avenue for future research. Because of the inherent nature of cosmetics products (i.e., specifically designed to beautify and thus attractiveness-centered by definition), it is very likely that only highly attractive models are used as executional elements. Therefore, our results may not apply to female models selected for product categories that are not so closely associated with attractiveness, such as coffee or personal computers. Bower and Landreth (2001) found that normally attractive models—those whose features are attractive but more representative of average women than the idealized beauty of very attractive models—can be more effective when products are not attractiveness-related (this finding indirectly supports the match-up hypothesis, which assumes the message effectiveness when the endorser's image and the image of the product are congruent on an attractiveness basis; see Kahle & Homer, 1985, and Kamins, 1990, for general overviews of the concept). Accordingly, future research should explore whether and to what extent specific physical features are associated with different beauty types in advertisements for products that are not inherently beauty-related.

It also needs to be noted that a distinctive characteristic of the beauty-focused advertising research has been the predominant emphasis on female models. Although there is a recent trend toward increasing investigations of male portrayals in advertisements (e.g., Leppard, Ogletree, & Wallen, 1993; Rohlinger, 2002), few studies have looked at the types and definitions of masculine attractiveness found therein. Hence, another direction for future research is to examine whether advertisements contain certain templates of male handsomeness and which, if any, physical features are associated with them.

Finally, although content analytic studies can reveal a wealth of descriptive data, they are of limited value in helping marketers and researchers predict consumer responses, such as brand attitude and behavioral intention. For this reason, further investigations exploring beauty-in-advertising issues should accompany consumer research using such techniques as surveys, experiments, focus groups, and in-depth interviews (with advertising practitioners or consumers) to appreciate the dynamic cultural interplays between advertisements and their receivers, which cannot be known by content analyses alone. Suggested focuses for such future explorations include how consumers develop their own ingrained, implicit beliefs about the physical characteristics that make up female beauty; to what extent these beliefs match the beauty images portrayed in advertisements; and how such perceptions influence consumers' advertising and brand evaluations. In this respect, the present study encourages further efforts to enhance our understanding of the intricate relations among beauty, culture, and consumers.

REFERENCES

Agrawal, M. (1995). Review of a 40-year debate in international advertising: Practitioner and academician perspectives to the standardization/adaptation issue. *International Marketing Review, 12,* 26–48.

Baker, M. J., & Churchill, G. A., Jr. (1977). The impact of physically attractive models on advertising evaluations. *Journal of Marketing Research, 14,* 538–555.

Banet-Weiser, S. (1999). *The most beautiful girl in the world: Beauty pageants and national identity.* Berkeley, CA: University of California Press.

Bartsch, R. A., Burnett, A. T., Diller, T. R., & Rankin-Williams, E. (2000). Gender representation in television commercials: Updating an update. *Sex Roles. 43,* 735–743.

Bassili, J. N., & Reil, J. E. (1981). On the dominance of the old age stereotype. *Journal of Gerontology, 36,* 682–688.

Belkaoui, A., & Belkaoui, J. M. (1976). A comparative analysis of the roles portrayed by women in print advertisements—1958, 1970, 1972. *Journal of Marketing Research, 12,* 168–172.

Bernstein, I. H., Lin, T., & McClellan, P. (1982). Cross- vs. within-racial judgments of attractiveness. *Perception and Psychophysics, 32,* 495–503.

Bittar, C. (2003, June). Beauty in the eyewash of the beholder. *Brandweek, 44,* 550–551.

Bower, A. B. (2001). Highly attractive models in advertising and the women who loathe them: The implications of negative affect for spokesperson effectiveness. *Journal of advertising, 30,* 51–63.

Bower, A. B., & Landreth, S. (2001). Is beauty best? Highly versus normally attractive models in advertising. *Journal of Advertising, 30,* 1–12.

Busby, L. J., & Leichty, G. (1993). Feminism and advertising in traditional and nontraditional women's magazines: 1950s–1980s. *Journalism Quarterly, 70,* 247–265.

Caballero, M. J., Lumpkin, J. R., & Madden, C. S. (1989). Using physical attractiveness as an advertising tool: An empirical test of the attraction phenomenon. *Journal of Advertising Research, 29,* 16–22.

Caballero, M. J., & Pride, W. M. (1984). Selected effects of salesperson sex and attractiveness in direct mail advertisements. *Journal of Marketing, 48,* 94–100.

Caballero, M. J., & Solomon, P. J. (1984). Effects of model attractiveness on sales response. *Journal of Advertising, 13,* 17–24.

Cheng, H. (1997). Holding up half the sky? A sociocultural comparison of gender-role portrayals in Chinese and US advertising. *International Journal of Advertising, 16,* 295–319.

Chestnut, R. W., LaChance, C. C., & Lubitz, A. (1977). The 'decorative' female model: Sexual stimuli and the recognition of advertisements. *Journal of Advertising, 6,* 11–14.

Cunningham, M. R., Roberts, A. R., Barbee, A. P., Druen, P. B., & Wu, C. (1995). "Their ideas of beauty are, on the whole, the same as ours": Consistency and variability in the cross-cultural perception of female physical attractiveness. *Journal of Personality and Social Psychology, 68,* 261–279.

DeBono, K. G., & Telesca, C. (1990). The influence of source physical attractiveness on advertising effectiveness: A functional perspective. *Journal of Applied Social Psychology, 20,* 1383–1395.

Donohue, G. A., Tichenor, P. J., & Olien, C. N. (1972). Gatekeeping: Mass media systems and information control. In F. G. Kline & P. J. Tichenor (Eds.), *Current perspectives in mass communication research* (pp. 41–70). Beverly Hills, CA: Sage.

Downs, A. C., & Harrison, S. K. (1985). Embarrassing age spots or just plain ugly? Physical attractiveness stereotyping as an instrument of sexism on American television commercials. *Sex Roles, 13,* 9–19.

Eagly, A. H., Ashmore, R. D., Makhijani, M. G., & Longo, L. (1991). What is beautiful is good, but ... : A meta-analytic review of research on the physical attractiveness stereotype. *Psychological Bulletin, 110,* 109–128.

Englis, B. G., Solomon, M. R., & Ashmore, R. D. (1994). Beauty before the eyes of beholders: The cultural encoding of beauty types in magazine advertising and music television. *Journal of Advertising, 23,* 49–64.

Feingold, A. (1990). Gender differences in effects of physical attractiveness on romantic attraction: A comparison across five research paradigms. *Journal of Personality and Social Psychology, 59,* 981–993.

Ferguson, J. H., Kreshel, P. J., & Tinkham, S. F. (1990). In the pages of Ms.: Women in advertising. *Journal of Advertising, 19,* 40–51.

Festinger, L. (1954). A theory of social comparison processes. *Human Relations, 7,* 117–140.

Ford, J. B., Kramer, P., Honeycutt, E. D., Jr., & Casey, S. L. (1998). Gender role portrayals in Japanese advertising: A magazine content analysis. *Journal of Advertising, 27,* 113–124.

Frith, K. T., & Mueller, B. (2003). *Advertising and societies: Global issues.* New York: Peter Lang.

Furnham, A., & Alibhai, N. (1983). Cross-cultural differences in the perception of female body shapes. *Psychological Medicine, 13,* 829–837.

Furnham, A., & Baguma, P. (1994). Cross-cultural differences in evaluation of male and female body shapes. *International Journal of Eating Disorders, 15,* 81–89.

Gilly, M. C. (1988). Sex roles in advertising: A comparison of television advertisements in Australia, Mexico, and the United States. *Journal of Marketing, 52,* 75–85.

Hall, E. T. (1981). *Beyond culture.* New York: Anchor.

Henss, R. (1991). Perceiving age and attractiveness in facial photographs. *Journal of Applied Social Psychology, 21,* 933–946.

Hofstede, G. (1997). *Culture's consequences: Comparing values, behaviors, institutions and organizations across nations.* Thousand Oaks, CA: Sage.

Joseph, W. B. (1982). The credibility of physically attractive communicators: A review. *Journal of Advertising, 11,* 15–24.

Kahle, L. R., & Homer, P. M. (1985). Physical attractiveness of the celebrity endorser: A social adaptation perspective. *Journal of Consumer Research, 11,* 954–961.

Kamins, M. A. (1990). An investigation into the 'match-up' hypothesis in celebrity advertising: When beauty may be only skin deep. *Journal of Advertising, 19,* 4–13.

Kassarjian, H. H. (1977). Content analysis in consumer research. *Journal of Consumer Research, 4,* 8–18.

Kolbe, R. H., & Burnett, M. S. (1991). Content-analysis research: An examination of applications with directives for improving research reliability and objectivity. *Journal of Consumer Research, 18,* 243–250.

Lakoff, R. T., & Scherr, R. L. (1984). *Face value: The politics of beauty.* Boston: Routledge & Kegan Paul.

Lee, S. (2002). The concept of female sexuality in Korean popular culture. In L. Kendall (Ed.), *Under construction: The gendering of modernity, class, and consumption in the Republic of Korea* (pp. 141–164). Honolulu, HI: University of Hawaii Press.

Leppard, W., Ogletree, S. M., & Wallen, E. (1993), Gender stereotyping in medical advertising: Much ado about something? *Sex Roles, 29,* 829–838.

Lewin, K. (1947). Frontiers in group dynamics II: Channels of group life; social planning and action research. *Human Relations, 1,* 143–153.

Liggett, J. (1974). *The human face*. New York: Stein & Day.

Maret, S. M., & Harling, C. A. (1985). Cross-cultural perceptions of physical attractiveness: Ratings of photographs of Whites by Cruzans and Americans. *Perceptual and Motor Skills, 60,* 163–166.

Martin, M. C., & Gentry, J. W. (1997). Stuck in the model trap: The effects of beautiful models in ads on female pre-adolescents and adolescents. *Journal of Advertising, 26,* 19–33.

Martin, M. C., & Kennedy, P. F. (1993). Advertising and social comparison: Consequences for female preadolescents and adolescents. *Psychology and Marketing, 10,* 513–530.

McCracken, G. (1996). *Big hair: A journey into the transformation of the self.* New York: Overlook Press.

Michell, P. C. N., & Taylor, W. (1990). Polarising trends in female role portrayals in U.K. advertising. *European Journal of Marketing, 24,* 41–49.

Milner, L. M., & Collins, J. M. (2000). Sex-role portrayals and the gender of nations. *Journal of Advertising, 29,* 67–79.

Moon, Y. (2002). Gender portrayal in Korean and Hong Kong television commercials. *Korean Journal of Advertising, 13,* 7–23.

Patzer, G. L. (1985). *The physical attractiveness phenomenon.* New York: Plenum.

Pederson, E. L., Markee, N. L., & Salusso, C. J. (1994). Gender differences in characteristics reported to be important features of physical attractiveness. *Perceptual & Motor Skills, 79,* 1539–1544.

Perlini, A. H., Bertolissi, S., & Lind, D. L. (1999). The effects of women's age and physical appearance on evaluations of attractiveness and social desirability. *Journal of Social Psychology, 139,* 343–354.

Pollay, R. W. (1986). The distorted mirror: Reflections on the unintended consequences of advertising. *Journal of Marketing, 50,* 18–36.

Reid, L. N., & Soley, L. C. (1981). Another look at the 'decorative' female model: The recognition of visual and verbal ad components. *Journal of Current Issues and Research in Advertising, 4,* 123–133.

Rich, M. K., & Cash, T. F. (1993). The American image of beauty: Media representations of hair color for four decades. *Sex Roles, 29,* 113–124.

Richins, M. L. (1991). Social comparison and the idealized images of advertising. *Journal of Consumer Research, 18,* 71–83.

Rohlinger, D. A. (2002). Eroticizing men: Cultural influences in advertising and male objectification. *Sex Roles, 46,* 61–74.

Samuels, C. A, & Ewy, R. (1985). Aesthetic perception of faces during infancy. *British Journal of Developmental Psychology, 3,* 221–228.

Schramm, W. (1949). The gatekeeper: A memorandum. In W. Schramm (Ed.), *Mass communications* (pp. 175–177). Urbana, IL: University of Illinois Press.

Shoemaker, P. J. (1991). *Gatekeeping.* Newbury Park, CA: Sage.

Singh, D. (1994). Ideal female body shapes: Role of body weight and waist-to-hip ratio. *International Journal of Eating Disorders, 16,* 283–288.

Singh, D., & Luis, S. (1995). Ethnic and gender consensus for the effect of waist-to-hip ratio on judgment of women's attractiveness. *Human Nature, 6,* 51–65.

Singh, D., & Young, R. K. (1995). Body weight, waist-to-hip ratio, breasts, and hips: Role in judgments of female attractiveness and desirability for relationships. *Ethology and Sociobiology, 16,* 483–507.

Soley, L. C., & Kurzbard, G. (1986). Sex in advertising: A comparison of 1964 and 1984 magazine advertisements. *Journal of Advertising, 15,* 46–64.

Solomon, M. R., Ashmore, R. D., & Longo, L. C. (1992). The beauty match-up hypothesis: Congruence between types of beauty and product images in advertising. *Journal of Advertising, 21,* 23–34.

Solomon, M. R., & Greenberg, L. (1993). Setting the stage: Collective selection in the stylistic content of commercials. *Journal of Advertising, 22,* 11–24.

Stats speak for themselves. (2002, June). *Cosmetic Surgery Times, 5,* 4.

Striegel-Moore, R. H., Silberstein, L. R, & Rodin, J. (1986). Toward an understanding of risk factors for bulimia. *American Psychologist, 41,* 246–263.

Synnott, A. (1987). Shame and glory: A sociology of hair. *British Journal of Sociology, 38,* 381–413.

Synnott, A. (1989). Truth and goodness, mirrors and masks—part I: A sociology of beauty and the face. *British Journal of Sociology, 40,* 607–636.

Tassinary, L. G., & Hansen, K. A. (1998). A critical test of the waist-to-hip ratio hypothesis of female physical attractiveness. *Psychological Science, 9,* 150–155.

Thakerar, J. N., & Iwawaki, S. (1979). Cross-cultural comparisons in interpersonal attraction of females toward males. *Journal of Social Psychology, 108,* 121–122.

Wimmer, R. D., & Dominick, J. D. (2003). *Mass media research* (7th ed.). Belmont, CA: Wadsworth/Thomson Learning.

Wolf, N. (1991). *The beauty myth: How images of beauty are used against women.* New York: Morrow.

Wolin, L. D. (2003). Gender issues in advertising—an oversight synthesis of research: 1970–2002. *Journal of Advertising Research, 43,* 111–129.

Yale, L., & Gilly, M. C. (1988). Trends in advertising research: A look at the content of marketing-oriented journals from 1976 to 1985. *Journal of Advertising, 17,* 12–22.

Part IV—Corporate Image

A positive and superior corporate image is important for enhancing the competitive advantage of any organization or business. Corporate image is multi-dimensional in nature: There are multiple stakeholders, and corporate image can be observed from different perspectives such as from that of consumers, employees, and other shareholders. Furthermore, corporate image can be enhanced by sponsorship marketing, and there is a positive effect if the sponsorship is valid to the brand. In this section, the first two chapters examine the conceptualization of corporate image from various stakeholders' perspectives (i.e., customers, employees, shareholders, etc). The last chapter provides a new theoretical framework based on information processing for the conceptualization of corporate sponsorship.

CHAPTER FOURTEEN

Well-Matched Employees Make Customers Happy: Effects of Brand–Employee Congruence

Youjae Yi
Seoul National University

Suna La
Korea National Open University

Companies are exerting their efforts to increase the number of loyal customers, who will evolve into brand apostles in the future (Yi & Jeon, 2003; Yi & La, 2004). Inside the company, however, they have not realized the importance of employees' perception of the brand.

A survey shows that about 30% of U.K. employees are brand neutral or are just not interested in their company's brand, and a further 22% are brand saboteurs, actively working against the brand culture (Hiscock, 2002). Companies should make sure that internal customers understand the brand and communicate it well to external customers. In this sense, Hiscock (2002) suggested that companies use more idiosyncratic methods to make the brand a living reality. Particularly, for companies whose brand is based more on service than product, it is even more important to keep employees who are the brand embassy.

Management should have a well-motivated team that comprehends and communicates the brand promise. Recently, corporations are finally realizing that employees are their vital assets. Successful organizations are able to interconnect their employees' personalities into a strong brand culture that expresses their brand promise (Ellwood, 2001).

Berry (2000) stated that, in most cases, consumers are aware of a service brand as the brand name of its company, which is a distinctive characteristic of service brands compared with product brands. For this reason, the management of a service company needs to realize the importance of brand image and brand identity of the company. For consumers, corporate brand messages of a service firm are embedded in the employees at every contact point. Thus, the attitudes and behaviors of service personnel can be critical communication messages. An employee's attitudes and behaviors have a close relation with his or her personality. There is a need for more research on employee personality especially in services settings. In this context, we propose an integrated model that investigates the relations among brand personality, employee–brand identification, employee satisfaction, and customer satisfaction (CS) effort with an internal marketing approach.

LITERATURE REVIEW

Internal Marketing

In the past research on employee satisfaction (ES), there have been two main approaches to increase customer satisfaction via ES. One is emphasizing the way of identifying and recruiting people whose personalities are appropriate for the job characteristics. The other is the internal marketing approach, which proposes to regard employees as internal customers (Gremler, Bitner, & Evans, 1994; Lewis & Entwistle, 1990; Rust, Stewart, Miller, & Pielack, 1996). The philosophy of the internal marketing approach is based on the idea that happy employees make customers happy.

On the internal marketing perspective, effectively measuring and improving employee satisfaction is a critical function of contemporary management. Because businesses are becoming more competitive and because employees with the skills and abilities needed to obtain competitive advantages are becoming scarcer, management can no longer afford to see employees as replaceable inputs (Miles & Creed, 1995).

Management should view employees as valuable contributors whose opinions and perceptions are important sources of knowledge. This view requires the development of relationships that go outside the bounds of traditional hierarchy as well as the acknowledgment that employee retention is dependent on a continuing exchange of agreements and contributions between employees and firms (Rousseau & Parks, 1992). In this sense, employees are similar to customers, and their satisfaction and retention are critical (Rust et al., 1996).

Berry (1981) mentioned that whether managing customers or employees, the central purpose remains the same: the attraction of patronage through the satisfaction of needs and wants. Rust et al. (1996) emphasized that particularly for the service firms, the frontline employee must be viewed not just as someone who must listen to management but also as someone to whom management must listen.

As mentioned earlier, satisfied employees are likely to produce satisfied customers. For example, supportive supervisors, technology, and empowerment have been considered the important variables for enhancing employee satisfaction (Schneider, Wheeler & Cox, 1992; Sergeant & Frenkel, 2000).

The model of service profit chain (Heskett, Jones, Loveman, Sasser, & Schlesinger, 1994; Heskett, Sasser & Schlesinger, 1997) includes several relations among firm profitability, customer loyalty, and employee satisfaction. Employee satisfaction is fostered by effective support services and policies that assist contact employees in their dealings with customers. Although the model has simple but strong conceptual value, the service profit chain had not been tested rigorously across different types of service organizations.

In fact, the measurement of CS corresponding to individual ES is hard to obtain. For the purpose of convenient measurement, a proxy for CS has been frequently used. Customer orientation and capacity to satisfy customers are widely adopted measures. Inconsistent results are found across various studies investigating the direct relation between ES and CS. Sergeant and Frenkel (2000) did not find the direct effect of job satisfaction on employees' capacities to satisfy customers. Researchers and practitioners are keenly interested in this issue because if ES does not guarantee CS, they should find a new determinant of CS inside the company.

Determinants and Consequences of ES

Burnout. Job satisfaction has been the topic of extensive study in seeking to understand employee behaviors and attitudes. Main issues are the relations among job satisfaction, job stress, burnout, performance, personality, and customer orientation.

The combined effect of several sources of job stress may exceed the person's capacity to cope and initiate the burnout process (Singh, Goolsby, & Rhodes, 1994). Burnout is defined as the state of fatigue and frustration arising from unrealistic, excessive demands on personal resources and leading to physical and mental exhaustion (Freudengerger, 1974). Burnout, therefore, is a syndrome of emotional exhaustion, depersonalization, and reduced personal accomplishment that can occur among individuals who work with people in some capacity (Brewer & Clippard, 2002; Maslach, Jackson, & Leither, 1996). Individuals in boundary-spanning positions are especially susceptible to emotional exhaustion (Cordes & Doughterty, 1993; Leiter & Maslach, 1988). Emotional exhaustion has been found to be related to attitudes and behaviors (Lee & Ashforth, 1990, 1996).

Possible effects of burnout at the organizational level are increase in job turnover and absenteeism as well as decreased employee involvement with the job, organizational commitment, and job satisfaction (Bakacus, Cravens, Johnston, & Moncrief, 1999; Belicki & Woolcott, 1996; Lee & Ashforth, 1996; Maslach, Jackson, & Leither, 1996; Singh et al., 1994).

Role Ambiguity and Role Conflict. Role ambiguity and role conflict are regarded as main sources of job stress, which result in the negative relation with job satisfaction (Sumrall & Sebastianelli, 1999). Previous research has empirically demonstrated that job satisfaction of employees can be increased by enhancing role clarity, decreasing role conflict, and reducing job tension (Churchill, Ford, & Walker, 1974, 1976, 1985; Kelly, Gable, & Hise, 1981; Rogers, Clow, & Kash, 1994; Walker, Churchill, & Ford, 1975). Among them, the initiative factor of increasing employee satisfaction is role clarity. It means that employees need to understand their roles within the firm clearly. Corporate brand message can be a tacit guide for employees' role in the firm.

Personality. Many researchers suggest that burnout is linked to personality factors (Burke & Richardsen, 1996; Cordes & Doughterty, 1993; Layman & Guyden, 1997; Maslach et al., 1996; Westman & Eden, 1997). Greater congruence between characteristics of people and situations is believed to create a more productive work environment and reduce role conflict (Aronoff & Wilson, 1985; Getzels & Guba, 1954). Especially, a number of studies suggest that the congruence between employee personality and his or her role is much more important in boundary-spanning positions (Hurley, 1998). Incongruence between employee personality and corporate brand personality could be a possible source of job stress for service employees and could be a possible cause of low job satisfaction.

Self-Esteem. Self-esteem is negatively related to burnout (Golembiewski & Kim, 1989). It is, in turn, positively related to job satisfaction. However, based on behavioral plasticity theory, researchers proposed that self-esteem is a buffer to protect individuals from becoming burned out (Pierce, Gardner, Dunham, & Cummings, 1993; Rosse, Bass, Johnson, & Crown, 1991).

Self-esteem has been recognized as a multifaceted and a hierarchical construct (Song & Hattie, 1985). Global self-esteem is conceptualized as an overall evaluation of self-worth and expresses an attitude of approval or disapproval of self (Korman, 1976; Wells & Marwell, 1976). Pierce, Gardner, Cummings, and Dunham (1989 p. 280) initially defined organization-based self-esteem as "the degree to which organizational members believe that they can satisfy their needs by participating in roles within the context of an organization."

There are various types of self-perceptions, including self-esteem, self-worth, and self-efficacy, and they are closely linked with one another. Self-consistency theory posits that individuals with high self-esteem are motivated to maintain that high level, and as a result they exert to perform well (Korman, 1976). Their high sense of self-esteem stems from self-efficacy, and it results in strong job performance (Gardner & Pierce, 1998). Especially, self-esteem is considered necessary for most service professions.

Self-esteem is closely associated with brand identification especially when a brand holds social reputation or status. It thus serves social recognition and social approval (Lassar, Mittal, & Sharman, 1995; Río, Vázquez, & Iglesias, 2001).

Customer Orientation and Capacity to Satisfy Customers. Customer orientation is a widely adopted dependent variable of job satisfaction. The key measure of customer orientation is the sales orientation-customer orientation (SOCO) scale, which is conceptualized as the employee's desire to help customers make satisfactory purchase decisions, to help customers assess their needs, to offer service that will satisfy those needs, to describe service accurately, to avoid deceptive or manipulative influence tactics, and finally to avoid the use of high-pressure tactics (Hoffman & Ingram, 1992).

The first attempt to measure customer orientation directly at the individual level was made by Saxe and Weitz (1982). They tried to measure the extent to which a salesperson seeks to increase long-term customer satisfaction. Brown, Mowen, Donavan, and Licata (2002) regarded customer orientation as an employee's tendency or predisposition to meet customer needs in an on-the-job context.

Sergeant and Frenkel (2000) developed the concept of capacity to satisfy customers (CSC). Contact employees' CSC is a subjective and self-rating evaluation of their relationships with customers, and in particular the ability to satisfy customers.

Even though there has been little evidence on the direct positive relation between ES and CS, general findings of past research converge on the point that job satisfaction is positively related to customer orientation or capacity to satisfy customers.

Brand Personality

Brand personality is defined as the set of human characteristics or traits that consumers attribute to a brand (Aaker, 1997). In the past, the "Big Five" scale had been used for measuring brand personality including agreeableness, extroversion, conscientiousness, culture, and neuroticism (Digman, 1990). Recent work of Aaker (1997) recognized five dimensions of brand personality. The five dimensions are sincerity, excitement, competence, sophistication, and ruggedness (see Table 14.1).

TABLE 14.1

Five Dimensions of Brand Personality

Competence	Sincerity	Excitement	Sophistication	Ruggedness
Reliable	Down-to-earth	Daring	Upper-class	Outdoorsy
Hard-working	Family oriented	Trendy	Glamorous	Masculine
Secure	Small-town	Exciting	Good-looking	Western
Intelligent	Honest	Spirited	Charming	Tough
Technical	Sincere	Cool	Feminine	Rugged
Corporate	Real	Young	Smooth	
Successful	Wholesome	Imaginative		
Leader	Original	Unique		
Confident	Cheerful	Up-to-date		
	Sentimental	Independent		
	Friendly	Contemporary		

Note. Aaker (1997)

Brand personality is closely related to symbolic consumption. It can function as a social display, which contributes to consumers' needs for consuming as classification or consuming as integration (Holt, 1995). For the purpose of classification or integration with a brand during consumption, consumers' identification with a brand personality becomes more important. Consumers often try to belong to their desired social world by making the image of a certain brand congruent with self-images or by making themselves adapted to the image of a certain brand (Schouten, 1991).

Aaker (1996) emphasized that a brand is more than a set of functional attributes of a product and that a brand should approach customers by giving emotional and self-expressive benefits. Keller (1993, 2001) argued that brand associations regarding the benefits are functional, experiential, and symbolic associations. Symbolic association of a brand is related to the needs for social approval, personal expression, or outer-directed self-esteem. Symbolic value is determined by prestige, exclusivity, or fashionability that a brand holds (Solomon, 1983). The physical benefits or attributes of a product or service perform utilitarian functions, whereas brand personality performs a symbolic function (Shavitt, 1990).

HYPOTHESIS

Impact of Brand Personality on Brand Identification

Consumers have a tendency to express their self-images effectively by choosing a certain brand that is perceived to be self-congruent (Kassarjian, 1971; Sirgy, 1982). Berry (2000) argued that a strong brand can be built by acquiring core values that customers think crucial and making an emotional connection with customers through communication. Underwood, Bond, and Baer (2001) proposed social identity as a mechanism of emotional connection between brand and customers. Social identity theory (Tajfel, 1982) is based on self-concept. Self-concept, which is an individual's ideas and feelings about self, consists of personal identity and social identity. Personal identity is a categorization of self based on certain traits such as being kind and being intellectual. Social identity is a categorization of self into a certain social group or social class. Social identity can be divided into public self and collective self, both of which are shown to social others or audience (Eagly & Chaiken, 1993).

People feel a sense of self-definition by using a brand and communicate it to others. Therefore, people feel identification with a brand whose image is congruent with their self-concepts and prefer to use the brand. In this sense, brand identification is considered as an antecedent and the consequence of brand equity (Gladden, Milne, & Sutton, 1998; Keller, 1993).

Symbolic consumption is rooted in self-concept. It is interpreted as the behaviors motivated from self-enhancement, maintenance of self-esteem, expression of one's values, or facilitation of social adaptation (Greenwald, 1989; Shavitt, 1989, 1990).

As reviewed previously, most research on brand personality and brand identification has focused on consumer–brand relationship. In this chapter, we examine the concept of brand identification in an inner-organization setting.

Brand identification can be divided into two categories. One is personal identification, and the other is social identification (Río et al., 2001). Personal identification starts from having affinity between a brand and self, which is related to personal identity. Social identification increases when a brand expresses the membership of one's social group to which he or she aspires to belong or presently belongs (Long & Schiffman, 2000).

Like the consumer–brand relation, employees are likely to feel both personal and social identification with the brand personality of their company when it is congruent with their personal or social identity. This idea leads to two hypotheses:

H1:   Certain aspects of the brand personality of a company will increase employees' personal identification with the brand.

H2:   Certain aspects of the brand personality of a company will increase employees' social identification with the brand.

Impact of Brand Identification on ES and CS Effort

Tracy (1986) insisted that managers should enhance their employees' self-concepts to assure a high level of performance and job satisfaction, because if people act in a manner inconsistent with these self-concepts, they move out of their comfort zones and experience stress and anxiety. Self-esteem will result in less stress and greater employee satisfaction (Howell, Bellenger, & Wilcox, 1987).

Consumers tend to be highly satisfied when the brand is image congruent or when the brand enriches, protects, or enhances self-image (Sirgy, 1982). With a similar rationale, we can say that employees as internal customers are likely to feel job satisfaction and to exert CS effort when the brand personalities of their companies are congruent with their personalities and enhance their self-images.

There could be a direct effect of brand identification on CS efforts as well as an indirect effect via ES. In other words, we posit that ES is a partial mediator in the proposed model. In addition, we hypothesize that personal identification affects social identification because personal identity cannot be independent of social identity. Once personal identification is attained, people want a higher level of identification. Maslow's hierarchy of needs offers a rationale for it.

We thus propose additional hypotheses:

H3:   Employees' personal identification with the brand will have a positive influence on social identification with the brand.

H4: As employees' personal identification with the brand increases, employee satisfaction will increase.

H5: As employees' social identification with the brand increases, employee satisfaction will increase.

H6: As employees' personal identification with the brand increases, employees' CS effort will increase.

H7: As employees' social identification with the brand increases, employees' CS effort will increase.

Impact of ES on CS Effort

Customer satisfaction and employee contentment have been gaining prominence since the 1990s. Employee satisfaction results in higher levels of quality, productivity, and business performance (Deming, 1985; Ishikawa, 1985). Heskett et al. (1997) captured the relation between employee and customer satisfaction with their analogy of satisfaction mirror.

Links between ES and CS have also repeatedly been proposed in the service quality literature (Carlzon, 1987; Hostage, 1975). Schneider and Bowen (1985, 1993) documented evidence of the relation between employee satisfaction and customer satisfaction. Satisfaction mirror, however, has been shattered (Silvestro & Cross, 2000), because even though the idea of service profit chain is intuitive, there has been a lack of strong empirical evidence supporting the links (Loveman, 1998; Silvestro & Cross, 2000).

Nonetheless, no one raises doubt about the idea that employees will treat their customers as they are treated. According to Gronroos (1990), service quality consists of technical and functional dimensions. Functional quality is determined by interpersonal contributions during the service encounter (Kelly, Donnelly, & Skinner, 1990). If so, for service firms, every department and level throughout the organization must adopt and act on the principles of internal customer satisfaction (Nichol, 1992).

Overall job satisfaction is positively correlated with customer-oriented behavior. Some researchers argue that intrinsic rewards may play a more important role in customer-oriented behavior than their extrinsic counterparts such as pay (Hoffman & Ingram, 1992). Brand–employee congruence in personalities can be viewed as an intrinsic factor to satisfy employees. Brown et al.'s (2002) results show that customer orientation partially mediates the impact of personality traits on performance.

Past research on ES or job satisfaction reveals little research on brand personality–employee personality congruence. Most relevant research has dealt with employee personality and job congruence, and certain personality traits are highly correlated with employee satisfaction, customer orientation, and performance (Comer & Dubinsky, 1985; Hurley, 1998).

Sergeant and Frenkel (2000) developed the concept of CSC (i.e., employee's capacity to satisfy customers) on the ground of Heskett et al.'s (1997) notion of customer contact employee capability. CSC is a measure of the extent to which customer contact employees achieve the goals of quality-service provision and receive some positive feedback about this.

In sum, we can see that higher ES can result in higher customer orientation or higher capacity regarding customer satisfaction, even though it does not capture customer-rated satisfaction directly. Thus, we hypothesize:

H8:   As employee satisfaction increases, employees' CS effort will increase.

Relative Impact of Personal and Social Identifications on ES and CS Effort

Personal identification is focused on private self, whereas social identification is focused on social self that is susceptible to social others (Eagly & Chaiken, 1993). Personal identity comprises one's values, personalities, self-pride, and lifestyle (Río et al., 2001). Social identity, on the contrary, seeks social respect and social status by having or using a badge brand (Lassar et al., 1995). Therefore, we can predict that personal identification has a greater influence on ES than on CS effort, whereas social identification has a greater impact on CS efforts than on ES. ES seems to be more personal and inner-directed feelings, but CS efforts are seen by others, so one should be aware of social context and one's social images. We thus hypothesize:

H9:   The impact of personal identification on ES will be greater than that of social identification.

H10:   The impact of social identification on CS effort will be greater than that of personal identification.

Figure 14.1 shows the conceptual model of the present study.

METHODOLOGY

We conducted an empirical study to investigate the structural relations among brand personality, brand identification, ES, and CS effort. Our proposed model was tested with Bank of NACF, one of the biggest retail banks in Korea. We did a survey with employees of Bank of NACF across the country. They were asked to respond to a brand image and employee satisfaction survey.

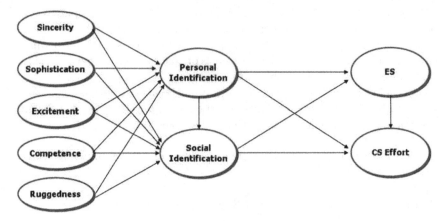

FIG. 14.1.   The conceptual model.

Respondents

The sample consisted of 515 respondents including frontline employees (58%) and middle-level employees (42%) who also contact customers during the work time. The male–female ratio of the sample was 63/37, respectively. The age range was from 20s to 50s. The age bracket of 20s included 27%, 30s had 42%, 40s had 25%, and 50s contained 6% of the sample. The branches of the bank were all over the country, and the respondents were employees of branches located in 10 provinces, including metropolitan cities of Korea.

Measures

Brand Personality.   We adopted Aaker's (1997) five dimensions of brand personality in the proposed model. We used two items for each dimension of the brand personality. Items were selected through a pilot test to reduce the possibility of misunderstanding in translation and to enhance model parsimony. Final items were as follows: sophisticated and elegant for "sophistication," sincere and friendly for "sincerity," spirited and exciting for "excitement," competent and successful for "competence," and rugged and tough for "ruggedness."

We asked how much each participant agreed with a series of statements. For example, for measuring the dimension of sophistication, the statements were as follows; "I think that the image of Bank of NACF is sophisticated" and "I think that the image of Bank of NACF is elegant." The 7-point scales were used for the responses. They were anchored as *not at all* (1) and *quite a lot* (7).

Brand Identification.   We categorized brand identification into personal and social identifications (Lassar, et al., 1995; Río et al., 2001). To measure personal identification, we provided the following three statements: "The image of Bank of NACF fits my personality," "The image of Bank of NACF represents my values well," and "The image of Bank of NACF matches my lifestyle." For measuring social identification, two statements were used: "The image of Bank of NACF gives me social recognition and respect" and "The image of Bank of NACF enhances my social status." The 7-point scales were used for each response. They were anchored as *not at all* (1) and *quite a lot* (7).

Employee Satisfaction.   Job satisfaction refers to an individual's attitude toward various aspects of his or her job as well as the job in general (Rogers et al., 1994). Generally job satisfaction has been measured by using multiple items including satisfaction with supervisors, work conditions, promotional opportunities, pay, coworkers, and customers (Churchill et al., 1974; Comer, Machleit, & Lagace, 1989). Service providers' job satisfaction has often been measured via the job descriptive index (JDI), which includes five dimensions of job satisfaction: satisfaction with the work itself, with supervision, with coworkers, with promotion opportunities, and with pay (Smith, Kendall, & Hulin, 1969). Another measure of job satisfaction is the job satisfaction scale (JSS). JSS, created by Koeske, Kirk, Koeske, and Rautkis (1994), measures job satisfaction in the human service field with attention to three dimensions: intrinsic satisfaction including opportunity to help clients, challenge derived from the job, and feeling of professional success; organizational satisfaction; and salary and promotion.

In most cases, overall job satisfaction has been measured. Jonge et al. (2001) assessed job satisfaction with a single item (i.e., "I'm satisfied with my present job") because it has been shown that a global index of overall job satisfaction is a valid measure of job satisfaction (Scarpello & Campbell, 1983; Wanous, Reichers, & Hudy, 1997).

We used the overall satisfaction measure for ES because specific dimensions of job satisfaction measures were not necessary for the present study. Two questions were asked: "Are you satisfied with your present job?" and "Do you feel happy when you are working?" The 7-point scales were used for each response. They were anchored as *not at all* (1) and *quite a lot* (7).

CS Effort.   Brown et al. (2002) used customer orientation as a self-assessment of an employee's tendency to try to meet customer needs and the degree to which he or she enjoys doing so, rather than a measure of service actions or on-the-job performance. The measure of contact employees' CSC, developed by Sergeant and Frenkel (2000), consists of 3 items: "You are not confident about your ability to satisfy customers," "You are not making customers happy," and finally, "You cannot satisfy customer requirements."

Based on these measures, we modified the scale by focusing on employees' CS activities. We asked how much each person agreed with the following two statements: "I do my best to satisfy my customers" and "I am exerting myself to make customers happy." The 7-point scales were used for the responses, anchored as *not at all* (1) and *quite a lot* (7).

ANALYSIS AND RESULTS

Factor Analysis

We adopt Aaker's five dimensions of brand personality in the present research. To confirm that five dimensions are valid for Bank of NACF, we conducted factor analysis in the first phase of the study.

Ten selected items were used as input. Before factor analysis, we examined the correlation matrix of 10 traits. Respective correlations of two items that were supposed to measure the same factor were mostly high, whereas the other correlations were relatively low. Pearson correlations of the items are as follows: .794 (sophisticated–elegant), .785 (rugged–tough), .595 (exciting–spirited), .648 (sincere–friendly), and .569 (competent–successful). Thus, the correlation matrix seems to be appropriate for factor analysis.

We used the principal component model as an extraction method and designated the number of factors as five according to Aaker (1997). For the purpose of ensuring clear interpretation and discriminant validity, we chose orthogonal rotation method.

As shown in Table 14.2, factor loadings on each factor are high, ranging from .602 to .904, which show high convergent validity. Cumulative variance explained by the 5 factors is 84.79%.

TABLE 14.2

Rotated Component Matrix

	Component				
	Sophistication	Sincerity	Excitement	Competence	Ruggedness
Sophisticated	.890	7.922E-02	.205	.167	.103
Elegant	.861	.126	.193	.142	.239
Sincere	.105	.904	.152	.101	9.573E-02
Friendly	.122	.799	.196	.308	.103
Spirited	.245	.119	.850	9.767E-02	.136
Exciting	.179	.257	.785	.189	.163
Competent	.398	.211	.153	.814	2.016E-02
Successful	3.551E-02	.320	.201	.709	.434
Rugged	.519	.144	.314	.163	.672
Tough	.596	.175	.231	.261	.602

Note. Extraction method: principal component analysis. Rotation method: Varimax with Kaiser normalization.

Reliability Check

To check the reliability of measures, we assessed Cronbach's α (Cronbach, 1951). Cronbach's α of brand personality was as follows: Competence (.72), Sincerity (.79), Sophistication (.89), Ruggedness(.93), and Excitement (.74), Cronbach's α of brand identification was as follows: personal identification (.90), and social identification (.93); Cronbach's α of ES and CS efforts are .93 and .82 respectively. In sum, all the measures showed a satisfactory level of reliability.

Hypothesis Test

The entire structural model was run with LISREL 8.0. We used correlation data as input. The results are presented in Fig. 14.2. The overall model showed satisfactory fit: χ^2(d.f. = 126) = 364.553 p < .001, the non-normed-fit index (NNFI)= .95, the comparative fit index (CFI) = .97, and the root mean-squared residual (RMR) = .046. Taken together, the findings indicated a satisfactory fit between the proposed model and the data (Bagozzi & Yi, 1988).

The estimates for individual path coefficients of brand personality on brand identification show interesting findings. Two dimensions of brand personality, namely, competence and excitement, affect personal identification of the employees at the Bank of NACF. Social identification is influenced by sincerity only among the five dimensions of brand personality. These results support H1 and H2. In fact, H1 and H2 had an exploratory nature to some degree. We found that among the brand personality of the bank, the three dimensions of competence, sincerity, and excitement influenced brand identification. In fact, six traits for these three dimensions showed relatively high means above the midpoint on the 7-point Likert scale. The means of competent and successful were 4.34 and 4.88. The means of spirited and exciting were 4.19 and 4.16, and those of sincere and friendly were 5.31 and 5.07, respectively.

All the other path coefficients were statistically significant. These results were consistent with H3 through H8. Thus, we can conclude that personal identification affects social identification, and both personal and social identifications affect employee satisfaction as well as CS effort. An interesting result was the influence of ES on CS effort. This result provides indirect support for the link between ES and CS, which has been a controversy among researchers and practitioners.

Next, the relative impacts of two types of brand identification on ES and CS effort were compared. Regarding the path from brand identification to ES, there was a significant difference between personal identification and social identification (personal identification = .54 versus social identification = .31; χ^2_d (1) = 4.80, p < .05). That is, for the path from brand identification to ES, the path coefficient of personal identification was significantly higher than that of social identification. H9 was thus supported. However, for the path from brand identification to CS effort,

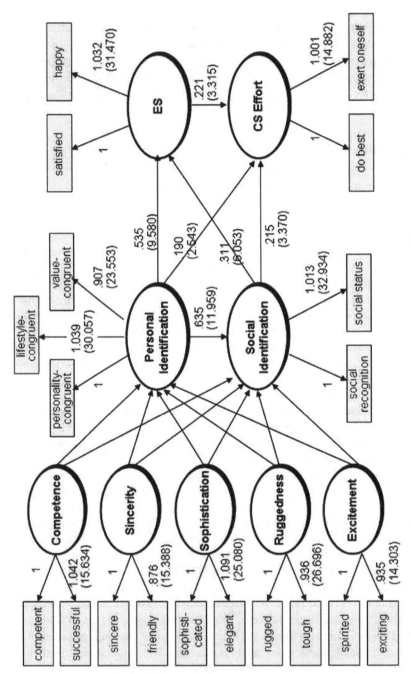

FIG. 14.2.   Results for the empirical model.

236

TABLE 14.3

Summary of Research Findings

Hypothesis		Result
H1	Certain aspects of the brand personality of a company will increase employees' personal identification with the brand.	Supported
H2	Certain aspects of the brand personality of a company will increase employees' social identification with a brand.	Supported
H3	Employees' personal identification with the brand will have a positive influence on social identification with the brand.	Supported
H4	As employees' personal identification with the brand increases, employee satisfaction will increase.	Supported
H5	As employees' social identification with the brand increases, employee satisfaction will increase.	Supported
H6	As employees' personal identification with the brand increases, employees' CS effort will increase.	Supported
H7	As employees' social identification with the brand increases, employees' CS effort will increase.	Supported
H8	As employee satisfaction increases, employees' CS effort will increase.	Supported
H9	The impact of personal identification on ES is greater than that of social identification.	Supported
H10	The impact of social identification on CS effort is greater than that of personal identification.	Not supported

the estimate of path coefficient of social identification was not significantly different from that of personal identification (social identification = .22 vs. personal identification = .19; $\chi^2_d(1) = .04, p > .10$). Accordingly, H10 was not supported. Research findings are summarized in Table 14.3.

DISCUSSION

Employee satisfaction has become an important construct for managers of service business because an increase in employee satisfaction among customer contact personnel from a firm will have a carry-over effect on customer care (Rogers et al., 1994). In this sense, the study described here provides several theoretical and managerial contributions. Our study is the first study that has examined brand personality and brand identification as the antecedents of employee satisfaction. Most research regarding employee personality was focused only on the employee's personality with little regard to corporate brand personality, and the main objective was finding personality traits for customer orientation. In contrast, our study focused on personality congruence between employees and the corporate brand. Another theoretical contribution is that the study presented here shows a positive impact of ES on CS effort. If an employee's CS effort serves as a proxy of true CS, then the shattered satisfaction mirror can be restored. This study also offers new managerial ideas about hiring and training employees as well as brand communication directed to internal and external customers.

Reviewing the previous research, employee personality is crucial for enhancing CS. For the position of frontline employees, service-oriented personality traits or interpersonal orientation are critical. It is generally recommended for service companies to hire individuals as employees who are highly empathetic and agreeable by nature because such personalities bring higher customer orientation and less job conflict. The next stage after cautious screening is training current employees to be empathetic. Additional managerial support can be, for example, providing employees with clear job descriptions or empowering employees within the customer–employee dyad to make decisions that will result in higher customer satisfaction with the service (Carlzon, 1987; Rogers et al., 1994). As the importance of hiring the right employees has attracted wide attention, companies have started to use a suite of personality tests for screening employees for job positions. Bernardin (1987) presented evidence that deliberate distortion is a problem with the transparent personality instruments when used for the screening purpose.

To cope with this problem, we recommend that companies test the degree of congruence between the corporate brand personality and employees' personalities. Employees who carry brand personality and convey it properly to customers are needed because employees are the face of the service company. Furthermore, the congruence of brand–employee personalities can influence employees' general attitudes and behaviors.

Alvesson and Willmott (2002) proposed that management should consider how employees are enjoined to develop self-images that are deemed congruent with managerially defined objectives. This suggestion implies that marketing effort for brand communication should be implemented both for internal and external customers and that it should make employees' self-images congruent with the company-defined brand images. For most types of service organizations, individual service workers are direct participants in implementing the marketing concepts (Brown et al., 2002).

Service employees are often called emotional laborers. They face many occasions to experience emotional dissonance, which is the conflict between emotions experienced by the employee and those required by the organization (Abraham, 1999). Emotional dissonance occurs when expressed emotions are in conformity with organizational norms but clash with true feelings (Rafaeli & Sutton, 1987). Corporate climate is a reflection of corporate brand personality, which is a sort of tacit norm to employees.

Customers' experiences with the staff at a company affect brand image as much as any advertising campaign. Therefore, employees of boundary-spanning positions are major tools for building brands. They should communicate brand message and express the intended brand personality consistently. For this purpose, employees should have the same personality as the corporate brand. This cohesiveness may be accomplished by recruiting and training. Especially, recruitment is a means of conveying marketing messages. With a psychological approach, management can build a strong brand personality that genuinely reflects the desires of the people who define the business (Ellwood, 2001).

Our study has several limitations, which suggest interesting issues for future research. We adopted Aaker's (1997) five dimensions of brand personality for a Korean retail bank. Aaker, Benet-Martinez, and Garolera (2001) recognized culture-specific dimensions of brand personality. In Japan, ruggedness was replaced by peacefulness and in Spain, peacefulness and passion were substituted for competence and ruggedness. These findings imply that unique dimensions of brand personality may reflect the Korean culture. Thus, one could explore to find Korean brand personality. Another limitation is that the present study adopted just two personality traits for each dimension. Aaker (1997) originally proposed multiple traits over five items for each dimension. An investigation of many traits may be needed for more reliable results.

REFERENCES

Aaker, D. A. (1996). *Building strong brands*. New York: The Free Press.
Aaker, J. L. (1997). Dimensions of brand personality. *Journal of Marketing Research, 34,* 347–356.
Aaker, J. L., Benet-Martinez, V., & Garolera, J. (2001), Consumption symbols as carriers of culture: A study of Japanese and Spanish brand personality constructs. *Journal of Personality & Social Psychology, 81,* 492–508.
Abraham, R. (1999). Emotional dissonance in organizations: Conceptualizing the roles of self-esteem and job-induced tension. *Leadership & Organization Development Journal, 20,* 18–31.
Aronoff, J., & Wilson, J. P. (1985). *Personality in the social process*. Hillsdale, NJ: Lawrence Erlbaum Associates.
Bagozzi, R., & Yi, Y. (1988). On the evaluation of structural equation models. *Journal of the Academy of Marketing Science, 16,* 74–94.
Bakacus, E., Cravens, D. W., Johnston, M., & Moncrief, W. C. (1999). The role of emotional exhaustion in sales force attitude and behavior relationships. *Journal of the Academy of Marketing Science, 27,* 58–70.
Belicki, K., & Woolcott, R. (1996). Employee and patient designed study of burnout and job satisfaction in a chronic care hospital. *Employee Assistance Quarterly, 12,* 37–45.
Bernardin, H. J. (1987). Development and validation of a forced choice scale to measure job-related discomfort among customer service representatives. *Academy of Management Journal, 30,* 162–173.
Berry, L. (1981). The employee as customer. *Journal of Retail Banking, 3,* 33–40.
Berry, L. (2000). Cultivating service brand equity. *Journal of the Academy of Marketing Science, 28,* 128–137.
Brewer, E. W., & Clippard, L. F. (2002). Burnout and job satisfaction among student support services personnel. *Human Resource Development Quarterly, 13,* 169–186.
Brown, T. J., Mowen, J. C., Donavan, D. T., & Licata, J. W. (2002). The customer orientation of service workers: Personality trait effects on self-and supervisor performance ratings. *Journal of Marketing Research, 34,* 110–119.
Burke, R. J., & Richardsen, A. M. (1996). Stress, burnout, and health. In C. L. Cooper (Ed.), *Stress, medicine, and health* (pp. 101–117). Boca Raton: CRC Press.

Carlzon, J. (1987). *Moments of truth*. Cambridge, MA: Ballinger.

Churchill, G. A., Ford, N. M., & Walker, O. C. (1974). Measuring the job satisfaction of industrial salesmen. *Journal of Marketing Research, 11*, 254–260.

Churchill, G. A., Ford, N. M., & Walker, O. C. (1976). Organizational climate and job satisfaction in the salesforce. *Journal of Marketing Research, 13*, 323–332.

Churchill, G. A., Ford, N. M., & Walker, O. C. (1985). The determinants of salesperson performance: A meta-analysis. *Journal of Marketing Research, 22*, 103–118.

Comer, J. M., & Dubinsky, A. J. (1985). *Managing the successful sales force*. Lexington, MA: Lexington Books.

Comer, J. M., Machleit, K. A., & Lagace, R. R. (1989). Psychometric assessment of a reduced version of INDSALES. *Journal of Business Research, 18*, 291–302.

Cordes, C. L., & Doughterty, T. W. (1993). A review of an integration of research on job burnout. *Academy of Management Review, 18*, 621–656.

Deming, W. E. (1985). *Out of the crisis, center for advanced engineering study*. Cambridge: MA: Massachusetts Institute of Technology.

Digman, J. M. (1990). Personality structure: Emergence of the five-factor model. *Annual Review of Psychology, 41*, 417–440.

Eagly, A., & Chaiken, S. (1993). *Psychology of attitudes*. Fort Worth, TX: Harcourt Brace Jovanovich.

Ellwood, I. (2001). How psychology can help create a brand culture. *Marketing, June*, 24.

Freudengerger, H. J. (1974). Staff burnout. *Journal of Social Issues, 30*, 159–165.

Gardner, D. G., & Pierce, J. L. (1998). Self-esteem and self-efficacy within the organizational context. *Group & Organization Management, 23*(1), 48–70.

Getzels, J. W., & Guba, E. G. (1954). Role, role conflict and effectiveness. *American Sociological Review, 19*, 164–75.

Gladden, J. M., Milne, G. R., & Sutton, W. A. (1998). A conceptual framework for assessing brand equity in Division 1 college athletics. *Journal of Sport Management, 12*, 1–9.

Golembiewski, R. T., & Kim, B. S. (1989). Self-esteem and phases of burnout. *Organizational Development Journal, 7*, 51–58.

Greenwald, A. G. (1989). Why attitudes are important: Defining attitude and attitude theory twenty years later. In A. R. Pratkanis, S. J. Breckler, & A. G. Greenwald (Eds.), *Attitude structure and function* (pp. 429–440). Hillsdale, NJ: Lawrence Erlbaum Associates.

Gremler, D. D., Bitner, M. J., & Evans, K. R. (1994). The internal service encounter. International *Journal of Service Industry Management, 5*, 34–56.

Gronroos, C. (1990). *Service marketing and management*. Lexington, MA: Lexington Books.

Heskett, J. L., Jones, T. O., Loveman, G. W., Sasser, W. E., & Schlesinger, L. A. (1994). Putting the service-profit chain to work. *Harvard Business Review, 72*, 164–175.

Heskett, J. L., Sasser, W. E., & Schlesinger, L. A. (1997). *The service profit chain: How leading companies link profit and growth to loyalty, satisfaction, and value*. New York: The Free Press.

Hiscock, J. (2002). The brand insiders. *Marketing* (May), 23–24.

Hoffman, K. D., & Ingram, T. N. (1992). Service provider job satisfaction and customer-oriented performance. *The Journal of Service Marketing, 6*, 68–83.

Holt, D. B. (1995). How consumers consume: A typology of consumption practices. *Journal of Consumer Research, 22*, 1–16.

Hostage, G. M. (1975). Quality control in a service business. *Harvard Business Review, 53*, 98–106.

Howell, R. D., Bellenger, D. N., & Wilcox, J. B. (1987). Self-esteem, role stress, and job satisfaction among marketing managers. *Journal of Business Research, 15*, 71–85.

Hurley, R. F. (1998). Customer service behavior in retail settings: A study of the effect of service provider personality. *Journal of Academy of Marketing Science, 26,* 115–127.

Ishikawa, K. (1985). *What is total quality control? The Japanese way.* Englewood Cliffs, NJ: Prentice-Hall.

Jonge, J., Dormann, C., Janssen, P. M., Dollard, M. F., Landeweerd, J. A., & Nijhuis, F. J. N. (2001). Testing reciprocal relationships between job characteristics and psychological well-being: A cross-lagged structural equation model. *Journal of Occupational and Organizational Psychology, 74,* 29–46.

Kassarjian, H. H. (1971). Personality and consumer behavior: A review. *Journal of Marketing Research, 8,* 409–418.

Keller, K. L. (1993). Conceptualizing, measuring, and managing customer-based brand equity. *Journal of Marketing, 57,* 1–22.

Keller, K. L. (2001). Building customer-based brand equity. *Marketing Management, July/August,* 15–19.

Kelly, J. P., Gable, M., & Hise, R. T. (1981). Conflict, clarity, tension and satisfaction in chain store manager roles. *Journal of Retailing, 57,* 27–42.

Kelly, S. W., Donnelly, J. H., & Skinner, S. J. (1990). Customer participation in service production and delivery. *Journal of Retailing, 66,* 315–335.

Koeske, G. F., Kirk, S. A., Koeske, R. D., & Rauktis, M. B. (1994). Measuring the Monday blues: Validation of a job satisfaction scale for human services. *Social Work Research, 18,* 27–35.

Korman, A. K. (1976). Hypothesis of work behavior revisited and an extension. *Academy of Management Review, 1,* 50–63.

Lassar, W., Mittal, B., & Sharma, A. (1995). Measuring customer-based brand equity. *Journal of Consumer Marketing, 12,* 11–19.

Layman, E., & Guyden, J. A. (1997). Reducing your risk of burnout. *Health Care Supervisor, 15*(3), 57–69.

Lee, R. T., & Ashforth, B. E. (1990). On the meaning of Maslach's three dimensions of burnout. *Journal of Applied Psychology, 75,* 743–747.

Lee, R. T., & Ashforth, B. E. (1996). A meta-analysis examination of the correlates of the three dimensions of burnout. *Journal of Applied Psychology, 81,* 123–133.

Leiter, M. P., & Maslach, C. (1988). The impact of interpersonal environment on burnout and organization commitment. *Journal of Organizational Behavior, 9,* 297–308.

Lewis, B., & Entwistle, T. (1990). Managing the service encounter: A focus on the employee. *International Journal of Service Industry Management, 1*(3), 41–52.

Long, M. M., & Schiffman, L. G. (2000). Consumption values and relationships: Segmenting the market for frequency programs. *Journal of Consumer Marketing, 17,* 214–232.

Loveman, G. W. (1998). Employee satisfaction, customer loyalty, and financial performance: an empirical examination of the service profit chain in retail banking. *Journal of Service Research, 1,* 18–31.

Maslach, C., Jackson, S. E., & Leither, M. P. (1996). *Maslach burnout inventory manual* (3rd ed.). Palo Alto, CA: Consulting Psychologists Press.

Miles, R. E., & Creed, W. E. D. (1995). Organizational forms and managerial philosophies: A descriptive and analytical review. *Research in Organizational Behavior, 17,* 333–372.

Nichol, G. (1992). Motivating employees. *Managing Service Quality, July,* 259–261.

Pierce, J. L., Gardner, D. G., Cummings, L. L., & Dunham, R. B. (1989). Organization-based self-esteem: Construct definition, measurement, and validation. *Academy of Management Journal, 32,* 622–648.

Pierce, J. L., Gardner, D. G., Dunham, R. B., & Cummings, L. L. (1993). Moderation by or-ganization-based self-esteem of role condition-employee response relationships. *Academy of Management Journal, 36,* 271–288.

Rafaeli, A., & Sutton, R. I. (1987). Expression of emotion as part of the work role. *Academy of Management Review, 12,* 23–37.

Río, A. B., Vázquez, R., & Iglesias, V. (2001). The effect of brand associations on consumer response. *Journal of Consumer Marketing, 18,* 410–425.

Rogers, J. D., Clow, K. E., & Kash, T. J. (1994). Increasing job satisfaction of service person-nel. *Journal of Service Marketing, 8,* 14–26.

Rosse, J. J., Boss, R. W., Johnson, A. E., & Crown, D. F. (1991). Conceptualizing the role of self-esteem in the burnout process. *Group & Organization Studies, 16,* 428–451.

Rousseau, D. M., & Parks, M. J. (1992). The contracts of individuals and organizations. *Research in Organizational Behavior, 15,* 1–43.

Rust, R. T., Stewart, G. L., Miller, H., & Pielack, D. (1996). The satisfaction and retention of frontline employees: A customer satisfaction measurement approach. *International Journal of Service Industry Management, 7,* 62–80.

Saxe, R., & Weitz, B. A. (1982). The SOCO scale: A measure of the customer orientation of salespeople. *Journal of Marketing Research, 19,* 343–351.

Scarpello, V., & Campbell, J. P. (1983). Job satisfaction: Are the parts there? *Personal Psychology, 36,* 577–600.

Schneider, B., & Bowen, D. (1985). New services design, development and implication and the employee. In W. R. George & C. Marshall (Eds.), *New services* (pp. 82–101). Chi-cago: American Marketing Association.

Schneider, B., & Bowen, D. (1993). Human resource management is critical. *Organizational Dynamics,* 39–52.

Schneider, B., Wheeler, J. K., & Cox, J. (1992). A passion for service: Using content analysis to explicate service climate theme. *Journal of Applied Psychology, 77,* 705–716.

Schouten, J. (1991). Selves in transition. *Journal of Consumer Research, 17,* 412–425.

Sergeant, A., & Frenkel, S. (2000). When do customer contact employees satisfy customers? *Journal of Service Research, 3,* 18–34.

Shavitt, S. (1989). Operationalizing functional theories of attitudes. In A. R. Pratkanis, S. J. Breckler, & A. G. Greenwald (Eds.), *Attitude structure and function* (pp. 311–338). Hillsdale, NJ: Lawrence Erlbaum Associates.

Shavitt, S. (1990). The role of attitude objects in attitude functions. *Journal of Experimental Social Psychology, 26,* 124–148.

Silvestro, R., & Cross, S. (2000). Applying the service profit chain in a retail environment challenging the "satisfaction mirror." *International Journal of Service Industry Manage-ment, 11,* 244–268.

Singh, J., Goolsby, J. R., & Rhodes, G. K. (1994). Behavioral and psychological conse-quences of boundary spanning burnout for customer service representatives. *Journal of Marketing Research, 31,* 558–569.

Sirgy, M. J. (1982). Self-concept in consumer behavior: A critical review. *Journal of Consumer Research, 9,* 287–299.

Smith, P. C., Kendall, L. M., & Hulin, C. L. (1969). *The measurement of satisfaction in work and retirement.* Chicago: Rand McNally.

Solomon, M. R. (1983). The role of products as social stimuli: A symbolic interactionism perspective. *Journal of Consumer Research, 10,* 319–329.

Song, I-S., & Hattie, J. (1985). Relationships between self-concept and achievement. *Journal of Research in Personality, 19,* 365–372.

Sumrall, D. A., & Sebastianelli, R. (1999). The moderating effect of managerial sales orientations on salespersons' role stress-job satisfaction relationships. *Journal of Marketing Theory and Practice, 3,* 72–79.

Tajfel, H. (1982). Social psychology of intergroup relations. *Annual Review of Psychology, 23,* 1–39.

Tracy, B. S. (1986). "I can't, I can't": How self-concept shapes performance. *Management World, April/May,* 1–2.

Underwood, R., Bond, E., & Baer, R. (2001). Building service brands via social identity: Lessons from the sports marketplace. *Journal of Marketing Theory and Practice* (Winter), 1–13.

Walker, O. C., Jr., Churchill, G. A., Jr., & Ford, N. M. (1975). Organizational determinants of the industrial salesman's role conflict and ambiguity. *Journal of Marketing, 39,* 32–39.

Wanous, J. P., Reichers, A. E., & Hudy, M. J. (1997). Overall job satisfaction: How good are single item measures? *Journal of Applied Psychology, 82,* 247–252.

Wells, L. E., & Marwell, G. (1976). *Self-esteem.* London: Sage.

Westman, M., & Eden, D. (1997). Effects of a respite from work on burnout: Vacation relief and fade-out. *Journal of Applied Psychology, 82,* 516–527.

Yi, Y., & Jeon, H. (2003). Effects of loyalty programs on value perception, program loyalty, and brand loyalty. *Journal of the Academy of Marketing Science, 31,* 229–240.

Yi, Y., & La, S. (2004). What influences the relationship between customer satisfaction and repurchase intention? Investigating the effects of adjusted expectations and customer loyalty. *Psychology & Marketing, 21,* 351–373.

CHAPTER FIFTEEN

Managing the Multidimensionality of Corporate Image: From the Stakeholders' Multilayered Experience Perspective

Chung-Hyun Kim
Sogang University

Taewon Suh
Texas State University–San Marcos

CORPORATE IMAGE AND STAKEHOLDER MANAGEMENT

The management of corporate image may be best accomplished when it is done in the line of stakeholder management. A superior corporate image, which is an intangible asset, is an important source of strategic competitive advantage, enhancing the long-term ability of a corporation to create value (Caves & Porter, 1977). Although resources such as technological leadership may be short-lived due to successive generations of innovation, favorable corporate image can be extremely long-lived. Most of the successful companies have maintained high-quality reputations over a long period of time. A superior corporate image provides the firm with advantages that may lead to positive results in several domains, such as pricing concessions by suppliers, improved employee morale, reduced risk for investors, increased strategic flexibility, and, not least, enhanced financial performance (Fombrun, 1996; Fombrun & Shanley, 1996). Furthermore, positive corporate image invites profitable marketing opportunities and increases the market value of the firm (Chauvin & Hirschey, 1994; Miles & Covin, 2000).

On the other hand, the concept of stakeholder management has become commonplace in the business literature. Whereas the conventional model of the corporation (i.e., the input–output model, which is unidirectional; refer to Donaldson and Preston, 1995, for details), in both legal and managerial forms, has failed to discipline self-serving managerial behavior, the stakeholder theory entails comprehensive restrictions on such behavior (Donaldson & Preston, 1995). The stakeholder theory views the corporation as an organizational entity through which numerous and diverse participants accomplish multiple and not always entirely congruent purposes. Thus, in the broad definition of the stakeholder theory, anything influencing or influenced by the firm is included in the realm of stakeholder (Freeman, 1984). Without support from those groups, the organization would cease to exist. Figure 15.1 depicts the model of the corporation as explained in the stakeholder theory. All persons or groups with legitimate interests participating in an enterprise do so to obtain benefits (Donaldson & Preston, 1995). In highly successful companies such as Hewlett-Packard and Wal-Mart, almost all the managers care strongly about people who have a stake in the business—customers, employees, stockholders, suppliers, and others (Kotter & Heskett, 1992).

Although more than often discussed separately, the two concepts, the management of corporate image and the stakeholder management, are obviously perceived to be indivisible. The accord of the two concepts can be induced in a few points. First, corporate image, because it is such a valuable asset, should be managed to take best advantage from a strategic point of view. The framework to manage such a strategic asset can best be provided by the stakeholder management. In the marriage of the concepts, the establishment should be a framework for examining the connections between the practice of stakeholder management and the achievement of various corporate performance goals. More specifically, a second point, the

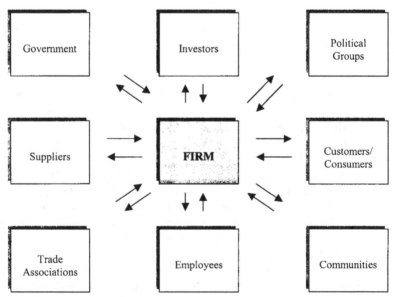

FIG 15.1. "The model of the corporation": The view of the stakeholder theory. From Donaldson and Preston (1995).

multidimensionality, which is one of the fundamental characteristics of corporate image, is the gist of managing corporate image. And, one side of the concept of multidimensionality can be rightly explained by the stakeholder theory. That is, corporate image should be assessed in terms of the diverse stakeholders influencing or influenced by the firm. In managing corporate image, it is important to include and consider the varied stakeholders at its general stage, as stakeholder management requires simultaneous attention to the legitimate interests of all appropriate stakeholders. This notion is extensively discussed in the following section.

MULTIDIMENSIONALITY OF CORPORATE IMAGE

Assessing corporate image without considering the various stakeholders or public may leave serious problems unsolved. A reciprocal multidimensionality exists in the relation between the corporate image and stakeholders of a firm. Corporate image has subdimensions related to each of the diversified characteristics and activities of a firm. For instance, corporate image can be assessed according to specific qualitative and technical attributes and is best illustrated by the annual survey by *Fortune* magazine. Measurement in the *Fortune* survey includes factors such as innovativeness; quality of management; value as a long-term investment; community and environmental responsibility; ability to attract, develop, and keep talented people; quality of products or services; financial soundness; and use of corporate assets (Fisher, 1996; Robinson, 1997).

However, it goes without saying that each subfactor is not always important and meaningful. Corporate image is a multidimensional concept at the point that it is developed in the relations with the specific parts of the society, which are stakeholders (Haedrich, 1993). The stakeholder theory suggests that the organization is managed by considering the often-conflicting needs and interests of all relevant stakeholders. A corporate image, roughly speaking, is the sum of the perceptions of its relevant stakeholders, including: (a) owners, (b) society and community including local and international and current and future generations, (c) customers, (d) employees, (e) suppliers and strategic partners, (f) government and inter-government agencies, (g) banks and other leaders, and (h) special interest nongovernmental organizations (Carroll, 1996). What is unique to a specific group of stakeholders is closely related to the decisive factor in their perception of the image of a firm. Therefore, it is impossible to assess the contingent structure of corporate image meaningfully without considering the characteristics of stakeholders who perceive the image. An image assessment that does not clearly distinguish the various stakeholders will fail to provide the specific information needed to provide strategic breakthrough into a problematic situation. For instance, consumers will deduce their image perception in many cases from their own experience with a product or service of a firm. On the other hand, stakeholders in local communities may infer their perceptions toward a firm from the contribution that the firm has made to the communities. Each stakeholder will draw a perception about the image of the firm in terms of his or her own resources of experience. The stakeholders' roles, norms, and values, therefore, will determine which factor is important in assessing the reputation of the firm (Dowling, 1988, 1993).

Furthermore, the multidimensionality of corporate image is related not only to the various social constituencies but also to the various identities of a person (Moffitt, 1994a, 1994b). Hall's (1986) articulation model of meaning, Moffitt's (1994a, 1994b) conceptualization of image explains how each individual can have unique and different images reflected from a unique intersection and combination of social and historical factors:

> The articulation model conceptualized image as any single opinion, attitude, behavior, or feeling about the corporation held by any person at any point time. That is, an individual may at one moment admire a corporation for its charity work in the community but, even moments later, change to a negative image of the same corporation when discussing the corporation's negative treatment of its employees. (Moffit, 1994a, p. 162)

This expanded model assumes that an individual will move in and out of the diverse memberships in a society almost simultaneously and therefore will choose one particular perception from many potential alternatives. It implies that the importance of a particular attribute of corporate image varies according to the varied situations of a firm.

These contingent perspectives in corporate image are needed for reflecting the multidimensionality of the concept. The subfactors of a contingency definition of image are differentiated along with the social contexts as well as the characteristics of assessing stakeholders. This approach to investigating the function or impact of corporate image perceived by a specific public or group of stakeholders solves the semantic problem encountered by using the general concepts that have been set forth in previous research. Assessment of corporate image should be structured in a specific context.

For instance, consider a situation in which consumers should choose a brand new product when they have little or no knowledge about that product. In this case, they may use corporate image as a summary construct to make their judgments in a heuristic way. Hence, to investigate the role of corporate image in similar situations, if all the subfactors are considered in the same way without different weight reflecting contingencies, the unique value of corporate image as a summary construct is undermined. The consumers may have constructed corporate image by giving more weight on their consumption experience.

A good example of a concept reflecting this contingent view, in which the reputation of a firm depends on the particular offering and the particular public, was offered by Barich and Kotler (1991). They presented a concept called "marketing image," defined as "the way people view the quality of the company's overall marketing offer and marketing mix" (p. 95), that can effectively reveal the effectiveness of corporate reputation in a marketing situation. Marketing image, according to the authors, consists of "how customers and other publics rate the exchange value of the company's offering compared to that of competitors" (p. 96). Merely good corporate reputation without a good marketing image cannot guarantee its contribution to sales. Customers may not overlook any drawbacks in marketing or the products of a firm although the firm is superior in activities of social and environmental responsibility.

It is vital to monitor the ever-shifting background of different audiences' needs and criteria for judging companies. There are many reasons for segmenting opinion leaders in research rather than lumping them together. One is that they have different expectations, different standards and issues by which they search their judgment of a company (Lewis, 2001).

A STRATEGIC CONCEPTION OF CORPORATE IMAGE

Although it is understood that corporate image should be managed in the realm of stakeholder management, a manager may feel the need to interpret corporate image into a manageable term. Based on the broad literature on corporate image, Suh and Amine (2002) proposed an integrate framework named the reputational capital model, incorporating the various concepts in the study of corporate image such as public awareness, favorability, corporate personality, corporate reputation, and perception of specific corporate behavior (see Fig. 15.2). Each component of the model is discussed briefly (for details, refer to Suh & Amine, 2002).

First, as an aggregate concept, public awareness simply means the degree to which a company is known to the public or the boundary within which public knows the company. Because it is a result of sheer exposure or perception rather than a fabrication of judgments, public awareness is differentiated from the general definition of awareness in psychology, which includes something beyond memory, that is, favorable attitude. Some researchers do not distinguish public awareness from reputation (e.g., Levitt, 1996) and sometimes consider it as a subfactor of corporate image (e.g.. Avenarius, 1993). Second, favorability denotes a favorable attitude toward the corporation, frequently measured by overall attitude. It is not factual knowledge—or at least not factual knowledge alone—that creates the sense of knowing a company (Lewis, 2001). Bromley (1993) regarded it as a subfactor of corporate image and related it to corporate reputation that is, in a commercial view, considered as one of the resources of an organization. Yet, mere summation of subimage or reputation factors may not be equal to overall attitude toward the organization. That is, favorability of public toward a corporation, a gestalt or a holistic type of attitudinal concept, is different from the simple total of all the subattributes. Third, the image construct may be interchangeably used with the concept of corporate personality (Preece, Fleisher, & Toccacelli, 1995). Corporate personality means a way of perceiving a firm in similar dimensions to those typically included in measures assessing an individual's personality. Although one can utilize all the theoretical approaches used for measuring personalities of people (Batra, Lehmann, & Singh, 1993), the trait approach is most

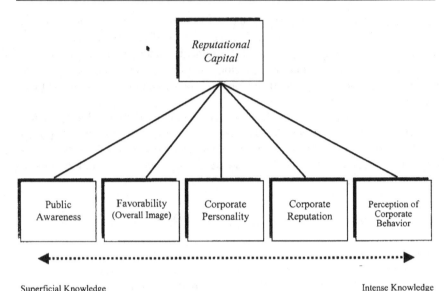

FIG 15.2.   The reputational capital model. From Suh and Amine (2002).

frequently used. Fourth, corporate reputation is here defined as the overall perception by the public of the performance of a firm, partly based on its ability to satisfy the specific needs and interests of the public (Riordan, Gatewood, & Bill, 1997). It is assessed by specified and technical attributes and is best illustrated in the annual survey on reputation published by *Fortune*, a survey that includes subfactors such as innovativeness; quality of management; value as a long-term investment; community and environmental responsibility; ability to attract, develop, and keep talented people; quality of products or services; financial soundness; and use of corporate assets (Fisher, 1996; Robinson, 1997). Last, the perception of specific corporate behavior is definitely distinct from other reputational factors because it is issue sensitive and relatively transient. However, in a long-term sense, this perception may converge with corporate reputation or other factors in reputational capital. As an issue is defined as "a gap between the expectations of a stakeholder regarding corporate behavior and the same stakeholder's perceptions of actual corporate behavior" (Nigh & Cochran, 1987, p. 6), the perception of specific corporate behavior is closely related to issues management. Each level in the reputational capital model explains a unique, strategic factor in managing corporate image. Also, the model provides the framework to illustrate the need for coordination and integration of activities in managing corporate image by managers.

The following section offers an example of a research piece, providing one facet of how the multidimensionality of corporate image is researched and thus managed from the consumers' multilayered experience. This study, following the definitions of the reputational capital model (Suh & Amine, 2002), focuses on favorability as an overall image construct.

A CASE OF STAKEHOLDERS' MULTILAYERED EXPERIENCE PERSPECTIVE

As explained in the previous section, overall image of a company is determined in a contingent manner, reflecting the multidimensionality of stakeholders. This study, using data collected from ordinary consumers and the public, empirically tests competing influences of factors from consumers' multilayered experience. The experience is categorized into three dimensions here: personal experience, indirect experience from media exposure, and experience from public sphere. These multiple factors in a consumer's experience may influence corporate image respectively at a different degree.

Personal experience with a particular company, such as satisfaction from interaction with a company, mutual benefits from the relationship with a company, and some kind of dealings with a company, are significant factors associated with overall corporate image. Although indirect, consumer experience from media exposure may exert a significant influence on overall corporate image. This is particularly true for perceived capability of top management and social responsibility of a company because media pay much attention to this type of company activities promoted by publicity programs and thus the company is well received by the consumer public. Also, consumers' and public's perceived integrity of a company, which includes the company's fair treatment of people, sound principles, straightforwardness, and honesty, also is associated with overall corporate image, although it may be hard to be perceived objectively from a consumer/public perspective. Because the research sample of this study only includes lay consumers and excludes opinion leaders and experts in business-related fields, overall corporate image should be influenced more heavily by personal experience and indirect experience from media exposure than by experience in the public sphere, defining more objective perceptions about a company.

Based on this discussion, the following hypotheses are proposed:

H1:   Consumers' satisfaction from relationship with a company is significantly associated with overall image of the company.

H2:   Consumers' perceived capability of top management of a company is significantly associated with overall image of the company.

H3:   Consumers' perceived social responsibility of a company is significantly associated with overall image of the company.

H4:   Consumers' perceived integrity of a company is associated with overall image of the company.

H5:   Consumers' overall image of the company is more heavily influenced by their personal experience and indirect experience from media exposure than by experience from public sphere.

Method

Originally developed in English, the questionnaire had to be translated into Korean to use it for the Korean sample. A bilingual expert, therefore, translated the questionnaire into Korean and then another bilingual expert back-translated it into English to ensure consistency with the original and cross-cultural equivalence of measures (Berry, 1980; Douglas & Craig, 1983).

All constructs were measured using multiple items with 5-point scales. Each measurement item of the five constructs used for this study is presented in Table 15.1. Also, descriptive statistics, construct reliability (alpha coefficients), and construct correlations are summarized in Table 15.2.

Data were collected through a survey of 400 convenient samples for two weeks, and approximately 80% of questionnaires were collected. The final usable research sample consists of 269 Korean consumers. The distribution of respondents well represented the Korean population, only slightly skewed to the high-resource population (i.e., younger, well educated, high income, etc). The 269 respondents were asked each measurement item for three companies. The three Korean companies (A, B, and C) selected are top ranked in terms of size and performance and are well known to general consumers in Korea. Company A is a major private manufacturer

TABLE 15.1

Measurement Items

Construct	Items
Overall image construct	Overall, I have a favorable image toward this company.
	Overall, I think this company is respected and admired in the society.
	Overall, I think this company will continuously grow.
Perceived integrity	Sound principles seem to guide this company's behavior.
	This company does not mislead people.
	This company treats people fairly and justly.
Perceived social responsibility	This company is interested in the welfare of society.
	This company is doing a lot of things for society.
	This company constantly spends money on socially responsible projects for the public's well being.
Satisfaction	I am satisfied with my interactions with this company.
	Both this company and I mutually benefit from the relationship.
	I enjoy dealing with this company.
Perceived capability of top management	Top management of this company has a clear vision.
	Top management of this company has expertise in their business area.
	Top management of this company has innovative ideas.
	Top management of this company has the ability to quickly adapt into ever-changing environment.
	Top management of this company is respected worldwide.

TABLE 15.2

Descriptive Statistics of Independent Variables for Three Data Sets

<Company A>	*Mean*	*S.D.*	*AC*[a]	*1*	*2*	*3*
1. Satisfaction	3.24	.72	.69			
2. Top management	3.33	.66	.74	.38		
3. Social responsibility	2.85	.78	.74	.41	.41	
4. Integrity	2.76	.63	.71	.48	.36	.44
<Company B>	*Mean*	*S.D.*	*AC*[a]	*1*	*2*	*3*
1. Satisfaction	3.09	.70	.68			
2. Top management	3.10	.52	.70	.43		
3. Social responsibility	2.62	.67	.73	.39	.43	
4. Integrity	2.68	.60	.67	.48	.47	.55
<Company C>	*Mean*	*S.D.*	*AC*[a]	*1*	*2*	*3*
1. Satisfaction	2.77	.61	.68			
2. Top management	2.90	.61	.75	.40		
3. Social responsibility	2.72	.74	.77	.56	.56	
4. Integrity	2.85	.56	.70	.44	.40	.46

Note. Construct correlations, italicized, are located off the diagonal in the last three columns.
[a] alpha coefficients

and marketer of semiconductor and electronic appliances and is highly regarded as a quality organization. Company B is an industry leader in telecommunications, serving mobile communication services, and has successfully turned from a public company to a private one in recent years. The growth of this company has been remarkable, and the company is widely known to consumers from their experience in service and through heavy marketing communication such as advertising and promotions. Company C is a world-wide iron and steel manufacturing public company that is in the process of privatization. This company has been using a soft-tone corporate image advertising campaign intensively to change its current corporate image of a hard-steel manufacturing company into a soft and friendly image. Using three data sets of diverse companies (e.g., consumer vs. industrial company; private vs. public company) enhances the validity of the model by canceling out any biased impact of specific factors originating from a particular company. If the three-company models show similar patterns in the results, the validity of our research model can be justified.

Results of Analysis

The results from a series of OLS regressions are summarized in Table 15.3. With the research model fitting well to all data, all the hypotheses are well supported. First, as predicted in the first hypotheses, perceived satisfaction from the relation-

TABLE 15.3

OLS Analysis Results

	Company A	Company B	Company C
Satisfaction	.33***	.23***	.23**
	(5.60)	(4.43)	(3.36)
Top management	.35***	.44***	.41***
	(5.74)	(6.29)	(6.05)
Social Responsibility	.17**	.13*	.14*
	(3.19)	(2.26)	(2.32)
Integrity	.07	.08	.06
	(1.06)	(1.24)	(.88)
(Constant)	.72**	.87***	1.09***
	(3.37)	(4.34)	(5.25)
F	50.23***	45.98***	41.34***
Adjusted R^2	.43	.41	.38

Note. t statistic in parentheses. *p < .05, **p < .01, ***p < .001.

ship with a company is significantly associated with overall image of the company in all three data sets (A company: $t = 5.60$, $p < .001$; B company $t = 4.43$, $p < .001$; C company : $t = 3.36$, $p < .01$). The second hypothesis, predicting an association between overall corporate image and perceived capability of top management, was well supported (A company: $t = 5.74$, $p < .001$; B company: $t = 6.29$, $p < .001$; C company: $t = 6.05$, $p < .001$). The influence of perceived social responsibility (H3) was also significant (A company: $t = 3.19$, $p < .01$; B company: $t = 2.29$, $p < .05$; C company: $t = 2.32$, $p < .05$). Contrary to prediction, an association between perceived integrity of a company and its overall corporate image was not significant (A company: $t = 1.06$, $p > .05$; B company: $t = 1.24$, $p > .05$; C company: $t = .88$, $p > .05$), failing to support H4. Last, the coefficients of satisfaction, perceived ability of top management, and social responsibility are greater than the coefficient of perceived integrity of the company (i.e., insignificant), suggesting the influences from personal experience and indirect experience are more important than experience from public sphere.

Summary and Discussion

The results of the analysis show that overall corporate image is influenced by consumers' personal experience from their transactions with the company and their perception about the company mainly from their exposure to mass media. First, to lay people, personal experience related to consumption or business must be one of the most important factors in perceiving corporate image (Moffitt, 1994b). Second, consumers' perception about a company's social responsibility and the capability of top management must have been constructed by media messages. For lay people, mass media is the most important factor influencing the corporate image they hold. The tools for this route of influence are the image campaigns (i.e., corporate image advertising) and publicity (of the CEO) of the company, which are effective at least for enhancing overall image. Particularly, the role of the CEO for the overall image of the company may be unique. The CEO does indeed set the tone at the top in terms of corporate image. It seems that members of the general public are quite willing to participate in anthropomorphic thinking, equating whole companies with the personal characteristics of the CEO and then choosing to support or criticize a company based on that judgment. The CEO faces a complex challenge in supervising corporate image while also conducting him- or herself as an indispensable component of the image of the company.

On the other hand, although the integrity of a company is a critical factor in building long-lasting, successful relationships in business, it is not so powerful an influence on consumers' perception of the overall image of a company because lay consumers seldom have the information regarding the internal policies and activities of a firm. It seems that the perceived integrity of a company, which represents consumer experience from the public sphere, is hardly related to corporate image because the information regarding the internal policies, activities, and business practices of the firm is often unavailable to consumers and they seldom have expertise to understand the policies, activities, and practices critically. In addition, the integrity of a company is not often publicized in media because it is subtle and sensitive to communicate to the public. However, it will be interesting if experts (e.g., opinion leaders and experts such as business journalists, professors, and consultants) have the same perception with general consumers on this issue.

It is clear that influence from personal experience and indirect experience from media exposure is more critical than influence from experience from the public sphere in overall corporate image. Appreciating that consumers' personal or media experience can largely determine overall corporate image calls into question established theories of the process of image building by its stakeholders.

These results are evident in the three data sets, suggesting the robust relations among the constructs. Only four constructs, however, from consumers' experience are considered in the model of corporate image employed in this study, although more constructs and factors are necessary to explain the overall corporate image. However, the main focus of this study is not to build a model of overall corporate image and to explain it; rather, the objective of the current research is to explore the relations among overall corporate image and consumers' multilayered personal experience. Consequently, the variance in corporate image explained by the model is only 40% with the four constructs. Future research is expected to explore a whole picture of corporate image utilizing the reputational capital model.

REFERENCES

Avenarius, H. (1993). Introduction: Image and public relations practice. *Journal of Public Relations Research,5*(2), 65–70.
Barich, H., & Kotler, P. (1991). A framework for marketing image management. *Sloan Management Review, 32,* 94–104.

Batra, R., Lehmann, D. R., & Singh, D. (1993). The brand personality component of brand goodwill: Some antecedents and consequences. In D. A. Aaker & A. L. Biel (Eds.), *Brand equity & advertising: Advertising's role in building strong brands* (pp. 83–96, Hillsdale, NJ: Lawrence Erlbaum Associates.

Bromley, D. B. (1993). *Reputation, image, and impression management.* Chichester: Wiley.

Carroll, A. B. (1996). *Ethics and stakeholder management.* Cincinnati: Southwestern.

Caves, R., & Porter, M. (1977). From entry barriers to mobility barriers. *Quarterly Journal of Economics, 91,* 421–434.

Chuvin, K. W., & Hirschey, M. (1994). Goodwill, profitability, and the market value of the firm. *Journal of Accounting and Public Policy, 13,* 159–180.

Donaldson, T., & Preston, L. E. (1995). The stakeholder theory of the corporation: Concepts, evidence, and implications. *Academy of Management Review, 29*(1), 65–91.

Dowling, G. R. (1988). Measuring corporate images: A review of alternative approaches. *Journal of Business Research, 17,* 27–34.

Dowling, G. R. (1993). Developing your company image into a corporate asset. *Long Range Planning, 26*(2), 101–109.

Fisher, A. B. (1996, March 6). Corporate reputations comebacks and comeuppances. *Fortune,* 90–98.

Fombrun, C. (1996). *Reputation: Realizing value from the corporate image.* Boston: Harvard Business School Press.

Fombrun, C., & Shanley, M. (1996).What's in a name? Reputation building and corporate strategy. *Academy of Management Journal, 33*(2), 233–258.

Freeman, R. E. (1984). *Strategic management: A stakeholder approach.* Boston: Pitman.

Haedrich, G. (1993). Image and strategic corporate and marketing planning. *Journal of Public Relations Research, 5*(2), 83–93.

Hall, S. (1986). On postmodernism and articulation. *Journal of Communication Inquiry, 10*(2), 45–60.

Kotter, J., & Heckett, J. (1992). *Corporate culture and performance.* New York: Free Press.

Levitt, T. (1996, Fall). Communications and industrial selling. *Marketing Management,* 44–49.

Lewis, S. (2001). Measuring corporate reputation. *Corporate Communications: An International Journal, 6*(1), 31–35.

Miles, M. P., & Covin, J. G. (2000). Environmental marketing: A source of reputational, competitive, and financial advantage. *Journal of Business Ethics, 23,* 299–311.

Moffitt, M. A. (1994a). Collapsing and integrating concepts of 'public' and 'image' into a new theory. *Public Relations Review, 20*(2), 159–170.

Moffitt, M. A. (1994b). A cultural studies perspective towards understanding corporate image: A case study of State Farm Insurance. *Journal of Public Relations Research, 6*(1), 41–66.

Nigh, D., & Cochran, P. L. (1987). Issues management and the multinational enterprise. *Management International Review, 27*(1), 4–12.

Preece, S., Fleisher, G., & Toccacelli, J. (1995). Building a reputation along the value chain at Levi Strauss. *Long Range Planning, 28*(6), 88–98.

Riordan, C. M., Gatewood, R. D., & Bill, J. B. (1997). Corporate image: Employee reactions and implications for managing corporate social performance. *Journal of Business Ethics, 16,* 401–412.

Robinson, E. A. (1997, March 3). America's most admired companies. *Fortune,* 68–76.

Suh, T., & Amine, L (2002). *Defining and managing corporate reputational capital in global markets: Conceptual issues, analytical frameworks, and managerial implications.* Paper presented at the 2002 Winter AMA Educators' Conference, Austin, TX.

CHAPTER SIXTEEN

Conceptualizing Sponsorship: An Item and Relational Information Account

Clinton S. Weeks
T. Bettina Cornwell
Michael S. Humphreys
University of Queensland, Australia

In recent years commercial sponsorship has grown to become commonplace at sporting events, both small and large, and is also prevalent at many cause-related and arts events (Cornwell & Maignan, 1998; Gwinner, 1997; Lardinoit & Derbaix, 2001; Marshall & Cook, 1992; Meenaghan, 2001b; Roy & Cornwell, 2004). It has been estimated that in 2004, sponsorship spending will reach $28 billion worldwide (International Events Group, 2003). Although many organizations appear to have a high level of acceptance and even dependence on sponsorship, a review of the literature suggests that this is not based on sponsorship being a conceptually understood or even theoretically validated business tool. Rather than basing decisions to invest in sponsorship on a sound understanding of its strategic potential, it appears that many organizations have simply followed the trend of adding sponsorship to their marketing programs in an attempt to mirror the apparent success others have reportedly experienced. Undoubtedly, this situation has been perpetuated by researchers failing to provide clear theory-based conceptualizations of sponsorship and its effects.

Although there have been attempts in the literature to conceptualize sponsorship, few studies have gone so far as to provide comprehensive psychological explanations of how sponsorship works to affect its audiences. It is the purpose of this chapter to outline a theoretical framework of how sponsorship operates when used to achieve image-related and awareness objectives and to provide guidance for enhancing sponsorship practices based on this framework.

257

DEFINING SPONSORSHIP

In one of the earliest managerial conceptualizations of commercial sponsorship, Gardner and Shuman (1987, 1988) explained that sponsorship can be used to support both corporate and marketing objectives. Corporate objectives are those aimed at enhancing or altering the image of a company, whereas marketing objectives are aimed at increasing brand or product awareness. Cornwell (1995) described sponsorship as " ... investing in causes and/or events to support overall corporate objectives and/or marketing objectives" (p. 15) and went on to note that the realization of sponsorship objectives may be dependent on related marketing efforts. She defined sponsorship-linked marketing as the " ... orchestration and implementation of marketing activities for the purpose of building and communicating an association (link) to a sponsorship" (p. 15).

Although sponsorship may share similarities with some forms of advertising, for example celebrity-endorser advertising (Gwinner, 1997; Keller, 1993; McDaniel, 1999), it differs both conceptually and operationally from traditional message-based advertising (Meenaghan, 1991). Message-based advertising seeks to promote some organizational or product attribute directly in a well controlled and explicit manner and often assumes that the audience is fully attending to the information presented (Crimmins & Horn, 1996; McDaniel, 1999). In contrast, sponsorship takes an indirect approach toward promoting the organization or product, often with the sponsor having less control over the information uptake process, and is assumed to operate at much lower attentional levels (Crimmins & Horn, 1996; Meenaghan, 2001a, 2001b; McDaniel, 1999). Thus, although both advertising and sponsorship aim to persuade consumers, advertising often attempts to do this quite overtly, whereas sponsorship is usually more subtle (Meenaghan, 2001a, 2001b). Because of these conceptual and operational differences, the theoretical frameworks used in advertising research may not always be applicable to sponsorship, and a theoretical framework of how sponsorship operates is needed.

SPONSORSHIP RESEARCH

In accordance with the growth in sponsorship activity over the last two to three decades, research in the area has also become more prevalent (Cornwell, 1999; Cornwell & Maignan, 1998; McDaniel, 1999; Meenaghan, 2001a, 2001b; Roy & Cornwell, 2004; Speed & Thompson, 2000). Despite this, however, only a small number of studies have directly sought to identify the conceptual basis of how sponsorship works. In one such study, Johar and Pham (1999) found that consumers tended to identify event sponsors, either correctly or incorrectly, as those organizations with greater perceived market share and for which there was a semantic relation, or congruence, between the sponsor and the event. Pham and Johar (2001) found in a subsequent experimental study that these biases were more evident when sponsorship information was difficult to learn, such as when it was not made salient through related marketing efforts. Based on these findings, Pham and Johar proposed that consumer memory for sponsorship information may be an inherently constructive process, particularly when sponsors fail to promote adequately or to make salient their presence as event sponsor.

Other researchers (e.g., Gwinner, 1997; Gwinner & Eaton, 1999; Meenaghan, 2001b; Speed & Thompson, 2000) have proposed that sponsorship operates primarily through promoting associations between sponsor and event in such a way that a sponsor takes on the favorable attributes of an event. Speed and Thompson (2000) examined sponsorship using a classical conditioning framework but did not go so far as to describe sponsorship as classical conditioning per se. They found that positive attitudes and favorable perceptions relating to an event were more likely to be associated with a sponsor if the sponsor was not previously perceived negatively, if the sponsor–event match was semantically congruent, and if the sponsor did not support a large number of events simultaneously. Although such studies have provided insight into processes relating to sponsorship, lacking in the literature is a comprehensive explanation of the psychological underpinnings of sponsorship.

As a way of summarizing existing understanding on the topic of sponsorship and to provide a basis for future research, Cornwell, Weeks, and Roy (2005) offered a model of consumer-focused sponsorship-linked marketing communications. The model is a synthesis of research from the area of sponsorship, considering work done in relation to information processing mechanics, individual and group level factors, market factors, and management factors, and discusses research on various theorized sponsorship outcomes. Such a model is particularly useful for highlighting processes that researchers have shown to be relevant to sponsorship contexts while illustrating that theoretical understanding in the area remains limited.

The remainder of this chapter is devoted to developing an item and relational information conceptualization of how sponsorship works to influence its audiences. Based on this theoretical perspective, strategies for enhancing the effectiveness of sponsorships, such as drawing attention to overall sponsor–sponsee relationships and to the individual components of such relationships, are outlined. The use of sponsorship as part of an integrated marketing communications program is also addressed.

ITEM AND RELATIONAL INFORMATION

In regard to the marketing goals of increasing brand or product awareness and the corporate goals of enhancing or altering brand image (Cornwell, 1995; Gwinner, 1997; Marshall & Cook, 1992; Meenaghan, 1991), sponsorship has traditionally been seen as important in two main respects. Firstly, sponsorship is said to increase brand or product awareness by serving as an exposure medium for core brand or product information such as name or logo (Pham & Vanhuele, 1997). This exposure, whether consciously processed or not, is assumed to affect consumer memory and subsequent purchase behavior by increasing familiarity and preference for that brand or product (Bennett, 1999; Janiszewski, 1993; Olson & Thjomoe, 2003). Zajonc's (1980) mere exposure effect, where preference is said to develop unconsciously as a result of repeated exposure, is often used as an explanation for this effect. Secondly, sponsorship may enhance or alter brand image by creating an association between the sponsor and sponsee, such that various attributes of one become associated with the other (Gwinner, 1997; Keller, 1993; Javalgi, Traylor, Gross, & Lampman, 1994). Further, this association may also assist in brand or product awareness in that once associated, exposure to the sponsee may prompt memory or additional thought about the sponsor, or vice versa (Keller, 1993). It is useful to bear these ideas in mind when reviewing the following sections on item and relational information processing.

In explaining memory phenomena, researchers have found it useful to distinguish between item and relational information. Item information can be described as that which is utilized when remembering a specific object or event (Humphreys, 1976, 1978; Hunt & Einstein, 1981; Kelley & Wixted, 2001; Murdock, 1974). Relational information, on the other hand, is used to remember the relation between objects or events (Humphreys, 1976, 1978; Hunt & Einstein, 1981; Kelley & Wixted, 2001; Murdock, 1974). A great deal of empirical research supports the distinction between these two types of information and, in particular, with respect to differential encoding and retrieval processes (e.g., Bain & Humphreys, 1988; Clark, 1992; Clark & Shiffrin, 1992; Gronlund & Ratcliff, 1989; Hockley, 1994; Hockley & Cristi, 1996; McGee, 1980; Yonelinas, 1997). Clark and Gronlund (1996) offer a detailed review of research in this area.

Although often distinguished on the basis of arguments that they involve differential recognition and recall processes, item and relational information have also been conceptualized as differing in how they are encoded (e.g., Bain & Humphreys, 1988; Begg, 1978; Einstein & Hunt, 1980; Hockley & Cristi, 1996; Hunt & Einstein, 1981; McGee, 1980). In developing an understanding of how sponsorship may operate in terms of item and relational information, Einstein and Hunt's (1980; Hunt & Einstein, 1981) findings are particularly useful. In the early 1980s these researchers sought convergence between two streams of memory research that had traditionally been viewed as incompatible. They integrated organizational memory theory and levels-of-processing theory, using the framework of item and relational information, to produce a general explanation of how optimal memory performance may function.

Organizational Memory Perspective

Early organizational memory theorists (e.g., Bower, 1970; Mandler, 1967; Puff, 1979) claimed that good memory performance requires an episode be encoded in an organized manner, based on similarities across items of information. If a memory representation can be thought of as a set of encoded features, organizational theorists would argue that similar features across various items produce overlap across representations in memory. Such overlap results in the various related items within an episode being encoded as a single, organized, and integrated holistic representation. This type of storage is assumed to facilitate retrieval by reducing the necessary search process in that, given some type of environmental memory cue, overlapping or related memory representations are activated. Because only related representations have been activated, the search process is essentially limited to just a particular class or category of relevant information, and so retrieval is more efficient. Without such a class activation process, each time memory for a particular event is sought, all stored memory traces would need to be searched, resulting in an extensive and inefficient retrieval process.

Levels-of-Processing Perspective

In contrast to organizational memory theorists, levels-of-processing theorists (e.g., Craik & Lockhart, 1972; Craik & Tulving, 1975; Lockhart, Craik, & Jacoby, 1976; Nelson, 1979) claimed that good memory performance results from attending to the differences across items of information in an episode. Each item is encoded as a discrete representation, with attention being given to encoding the distinctive features of each item. Items are stored as unique representations in memory, identifiable through a lack of overlapping features or lack of integration across representations. This lack of overlap assists retrieval, with the distinctiveness of a particular representation serving a discriminatory function, allowing it to be distinguished from all other stored traces. Without encoding being based on differences across pieces of information, identification of the appropriate memory representation at retrieval would not be possible, due to a lack of ability to differentiate between similar representations.

Integration of Perspectives

Whereas organizational memory theorists claimed that memory involves encoding similarities between items, levels-of-processing theorists argued that it is instead based on encoding differences. Although these seem to be competing perspectives, somewhat paradoxically, both organizational and levels-of-processing memory theories have been empirically supported (e.g., Bower, 1970; Craik & Lockhart, 1972; Craik & Tulving, 1975; Lockhart et al., 1976; Mandler, 1967; Nelson, 1979; Puff, 1979). Einstein and Hunt (1980; Hunt & Einstein, 1981) proposed that these contrasting operations may actually function together, such that optimal memory performance occurs when both forms of processing occur at encoding and are used in conjunction at retrieval.

Reconsidering these theories from an item and relational memory perspective, Einstein and Hunt (1980; Hunt & Einstein, 1981) argued that distinctiveness encoding, as suggested by levels-of-processing theorists, may apply to the processing of item information, whereas similarity encoding, as suggested by organizational theorists, may apply to the processing of relational information. It was proposed that relational information serves primarily a generative function by activating the general class or category to which a specific stimulus belongs. Item information may then be used to search within this limited group of representations, with the discriminatory function enabling the correct representation to be distinguished from other related information. In this way Einstein and Hunt proposed that relational and item information each contribute to memory retrieval processes but in different ways.

To illustrate with a practical example, if someone is asked the question, "Which brand is the major sponsor of tennis player Lleyton Hewitt?" both relational and item processing may be used to provide an answer. Relational processing is required to activate those memory representations that relate to the category of "Lleyton Hewitt." This information alone, however, may not be enough to enable the person to provide a precise response, and so the use of item processing is also required. Item processing would be used to discriminate among all those activated representations in the "Lleyton Hewitt" category to identify the one encoded with the distinctive feature of "major sponsor." Thus, although either relational or item processing alone might be used to retrieve relevant information from memory, their conjunctive use can facilitate retrieval in terms of efficiency and precision.

Although this example outlines how item and relational processes may occur when memory is explicitly cued, these processes can also operate at an implicit level (Hunt & McDaniel, 1993). For example, consider the situation in which a person has just been watching a swimming race where the winner was sponsored by Speedo. If that person then had to make some value judgment about various swimwear products, say in a purchase-decision environment, relational and item information may again come into play. When confronted with the Speedo brand, relational information would be used to activate at an implicit level various attributes relating to Speedo. Item information would then be used to discriminate among all Speedo-related memory traces to identify just those relevant to the decision, namely representations that had been encoded with features such as quality, speed, or success. Although occurring at an implicit level, relational and item information processing have nonetheless been used to affect the person's judgment. In this way Einstein and Hunt (1980; Hunt & Einstein, 1981) were able to integrate, using an item and relational information framework, two seemingly competing theories of memory and to put forward an explanation of optimal memory performance.

Determinants of the Processing of Item and Relational Information

An important point that Einstein and Hunt (1980; Hunt & Einstein, 1981) made in their research was that for item and relational information to be utilized at retrieval, both must have been earlier encoded. They explained that the encoding of each type of information is dependent on two influences: semantic relatedness and orientation toward encoding. Semantic relatedness refers to how obviously related the items of information in the episode are, or the extent to which they are perceived to share common attributes. Einstein and Hunt argued that when an episode involves obviously related items, where similarities between items are salient, then relational information will be encoded automatically. For episodes with seemingly unrelated items, however, where differences are more salient then similarities, item information will be encoded automatically. This aspect of encoding is both automatic and obligatory in that, depending on the semantic relatedness between items, either relational or item information will always be processed.

Orientation toward encoding refers to the way in which the person, at encoding, is induced to attend to either the relatedness or the distinctiveness of the items involved (Einstein & Hunt, 1980; Hunt & Einstein, 1981; Hunt & McDaniel, 1993). If a person is induced to attend to similarities between items in an episode, then relational information will be encoded. If they are induced to attend to differences between items, however, then item information will be encoded. This nonautomatic aspect of encoding is in addition to the automatic semantic relatedness encoding and ultimately is the determinant of whether the person encodes an episode as just one type of information or as both (Hunt & McDaniel, 1993). Thus, although Hunt and Einstein proposed that optimal memory retrieval results from a combination of the generative functions of relational processing and the discriminative functions of item processing, the encoding of both types of information so that they are available at retrieval does not always occur. As is often the case, only the automatic processing of semantic relatedness may occur, resulting in the encoding of just one type of information.

Empirical Support

In developing their arguments, Einstein and Hunt (1980; Hunt & Einstein, 1981) used research findings from a number of earlier studies, such as those by Bellezza, Cheesman, and Reddy (1977), Begg (1978), and Epstein, Phillips, and Johnson (1975). Bellezza et al. gave participants a list of semantically unrelated words (which should be automatically encoded as item information) and instructed half to generate a distinct and separate sentence for each word (which should orient participants toward encoding further item information) and the other half to generate a sentence for each word but to make the sentences form a general storyline (which should orient participants toward encoding relational information). Those participants forming distinct and separate sentences for each word should thus encode only item information, whereas those forming sentences as part of a general storyline should encode both item and relational information. Results showed that recall was typically higher for those participants who formed sentences as part of a general storyline than for those who formed discrete sentences. Thus, in accordance with Einstein and Hunt's encoding arguments, those participants who were oriented toward encoding relational information, in addition to the automatically encoded item information, showed better memory performance than those who were oriented toward encoding further item information.

Using a different experimental technique, Begg (1978) showed that conceptually related word pairs were better remembered if participants were instructed to attend to differences between the words. In contrast, conceptually unrelated word pairs were better remembered when participants were instructed to attend to similarities between the words. Thus, while related words would automatically be encoded using relational processing, the induction of additional item processing through making differences salient, facilitated memory. Similarly, for unrelated word pairs that would automatically be encoded using item processing, the induction of relational processing through making similarities salient improved memory performance. When the automatic encoding resulting from semantic relatedness was congruent with the nonautomatic encoding induced through instructions (i.e., when the semantic relatedness and orientation toward encoding involved the processing of the same type of information), there was little improvement in memory performance. Similar findings were reported by Epstein et al. (1975).

Studies employing encoding techniques involving the use of mental imagery have also shown supporting results (e.g., Bain & Humphreys, 1988; Hockley & Cristi, 1996; McGee, 1980). Typically, when participants are instructed to encode semantically unrelated word pairs by forming separate mental images for each one, subsequent recognition of the individual items is good, but recognition for the word pairs is poor. When instructed to form an image incorporating both unrelated words from the pair, however, recognition of the individual items remains good, and pair recognition improves significantly. Thus, in accordance with Einstein and Hunt (1980; Hunt & Einstein, 1981), research has typically shown that when unrelated word pairs are encoded using mental imagery tasks that promote either item or relational processing, item information is generally available at retrieval. Relational information, however, is more readily available for the unrelated items only following the relational processing task.

Einstein and Hunt's (1980; Hunt & Einstein, 1981) series of studies provide perhaps the most direct support for their integrated theory perspective and demonstrates the separate influences of semantic relatedness and orientation toward encoding. In these studies, participants were exposed to lists of words from either five obvious categories (e.g., animals, fruits, etc.) or five obscure categories (e.g., things that make noise, things that women wear, etc.). Words in the obvious category list were assumed to be encoded automatically as relational information, and words in the obscure category list were assumed to be encoded automatically as item information. An incidental learning technique was used, with half the participants instructed to rate each word in the list for pleasantness (to induce item processing) and half instructed to sort the items into categories (to induce relational processing). Results showed that words in the obvious category list were better recalled when rated for pleasantness than when sorted into categories, whereas words in the obscure category list were better recalled when sorted into categories than when rated for pleasantness. Thus, in line with the findings of other researchers and in support of their own propositions, Einstein and Hunt found that retrieval of related items was better when encoding involved item processing, whereas retrieval of unrelated items was better when encoding involved relational processing. Further support for the influences of semantic relatedness and orientation toward encoding on item and relational processing can be found in subsequent work by Hunt and colleagues (e.g., Hunt & Seta, 1984) and can also be inferred from more recent research (e.g., Prior & Bentin, 2003).

Summary

A brief summary of the key elements of Einstein and Hunt's (1980; Hunt & Einstein, 1981) relational and item theory follows.

Relational Information.   The encoding of relational information is suggested as being based around similarities and relations among items, such that overlapping features across items form a well organized, highly integrated, holistic representation in memory. At retrieval, this integration and organization facilitates the search process by enabling the generation of a limited category or class of related information from which an appropriate item response can be drawn. In this way, relational information serves a generative recall-like function (Hunt & McDaniel, 1993).

Item Information.   The encoding of item information is suggested as being based on differences among items, with each item encoded as a set of distinctive features. At retrieval, this distinctiveness serves a discriminatory function, enabling the appropriate representation to be distinguished from all others stored in memory. Here, item information plays a discriminative recognition-like role (Hunt & McDaniel, 1993).

Encoding.   Encoding of relational and/or item information is dependent on two influences, one automatic and the other nonautomatic. First, the apparent semantic relatedness between items determines whether relational or item information will be automatically encoded. Related items are encoded using relational information because of obvious similarities among the items, whereas unrelated items are encoded using item information because of salient differences among the items (Einstein & Hunt, 1980; Hunt & Einstein, 1981; Hunt & McDaniel, 1993). Second, if an individual is oriented to attend to similarities or differences among items, further encoding may occur, which is in addition to the automatic semantic relatedness encoding. If attention is drawn to similarities or relations among items, then relational processing will be induced. If attention is drawn to distinctive features or differences across the items, then item processing will be induced. Although any given episode may be encoded with just one type of information, if the semantic relatedness of items within that episode and the person's orientation toward encoding the items promote the processing of different types of information, then both item and relational information will be encoded.

Retrieval.   Provided that the automatic and nonautomatic encoding processes have led to both item and relational information being processed, then memory retrieval will be facilitated. In such an instance, given some memory cue, relational information will serve to generate the class or category of representations stored in memory relating to that cue. Item information will then enable precise discrimination within the generated set of representations to identify the appropriate trace. If, however, only automatic encoding based on semantic relatedness has occurred, or if both automatic and nonautomatic elements of encoding have resulted in only one type of information being encoded, then memory retrieval will be less reliable. Although either item or relational processing alone may be sufficient for memory to operate, performance is enhanced in terms of efficiency and precision when both item and relational information are processed at encoding and used in conjunction at retrieval (Hunt & McDaniel, 1993).

CONCEPTUALIZING SPONSORSHIP AS ITEM AND RELATIONAL INFORMATION

Whereas a great deal of research has been conducted to investigate item and relational information, theoretical research in the area of commercial sponsorship has been less extensive. Despite this, across these two areas there are a number of correspondences that provide support for conceptualizing sponsorship as item and relational information. The following sections outline how sponsorship can be viewed within such a framework and describe similarities across the two research paradigms.

As noted earlier, organizations can use sponsorship to fulfill a variety of awareness and image-related objectives (Cornwell, 1995; Gwinner, 1997; Marshall & Cook, 1992; Meenaghan, 1991). Sponsorship can increase brand or product awareness by serving as an exposure medium for core brand or product information such as name or logo (Pham & Vanhuele, 1997). It can enhance or alter brand image by creating an association between the sponsor and sponsee, such that various attributes of one become associated with the other (Gwinner, 1997; Gwinner & Eaton, 1999; Javalgi et al., 1994) and where memory for one may prompt memory for the other (Keller, 1993). Using an item and relational information framework, it is proposed that the capacity of a sponsorship to achieve these objectives rests in part with how audiences encode information at the time of exposure. As will become evident, Einstein and Hunt's (1980; Hunt & Einstein, 1981) suggestions about semantic relatedness and orientation toward encoding are particularly relevant to sponsorship.

Increasing Brand or Product Awareness

If the goal of an organization is to promote brand or product awareness, then typically the organization seeks to increase levels of exposure of the brand or product (Aaker, 1991; Gwinner, 1997). Many researchers have argued that such increases in exposure, whether consciously attended to or not, may promote levels of familiarity with the presented information, which may enhance preference for that information (e.g., Bennett, 1999; Janiszewski, 1993; Olson & Thjomoe, 2003; Zajonc, 1980). Such reasoning is usually justified in terms of the mere exposure effect (Zajonc, 1980). Thinking about sponsorship within an item and relational information framework, however, suggests that there is more to promoting brand or product awareness, and preference, than just mere exposure.

If the relationship between a sponsor and sponsee is perceived as one that is seemingly unnatural or illogical (i.e., semantically unrelated), as might be the case when a financial institution sponsors a football team, then it can be assumed that audiences will process these two entities using item information. If the sponsor can articulate a relationship, however, or draw attention to the similarities between the two entities, then the audience may also be oriented to process relational information (i.e., via orientation toward encoding). Alternatively, if the relationship between a sponsor and sponsee is perceived as more natural or logical, such as may be the case with an athletics shoe manufacturer sponsoring a track and field squad, relational information will be automatically encoded. Here the sponsor may benefit by drawing attention to each entity within this relationship, inducing additional item processing, which will help to differentiate both entities from other related items (e.g., other brands and events). In this way, both types of information will have been processed, and when confronted with a situation in which memory for the brand or product is required, retrieval of this information will be facilitated.

The processing of both relational and item information, in regard to promoting brand or product awareness, may be particularly important in combating the effects of ambush marketing and in developing a sponsorship into a distinctive competence for the sponsor. Ambush marketing occurs when some nonsponsor rival organization conducts a marketing campaign aimed at developing an association with an event and at obtaining those benefits assumed to come from sponsorship (Crow & Hoek, 2003; Meenaghan, 1994, 1998; O'Sullivan & Murphy, 1998). If a sponsor is able to establish a clear link between itself and its sponsee, such that the two are perceived as strongly related (i.e., relational information) and such that the sponsor is clearly distinguished from other similar information such as competing brands (i.e., item information), then audiences will be better able to identify the true sponsor from nonsponsors. In this way, the sponsorship can be developed into a distinctive competence for the sponsoring organization and can promote brand differentiation (Amis, Slack, & Berrett, 1999; Cornwell, Roy, & Steinard, 2001). This may also be relevant in reducing the prominence bias reported by Pham and Johar (2001), where those brands perceived to be prominent in the marketplace are said to be miscredited with sponsorships. Brand or product awareness, although traditionally sought through attempts at gaining greater exposure for brand or product information, can clearly benefit through ensuring that audiences process sponsorships as both item and relational information.

Enhancing or Altering Brand Image

Although the goal of enhancing or altering brand image differs from that of increasing brand or product awareness, in that a transfer of valence from event to sponsor is intended (Gwinner, 1997; Gwinner & Eaton, 1999), the concepts of item and relational processing are still pertinent. If sponsors, whether obviously related to the sponsee or otherwise, are able to encourage both item and relational processing, then not only will the attributes of the event be encoded in an holistic representation with those of the sponsor (i.e., relational information) but at the same time, the sponsor will be seen as a distinct entity in its own right (i.e., item information). Consider again the situation of a financial institution sponsoring a football team. If both item and relational information are processed, then not only will audiences encode the perceived similarities between the institution and the football team, such as the attributes of determination, fair play, and competitiveness (i.e., relational information), but the financial institution will be distinguished from other football-related information such as additional sponsors, having a sports orientation, and so forth (i.e., item information). Thus, while the financial institution will benefit by being associated with those image attributes of the football team that are made salient as similarities, it will also be clearly identifiable in the minds of consumers as a financial institution and sponsor.

Conceptualizing sponsorship in terms of item and relational information provides a clear explanation of how goals such as increasing product or brand awareness and enhancing or altering brand image may be achieved. Specifically, consideration must be given to the way in which audiences perceive the relationship between the sponsor and sponsee (i.e., semantic relatedness) and the way in which audiences are oriented to attend to aspects of the relationship (i.e., orientation toward encoding). This framework suggests that for a sponsorship to be most effective, both item and relational information must be encoded, so as to be available at retrieval. Sponsors who fail to promote the processing of both types of information ultimately leave their sponsorship at a disadvantage.

CORRESPONDENCES ACROSS PARADIGMS

Parallel notions to Einstein and Hunt's (1980, Hunt & Einstein, 1981) semantic relatedness and orientation toward encoding have been developed independently in the sponsorship literature. Many researchers in this field have argued that the effectiveness of a sponsorship is dependent on the perceived congruence between the sponsor and sponsee (e.g., Gwinner, 1997; Gwinner & Eaton, 1999; Johar & Pham,

1999; McDaniel, 1999) and the way in which audiences are encouraged to perceive this relationship (Crimmins & Horn, 1996; Dean, 1999). These correspondences across paradigms are highly supportive of an item and relational information conceptualization of sponsorship.

Researchers such as Gwinner (1997; Gwinner & Eaton, 1999; McDaniel, 1999) and Johar and Pham (1999) have claimed that semantic relatedness between a sponsor and sponsee can enhance the association between the two and can augment the transfer of valence from the sponsee to the sponsor. This is often referred to as a congruence or match-up effect (Johar & Pham, 1999; McDaniel, 1999). Varying explanations for how congruence or match-up enhances sponsorship effectiveness have been proposed in the sponsorship literature. For example it has been suggested that congruent relationships can be anchored better in the minds of consumers (Gwinner, 1997) and that matching relationships fit better with existing schemas of the sponsor or sponsee (McDaniel, 1999). Although the concept of semantic relatedness in the sponsorship literature was developed independently of that in the item and relational information literature, there is a clear correspondence between the two.

Sponsorship research has also addressed the item and relational information issue of orientation toward encoding, with several studies indicating that unrelated sponsor–sponsee pairings benefit when consumers are led to attend to some meaningful rationale for the pair (Crimmins & Horn, 1996; Dean, 1999). Although they were prescribing managerial sponsorship tactics rather than ways in which information encoding could be enhanced, Crimmins and Horn explained that when the relationship between a sponsor and sponsee is not obvious, sponsors benefit by using additional communications to explicitly "interpret" the relationship on behalf of the consumer. Experimental research by Dean led to a similar conclusion.

Although little sponsorship literature directly notes that a highly related sponsor–sponsee pairing may benefit from drawing attention to the specific entities within the relationship, this might be inferred from ambush marketing research (Meenaghan, 1994, 1998) and from Pham and Johar's (2001) prominence and relatedness biases work. When sponsor-specific item information encoding is induced, audiences should be more able to discriminate accurately between possible sponsors (e.g., those firms using an ambushing strategy, or which are prominent in the marketplace) and the actual sponsor because of the distinctive information stored in memory. Thus, in accordance with Einstein and Hunt's (1980, Hunt & Einstein, 1981) claims about orientation toward encoding, sponsorship researchers have noted similar issues.

Further empirical support for the semantic relatedness and orientation toward encoding notions, in a sponsorship context, have been provided in preliminary work by Cornwell, Humphreys, Maguire, and Tellegen (2003). Sponsor recall was improved for semantically unrelated or incongruent sponsor–event pairings when a relationship was explicitly articulated in the form of a press release. Recall remained unchanged however, for semantically related or congruent sponsor–event pairings when the same articulation manipulation was used. Thus, in support of the theoretical ideas of Einstein and Hunt (1980, Hunt & Einstein, 1981), Cornwell et al. (2003) have shown, using realistic sponsorship stimuli, that by inducing relational processing, memory for sponsor–sponsee pairings can be enhanced, but only for those where this information would not have automatically been encoded otherwise (i.e., incongruent pairings). In sum, clear correspondences appear across the item and relational memory literature and the sponsorship literature, providing strong support for the current conceptualization of sponsorship.

PRACTICAL IMPLICATIONS: ENSURING ITEM AND RELATIONAL PROCESSING

The presentation of sponsorship information can take many forms. For example, in a sporting context, sponsorship information may be presented as background material with brand names or logos displayed on perimeter fences, team uniforms, on features such as scoreboards, set amid seating, and so forth. Further exposure can be gained through such media as press releases detailing sponsorship information, Internet sites, point-of-purchase displays, thematically linked advertisements, and a number of other integrated marketing communications (Keller, 2001). Most interesting, however, is that the way in which such sponsorship information is encoded by audiences (i.e., as item information, relational information, or both) ultimately depends on how semantically related (or congruent) a sponsor and sponsee relationship is perceived to be and on how a sponsor uses its marketing communications efforts to articulate linkages between itself and its sponsee. As established previously, the way this information is encoded has repercussions for the subsequent effectiveness of retrieval.

Perhaps the most important implication of an item and relational information conceptualization of sponsorship for practitioners is that it provides an explanation of how sponsorships can be used to achieve corporate and marketing objectives. Not only is memory for the overall sponsorship enhanced through the processing of both item and relational information, but the processing of item information also promotes product and brand awareness and brand differentiation through increasing distinctiveness. The processing of relational information enables the sponsor to take on various attributes of the sponsee, enhancing brand image, and allowing one to prompt memory for the other.

Optimal sponsorship effectiveness can be expected when practitioners promote the processing of both item and relational information. For seemingly natural or logical sponsor–sponsee relationships, additional emphasis should be placed on promoting sponsor- and sponsee-specific information. This is not to say that the relationship between the sponsor and sponsee should be ignored or receive no promotional attention, however, because the relationship needs to remain salient to the audience. For seemingly unnatural or illogical sponsor–sponsee relationships, audiences should be made aware of some meaningful relationship. This awareness could be accomplished through integrated marketing communications efforts such as media advertising, direct and interactive advertising, point-of-purchase displays, trade promotions, consumer promotions, public relations efforts, and so forth (Keller, 2001). With such a diverse range of marketing communications tools available, practitioners have ample opportunity to promote or make salient the desired components of their sponsorships.

In a sponsorship involving strong semantic relatedness (i.e., congruence), such as would be the case with Nissan sponsoring a NASCAR (National Association of Stock Car Auto Racing) driver, marketing communications such as print or television advertising may help to promote item-specific sponsorship information. An advertisement, while drawing attention to the high semantic relatedness of the sponsorship, may seek to promote Nissan-specific information by denoting Nissan dealership locations, specific deals that the company is offering, and so forth. It is important that the Nissan–NASCAR relationship still remains salient, however, because ignoring it may impair the automatic processing of relational information. By promoting a sponsorship with strong semantic relatedness (where relational processing should be automatic) together with additional sponsor-specific information (where item processing is induced), memory for the sponsorship and the specific sponsor will be facilitated.

For weakly related (i.e., incongruent) sponsorships, such as may be the case if Kellogg's was to sponsor a NASCAR driver, integrated marketing communications efforts could be used to draw audience attention to some relationship between the two. For example, advertising or billboards may depict the driver eating Kellogg's breakfast cereals and snack products. Thus, integrated marketing communications programs, if used wisely and purposefully, can greatly assist in achieving the brand image and awareness objectives of sponsorship investments.

THE NEED FOR FURTHER EMPIRICAL WORK

One issue that must be addressed if the current theoretical framework is to be validated concerns the way sponsorship typically operates at low attentional levels. In the absence of integrated marketing communications, sponsorship information may be given very little conscious attention by consumers, particularly, for example, if presented simply as venue signage, logo displays, or brief press-release statements (Nebenzahl & Hornik, 1985; Pham & Vanhuele, 1997). Although empirical evidence supports the view that information processed at low levels of attention is still encoded and may be retrieved at a later time (Hasher & Zacks, 1984; Kausler, 1990; Kausler & Lichty, 1984; Kausler & Puckett, 1980; Kausler, Wright, & Hakami, 1981; Petty & Cacioppo, 1981; Petty, Cacioppo, & Schumann, 1983), the extent to which this applies to both item and relational information has yet to be demonstrated.

Research has shown that information such as frequency of occurrence, spatial location, and temporal location are encoded automatically, with little conscious effort, under conditions of both incidental and intentional learning (Hasher & Zacks, 1979, 1984; Kausler, 1990; Kausler & Lichty, 1984; Kausler & Puckett, 1980; Kausler et al., 1981). Although this type of research has primarily examined these variables in terms of item information, the findings may be generalizable to relational information if it is assumed that relational information is encoded as integrated and holistic representations. Studies employing incidental learning conditions such as those of Einstein and Hunt (1980, Hunt & Einstein, 1981) and Prior and Bentin (2003) have already demonstrated that relational information may be encoded in the absence of intention to learn, so this issue may be less problematic than it first appears.

Although any information learned under low levels of attention is likely to be poorer than if it were learned under higher levels of attention, relational information may suffer to a greater extent than item information, given that it involves the encoding and storage of more complex representations. Future research should investigate the extent to which this is the case and whether it can be overcome by such manipulations as repetition of exposure or variation in exposure context. This type of research will prove critical in supporting the current theoretical framework.

SUMMARY AND CONCLUSIONS

Although commercial sponsorship has grown dramatically in recent years, a conceptual understanding of how sponsorship works has not been clearly established in the literature. This chapter has sought to provide one such conceptual framework using item and relational memory theory from the psychological literature. This framework not only provides a basis for making predictions about sponsorship effectiveness but can also be used to guide sponsorship practices. Depending on the perceived semantic relatedness between the sponsor and sponsee and how audiences are led to understand either item-specific or relational aspects of this relationship, sponsorship effectiveness may vary. When both item and relational information about the sponsorship are processed, sponsorships should be more effective in achieving awareness and image-related objectives. Because relationships between sponsors and sponsees vary, as do audience perceptions, integrated marketing communications can be used to promote those aspects of the relationship desired by the sponsor.

As might be expected, the conceptualization provided here is not without its limitations. At a theoretical level, and as has been noted in the item and relational literature, is the issue of how distinct item and relational information really are (e.g., Hunt & Einstein, 1981). For example, is it feasible to assume that a strong semantic relationship does not involve the encoding of the individual items within that relationship? If not, how then is the strength of that relationship initially determined? Similarly, is it feasible to assume that a weak semantic relationship is processed primarily as item information, with little encoding of relational information? If so, then how is the context in which that information is set, which may be considered a form of relational information, excluded from the encoding process? At a sponsorship-specific level are the concerns regarding the way in which sponsorship information is processed at low levels of attention and how this may affect encoding and storage operations.

Despite these concerns, a psychologically-based, theoretical conceptualization of sponsorship has been lacking in the literature, and this chapter has gone some way to address this situation. Conceptualizing sponsorship as item and relational information offers a strong theoretical framework on which to build future research and to guide practical efforts. With sponsorship expected to continue to grow in future years, the provision of such frameworks will be useful in providing directions for future research and in ensuring that organizations have a sound basis for making tactical decisions regarding their sponsorship-linked marketing efforts.

REFERENCES

Aaker, D. A. (1991). *Managing brand equity: Capitalizing on the value of brand name*. New York: The Free Press.

Amis, J., Slack, T., & Berrett, T. (1999). Sport sponsorship as distinctive competence. *European Journal of Marketing, 33*(3/4), 250–272.

Bain, J. D. & Humphreys, M. S. (1988). Relational context: Independent cues, meanings or configurations? In G. M. Davies & D. M. Thomson (Eds.), *Memory in context: Context in memory* (pp. 97–137). Oxford, England: Wiley.

Begg, I. (1978). Similarity and contrast in memory for relations. *Memory & Cognition, 6,* 509–517.

Bellezza, F. S., Cheesman, F. L., & Reddy, G. (1977). Organization and semantic elaboration in free recall. *Journal of Experimental Psychology: Human Learning & Memory, 1,* 539–550.

Bennett, R. (1999). Sports sponsorship, spectator recall and false consensus. *European Journal of Marketing, 33*(3/4), 291–313.

Bower, G. H. (1970). Organizational factors in memory. *Cognitive Psychology, 1,* 18–46.

Clark, S. E. (1992). Word frequency effects in associative and item recognition. *Memory & Cognition, 20,* 231–243.

Clark, S. E. & Gronlund, S. D. (1996). Global matching models of recognition memory: How the models match the data. *Psychonomic Bulletin & Review, 3,* 37–60.

Clark, S. E. & Shiffrin, R. M. (1992). Cuing effects and associative information in recognition memory. *Memory & Cognition, 20,* 580–598.

Cornwell, T. B. (1995). Sponsorship-linked marketing development. *Sport Marketing Quarterly, 4*(4), 13–24.

Cornwell, T. B. (1999). Recent developments in international sponsorship research *Sponsorship Business Review, 2,* 36–42.

Cornwell, T. B. Humphreys, M. H., Maguire, A., & Tellegan, C. (2003). The role of articulation in sponsorship-linked marketing. *Proceedings of the Advertising & Consumer Psychology Conference 2003,* 8–9.

Cornwell, T. B. & Maignan, I. (1998). An international review of sponsorship research. *Journal of Advertising, 27*(1), 1–21.

Cornwell, T. B., Roy, D. P., & Steinard, E. A. (2001). Exploring managers' perceptions of the impact of sponsorship on brand equity. *Journal of Advertising, 30*(2), 41–51.

Cornwell, T. B., Weeks, C. S., & Roy, D. P. (2005). Sponsorship-linked marketing: Opening the blackbox. *Journal of Advertising, 34*(2), 23–45.

Craik, F. I. M. & Lockhart, R. S. (1972). Levels of processing: A framework for memory research. *Journal of Verbal Learning & Verbal Behavior, 11*, 671–684.

Craik, F. I. M. & Tulving, E. (1975). Depth of processing and retention of words in episodic memory. *Journal of Experimental Psychology: General, 104*, 268–294.

Crimmins, J., & Horn, M. (1996). Sponsorship: From management ego trip to marketing success. *Journal of Advertising Research, 36*(4), 11–20.

Crow, D., & Hoek, J. (2003). Ambush marketing: A critical review and some practical advice. *Marketing Bulletin, 14*, 1–14.

Dean, D. H. (1999). Brand endorsement, popularity, and event sponsorship as advertising cues affecting consumer pre-purchase attitudes. *Journal of Advertising, 28*(3), 1–12.

Einstein, G. O., & Hunt, R. R. (1980). Levels of processing and organization: Additive effects of individual-item and relational processing. *Journal of Experimental Psychology: Human Learning & Memory, 6*, 588–598.

Epstein, M. L., Phillips, W. D., & Johnson, S. J. (1975). Recall of related and unrelated word pairs as a function of processing level. *Journal of Experimental Psychology: Human Learning & Memory, 1*, 149–152.

Gardner, M. P., & Shuman, P. (1987). Sponsorship: An important component of the promotions mix. *Journal of Advertising, 16*(1), 11–17.

Gardner, M. P., & Shuman, P. (1988). Sponsorships and small businesses. *Journal of Small Business Management, 26*(4), 44–52.

Gronlund, S. D., & Ratcliff, R. (1989). Time course of item and associative information: Implications for global memory models. *Journal of Experimental Psychology: Learning, Memory, & Cognition, 15*, 846–858.

Gwinner, K. (1997). A model of image creation and image transfer in event sponsorship. *International Marketing Review, 14*(3), 145–158.

Gwinner, K., & Eaton, J. (1999). Building brand image through event sponsorship: The role of image transfer. *Journal of Advertising, 28*(4), 47–57.

Hasher, L., & Zacks, R. T. (1979). Automatic and effortful processes in memory. *Journal of Experimental Psychology: General, 108*, 356–388.

Hasher, L., & Zacks, R. T. (1984). Automatic processing of fundamental information: The case of frequency of occurrence. *American Psychologist, 39*, 1372–1388.

Hockley, W. E. (1994). Reflections of the mirror effect for item and associative recognition. *Memory & Cognition, 22*, 713–722.

Hockley, W. E., & Cristi, C. (1996). Tests of encoding tradeoffs between item and associative information. *Memory & Cognition, 24*, 202–216.

Humphreys, M. S. (1976). Relational information and the context effect in recognition memory. *Memory & Cognition, 4*, 221–232.

Humphreys, M. S. (1978). Item and relational information: A case for context independent retrieval. *Journal of Verbal Learning & Verbal Behavior, 17*, 175–187.

Hunt, R. R., & Einstein, G. O. (1981). Relational and item-specific information in memory. *Journal of Verbal Learning & Verbal Behavior, 20*, 497–514.

Hunt, R. R., & McDaniel, M. A. (1993). The enigma of organization and distinctiveness. *Journal of Memory & Language, 32*, 421–445.

Hunt, R. R., & Seta, C. E. (1984). Category size effects in recall: The roles of relational and individual item information. *Journal of Experimental Psychology: Learning, Memory, & Cognition, 10*, 454–464.

International Events Group. (2003). Sponsorship spending to increase 8.7 percent in 2004. *IEG Sponsorship Report, 22*(24), 1, 4.

Janiszewski, C. (1993). Preattentive mere exposure effects. *Journal of Consumer Research, 20*, 376–392.

Javalgi, R. G., Traylor, M. B., Gross, A. C., & Lampman, E. (1994). Awareness of sponsorship and corporate image: An empirical investigation. *Journal of Advertising, 23*(4), 47–58.

Johar, G. V., & Pham, M. T. (1999). Relatedness, prominence and constructive sponsor identification. *Journal of Marketing Research, 36*(3), 299–312.

Kausler, D. H. (1990). Automaticity of encoding and episodic memory processes. In E. A. Lovelace (Ed.), *Aging and cognition: Mental processes, self awareness and interventions* (pp. 29–68). Amsterdam: North-Holland.

Kausler, D. H., & Lichty, W. (1984). Frequency judgments for distractor items in a short-term memory task: Instructional variation and adult age differences. *Journal of Verbal Learning & Verbal Behavior, 23*, 660–668.

Kausler, D. H., & Puckett, J. M. (1980). Frequency judgments and correlated cognitive abilities in young and elderly adults. *Journal of Gerontology, 35*, 376–382.

Kausler, D. H., Wright, R. E., & Hakami, M. K. (1981). Variation in task complexity and adult age differences in frequency-of-occurrence judgments. *Bulletin of the Psychonomic Society, 18*, 195–197.

Keller, K. L. (1993). Conceptualizing, measuring, and managing customer-based brand equity. *Journal of Marketing, 57*(1), 1–22.

Keller, K. L. (2001). Mastering the marketing communications mix: Micro and macro perspectives on integrated marketing communications programs. *Journal of Marketing Management, 17*, 819–847.

Kelley, R., & Wixted, J. T. (2001). On the nature of associative information in recognition memory. *Journal of Experimental Psychology: Learning, Memory & Cognition, 27*, 701–722.

Lardinoit, T., & Derbaix, C. (2001). Sponsorship and recall of sponsors. *Psychology & Marketing, 18*(2), 167–190.

Lockhart, R. S., Craik, F. I. M., & Jacoby, L. L. (1976). Depth of processing, recognition, and recall. In J. Brown (Ed.), *Recognition and recall* (pp. 75–102). London: Wiley.

Mandler, G. (1967). Organization and memory. In K. Spence and J. Spence (Eds.), *The psychology of learning and motivation* (pp. 327–372). New York: Academic Press.

Marshall, D. W., & Cook, G. (1992). The corporate (sports) sponsor. *International Journal of Advertising, 11*, 307–324.

McDaniel, S. R. (1999). An investigation of match-up effects in sport sponsorship advertising: The implications of consumer advertising schemas. *Psychology & Marketing, 16*(2), 163–184.

McGee, R. (1980). Imagery and recognition memory: The effects of relational organization. *Memory & Cognition, 8*, 394–399.

Meenaghan, T. (1991). Sponsorship—Legitimizing the medium. *European Journal of Marketing, 25*(11), 5–10.

Meenaghan, T. (1994). Point of view: Ambush marketing: immoral or imaginative practice? *Journal of Advertising Research, 34*(5), 77–89.

Meenaghan, T. (1998). Ambush marketing: Corporate strategy and consumer reaction. *Psychology & Marketing, 15*, 305–322.

Meenaghan, T. (2001a). Sponsorship and advertising: A comparison of consumer perceptions. *Psychology & Marketing, 18*, 191–215.

Meenaghan, T. (2001b). Understanding sponsorship effects. *Psychology & Marketing, 18*, 95–122.

Murdock, B. B. (1974). *Human memory: Theory and data*. Hillsdale, NJ: Lawrence Erlbaum Associates.

Nebenzahl, I., & Hornik, J. (1985). An experimental study of the effectiveness of commercial billboards in televised sports arenas. *International Journal of Advertising, 4,* 27–36.

Nelson, D. L. (1979). Remembering pictures and words: Appearance, significance, and name. In L. S. Cermak & F. I. M. Craik (Eds.), *Levels of processing in human memory* (pp. 46–76). Hillsdale, NJ: Lawrence Erlbaum Associates.

Olson, E. L., & Thjomoe, H. M. (2003). The effects of peripheral exposure to information on brand performance. *European Journal of Marketing, 37,* 243–255.

O'Sullivan, P., & Murphy, P. (1998). Ambush marketing: The ethical issues. *Psychology & Marketing, 15,* 349–366.

Petty, R. E., & Cacioppo, J. T. (1981). *Attitudes and persuasion: Classic and contemporary approaches.* Dubuque, IA: William C. Brown.

Petty, R. E., Cacioppo, J. T., & Schumann, D. (1983). Central and peripheral routes to advertising effectiveness: The moderating role of involvement. *Journal of Consumer Research, 10,* 135–146.

Pham, M. T., & Johar, G. V. (2001). Market prominence biases in sponsor identification: Processes and consequentiality. *Psychology & Marketing, 18,* 123–143.

Pham, M. T., & Vanhuele, M. (1997). Analyzing the memory impact of advertising fragments. *Marketing Letters, 8,* 407–417.

Prior, A., & Bentin, S. (2003). Incidental formation of episodic associations: The importance of sentential context. *Memory & Cognition, 31,* 306–316.

Puff, C. R. (1979). *Memory organization and structure.* New York: Academic Press.

Roy, D. P., & Cornwell, T. B. (2004). The effects of consumer knowledge on responses to event sponsorships. *Psychology and Marketing, 21,* 185–207.

Speed, R., & Thompson, P. (2000). Determinants of sports sponsorship response. *Journal of the Academy of Marketing Science, 28*(2), 226–238.

Yonelinas, A. P. (1997). Recognition memory ROCs for item and associative information: The contribution of recollection and familiarity. *Memory & Cognition, 25,* 747–763.

Zajonc, R. B. (1980). Feeling and thinking preferences need no inferences. *American Psychologist, 35,* 151–175.

Part V—Individual Characteristics and Culture

Image can be related to individual characteristics and culture in a number of ways. For example, personal values and culture of an individual can affect the individual's perception of a brand and influence consumer behavior in purchase decisions of various products or services. This section covers the implications of individual characteristics and culture in consumer buying and consumption behavior in various settings. This section also includes cross-cultural studies on individual characteristics (i.e., individual brand personality), cultures of different groups of individuals, and consumption patterns in different countries.

CHAPTER SEVENTEEN

Values, Brands, and Image

Woo-Sung Kim
Youngsan University, S. Korea

David M. Boush, Adam Marquardt, and Lynn R. Kahle
University of Oregon

Recently brands have received increased interest and attention from managers, consumers, and researchers. A brand has been considered as one of the most powerful assets that a company has (D. Aaker, 1996). The power of a brand comes from many sources, such as overall quality, brand loyalty, brand awareness, brand image, and personal values associated with a brand (Keller, 1998).

Schmitt (1999) suggested three new marketing trends: a) the omnipresence of information technology, b) the supremacy of the brand, and c) the ubiquity of integrated communications and entertainment. In these important trends, the focus should be on brands, consumers, the relationship between a brand and a consumer, overall brand image, fulfillment of consumer needs and wants, personal values, and the synergy of promotional tools.

A brand and a product are different. According to Kotler (2003), a product is anything that can be offered to a market to satisfy a need or want. A product can be a physical good, service, retail store, person, place, or an idea. According to the American Marketing Association (AMA), a brand is a name, a term, a sign, a symbol, a design, or a combination of them, intended to identify the product of one seller and to differentiate it from those products of the competition. In modern marketing, a brand is treated as a complex idea, including symbolic and psychosocial meaning that consumers assign to a brand, and can be described as a network of interconnected concepts manifesting in the consumer's mind. A brand can be related to attributes, benefits, values, culture, personality, and users (Kotler, 2003). In contrast to a product, a brand cannot be easily duplicated by competitors, and a well-managed brand can seemingly take on a life of its own.

The power of a brand is often expressed by brand equity. Brand equity is defined in terms of a net asset (D. Aaker, 1991) or the differential effect of brand knowledge on consumer responses to the marketing of a brand (Keller, 1993, 2003b). Keller (1993, 2003b) emphasized the importance of the consumer mind in brand perception. According to Keller, two sources of brand equity are brand awareness and brand image. A positive brand image is created by creating strong, favorable, unique, and consistent brand associations. For example, the brand image of Body Shop is strongly associated with personal care and environmental concern (Keller, 2003b).

Schmitt (1999) considered brands as experience providers. Schmitt proposed experiential marketing as marketing integrating five types of customer experiences: sense, think, feel, act, and relate. Experiential marketing focuses on how a brand can enrich a customer's life (Post, 2000). In experiential marketing, real experiences of a product or service, personal values and lifestyles of customers, the relationships between a brand and customers, and emotional aspects of a brand are emphasized. According to the paradigm of experiential marketing, a brand competes not only with other brands in its product category but also with those brands in a broader category defined not by attributes or benefits but by product usages or consumption situations that are closely related to customers' personal values. For example, McDonald's competes with not only Burger King and Wendy's but also Domino's Pizza, Subway, and Kentucky Fried Chicken. Brand images of some brands are based on strong and persistent personal values associated in effective advertisements with the brands (e.g., sense of accomplishment value in Nike, self-fulfillment in U.S. Army, excitement in Pontiac, security in Volvo).

In this chapter, we deal with brands and two related concepts, an image and a personal (or social) value. Specifically, we organize the chapter in terms of three relationships: a) values and images, b) brands and images, and c) brands and values.

VALUES AND IMAGE

Two Types of Values

A value has many different meanings. The meaning of a value in marketing can be classified into two main categories, a *utilitarian value* and a *personal value*. A utilitarian value is defined in terms of what one gets as worthy things, and a personal value is defined in terms of what one believes to be important in his or her life (e.g., happiness, fun). Zeithaml (1988) classified definitions of the utilitarian value into four kinds: a) low price, b) whatever I want in a product, c) quality I get for the price, and d) what I get for what I give. She defined perceived utilitarian value as "a consumer's overall assessment of the utility of a product, based on perceptions of what is received vs. what is given" (p. 14).

A personal value is "an enduring belief that a specific mode of conduct or end-state of existence is personally or socially preferable to an opposite mode" (Rokeach, 1973, p. 5). A personal value becomes a *social value* when all or many members of a society share the same value. Kahle (1996) viewed a social value, which comes from groups of personal values, as the most abstract type of social cognition, useful for storing and guiding responses to stimuli.

Personal values are helpful in a consumer's determining choice criteria for evaluating brands in a product category (Howard & Woodside, 1984). Personal values include *instrumental values* and *terminal values*. Terminal values are the preferred end states of existence, and instrumental values are the modes of behavior that are means to the end states (Rokeach, 1973). In this chapter, we focus on personal (or social) terminal values when we use the word *value*.

Values, personality, and lifestyles are the three basic components of psychographics, a psychological and behavioral description of consumers. Values are useful in understanding consumption patterns of consumers, planning market segmentation, and designing and executing marketing strategies.

Brand Image

Brand image is a general picture derived from attributes and associations of a brand. Biel (1993) defined brand image as "a cluster of attributes and associations that consumers connect to the brand name" (p. 71). Similarly, Keller (1993) defined brand image as "perceptions about a brand as reflected by brand associations in a consumer's memory" (p. 3). According to Biel (1993), brand image has three subimages: a) corporate image, b) user image, and c) the image of the product or service itself.

Many inputs contribute to brand image: perceived quality, brand attitudes, perceived value, feelings, brand associations, and attitude toward an ad (Kirmani & Zeithaml, 1993). Reynolds and Gutman (1984) viewed brand image in several ways: general characteristics, feelings, or impressions; perceptions of products; beliefs and attitudes; brand personality; and linkages between characteristics and feelings.

Brand personality is a concept closely related to brand image. Brand personality is "the set of human characteristics associated with a brand" (D. Aaker, 1996; J. Aaker, 1997, p. 347). J. Aaker (1997) developed and verified five dimensions of brand personality (i.e., sincerity, excitement, competence, sophistication, and ruggedness). Brand image is a broader and more encompassing term than brand personality because brand image includes other attributes and benefits as well as brand personality (Batra, Lehmann, & Singh, 1993).

Relations Between Value and Image

Users of a brand have values. A personal value is general and at one end in the means–end hierarchy. A means–end chain is a concept relating values (i.e., the end) through consequences (i.e., benefits) to attributes of a product or service. When you ask consumers why they buy a brand, they typically answer with an attribute or benefit. For example, a consumer buys toothpaste because it has fluoride. When you continue the questioning with asking why the attribute or benefit matters, consumers typically answer with a consequence. For example, fluoride prevents cavities. If you ask yet again why the consequences matter, typically consumers respond with a value. For example, health is associated with a lack of cavities, which is necessary to accomplish what you want in life. Thus, the core reason consumers purchase a particular brand is typically a value (Homer & Kahle, 1988; Reynolds & Gutman, 1984). Brand personality and attributes (J. Aaker, 1997) represent an intermediate rather than ultimate step in the decision process. When areas of customer-desired value are successfully identified, integrated, and communicated, consumers will be more likely to buy the brand, often paying a premium price in the process (Keller, 1993; Romaniuk, 2001). Keller (2003b) posited the importance of congruence between user imagery and brand personality in building brand image and suggested that this congruence is particularly relevant regarding the more extrinsic benefits associated with symbolic brands.

Image is an abstraction of associations related to a thing, an object, or a person. Image can be applied to a brand (e.g., image of BMW, image of Beetle), a product (e.g., image of perfume), or a service (e.g., image of a medical office). Image can be based on concrete attributes, abstract attributes, benefits, or personal values; thus, a personal value is one of many factors contributing to image, and it is the most fundamental.

BRAND AND IMAGE

Self-Concept and Brand Image

A person's image is often reflected in self-concept. Self-concept has received some attention in consumer research in the past. A product can be viewed as something with a set of attributes having different importance to different types of consumers (Alpert, 1972). People show greater similarity of self-concept and the most preferred images of a brand than self-concept and the least preferred images (Dolich, 1969). Consumers buying different brands perceive themselves to have significantly different self-concepts (Grubb & Hupp, 1968). Some possessions can even be viewed as being a part of the self (i.e., "extended self") beyond representing oneself (Belk, 1988).

In spite of some research showing relations between self-concept and the preference for matching brand images, the exact relation between self-concept and brand image has been somewhat weak and inconclusive. Sirgy (1982) summarized self-concept research as "fragmented, incoherent, and diffuse" (p. 287).

Some recent studies dealing with the relations between self-concept or self-image and brand image show more consistent findings. Using four test stimuli (i.e., two for cars and two for shampoo), Hong and Zinkhan (1995) found that brand preference and purchase intention were influenced by the consumer's congruence level with an ad. Graeff's (1997) study showed that marketers could manage the effects of image congruence between brand image and self-image by promoting different consumption situations, and a dynamic concept of situational ideal self-image was a better predictor of brand attitudes than a static concept of self-image.

Self-Expressive Function of a Brand

D. Aaker (1996) explained how a brand image or personality could create brand equity as three models: a) the self-expression model, b) the relationship model, and c) the functional benefit representation model. According to the self-expression model, people express their actual or ideal identities through brands. For example, users of Nike products express their identities in buying and using Nike products with a spirited, tough, and rebellious image. Endorsers (e.g., Michael Jordan, Tiger Woods) and advertising campaigns (e.g., "Just Do It") contributed to Nike's unique and strong image.

Types of Brand Images

Park, Jaworski, and MacInnis (1986) proposed three kinds of brand image (i.e., functional, symbolic, and experiential) and recommended strategies for each brand image. Functional brand image refers to an image related to performance and practicality. Functional brand image is often derived from a concrete attribute of a brand and comes from externally generated needs. Symbolic brand image refers to an image associated with a desired group, role, or self-image. Experiential brand image is defined as an image related to sensory pleasure, variety seeking, and cognitive stimulation. Both experiential image and symbolic image come from internally generated needs.

Tybout and Carpenter (2001) compared and contrasted three brand types (i.e., functional brand, image brand [the equivalent of symbolic brand], and experiential brand). Functional brands (e.g., Dell computer) are differentiated on the basis of performance or price and mainly relate to physiological need or security need. Image brands (e.g., Nike) are differentiated on the basis of desirable image and mainly relate to social need or self-esteem need. Experiential brands are differentiated on the basis of unique and impressive experiences and mainly relate to self-actualization need.

Among the three brand images, functional image and symbolic image can be clearly contrasted in terms of a cognitive versus affective dichotomy. Functional image belongs to the cognitive side of the dichotomy, and symbolic image belongs to the affective side of the dichotomy. Kim (2001) contrasted functional brand image and symbolic brand image in terms of the level of abstraction, the components of brand image, cues, benefits, a processing mode, the basis of quality, and a main motive. For example, in the level of abstraction, functional brand image is mainly related to lower levels (e.g., a concrete attribute), but symbolic image is mainly related to a more abstract level. Functional brand image is often related to functional benefits, whereas symbolic image is mainly related to psychosocial benefits. In the processing mode, whereas functional brand image is often processed sequentially and analytically, symbolic brand image is processed holistically and emotionally (Keller, 1998; Kim, 2001).

Symbolic image and functional brand image have different implications in consumer behavior and advertising. Kirmani and Zeithaml (1993) recommended different advertising strategies for a functional brand and a symbolic brand: concentrating on intrinsic attributes related to performance or purpose for a functional brand and a focus on conveying image by using extrinsic cues for a symbolic brand. In Roth's (1995) study, strategies based on functional brand image were more effective than those strategies based on social image (i.e., applying symbolic image to a group) in individualist countries, but social strategies were more effective than functional strategies in collectivist countries. According to Lawson and Balakrishnan (1998), functional image was related more to education, environmental awareness, power, and safety, whereas symbolic image was related more to achievement, affiliation, ego enhancement, and power.

BRAND AND VALUES

Brand Related to Personal Value

A brand related to a relevant, strong, and consistent value can be a powerful tool, and connecting product attributes and benefits to consumers' values an important driver of brand success. Pontiac is a good example of a brand strongly associated with one of the core personal values of many consumers (i.e., excitement).

The successful "milk mustache" campaign ads are good examples of managing consistent image and employing simple but well-designed integrated marketing communication (IMC) strategies. Thanks to the campaigns, milk is now considered a hip, intelligent, funny product (Manning, 2003). From a humble beginning 10 years ago at the time of launching the campaigns, milk as a brand has been revitalized and is looking and acting more like a vibrant, power-packed brand (Manning, 2003). For the campaigns, many celebrities including supermodels (e.g., Naomi Campbell and Christie Brinkley), actors (e.g., Jennifer Aniston and Jackie Chan), sports stars (e.g., Mark McGuire and Mohammad Ali), and other famous personalities (e.g., Spike Lee and LeAnn Rimes) have appeared as models in the commercials and candidly displayed benefits related to their own lifestyles and values. In 2004, the milk mustache campaign celebrated its 10-year anniversary and its 200th celebrity sporting the now famous white upper lip. The campaign ads have been very exciting, sincere, and unique, as reflected by public sentiment and the strength of the campaign.

Some of recent trends in advertising are using more "feel" or transformational advertisements, increasing corporate advertisements focusing on the values of companies and societal orientation, and using "multi advertisement" (i.e., showing two or more separate, related advertisements of a brand such as the successful targeting of television advertisements for the Renault–Samsung SM3 car in Korea, aimed at men and women, respectively).

Lifestyle brands are brands based on strong lifestyles and values. Some examples are Nike, Virgin, and Coca-Cola (Schmitt, 1999). To satisfy customers' needs fully, products are defined in terms of values, not attributes or benefits. For example, cosmetic products can be defined as products that make people beautiful and happy. Kochan (1997) argued that in the future, the brands that succeed will be those brands that communicate clear values stretching across a number of products.

Relationship Function of a Brand

Relate is one of five types of customer experiences (Schmitt, 1999). D. Aaker and Joachimsthaler (2000) suggested brand management based on a customer relationship model. In their model, deep and insightful understanding of a customer's "sweet spot," which consists of values and beliefs, activities and interests, and possessions, is likely to be effective.

Recent emphasis on relationship marketing or customer relationship management (CRM) has led to more attention to a reciprocal and long-term relationship between a brand and a person. Fournier (1998) suggested reciprocal, active, and dynamic relationships between a brand and a consumer. The 15 relationship types of Fournier (1998) are arranged marriages, casual friends or buddies, marriages of convenience, committed partnerships, best friendships, compartmentalized friendships, kinships, rebounds and avoidance-driven relationships, childhood friendships, courtships, dependencies, flings, enmities, secret affairs, and enslavements. For example, the relationship between Saturn car and a consumer can be described as best friendship.

Deep and long-term relationships between a brand and a customer can develop into the relationships among a brand and many dedicated customers. Muniz and O'Guinn (2001) introduced the idea of brand community, which is a specialized, nongeographically bound community, based on social relationships among admirers of a brand and marked by a shared consciousness, rituals and traditions, and a sense of moral responsibility. They found evidence of the main characteristics of brand communities, after investigating the brand communities of Ford Bronco, Macintosh, and Saab, by using ethnographic and computer-mediated data.

Brand as a Family

We can consider related products, especially related products with the same brand name, as a family of products. According to Gutman (1982), one major benefit of categorization is to simplify things or objects. Gutman (1982) argued that in addition to conventional product-type of product categories (e.g., a toothbrush), consumers often create new categories based on product functions (e.g., whitening teeth). Some researchers consider a parent brand and all its extensions as a brand category (e.g., Boush, 1993; Joiner & Loken, 1998). Consumers often think of all the products under the same brand name as one brand category and may further extend basic inferred characteristics to new brand extensions (Joiner & Loken, 1998).

A brand category can be based on different levels of abstraction of brand knowledge. Logically, a category includes more diverse products if a higher level of abstraction (e.g., terminal value) is used.

Values and Preference for Products or Brands

A value can affect attitudes towards particular brands or products and choice of brands or products. Persons who emphasize different values usually have preferences for different brands or products. Similarly, different generations have different values. A change in values on the part of Generation Y consumers may make some brands such as Mountain Dew or Van (a shoe brand) succeed and some traditional power brands (e.g., Levi's, Nike, Coke) struggle in total sales ("Generation Y," 1999).

Means–End Chain (MEC) Model

The means–end chain (MEC) model is based on a micro approach dealing with the application of a value perspective to marketing of consumer products (Reynolds & Gutman, 1988). The MEC model explains how people's choice of a product or service relates to achieving their desired values. This approach argues that product information can be stored and processed at different levels of abstraction and these levels are hierarchically ordered from the lowest to the highest level of abstraction (Gutman & Reynolds, 1979; Myers & Shocker, 1981; Olson & Reynolds, 1983; Young & Feigin, 1975).

In the MEC model, a higher level of product knowledge can be generalized to more different product categories. According to Zeithaml (1988), as attributes become more general, they become common to more alternatives. There are a small number of products which have a particular concrete attribute; however, many products are related to a particular personal value (e.g., happiness). According to Johnson (1984), because noncomparable alternatives (e.g., a refrigerator vs. a computer) cannot be compared at the same concrete attribute level, comparison at a more general level (e.g., necessity) should be done. In his experiments, consumers abstracted product representations to a higher level at which comparisons were possible.

In hedonic or experiential products or brands, personal values may directly influence consumers' consumption motivation. Mort and Rose (2004) investigated the effects of product type (i.e., utilitarian vs. hedonic) on value linkages in the MEC. As they hypothesized, personal values were related through benefits to attributes in consumers' motivation to consume utilitarian products (orange juice in their study), and, in contrast, consumers' values directly stimulated the motivation to consume hedonic products (fashion and leisure travel in their study).

Advantages of Values in Brand Extension

In brand extension, the strength of existing, strong, directional associations at lower levels in means–end chains may limit the extendibility of brands (e.g., "washing windows" strongly associated with the Windex brand; Farquhar & Herr, 1993).

D. Aaker and Keller (1990) suggested that abstract attributes transfer to broader product classes than concrete attributes. Nakamoto, MacInnis, and Jung (1993) investigated the effects of attribute-based and quality-based brand equity on extension products (i.e., relevant and irrelevant extension products) through advertising and brand evidence. Two core products were used: a stereo and yogurt. Their results supported their hypothesis (H1) that brand extensions for products whose equity was based on a specific attribute claim would benefit only when that attribute was relevant. However, for the superiority of specific-attribute-based brand equity for the extension to relevant extension products (H3), the results gave only mixed support, and for the superiority of quality-based brand equity for the extension to irrelevant extension products (H2), the results gave only directional support.

Rangaswamy, Burke, and Oliva's (1993) study consisted of a conjoint task and a brand-extension evaluation task. Real brand names in four product categories (i.e., yogurt, mouthwash, shampoo, and breakfast cereal) were used for possible extension to within-category (i.e., line), related, and distant products. Although the results were somewhat mixed, they generally supported their model. Rangaswamy et al. (1993) suggested that for maximizing future extendibility, a brand should associate with its name general characteristics such as quality, style, and durability.

Kim (2001) investigated the effects of generality levels in terms of the means–end chain model on brand extendibility. Under unmatched conditions, a salient, more general level in terms of the MEC had higher similarity scores than a more specific level, as expected. In terms of dependent measures, both the superiority effect of a salient, more general level over a salient, more specific level under unmatched conditions and the superiority effect of a salient, more specific level over a salient, more general level under matched conditions were partly supported.

CONCLUSION

In his recent article, Keller (2003a) suggested a broader and more holistic perspective synthesizing the multidimensionality of brand knowledge, beyond brand awareness and brand image or associations (Keller, 1993). In this perspective, people, places, things, or other brands are included as a means to understand and improve brand equity. Brand image is still one of the eight dimensions of Keller's (2003a) brand knowledge, and personal values are included in the benefits dimension.

The relationship between a brand and a consumer is very important in the long-term management of a brand. In the brand concept management (BCM) framework (Park et al., 1986), the most appropriate brand image is carefully selected and managed over three stages (i.e., introduction, elaboration, and fortification). Personal values are often reflected in a consumer's attitude toward, perception of, and actual choice of a brand. Consumers often buy a particular brand because that brand has important and useful attributes or benefits related to terminal values in the end.

Management of brand image is important. Organizations use a unique, favorable, and strong brand image in advertising campaigns or brand positioning. Brand image has a direct effect on sales and a moderating effect on the relationship between product life cycle (PLC) strategies and sales (Park et al., 1986). The consumer's personal values are important because related products can be thought of and united in a personal value (especially, a terminal value), and emphasis on a value is helpful in successfully extending to more diverse and distant products.

REFERENCES

Aaker, D. A. (1991). *Managing brand equity.* New York: The Free Press.
Aaker, D. A. (1996). *Building strong brands.* New York: The Free Press.
Aaker, D. A., & Joachimsthaler, E. (2000). *Brand leadership.* New York: The Free Press.
Aaker, D. A., & Keller, K. L. (1990). Consumer evaluations of brand extensions. *Journal of Marketing, 54,* 27–41.
Aaker, J. L. (1997). Dimensions of brand personality. *Journal of Marketing Research, 34,* 347–356.
Alpert, M. I. (1972). Personality and the determinants of product choice. *Journal of Marketing Research, 9,* 89–92.
Batra, R., Lehmann, D. R., & Singh, D. (1993). The brand personality component of brand goodwill: Some antecedents and consequences. In D. A. Aaker & A. Biel (Eds.), *Brand equity and advertising* (pp. 83–96). Hillsdale, NJ: Lawrence Erlbaum Associates.
Belk, R. W. (1988). Possessions and the extended self. *Journal of Consumer Research, 15,* 139–168.
Biel, A. (1993). Converting image into equity. In D. A. Aaker & A. Biel (Eds.), *Brand equity and advertising* (pp. 67–82). Hillsdale, NJ: Lawrence Erlbaum Associates.
Boush, D. M. (1993). Brands as categories. In D. A. Aaker & A. Biel (Eds.), *Brand equity and advertising* (pp. 299–312). Hillsdale, NJ: Lawrence Erlbaum Associates.
Dolich, I. J. (1969). Congruence relationships between self images and product brands. *Journal of Marketing Research, 6,* 80–84.
Farquhar, P. H., & Herr, P. M. (1993). The dual structure of brand associations. In D. A. Aaker & A. Biel (Eds.), *Brand equity and advertising* (pp. 263–277). Hillsdale, NJ: Lawrence Erlbaum Associates.
Fournier, S. (1998). Consumers and their brands: Developing relationship theory in consumer research. *Journal of Consumer Research, 24,* 343–373.
Generation Y. (1999, Feb. 15). *Business Week,* 80–84.
Graeff, T. R. (1997). Consumption situations and the effects of brand image on consumers' brand evaluations. *Psychology & Marketing, 14,* 49–70.

Grubb, E. L., & Hupp, G . (1968). Perception of self, generalized stereotypes, and brand selection. *Journal of Marketing Research, 5,* 58–63.

Gutman, J. (1982). A means-end chain model based on consumer categorization processes. *Journal of Marketing, 46,* 60–72.

Gutman, J., & Reynolds, T. (1979). An investigation of the levels of cognitive abstraction utilized by consumers in product differentiation. In J. Eighmey (Ed.), *Attitude research under the sun* (pp.128–150). Chicago: American Marketing Association.

Homer, P. M., & Kahle, L. R. (1988). A structural equation test of the value–attitude–behavior hierarchy. *Journal of Personality and Social Psychology, 54,* 638–646.

Hong, J. W., & Zinkhan, G. M. (1995). Self-concept and advertising effectiveness: The influence of congruency, conspicuousness, and response mode. *Psychology & Marketing, 12,* 53–77.

Howard, J. A., & Woodside, A. G. (1984). Personal values affecting consumer psychology. In R. E. Pitts, Jr. & A. G.. Woodside (Eds.), *Personal values and consumer psychology* (pp. 3–12). Lexington, MA: Lexington Books.

Johnson, M. D. (1984). Consumer choice strategies for comparing noncomparable alternatives. *Journal of Consumer Research, 11,* 741–753.

Joiner, C., & Loken, B. (1998). The inclusion effect and category-based induction: Theory and application to brand categories. *Journal of Consumer Psychology, 7,* 101–129.

Kahle, L. R. (1996). Social values and consumer behavior: Research from the list of values. In C. Seligman, J. M. Olson, & M. P. Zanna (Eds.), *The psychology of values: The Ontario symposium, Vol. 8* (pp. 135–151). Mahwah, NJ: Lawrence Erlbaum Associates.

Keller, K. L. (1998). *Strategic brand management: Building, measuring, and managing brand equity.* Upper Saddle River, NJ: Prentice-Hall.

Keller, K. L. (1993). Conceptualizing, measuring, and managing customer-based brand equity. *Journal of Marketing, 57,* 1–22.

Keller, K. L. (2003a). Brand synthesis: The multidimensionality of brand knowledge. *Journal of Consumer Research, 29,* 595–600.

Keller, K. L. (2003b). *Strategic brand management* (2nd Ed.). Upper Saddle River, NJ: Prentice-Hall.

Kim, W. (2001). Product quality, image, and salient association levels as factors in brand extendibility. Unpublished doctoral dissertation, University of Oregon, Eugene.

Kirmani, A., & Zeithaml, V. (1993). Advertising, perceived quality, and brand image. In D. A. Aaker & A. Biel (Eds.), *Brand equity and advertising* (pp.143–161). Hillsdale, NJ: Lawrence Erlbaum Associates.

Kochan, N. (1997). *The world's greatest brands.* New York: New York University Press.

Kotler, P. (2003). *Marketing management* (11th Ed.). Upper Saddle River, NJ: Prentice-Hall.

Lawson, R., & Balakrishnan, S. (1998). Developing and managing brand image and brand concept strategies. In D. Grewal & C. Pechmann (Eds.), *AMA Winter Educators' Conference Proceedings, Vol. 9* (pp. 121–126). Chicago, IL: American Marketing Association.

Manning, J. (2003). Got milk? A decade of lessons pours in. *Brandweek, 44*(22), 24–26.

Mort, G. S., & Rose, T. (2004). The effect of product type on value linkages in the means–end chain: Implications for theory and method. *Journal of Consumer Behavior, 3,* 221–234.

Muniz, A. M., Jr., & O'Guinn, T. C. (2001). Brand community. *Journal of Consumer Research, 27,* 412–432.

Myers, J. H., & Shocker, A. D. (1981). The nature of product-related attributes. In J. N. Sheth (Ed.), *Research in Marketing, Vol. 5* (pp. 211–236). Greenwich, CT: JAI.

Nakamoto, K., MacInnis, D. J., & Jung, H. (1993). Advertising claims and evidence as bases for brand equity and consumer evaluations of brand extensions. In D. A. Aaker & A. Biel

(Eds.), *Brand equity and advertising* (pp. 281–297). Hillsdale, NJ: Lawrence Erlbaum Associates.

Olson, J. C., & Reynolds, T. J. (1983). Understanding consumers' cognitive structures: Implications for advertising strategy. In L. Percy & A. Woodside (Eds.), *Advertising and consumer psychology* (pp. 77–90). Lexington, MA: Lexington Books.

Park, C. W., Jaworski, B. J., & MacInnis, D. J. (1986). Strategic brand concept–image management. *Journal of Marketing, 50* (October), 135–145.

Post, P. (2000). Beyond brand—The power of experience branding. *ANA/The Advertiser,* October/November.

Rangaswamy, A., Burke, R. R., &. Oliva, T. A. (1993). Brand equity and the extendibility of brand names. *International Journal of Research in Marketing, 10,* 61–75.

Reynolds, T. J., & Gutman, J. (1984). Advertising is image management. *Journal of Advertising Research, 24,* 27–37.

Reynolds, T. J., & Gutman, J. (1988). Laddering theory, method, analysis, and interpretation. *Journal of Advertising Research, 28*(1), 11–31.

Rokeach, M. J. (1973). *The nature of human values.* New York, NY: The Free Press.

Romaniuk, J. (2001). Brand positioning in financial services: A longitudinal test to find the best brand position. *Journal of Financial Services Marketing, 6,* 111–121.

Roth, M. S. (1995). The effects of culture and socioeconomics on the performance of global brand image strategies. *Journal of Marketing Research, 32*(May), 163–175.

Schmitt, B. (1999). *Experiential marketing: How to get customers to sense, feel, think, act, relate to your company and brands.* New York: The Free Press.

Sirgy, M. J. (1982). Self-concept in consumer behavior: A critical review. *Journal of Consumer Research, 9*(Dec.), 287–300.

Tybout, A. M., & Carpenter, G. (2001). Creating and managing brands. In D. Iacobucci (Ed.), *Kellogg on marketing* (pp. 74–102). Hoboken, NJ: Wiley.

Young, S., & Feigin, B. (1975). Using the benefit chain for improved strategy formulation. *Journal of Marketing, 39*(July), 72–74.

Zeithaml, V. A. (1988). Consumer perceptions of price, quality, and value: A means–end model and synthesis of evidence. *Journal of Marketing, 52*(July), 2–22.

CHAPTER EIGHTEEN

Image Attributes of Automobiles and Their Influence on Purchase Price Decision

Keiko I. Powers
J. D. Power and Associates

Purchasing an automobile is possibly one of the most involving shopping processes we consumers experience. The purchase experience often requires both cognitive involvement (e.g., what functional features are needed, such as the size of the car, the number of seats, fuel economy, etc) and emotional involvement (e.g., do I like the shape of the car, or which color should I choose, etc). For some people, the choice of a car is a more functional one, and thus they methodologically compare, examine, and evaluate key functional features of the car (e.g., size of the car). On the other hand, for some other people, their cars are personal statements, and owning a car with an appealing image is an essential part of the purchase decision. In these cases, choosing the color of a car could be as important as selecting a car with high fuel economy, and as a result, there may exist differences in automobile purchase prices with respect to image attributes, such as color. The main purpose of the study reported here is to investigate if there are in fact price differences due to automobile image attributes.

The theme of the current study is relevant to several consumer behavior research fields, such as price versus emotion (e.g., O'Neill & Lambert, 2001), image attributes versus affect or emotion, and more broadly, cognition versus affect. These three topics are reviewed in detail in the next section.

PRICE AND COGNITIVE VERSUS AFFECTIVE PROCESSING

The relation between price and cognitive–affective processing has been studied from various perspectives. Lichtenstein, Bloch, and Black (1988) investigated the concept of price acceptability and found an inverse relationship between price consciousness and product involvement as well as a positive relationship between price

291

acceptability level and the width of the latitude of price acceptance. Their empirical study supported the idea that individual differences in price consciousness and product involvement are related to price acceptability. Both Campbell (1999) and Bolton, Warlop, and Alba (2003) examined perceived fairness or unfairness of product prices. For example, Campbell (1999) found that the inferred motive by a firm as well as inferred profit is an important factor for understanding perceived price unfairness by consumers. The study demonstrated that the reputation of the firm and the inferred profit influence the inferences of motive by the firm, which in turn influence perceived price fairness. Bolton et al. (2003) investigated various factors that may be related to price perception, such as past prices or competitor prices, and concluded that consumers lack accurate mental models of product costs and are unable to generate cost categories spontaneously.

Luce, Bettman, and Payne (2001), in their comprehensive monograph on emotional decisions, present a theoretical summary of model development on tradeoff difficulty and associated emotional responses in consumer choices. In the series of experiments they conducted (see also Luce, Payne, & Bettman, 1999), subjects were asked to perform trade-off tasks among various automobile attributes (e.g., safety is very good, good, average; price is $20,000, $30,000, $40,000; styling is good, average, very poor). They found that coping with potentially emotional choice trade-offs is a factor that can influence consumer choice strategies. For consumers, avoiding or coping with negative emotion is an important goal that guides their decision behavior.

O'Neill and Lambert (2001), in their study on emotion and price, introduced the concept of *price affect*, or the role of emotion with respect to prices. Based on their empirical studies, they confirmed the following hypotheses: As involvement increases, the highest price one is willing to pay likewise increases. As internal reference price increases, the magnitude of a price change sufficient to alter purchase intention likewise increases. Because of these relationships, people's emotional reactions to prices, or price affect, influence product choices through the mechanisms of involvement, price–quality associations, price consciousness, internal reference price, and price latitude.

COLOR, OTHER IMAGE ATTRIBUTES, AND AFFECT/EMOTION

Various emotional and nonfunctional attributes, such as color and music have close relations with consumer purchase behavior and decision. For example, a study found that the type of music played in a grocery store affects the consumers' buying behavior; consumers spends a longer time at the store when slow music is played (Milliman, 1982; see also Alpert & Alpert, 1990 for a review). Effects of music on advertising have been studied as well (e.g., Gorn, 1982). Bellizzi, Crowley, and Hasty (1983) introduced a comprehensive review of the physiological and psychological effects of color. In the study on the effect of environment color on purchase behavior (Bellizzi & Hite, 1992), retail environments were simulated using predominately red or blue colors. Their experiments corroborated the differential effects of red and blue that prior research suggested. The results indicated that the affective perception of color rather than the arousal dimension of color may be responsible for the outcome.

Desmet, Hekkert, and Jacobs (2000) investigated the relation between visually appealing image attributes of automobiles and emotional responses to these attributes in their effort to develop an instrument to measure product emotions. Literature on color perception of automobiles has a relatively long history. For example, Doehlert (1968) measured respondent perceptions of automobile colors and color preferences. The results of multidimensional scaling (MDS) perceptual map indicated that color substitution patterns were in general restricted to similar stimuli. These results are consistent with the idea that products or brands that are similar in consumer preferences are more likely to compete. However, Lonial and Auken (1982), in their replicated efforts of Doehlert's study, found no congruency between consumers' similarity judgement patterns and their preferences for automobiles. Based on their study results, Lonial and Auken suggested that MDS perceptual maps based on consumers' similarity ratings are unlikely to be useful for marketing strategy decisions.

For many automobile marketers and consumers, the importance of color for car purchase and ownership has been indisputable. Gimba (1998) emphasized the importance of color in the marketing environment and stated that color affects the mind and body in different ways. Certain colors convey different meaning not only to different cultures but also within a single culture. For example, black is interpreted differently even within the United States, depending on the geographic location (i.e., urban versus rural), ethnic group or occasion. A recent article at an automobile website described an interesting (but very likely unscientific) relation between the color of the vehicle and the owner's personality traits (Treganowan, 2001). For example, if you own a blue car, it means you are a team player, sociable and friendly, but lacking imagination. There is a definite trend in the popular colors for cars. In the 1980s, the most popular color was green, but currently, it is taken over by silver (Powers, 2003). The study also showed that color-loyal vehicle owners and color-trendy owners (i.e., those who switched from green to silver) display interesting differences in their demographic characteristics—for example, the color-trendy group tends to be older. The color-trendy group also prefers Asian automobiles with no significant difference between cars and trucks.

COGNITION VERSUS AFFECT

The issue of cognition and affect in the consumer behavior context has been the focus of many theoretical and empirical studies, and a comprehensive review is beyond the scope of this chapter. Therefore, the goal here is to present a more restricted review focusing on studies that specifically provide relevant information for the current study. Both Zajonc and Markus (1991) and Cohen and Areni (1991) provide excellent reviews on the role of affect in consumer behavior.

Many studies have emphasized the key role of affect or emotion in attitude formation and decision making. For example, Bodur, Brinberg, and Coupey (2000) focused on the debate related to affect and attitude—namely, whether affect and attitude are separate constructs and whether affect influences attitudes independently of cognitive structure. Results of their study indicated that affect in fact influences attitude directly and independently of cognitive structure. Kuykendall and Keating (1990) found that systematic processing of persuasive communications is reduced by positive but not by negative moods. Positive affect decreases systematic processing because people are content to experience positive states; however, for subjects induced to feel negatively, attitudes were more favorable following strong arguments. Their research results were consistent with motivational interpretations of affect and cognitive processing. Isen (2001), on the other hand, stated that the literature review indicates positive affect enhances problem solving and decision making. It is suggested that when the situation is important or interesting to the decision maker, positive affect facilitates systematic and careful cognitive processing and tends to make it more efficient and more thorough. Ruth (2001), based on her two experimental studies, concluded that the cognitive process using a knowledge-based consideration of the emotional benefits of a brand can influence consumers' beliefs about the brand and brand attitudes. Consumers perceive a difference in brands based merely on the categories of emotions associated with them. "For example, when told that the Pontiac Sunfire is driving excitement, ... the consumer accesses categorical knowledge linked with excitement (i.e., strongly positive with modest to high arousal) and associates it with the brand" (p. 101). Brands associated with relevant emotion benefits are evaluated more favorably than those associated with a different emotion.

Some other studies attempted to identify psychological constructs for affect formation. Mittal (1994) developed a concept of affective choice mode for decision processes for highly involving products that do not require extensive information processing. He compared his concept against the information processing mode (Bettman, 1979) and argued that these two models are two separate distinct concepts. They are negatively related, but they are not mirror images of each other. Affective involvement occurs when a person identifies a new stimulus with an exemplar and then automatically transfers that affect to the brand itself. Because of its processing scheme, product expressiveness—whether or not the product possesses affect-laden exemplars (i.e., the new stimulus is similar to something the consumer had emotional experience with)—is a critical factor for the affective process.

Westbrook and Oliver (1991) investigated the interrelations between consumption emotion and satisfaction judgments and identified five discriminable patterns of affective experience based on three independent affective dimensions: hostility,

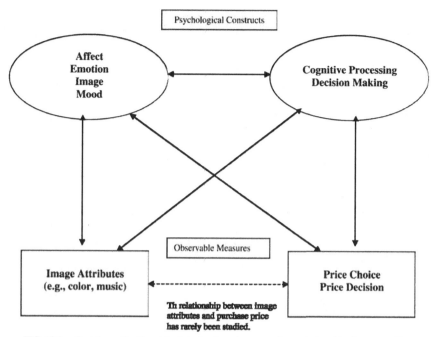

FIG. 18.1. Past theoretical/empirical studies focusing on various relationships between affect and decision making.

pleasant surprise and interest. Their results indicated that satisfaction measures vary in their ability to represent the affective content of consumption experiences. Pham (1998) argued that both representativeness and relevance of feelings are critical in decision making. The study indicated that for the feelings to influence the evaluation of a target, they must be perceived as genuine affective responses to the target, that is, the feelings are representatives of the target. In addition, reliance on feelings also depends on whether feelings toward the target are regarded as relevant. In particular, consumers are more likely to rely on their feelings when they have consummatory motives (i.e., linked to intrinsically rewarding behaviors, such as reading a novel for pleasure) than when they have instrumental motives (i.e., linked to behaviors for achieving some other goals, such as reading a tax manual to prepare a tax return).

Reviewing the past literature in these fields has revealed that, as O'Neill and Lambert (2001) claimed, few studies have explicitly investigated the relation between emotion/affect and price. As illustrated in Fig. 18.1, many studies have examined relations between emotion/affect and image attributes, such as color, purchase price decision in the context of consumer decision making, and at the higher conceptual level, relations between emotion/affect and consumer decision making in various contexts. The studies reviewed in the previous sections focused on one or more of these relations. The main focus of the study discussed here is to quantitatively assess the effect of emotionally appealing image attributes of automobiles on the final purchase price by comparing the prices paid to vehicles with different image attributes. By studying how image attributes and purchase price decision interact, we can provide more insight to the conceptual-level relation between emotion/affect and consumer decision making process.

In addition, from the methodological perspective, we analyze the point-of-sales data collected from auto retailers in the United States, and therefore, the analysis results enable us to better understand how consumers make purchase price decisions in real-life situations. As shown by the literature, many studies have focused on cognition and affect from various perspectives and with various empirical settings. However, one area that has been lacking in these empirical studies for cognition and affect is the validation in the real market. Most studies have been survey or experimental studies using samples obtained in the university setting. On the other hand, the current study uses data that reflect the consumer's purchase decisions in the real market environment.

STUDY OBJECTIVES

To the author's knowledge, this is the first attempt to investigate the relation between image attributes (i.e., color) and price (i.e., the price consumers actually paid for a new automobile) in the consumer behavior context explicitly and directly. Because of its exploratory nature, the following general analysis objectives are prepared as the guidelines of the empirical study.

- Are there differential effects of color on the purchase price of a new automobile?
- Are there differential effects of engine size (which represent the image of power) on the purchase price of a new automobile?
- Are there differential effects of body type (i.e., coupe versus convertible, where convertible represents 'cool,' 'trendy') on the purchase price of a new automobile?

In addition to studying the relations between automobile image attributes and price decision, this study addresses any moderating effects of consumer demographic backgrounds.

- Are there interaction effects between these image attributes and consumer age (e.g., baby boomers versus Generation X) on the purchase price?
- Are there interaction effects between these image attributes and consumer gender on the purchase price?

EMPIRICAL STUDY

Vehicle Point-of-Sales Data

This study uses a large database collected from automobile dealers and includes various analyses to understand what role image attributes play in automobile purchase. Power Information Network, LLC (PIN) has been collecting and archiving point-of-sale data from automobile retailers in the United States. The data are electronically sent to the PIN computer system daily. The data consist of new and used vehicles purchased by end consumers since 1996 and currently cover 26 key markets (e.g., New York, Florida, Detroit/Chicago area, Texas, California, etc.) with over 6,000 franchise retailer points providing data to PIN. The total cumulative number of transactions now exceeds 16 million records. These transaction records can be aggregated and summarized to produce historical data, which allows us to conduct various analyses to understand the impact of the image attributes on consumer behavior in automobile purchase. This study focuses on new vehicle sales in the California market during the time period from 1997 through mid 2001.

As an exploratory study, it was important to select automobile types where the image attributes are relevant. For example, it was reasonable to assume that the image of a car is not critical for selecting a full-size van when many consumers purchase a van for its cargo space or its functional features. On the other hand, for a consumer who is interested in purchasing a red convertible sports car, its image attributes and their heuristic how-it-makes-me-feel aspects are very important. For these reasons, those cars with functional features being the main importance were excluded, and sedans, coupes, and sports cars, with each type having a domestic and an Asian model, were chosen. As mentioned earlier, three vehicle image attributes, color, engine size, and body type (i.e., convertible vs. coupe), were selected for purchase price comparisons (see Table 18.1 for detailed setup).

Analysis Procedure

Unbalanced analysis of variance (ANOVA) was performed for each vehicle model separately with the complete factorial design using the following factors:

- Color (black, white, red, green, silver—with some differences based on the vehicle model—see Table 18.1 for details)
- Body type (i.e., coupe vs. convertible, for two vehicle models only—see Table 18.1 for details)
- Engine size (i.e., more or less power, for three models only—see Table 18.1 for details)
- Consumer gender

TABLE 18.1

Attributes of Automobiles Included in the Analysis

Automobile type	Country of origin	Vehicle price range based on Annual Average (1997–2000)	Sample size	Color	Engine size	Body type
Midsize sedan	Domestic	$18,740–18,916	1001	Black, green, red, silver, white	—	—
	Asian	$14,470–15,050	2953	Black, green, red, white	—	—
Midsize coupe	Domestic	$21,545–23,627	1070	Black, green, red, silver, white	6 cylinder vs. 8 cylinder	—
	Asian	$22,313–22,500	816	Black, red, silver, white	GS vs. GST (turbo)	Convertible vs. Coupe
Sports car	Domestic	$19,347–20,367	3421	Black, green, red, silver, white	6 cylinder vs. 8 cylinder	Convertible vs. Coupe
	Asian	$20,749–23,900	989	Black, blue, green, red, white	—	Convertible only

- Consumer age group (Generation X vs. Baby Boomer)—Generation X was defined as those whose age was between 20 and 35. Baby Boomer was defined as those who were 36–60 years old.

Both main effects and interaction effects were examined for the following dependent variables:

- Vehicle Price—The price the consumer paid toward the new vehicle. Prices for other items/services, such as an extended warranty, are not included.
- Vehicle Cost—Similar to the dealer invoice, or the dollar amount that the dealer paid for the vehicle.
- Profit Margin—The percentage of gross profit with respect to vehicle price , i.e., (vehicle price-vehicle cost)/vehicle cost.

The overall analysis procedure for the effect of color of each vehicle model is determined by the ANOVA results of vehicle cost. If there is no significant difference in vehicle cost due to color, then both vehicle price and profit margin are analyzed next; on the other hand if there is a significant difference due to color, then only profit margin is analyzed with ANOVA. If there were original price differences (i.e., vehicle cost is different) among vehicle colors, any vehicle price variation due to color would likely to be a reflection of the production cost differences for particular colors, rather than the consumers' pricing decision differences in choosing the color. In such a case, examining profit margin provides a better way to assess consumer response differences in price decision for different vehicle colors.

Both engine size and body type needed special consideration for a similar reason. Because there is a considerable difference in the original price with respect to these two vehicle attributes, examining the main effects of vehicle price and profit margin is unlikely to single out the price difference empirically due to the emotional power of these two image attributes. Therefore, analyses for these two attributes focused more on interaction effects between the vehicle attributes and consumer demographic characteristics.

Finally, to control for the possible time-related variation as well as the effect of an introduction of new model year vehicles, the study excluded transactions with very high days to turn and transactions of the previous model year after the new model year was introduced. For example, when a vehicle is sold after 12 months (i.e., days to turn = 365 days) rather than 10 days, it is very likely that the vehicle price is substantially affected by the retailer's desire to sell the vehicle quickly. This situation introduces unwanted variation in the vehicle price. An introduction of new model year is also a possible cause of unwanted variation in the vehicle price. Almost every year, manufacturers introduce a new model year of the same vehicle model, which comes with major to minor design changes. From the consumer's point of view, as soon as the new model year is introduced, the unsold older model year units become less appealing. As a result, retailers are likely to be willing to

TABLE 18.2

Price/Profit Differences Due to Vehicle Color

Automobile type	Country of origin	Significant color-related differences
Midsize sedan	Domestic	None
	Asian	Main effect: Color on price (p < .001), Color on profit (p < .01)
Midsize coupe	Domestic	Main effect: color on price (p < .05) Interaction effect: color × gender on price (p < .05)
	Asian	Interaction effect: color × age group on price (p < .05), color × age on group profit (p < .05)
Sports car	Domestic	Main effect: color on price (p < .01)
	Asian	Main effect: color on profit (p < .05)

give a bigger discount to these unsold vehicles. To control for these variations, the study excluded vehicles with a very high days to turn (i.e., > 365 days) and older model-year vehicles after the new model year was introduced.

RESULTS

All the main effects and interaction effects among the listed factors were tested simultaneously to ensure that observed price differences due to a particular factor, such as color or engine size, are adjusted for the moderating effects of other factors. For this reason, least-squares means were used for interpreting the ANOVA results.

Effects of Vehicle Color on Purchase Price

Table 18.2 provides a summary of ANOVA results. As can be seen, most of the vehicle models, except the domestic midsize sedan, had price differences or profit differences due to the vehicle color. Only main effects by color were observed for the midsize sedan and sport car segments, whereas the midsize coupe models had interaction effects between color and either gender or age group.

Figures 18.2 and 18.3 display mean vehicle prices and mean profit margins for the statistically significant differences for each vehicle model. Overall, the vehicle colors, red and black, are associated with a higher vehicle price. There seems to be an exception pattern for the Asian midsize coupe (in Fig. 18.3); however, though silver is higher priced than black or red for the Baby Boomer group, both black and red are priced higher than silver overall. The average price differences between the least and the most expensive color are, approximately, between $500 (for the Asian midsize sedan) to $1,200 (for the domestic sports car). There is a noteworthy gender-related difference in the color-related pattern for the domestic midsize coupe. When the interaction between color and gender is examined for the expensive color—black—and the inexpensive color—green—the bottom-right chart in Fig. 18.2 shows that females were on the average willing to pay more for a black car,

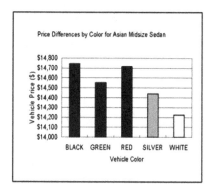

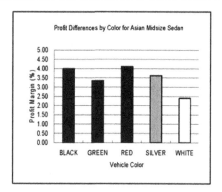

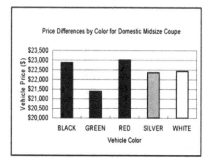

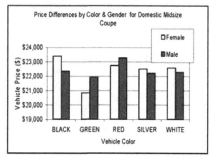

FIG. 18.2.   Vehicle price/profit margin differences due to color and customer demographic characteristics for Asian midsize sedan and domestic midsize coupe.

whereas males paid more for a green car. As for the color x age group interaction, Baby Boomers paid significantly more for the silver Asian midsize coupe than Generation X (see Fig. 18.3, the top-left chart). Implications of these results are discussed in a later section.

Effects of Engine Size and Body Type on Purchase Price

Table 18.3 provides a summary of ANOVA results for testing the relations between the vehicle price/profit and engine size as well as body type. As mentioned in the method section, three of the original six vehicle models were analyzed for engine size—more powerful versus less powerful. Two models, the Asian midsize coupe and the domestic sports car had the combination of various colors, two engine sizes, and different body types (i.e., coupe vs. convertible) with sufficient numbers of transactions. As with the analyses for color, main effects and interaction effects of these factors on vehicle cost or dealer invoice were tested with unbalanced ANOVA first. Because there were big differences in vehicle cost with respect to engine size and body type, main effects of these factors on vehicle price or profit margin were

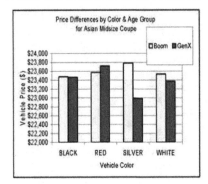
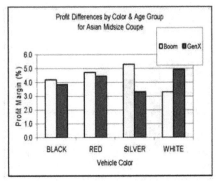

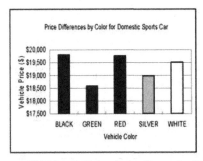
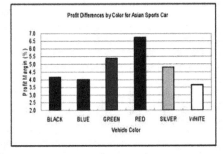

FIG 18.3.   Vehicle price/profit margin differences due to color and customer demographic characteristics for Asian midsize coupe, domestic sports car, and asian sports car.

hard to interpret. Therefore, only interaction effects were examined (see Table 18.3).

Only domestic sports car had a significant interaction effect between body type and age group on vehicle price. No engine size differences were found. Figure 18.4 depicts mean vehicle price for coupe and convertible by the age groups, Baby Boomer and Generation X. As can be seen, Baby Boomers paid approximately $200 more for the convertible than Generation X, whereas Generation X paid about $250 more for the coupe than Baby Boomers.

GENERAL DISCUSSION

Would consumers be willing to pay more for a car just because of its color? The analyses presented in this chapter suggest that consumers do, at least for image-oriented cars, such as sports cars.

Among the three image attributes considered here, the vehicle color showed more differences in vehicle price among the six models. All models except domestic midsize sedan had color-related differences in vehicle price or profit margin. Particularly interesting is the consistently higher price for red and black. This effect

TABLE 18.3

Interaction Effects of Vehicle Engine Size/Body Type and Consumer Age
on Vehicle Price and Profit Margin

Automobile type	Country of origin	Engine size	Body type	Significant interaction effects
Midsize coupe	Domestic	6 cylinder vs. 8 cylinder	—	None
	Asian	GS vs. GST (turbo)	Convertible vs. coupe	None
Sports car	Domestic	6 cylinder vs. 8 cylinder	Convertible vs. coupe	Interaction effect: body type × age group on vehicle price (p < .05)

may be because of the type of vehicles that were included, specifically coupes and convertibles. As mentioned in the method section, the study used the vehicle models that have many image features to examine the effects of the image attributes on consumer price decision in the most ideal situation possible. Because these models are in general perceived as cool or sporty, red and black are likely to be considered more desirable colors than the other colors. A possible explanation for the color-related difference is an application of the theory of emotional benefits by Ruth (2001) and the price affect idea by O'Neill and Lambert (2001). Both papers describe emotion as one of the key factors for decision making during highly involved purchase experiences. Applying these theories, we can infer that, due to emotion categories, both black and red are congruent with coolness and sportiness of the vehicle model, which results in more tolerance for a higher price. Therefore, for those who are image conscious and believe their car is their personal statement, having a particular color for their car is very critical to satisfy their drive to achieve the personal-statement goal. Because of this desire to choose a particular color, the color options become limited, and the consumer loses price negotiation power with

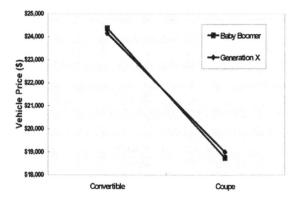

FIG. 18.4.   Baby boomers pay more for convertible (domestic sports car).

respect to the color. As a result, these consumers opt to pay a higher price for the car with the color of their choice. Naturally, confirming this logic would require more experimental studies, but the observed price differences due to color have opened up a lot of opportunities for debates on various affect–cognition theories.

The interaction effects between color and consumer characteristics for domestic midsize coupe and Asian midsize coupe also deserve attention. For example, there are substantial price differences for black and green between males and females for domestic midsize coupe. Females were on the average willing to pay more for a black car, whereas males paid approximately the same. As for the Asian midsize coupe, silver was the only color showing a substantial difference between Baby Boomers and Generation X. It is interesting to note that silver is the most popular color in recent years in the U.S. market (see Powers, 2003). The age group with the highest rate of automobile purchases is Baby Boomers, and therefore, this overall color preference seems to be reflecting the most favorite color among this age group. Because popular models among Baby Boomers are typically the ones that Generation X stay away from (O'Dell, 2003), it can be assumed that silver is the color that Generation Xers do not prefer. The price difference for silver is reflecting the difference in color preference between these two age groups.

These color-related differences and their patterns are consistent with various theories discussed in the earlier section. In fact, the close and consistent relation between vehicle color and price difference provides various implications to the other relationships depicted in Fig. 18.1. Particularly, the price difference due to color provides strong support to the notion that affect influences consumer decision making (Bodur et al., 2000). In this sense, the study provides evidence for the statement by Pham (1998), "affect may play a more central role in the decision-making process than previously recognized" (p. 144). As the next step, it is interesting to investigate further if there are any systematic patterns in the price differences. For example, applying the idea of psychophysics (see O'Neill & Lambert, 2001), it is possible that there is a systematic psychological threshold beyond which consumers start considering the price difference to be too high for the particular choice of color. Naturally, each individual consumer does not have a clear idea what other consumers were willing to pay for the particular color, and in this sense, there is no way for them to know objectively if they are getting the "good" price for the vehicle color. Therefore, if a consumer already has a very strong preference for a particular color and the drive to get a lower price is somewhat tarnished, then the resultant vehicle price should be the quantitative reflection of the person's emotional state. The effect of such an emotional state, or emotion elasticity on price, can be quantitatively measured by systematically comparing the final negotiated price for different colors among various vehicle models.

Compared to the results on color, the effects of the other two attributes, body type and engine size, on price decision were somewhat weak. Only the domestic sports car resulted in a noteworthy interaction effect between body type and age group. The lack of observed differences leaves some issues for future research. As indicated in the method section, because these two attributes already come with a substantial price difference, statistically decomposing purchase price differences to the part due to the production cost difference versus the part due to consumer's emotional response to, say a convertible or a coupe, is fairly difficult, if not impossible. Still, the age-related interaction effect found in this study provides an interesting pattern that deserves attention. On the average, Baby Boomers paid about $200 more than Generation X for the domestic convertible, whereas Baby Boomers paid about $250 less for the coupe of the same domestic model. These results are consistent with the commonly known mid-age crises idea, where a middle-aged man decides to buy a car with high image appeal, such as a red convertible sports car. Because he is highly involved with the image car, his emotional involvement with the convertible is particularly high. As a result, the Baby Boomers pay more than Generation X for a convertible. However, the same level of emotional involvement is not expected by the Baby Boomers for a coupe. Because of the lower level of emotional involvement, the Baby Boomers, who in general have better credit records, pay less than Generation X.

Although the results showed many interesting patterns that deserve further investigation, some caution in interpreting the results is needed. First, as the first attempt to explore the effect of image attributes on consumer price decision, this study had a setup that is as ideal as possible to find such price differences. For example, the number of vehicle models investigated was very small; six models are only a small fraction of the total number of models available in the U.S. market. In addition, only the models with possibly the highest level of image attributes were chosen. Only the California market, the market where the image or the psychological appeal from automobiles is likely to be very important, was studied. As noted in the method section, vehicles with a high days-to-turn and those sold after the new model year was introduced were excluded. Considering these restrictions, it is too early to generalize the relation between image attributes and price decision to all automobile purchase situations in the U.S. market. At the same time, the results of the current study have a direct application opportunity when an automobile manufacturer is ready to launch an advertising campaign for a new sports car. For such an occasion, it is expected that image attributes, particularly the automobile color, have a substantial influence in consumers' perceptions and evaluations of the new automobile.

Several related issues can be investigated with future research. For all the factors described here, such as possible effects of the vehicle type, the consumer geographic location, the time-related variation (i.e., days to turn), it is interesting to find out if they in fact display differential effects on the vehicle price–image attribute relation. Some other factors, such as the country of origin or the popularity trend (i.e., the overall market trend in the consumer preference, such as the shift from green to silver in the most popular automobile color) also deserve further research. Taken together, cumulative research efforts would provide to us a better understanding of the relation between the image attributes and price decision, which in turn would provide better insight into how affect and cognitive processing interact in a complex decision-making process.

CONCLUSIONS

As O'Neill and Lambert (2001) indicated, there have been limited research efforts that specifically address the emotional aspect of purchase price. The current study using point-of-sales automobile data is, to this author's knowledge, the first attempt to assess quantitatively the effect of affect, represented by the image attributes, on purchase price decision in the real-market setting. The analysis results based on six vehicle models with varying degrees of image appeal demonstrated that the automobile color can in fact influence consumers' purchase price decision. Naturally, the generalizability of the findings to other models and other situations, such as different demographic locations, is limited, and further investigation is needed to address many unanswered questions with respect to these various moderating factors. At the same time, although limited in its scope and its generalizability, this empirical study successfully demonstrated the existence of differential effect of emotion, represented by color, on purchase price decision and quantitatively assessed the price differences. Future studies along this line will benefit understanding of not only the relation between emotion and price per se but also the complex relation between affect and cognition as a whole.

REFERENCES

Alpert, J. I., & Alpert, M. I. (1990). Music influences on mood and purchase intentions. *Psychology and Marketing, 7*, 109–133.

Bellizzi, J. A., Crowley A. E., & Hasty, R. W. (1983). The effects of color in store design. *Journal of Retailing, 59*, 21–45.

Bellizzi, J A., & Hite, R. E. (1992). Environmental color, consumer feelings, and purchase likelihood. *Psychology and Marketing, 9*, 347–363.

Bettman, J. R. (1979). *An information processing theory of consumer choice.* Reading, MA: Addison-Wesley.

Bodur, H. O., Brinberg, D., & Coupey, E. (2000). Belief, affect, and attitude: Alternative models on the determinants of attitude. *Journal of Consumer Psychology, 9*, 17–28.

Bolton, L. E., Warlop, L., & Alba, J. W. (2003). Consumer perceptions of price (un)fairness. *Journal of Consumer Research, 29*, 474–491.

Campbell, M. C. (1999). Perceptions of price unfairness: Antecedents and consequences. *Journal of Marketing Research, 36*, 187–199.

Cohen, J. B., & Areni, C. S. (1991). Affect and consumer behavior. In T. S. Robertson & H. H. Kassarjian (Eds.), *Handbook of Consumer Behavior* (pp. 188–240). Englewood Cliffs, NJ: Prentice Hall.

Desmet, P. M. A., Hekkert, P., & Jacobs, J. J. (2000). When a car makes you smile: Development and application of an instrument to measure product emotions. *Advances in Consumer Research, 27*, 111–117.

Doehlert, D. H. (1968). Similarity and preference mapping: A color example. *In Proceedings of the Fall Conference.* Chicago: American Marketing Association.

Gimba, J .G. (1998). Color in marketing: Shades of meaning. *Marketing News, 32*, 6.

Gorn, G. J. (1982). The effects of music in advertising on choice behavior: A classical conditioning approach. *Journal of Marketing, 46,* 94–100.

Isen, A. M. (2001). An influence of positive affect on decision making in complex situations: Theoretical issues with practical implications. *Journal of Consumer Psychology, 11,* 75–85.

Kuykendall, D., & Keating, J. P. (1990). Mood and persuasion: Evidence for the differential influence of positive and negative states. *Psychology and Marketing, 7,* 1–10.

Lichtenstein, D. R., Bloch, P. H., & Black, W. C. (1988). Correlates of price acceptability. *Journal of Consumer Research, 15,* 243–252.

Lonial, S. C., & Auken, S. V. (1982). Perception and preference congruency: A color replication. *Decision Science, 13,* 60–70.

Luce, M. F., Bettman, J. R., & Payne, J. W. (2001). Emotional decisions: Tradeoff difficulty and coping in consumer choice. *Monographs of the Journal of Consumer Research* (1).

Luce, M. F., Payne, J. W., & Bettman, J. R. (1999). Emotional trade-off difficulty of choice. *Journal of Marketing Research, 36,* 143–159.

Milliman, R. E. (1982). Using background music to affect the behavior of supermarket shoppers. *Journal of Marketing, 46,* 86–91.

Mittal, B. (1994). A study of the concept of affective choice mode for consumer decisions. *Advances in Consumer Research, 21,* 256–263.

O'Dell, J. (2003, July 5), This is not your father's Toyota. *Los Angeles Times*, pp. C1, C5.

O'Neill, R. M., & Lambert, D. R. (2001). The emotional side of price. *Psychology and Marketing, 18,* 217–237.

Pham, M. T. (1998). Representativeness, relevance, and the use of feelings in decision making. *Journal of Consumer Research, 25,* 144–149.

Powers, K. I. (2003). Emotional effect of color on automotive purchase price. Presented at 2003 American Psychological Association Convention in Toronto, Canada.

Ruth, J. A. (2001). Promoting a brand's emotion benefits: The influence of emotion categorization processes on consumer evaluations. *Journal of Consumer Psychology, 11,* 99–113.

Treganowan, L. (2001). Car color: What's it say about you? Retrieved January 15, 2001, from Lucille's Garage at MSN UnderWire website http://www.cdnpaint.org/Auto_Adviser.htm.

Westbrook, R. A., & Oliver, R. L. (1991). The dimensionality of consumption emotion patterns and consumer satisfaction. *Journal of Consumer Psychology, 18,* 84–91.

Zajonc, R. B., & Markus, H. (1991). Affective and cognitive factors in preferences. In H. H. Kassarjian and T. S. Robertson (Eds.), *Perspectives in consumer behavior* (4th Ed., pp 240–252). Englewood Cliffs, NJ: Prentice Hall.

CHAPTER NINETEEN

Assessing the Influence of Cultural Values on Consumer Susceptibility to Social Pressure for Conformity: Self-Image Enhancing Motivations vs. Information Searching Motivation

Heonsoo Jung
Konkuk University

The phenomenon of conformity to social pressure has profound implications for individuals' social and buying behavior. Since Asch (1951), many social psychology and marketing researchers have explored the extent and characteristics of conformity to social pressure in a variety of contexts. Although these studies demonstrated that the conformity is widespread behavior, replications of the Asch-type experiment in various countries showed a disconcerting level of conformity. These results obviously imply the operation of country or over country characteristics in the social conformity process. In this review, I suggest a cultural values argument (CVA) that conformity is manifestation of certain cultural values. Based on extensive review of social psychology and marketing literature on conformity, I have documented the history of conformity studies and identified two major motivations of social conformity (i.e., self-image enhancing vs. information-seeking motivations) that govern social conformity process. Then I hypothesized that three cultural values (i.e., collectivism/individualism, uncertainty intolerance, and Confucian values) are moderating the social conformity impact in terms of magnitude and motivation types (i.e., self-image enhancing vs. information-seeking motivations).

CULTURAL VALUES AND SOCIAL CONFORMITY

Widespread movement into international markets by companies of all types has made an increasing number of product markets global or regional rather than domestic in scope. Markets that once were bounded by national limits today have assumed international dimensions (Douglas & Craig, 1995). As more companies move toward globalization, an understanding of how consumer behavior differs from one culture to another becomes essential for success in the worldwide market. Annals of international marketing overflow with horror stories arising from insufficient adaptation to different cultural regions. For example, Pepsi-Cola once translated its advertising slogan "Come alive with the Pepsi generation" into Chinese for the Taiwan market. The selling pitch became "Pepsi brings your ancestors back to life." In Japan, American Express' "Do you know me?" advertising slogan implies that its credit card should be used only one day a week (Yip, 1992).

Although it is well known among marketers that cultural values have influence on consumer behavior to a large extent, little is known about how cultural values translate into a variety of consumer behavior. Because culture often has subtle, oblique, and ephemeral effects, it is difficult to determine how and in what ways its impact is manifested (Douglas & Craig, 1995). Despite such difficulties, many consumer researchers have attempted to explore the nature and influence of culture on consumer behavior for the last several decades. According to Sojka and Tansuhaj (1995), cross-cultural consumer behavior publications that have appeared in four major marketing journals and proceedings for the last decade discussed a variety of consumer behavior topics in cross-cultural contexts. For example, the topics of consumer acculturation, adoption, decision processes, and diffusion have been frequently examined. Other topics discussed in more than one article include advertising, gift giving, family decision making, brand loyalty, and information processing.

As may be surmised from Sojka and Tansuhaj's (1995) finding, one critical area of consumer behavior that has not been considered by previous cross-cultural studies is consumer conformity under social pressure. Since Asch (1951), a stream of social psychology studies have shown that the impact of social pressure for conformity is a relatively clear-cut and common behavioral phenomenon. Although several studies showed the small impacts of social pressure for conformity, most studies have demonstrated that individual psychological processes are subject to social influence processes. Tajfel (1969) noted that one major limitation of previous social influence studies is the ignorance of cultural effects in social influence processes. It is possible that people with different cultural backgrounds show different levels or processes of conformity in a range of social situations.

Recently, several studies have replicated the Asch (1951) classical experiment in other countries (e.g., Japan, Brazil, South Africa, etc.). Although some studies conducted in small countries have shown that social pressure is stronger and conformity to such pressure is more prevalent in those countries than in United States, the studies conducted in other countries have demonstrated relatively similar results. The disconcerting levels of conformity found by these cross-country studies obviously indicate the operation of inherent country or over country characteristics in the social conformity process. The major limitation of the cross-country studies centers on the fact that they simply seek to test and confirm national stereotypes in controlled situations by the use of a standardized measure.

MANAGERIAL RELEVANCE OF SOCIAL CONFORMITY

Why should international marketers care about the different levels and characteristics of conformity found in various cultural regions when they develop international marketing strategies? Although the answer to this question is not easy, arguments emphasizing the importance of understanding consumer behavior as a basis for developing effective marketing strategies may provide clues.

As was emphasized by many marketing researchers, it is crucial for marketers to gain an understanding of customer needs and behavior before developing marketing strategies that aim at achieving certain marketing goals. In international markets where more heterogeneous consumer behavior patterns are likely to be observed, a greater emphasis on understanding differences and similarities in customer behavior and response patterns in diverse settings would be required. Douglas, Morrin, and Craig (1994) noted that conducting cross-cultural consumer studies involves certain practical managerial purposes, namely to assess similarities and differences in consumer behavior and patterns between countries. Such information provides key informational input to management in determining whether or not to introduce a new product or service into another country and if so, how far to adapt marketing strategies to idiosyncratic country characteristics.

The social psychology or marketing studies on social conformity generally suggest that in a consumer decision-making situation where no objective standards are present, individuals who are exposed to a group norm or judgment tend to conform to that group norm or judgment. These findings imply that in a certain situation (i.e., a situation where buyers do not have a clear idea about the real quality of the product), marketers can benefit from promoting their products through noncommercial communication channels (e.g., word of mouth). This would be especially true for the cultural region of which members show strong conformity.

If people in a certain cultural region have a strong tendency to conform under social pressure, then marketers may design marketing strategies that are more in line with such a tendency. The adapted marketing strategy would accelerate the consumer response and put the company in a better competitive market position.

CONFORMITY TO SOCIAL PRESSURE

A stream of social psychology studies have demonstrated that individual psychological processes are subject to social influence (Asch, 1951; Blake & Mouton, 1954; Bovard, 1951; Deutsch & Gerard, 1955; Sherif 1935, 1936). The operational definition of conformity that underlies most of these studies is the private or public agreement of individuals with an opinion that they had not held before it was presented to them. The existence of this phenomenon is, of course, the basis of all human society and undoubtedly accounts for the direction of the overwhelming majority of all human behaviors.

Sherif's (1935) early experiment on the autokinetic effect and Blake's experiments that ingeniously use real-life settings in a controlled manner have demonstrated that when people are exposed to social influences they tend to yield to them. In his seminal work, Asch (1951) devised an experimental situation in which he studied the susceptibility of individuals to social pressures for conformity. In the experiment, single individuals faced a well-structured situation in which they often found themselves in disagreement with a unanimous majority of seven to nine other individuals. The situation involved selecting from among three lines of different lengths presented on a single card. In all, 12 judgments were required, and for 7 of the judgments, the majority had been previously instructed to select the same incorrect line. Asch's results are of particular interest in view of the fact that control subjects, those judging alone, made relatively few errors in judgment, whereas one third of the judgments of experimental subjects, those judging in the group situation, conformed with the incorrect unanimous judgments of the group. These results show clearly the impact of social pressure for conformity even in some situations that are relatively clear-cut and unambiguous. Following Asch, many social psychology researchers have replicated the experimental paradigm in a variety of situations and found similar results.

MOTIVATION: SELF-IMAGE ENHANCING VERSUS INFORMATION SEEKING

Several social psychologists have explored motivations that govern individuals' conformity to social pressure. Deutsch and Gerard (1955) argued that two types of social influence, normative and informational, are operative in the experimental setting. They define a normative social influence as an influence to conform with the positive expectation of another, whereas an informational social influence is characterized as an influence to accept information obtained from another as evidence about reality. Through a modified series of the Asch experiment they demonstrated that when the normative social influence in the direction of an incorrect judgment is removed, more errors are made by experimental subjects than by a control group of people making their judgments alone. Thus, it seems that people, even if not normatively influenced, are influenced by others in the sense that the judgments of others are taken to be a more or less trustworthy source of information about the objective reality with which they and the others are confronted.

Kelman (1961), building on Deutsch and Gerard's (1955) finding, argued that social influence operates through one or more of three distinct processes, each characterized as a distinct set of antecedents and a distinct set of consequent conditions: (a) internalization, (b) identification, and (c) compliance. Internalization is said to occur when the individual accepts influence because it is perceived as inherently conducive to the maximization of values. Identification is said to occur when an individual adopts a behavior or opinion derived from another because the behavior is associated with a self-defining relationship to the other. Finally, compliance is said to occur when an individual conforms to the expectations of another to receive a reward or avoid a punishment mediated by that other. According to his argument, whereas internalization is expected to occur when others' judgments or behaviors are perceived as providing valuable information to one's decision making (i.e., informational influence), identification and compliance occur when one is motivated to realize social benefit from conformity or avoid a punishment mediated by another (i.e., normative influence).

Kelman's (1961) categorization is useful in the analysis of various influence situations and the resulting opinion changes. It should be particularly relevant when one is concerned with the motivational conditions that produced them. By tying together certain antecedents of influence with certain consequences, one can infer the motivation underlying a particular opinion from knowledge of its manifestations and predict the future course of an opinion from knowledge of the conditions under which it was formed.

In Kelman's informational influence process, the motivation that governs social conformity is the signaling value of others' judgments or behaviors. Because the opinion of the majority is more likely to reflect the reality, people conform to the opinion of the majority. On the other hand, the motivation governing the normative influence process relates to the self-image of social entities (i.e., people) confronting social pressure. Facing the unanimous opinion of the majority, people seek social benefit from conformity or avoid a punishment. Maintaining or enhancing their desirable self-images would be possible when they conform to the majority opinion. In this sense, Kelman's normative influence processes could be referred to as image-enhancing influence process.

Another noticeable, alternative argument regarding the motivation of social conformity is based on the social dissonance theory. Zimbardo (1960) noted that dissonance is created when an individual knows that another person—a communicator—holds an opinion contrary to his or her own. The magnitude of the dissonance created by the expression of a contrary opinion increases with increases in a) the credibility and attractiveness of the communicator, b) the extent of the discrepancy in opinion, and c) the importance of or involvement with the cognitive elements of the situation. In a social situation there are a number of potential channels of dissonance reduction, such as changing one's own opinion, changing the opinion of the communicator, making the communicator noncomparable to oneself, seeking further support for one's position, dissociating the source from the content of the communication, and distorting the meaning of communication. One of the major methods of reducing dissonance, then, is conformity or opinion change in the advocated direction. Thus, in case the other avenues of dissonance reduction are restricted, opinion change should be a function of the intensity of dissonance and importance of or involvement with the cognitive elements of the situation.

The other interesting alternative argument, which has a very different perspective from the previously reviewed studies, is the personality predisposition argument. The basic notion is that people tend to have different levels of inherent tendency (i.e., predisposition) to conform to social pressure. Thus, researchers in this area view people's conformity as a manifestation of personality, not behavior cued by situational factors. A number of studies deal with personality predisposition to conformity. Janis (1954) stated that people with low self-esteem tend to be more readily influenced than others. On the other hand, he found that people with acute symptoms of neurotic anxiety tend to conform less. Hoffman (1953) found that conformity has an anxiety-reduction function for compulsive conformists, that is, those whose conformity is based on nonrational needs to agree with one's peer group. Interestingly, he finds no difference in the frequency of conformity, whether compulsive or realistic conformity is involved. Crutchfeld's (1955) finding on personality correlates of conformity shows authoritarian attitudes and behavior to be positively correlated with conformity, a conclusion that agrees with those in the theory of authoritarian personality.

CONFORMITY IN CONSUMER BUYING CONTEXT

The laboratory studies of social conformity processes in social psychology have demonstrated that individuals are highly susceptible to group pressure. Although many social psychology studies explored the social conformity issue, relatively little attention has been given to this issue in the consumer buying context. As may be surmised from the review in the previous sections, the small group studies in social psychology were not concerned with group influence in buying situations. Because consumer buying situations are more complicated and involve more factors than Asch's judgment situation, one may not simply say that the findings in social psychology are applicable to consumer buying contexts. Assessing their relevance to buyer behavior after an exhaustive search of the social psychological literature, Howard (1963, p. 136) speculated about marketing situations as follows:

> Although knowledge about conformity to group norms in the marketplace is slight, common sense would lead us to conclude that consumer decision making takes place in an environment where conformity is a major force. However, the operation of group norms in many buying situations needs to be empirically established, and the social influence of groups on consumer behavior needs to be investigated systematically.

Venkatesan (1966), noting such needs for the marketing studies, devised and ran an experiment in which the consumer decision-making process would come close to an actual buying situation. The assigned task in the experiment was to evaluate and choose the best suit among three identical men's suits. All other means of identification were removed from the suits. Just like the Asch experiment, two different manipulations for the controlled and conformity conditions were executed. Venkatesan found that in consumer decision making, in the absence of any objective standard, individuals tend to conform to the group norm, which indicates the validity of Asch's predictions in the consumer buying context.

Burnkrant and Cousineau (1975) tested Kelman's three influence processes in a marketing context. Experimental subjects were exposed to evaluations of coffee that were attributed to either a similar or a dissimilar source. These evaluations were high in uniformity, low in uniformity, or of unknown uniformity. Participants then tested and evaluated the coffee. The evaluations were made either under a visible (i.e., identifiable) condition or an anonymous condition. Evidence from the experiments was provided to indicate that people use others' product evaluation as a source of information about the product. It appeared that, after observing others evaluating a product favorably, people perceive the product more favorably themselves than they would have in the absence of this observation. The people seemed to use the evaluations of others as a basis for inferring that the product is, indeed, a better product. Interestingly, although Burnkrant and Cousineau's (1975) study clearly indicates the informational influence process is operating in consumer decision making, it represents a departure from prior research, which suggests that the responses of others establish a norm with which people comply.

Park and Lessig (1977) examined two different samples consisting of housewives and students, respectively, in terms of differences in their susceptibility to reference group influence. The subjects were presented the 14 reference group manifestation statements with a listing of the 20 products and asked to indicate, for each product, the extent to which the situation described by the statement was relevant to consumer's brand selection. The results reveal significant differences between housewives and students in terms of the influence of the three types of reference groups (i.e., informational, utilitarian, and value expressive[1]) on brand selection. The findings raise a serious question concerning the external validity of studies that test students yet make generalizations to a broader population base.

Bearden and Etzel (1982) examined consumer perceptions of reference group influence on product and brand decisions using 645 members of a consumer panel and 151 respondents in a follow-up study. Based on consumer judgments, they first classified 16 products into the following four categories: public luxury, public necessity, private luxury, and private necessity. Then, as in Park and Lessig (1977), respondents were instructed to indicate their degrees of agreement with each item as it applied to product or brand selection decision. Differences for 16 products in informational, value-expressive, and utilitarian influence were investigated in a nested repeated-measures design. The results supported hypothesized differences in reference group influence between publicly and privately consumed products and luxury and necessities.

---

[1]Informational, utilitarian, and value expressive correspond to internalization, compliance, and identification, respectively.

Bearden, Netemeyer, and Teel (1989), building on personality disposition arguments in social psychology, argued that susceptibility to interpersonal influence is a general trait that varies across individuals and that a person's relative influencability in one situation tends to have a significant positive relation to his or her influencibility in a range of other social situations. Based on this notion, they developed a scale to assess consumer susceptibility to interpersonal influence. The construct was defined as the need to identify with or enhance one's image in the opinion of significant others through the acquisition and use of products and brands, the willingness to conform to the expectations of others regarding purchase decisions, and the tendency to learn about products and services by observing others or seeking information from others. Through a series of analyses, they identified 12 items—4 informational and 8 normative items. Their results support the discriminant and convergent validity of the informational factor in comparison with the value expressiveness and utilitarian factors. In addition, utilitarian and value expressive measures were combined into a single normative influence factor.

Bearden and Rose (1990), building on Lennox and Wolfe (1984), argued that the extent to which individuals are sensitive to social comparison cues relevant to their product choice and usage is a moderator of interpersonal influence. In other words, the influence that others have on individual decisions is often due to the person's concern or caring about reactions to his or her behavior (i.e., personality factor). To examine the role of an individual difference factor—attention to social comparison information (ATCSI)—in consumer interpersonal influence, they conducted four studies. The attention-to-social-comparison-information measure of Lennox and Wolfe (1984) was first selected as a means of classifying individuals according to their relative sensitivity to social comparison information. To provide a test of the ability of ATCSI to moderate the effects of normative influences on conformity, an experiment was conducted that required a behavioral response to conformity pressure. The task involved the selection of a shade from a choice of two colors that would best represent the university. The manipulation was intended to heighten perceptions of normative pressure by informing the subjects that one color was preferred by a negative reference group, whereas the other color was preferred by a positive reference group. Results showed that the subjects who scored high on the ATSCI scale exhibited greater conformity to the preferences of their peers than those subjects with lower scores on the scale, which confirmed their expectation that consumer susceptibility to interpersonal influence is moderated by the level of attention-to-social-comparison information.

The experimental studies that apply the operational criteria of social conformity in consumer buying contexts have shown that, overall, consumers are highly susceptible to group pressures in a variety of buying situations. However, unlike the social psychology studies, the marketing studies demonstrated that consumer buying situations are more complicated and involve more factors to consider. For example, as shown by Bearden and Etzel (1982), the strength and process of individuals' conformity to social pressure depend on the kind of products they evaluate (e.g., public vs. private, necessity vs. luxury). In addition, as Park and Lessig (1977) noted, the strength of conformity depends on who evaluates the object products (i.e., student vs. housewife). Among all, the most noticeable difference pertains to the judgment object. In a social psychology context, subjects are asked to judge the state of an object that has no psychological affiliation with the person, whereas in a consumer buying context, subjects are asked to evaluate the products that they may want to purchase to maintain or enhance their self-images.

SOCIAL CONFORMITY AND COUNTRY STEREOTYPING

Recent studies that replicated the Asch-type experiment in other countries revealed that the impact of social pressure for conformity is a common behavioral phenomenon across countries. Whittaker and Meade (1967) studied conformity in four countries—Brazil, Lebanon, Hong Kong, and Rhodesia. In three of the four countries, the frequency of yielding was remarkably similar to that found by Asch more than a decade earlier in the United States (33%): namely Brazil (34%), Lebanon (31%), and Hong Kong (32%). Only the Bantu subjects from Rhodesia, a tribe with extremely stringent sanctions for nonconformity, yielded to conformity significantly more often (51%). A replication of the Asch procedure in Fiji (Chandra, 1973) obtained a conformity rate of 36% among indigenous Fijians. The remarkable similarity of the findings across countries may indicate that regardless of national influences, some powerful experimental force produces the effect. Whittaker and Meade (1967) mentioned possible biases due to the fact that their samples consisted of volunteers. Another possibility is that because the subjects were all college students, they belong to a relatively homogenous subculture whose values transcend factors of national background.

Unlike Whittaker and Meade (1967), the experiments conducted in Germany (Timaeus, 1968) and in Japan (Frager, 1970) obtained significantly less conformity than was exhibited by Asch's American studies in the early 1950s. Timaeus (1968) predicted, on the basis of Lewin's (1948) and Hofstatter's (1963) analysis of the German personality in social situations, a lower level of conformity than for Americans. His sample of University of Cologne students indeed produced a lower conformity response (22%). However, it is possible that age was a factor, as the German students were considerably older (and therefore probably more independent) than the typical American participants.

Frager's (1970) study of Japanese conformity is surprising for two reasons. An analysis of the literature led him to expect that in Japan social pressures would be strong and therefore conformity responses prevalent; however, the frequency of conformity responses (25%) was somewhat lower than that found by researchers in other countries. Further, a strong anticonformity response was shown by 34% of the subjects; this is the tendency for a person during neutral trials to call the wrong answer deliberately when the majority give the correct answer—a phenomenon rarely observed in conformity research. This unexpected finding raises some important questions regarding the differing forms that conformity and anticonformity responses may take in various societies, such as whether such strong anticonformity is unique to Japanese populations.

An important consideration is the significance to a Japanese participant of an ad hoc group of strangers gathered together in the laboratory. Nakano (1970) and others have commented on the strong loyalty Japanese have to one group and to that group alone. It would be incorrect therefore to conclude on the basis of Frager's (1970) findings that the Japanese are in general nonconformist. The striking display of contrary behavior in response to a group of strangers leads to the conclusion that in Japan conformity can be elicited only by the natural group to which the individual already owes strong allegiance.

Ellis, Nel, and Rooyen (1992) compared the conformity behaviors of 50 Afrikaans- and 48 English-speaking early adolescents (age 12 to 14 years old) using a modified Asch experiment. The effects of sex, self-concept, and certain personality factors were also examined. No significant differences between the conformity scores of the two language groups were found, but boys and girls significantly differed with regard to their conformity scores. In addition, individuals with low self-concept scores did not have higher conformity scores than those with high self-concept scores.

Childers and Rao (1992) attempted to examine consumers' conformity under social pressures in two different countries. In the study, the influence of peers on individuals' product and brand decisions for products that range in degree of conspicuousness was examined for comparable samples in the United States and in Thailand to assess the validity of the Bearden and Etzel (1982) framework over time and across cultural contexts. Further, the influence of the family was addressed through an examination of intergenerational influences across the two cultures. The results of the study support Bearden and Etzel's (1982) framework. Also, they show that reference group influence may vary depending on the characteristic of the reference group (i.e., family vs. peer).

Although these cross-country studies on social conformity demonstrated that individuals' conformity to social pressures may be a quite common phenomenon across countries, the following comments can be made on the limitations of them. First, the exact intensity of social conformity in each country or culture has not been clearly determined by previous studies (i.e., there are confounding results) and probably needs to be explored further. As Gergen (1973) indicated, replication of Asch's experiment within a culture as well as across cultures is obviously called for, and on a variety of samples, not just students. Second, no study has ever attempted to examine the underlying conformity processes (i.e., whether an informational process or an image-enhancing process) in different cultures. As Mann (1980) noted, this issue is important because in some cultures conformity may be based on informational factors (e.g., rapidly changing societies in which the group defines social reality for its members) rather than normative pressures (e.g., traditional societies in which adherence to group norms is rigidly enforced). The Asch procedure and its variants tap predominantly the normative basis of conformity (Allen, 1965). Third, the previous cross-country studies on social conformity simply replicated the Asch experiment in other countries. Those studies sought to test and confirm national stereotypes in a controlled situation by the use of a standardized measure. Thus, their findings are limited in that they cannot explain why a certain country sample shows greater conformity compared to another country sample. By identifying cultural dimensions that may be related to social conformity and relating them to the intensity and process of individuals' conformity, researchers can explain why that happens.

Last, there are few studies (only one study, Childers & Rao, 1992) in marketing that examine social conformity issues in a cross-cultural context. Several marketing studies applied the Asch framework in consumer buying situations. Although their findings provide an understanding of the roles of social pressure in consumer decision making, the applicability of those findings to different cultural contexts is questionable.

PERSONAL PREDISPOSITION ARGUMENT VERSUS CULTURAL VALUES ARGUMENT

As mentioned before, personality predisposition arguments describe that people tend to have different levels of inherent tendencies (i.e., predisposition) to conform to social pressure. In other words, the operation of interpersonal processes is dependent on the individual attending to and acting on the beliefs, thoughts, and expectations of others. Bearden and Rose (1990), building on those arguments, stated that sensitivity to social comparison information (i.e., a kind of personality), motivated by such factors as a fear of negative social evaluation, is one moderating variable. If this argument is true (actually, it has been supported by several previous studies, e.g., Lennox & Wolfe, 1984; Miniard & Cohen, 1983), then we may argue that cultural values are also another possible moderating factor in social conformity processes. In other words, it is possible that people in different cultures have different tendencies to conform under social pressure. I refer to this idea as the cultural values argument.

Tylor (1874) defined culture as "that complex whole which includes knowledge, belief, art, morals, law, custom, and other capabilities and habits acquired by a man as a member of society." Different cultural groups tend to have different types of the man-made part of the environment, and based on the parts, the members in those cultural groups, through learning, may develop different types of disposition (i.e., different tendencies to respond to environmental stimuli; Herskovits, 1955). Whereas in a certain culture, people may conform to group norms more strongly because there has been a strict sanction for nonconformity (e.g., Rhodesian people; Whittaker & Meade, 1967), in other cultures people may conform to social pressure weakly because independence or self-esteem image has been more valued by the society for a long time (e.g., those with high self-esteem; Ellis et al., 1992). In a society where there has been a strict sanction, people are more likely to acquire a disposition to conform to the group norms. Hui and Triandis (1986) noted that one major cultural value, collectivism/individualism can be seen as a cultural variable as well as a personality variable. When there is a majority of collectivists (or individualists) in a culture, the society is labeled collectivist (or individualist). On the very basic level, however, it is the person's own feelings, emotions, beliefs, ideology, actions, and so forth that constitute collectivism.

Although cultural values appear to moderate the conformity impact and as a result of the intervention of cultural values people in different cultures tend to show heterogeneous social conformity patterns, the previous cross-country studies on social conformity did not fully address it. Researchers have not explicitly recognized such a role of cultural values, and they have not attempted to identify related cultural values in social conformity processes. In general, the validity of cross-cultural comparisons depends on the extent to which the entities arrayed for comparison can be accurately conceptualized and defined as cultures and not blurred with other entities (e.g., nations, socioeconomic classes, and rural–urban groups, etc.). If the aim is to relate phenomena on a cultural level to those on a social psychological (i.e., group) level, then the investigator must be alert to the definition of culture and the precise features of culture that are supposed to influence social behavior—language, economic factors, ecology, urbanization, level of education, belief system, and so on. Unfortunately, all the previous cross-country studies on social conformity either ignored this conceptual problem or confounded the operation of culture with some other factor.

Tajfel (1969) noted one of the main methodological problems in this area, from the psychologist's viewpoint, is to discover techniques that will allow the transition from the analysis of a cultural system to that of the regularities in behavior relating this process. When it is done, it is easy to understand how a cultural system of values and beliefs gives rise to individual variability. Tajfel also argued that cultural regularities undoubtedly exist, and it may be expected that the effects of cultural background become more marked as a function of the complexity and ambiguity of the available information and of the opportunities that an individual has to engage in his or her independent checking of what comes from social sources.

Reflecting the limitations of the previous research on conformity and recognizing that conformity is the manifestation of certain cultural values, I propose that cultural values modify individuals' conformity to social pressures. Certain cultural groups tend to exhibit different levels of strength and patterns of conformity compared to other cultural groups because they have inherently different cultural backgrounds. Figure 19.1 outlines the moderating role of cultural values in the social conformity process.

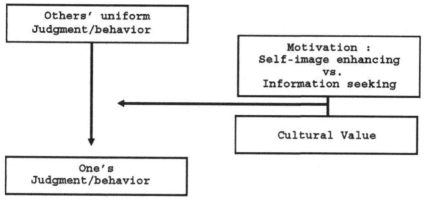

FIG. 19.1. The role of cultural values.

SOCIAL CONFORMITY AND RELATED CULTURAL VALUES

In the prior section I argued that cultural values moderate the social conformity impact and provided a rationale for the reasoning. In this section I explore plausible cultural dimensions that would be related to conformity to social pressure. One insight into this issue can be provided by a landmark piece of cross-cultural research, which has a tremendous amount of face validity. In 1980, Professor Geert Hofstede received permission from a major multinational corporation to carry out a multicultural attitude survey across the 53 countries in which the corporation was based, with over 10,000 employees. Hofstede sought to establish whether there were indeed cultural differences across national boundaries, and more important, whether there was a shared basis for regional cultural orientations such as those that may be shared by East Europeans, Asians, North Americans, etc. Not surprisingly, the study identified four dimensions of national cultures: individualism/collectivism, power distance, masculinity, and uncertainty avoidance. In addition, Bond, Leung, and Wan (1987) and Hofstede (1994) noticed the existence and value of the Confucian dynamic in Asian countries.

There are several reasons for using the five cultural dimensions. First, the behavioral or values approach used to identify these dimensions is useful for tackling the concept of national culture and raising the prominence of national culture as an important subject of scholarly inquiry. Second, Hofstede's (1980) study—from which four of the five dimensions were derived—is regarded as the most extensive examination of cross-national values. Third, validity for all dimensions but the Confucian dynamic was established through correlations from 38 other studies that compare between 5 and 39 countries (Hofstede, 1980). Fourth, studies note the existence and value of the Confucian dynamic (Hofstede, 1994), although there is a need for further empirical research to shed more light on this factor. Fifth, the validity of his analysis was supported by a plethora of previous research involving diverse types of cultural data.

Although all five cultural dimensions may be related to social conformity, the following three dimensions may be particularly relevant to the social conformity: a) individualism/collectivism, b) uncertainty avoidance, and c) Confucian dynamic. In the next section, I first explore how each of these three dimensions relates to social conformity, because, to reach the testable hypotheses, specific variables must be selected within a wide cultural context and their predicted effects on response must be articulated. Then I close the section by developing pertinent hypotheses based on identified cultural dimensions.

Collectivism/Individualism

The most appropriate cultural dimension that may be related to social conformity processes is collectivism/individualism. Hofstede (1980, p. 8–13) defined individualism as the emotional independence from "groups, organizations, or other collectivities and contrasted this with collectivist societies where people are born into extended families or kinship systems that protect them in exchange for loyalty. This dimension involves the extent to which an individual considers the requirement of the relevant group, as opposed to his or her individual requirements, in making decisions. Societies high in individualism have loose ties among members—everyone looks after his or her own interests and those of the immediate family. Examples include the United States, Great Britain, Canada, and Italy (Hofstede, 1980). Societies low in individualism, such as Japan, Iran, Taiwan, and South Korea, hold group values and beliefs and seek collective interests.

In light of Hofstede's conceptualization of the individualism/collectivism construct, I suggest that people from countries that are low on individualism tend to be more susceptible to the group than their counterparts from countries that are high on this construct. Because individuals in collectivist societies cannot easily distance themselves from the various groups to which they belong, they will most likely be influenced by the norms of these groups. According to Hofstede, these groups protect the interests of their members but in turn expect permanent loyalty. However, people from more individualist societies, who are more concerned with their own self-interests, tend to be influenced less by group norms. The socialization patterns that are found in collectivist cultures emphasize obedience, duty, sacrifice for the group, cooperation, favoritism toward the in-group, acceptance of in-group authorities, nurturing, and interdependence. The heightened importance of group solidarity in collectivist cultures may have a profound effect on social information processing. It may result in a stronger weight being attached to different types of input important to achieving the group's goal (Bond, Leung, & Wan, 1982). As a result, in collectivist cultures, the opinion of the majority may work as social pressure; it, in turn, is likely to lead to each individual's attitude change in an advocated direction.

On the other hand, the socialization patterns that are found in individualist cultures emphasize independence, self-reliance, creativity, and acceptance of disobedience if the child is especially competent. In individualist cultures, people are very good at entering and leaving groups and are insensitive to the problem of group cohesiveness. Thus, in individualist cultures where members emphasize the uniqueness of the individual, self-interest, and less concern about group, attitude change is less likely to occur under social pressure.

Hui and Triandis (1986) note that regardless of underlying influence process, collectivists are likely to pay more attention to the influencing agent than are individualists. Although the process may be more complicated, it may be safe to say that the former are more willing to go along with the group to avoid being rejected.

Regarding the underlying conformity process, individualists may conform under social pressure mainly due to the relevance of social information to their decision making. Traditionally, the term individualism has been used to refer to the feeling or conduct in which the guiding principle is the interest of the individual. More recently, Waterman (1984) contended that individualism was embodied in four psychological qualities: self-interest, self-actualization, internal locus of control, and post-conventional principled moral reasoning. Because individualists are less dependent on the group and are seeking self-interest, it is in their best interest to follow others only when they believe others' opinions would contribute to their judgments (i.e., when group's information is valuable). Thus, in an individualist culture the influence process is expected to occur to the extent that it is perceived as providing information relevant to decision making, that is, contribution to better decision making. Given this understanding, I suggest the following hypotheses:

Hypothesis 1a:

Other things being equal, a cultural difference (collectivism/individualism) should produce stronger conformity for the collectivists than the individualists when they are exposed to a reference group's uniform judgment or behavior.

Hypothesis 1b:

In a collectivist culture, consumer conformity occurs mainly due to social pressure (i.e., self-image enhancing motivation), whereas individualists' conformity occurs mainly due to the relevance of the information obtained from a reference group to their decision making (i.e., informational motivation).

Uncertainty Intolerance

One of Hofstede's (1980) cultural dimensions, uncertainty avoidance (uncertainty intolerance), centers on how societies deal with unknown aspects of the future. Cultures vary in the extent to which they are willing to tolerate ambiguity and uncertainty (Hofstede & Bond, 1984). Uncertainty about the future tends to create anxiety and stress, and societies differ in the extent such uncertainties exist and the extent to which the uncertainty and anxiety is avoided or tolerated. Generally speaking, high avoidance of uncertainty is more common among cultures that are experiencing a rapid change, such as new democracies, whereas more advanced societies, such as the older democracies, tend to have more tolerance for uncertainty. Hofstede (1980) found that although the United States was slightly higher than Hong Kong in uncertainty avoidance, both countries were well below the average. Ralston, Toyne, and Martinez (1992) found that U.S. managers were significantly more tolerant of ambiguity than their Hong Kong counterparts, and in turn, that the Hong Kong managers were significantly more tolerant than the PRC managers.

Similarly, Tse, Lee, Vertinsky, and Wehrung (1988) proposed that a culture may affect business decisions by generally influencing risk-taking patterns (e.g., promoting caution and discouraging gambling) or prescribing a pattern of tradeoffs between risk and return.

Vitell, Nwachukwu, and Barnes (1993), based on Hofstede's (1980) conceptualization of uncertainty avoidance, suggested that business practitioners from societies that are strong on uncertainty avoidance are more likely to be intolerant of any deviations from group or organizational norms than their counterparts from countries that have weak uncertainty avoidance. As an example, the United States and Canada are characterized as having weak uncertainty avoidance, whereas Japan is characterized as strong on this dimension. This characterization suggests that business practitioners in Japan (i.e., Oriental culture) are more likely to be intolerant of any deviations from group or organizational norms than their North American counterparts (i.e., Western culture). Because deviants are not expected to be tolerated, membership in most organizational groups in Japan is expected to be composed of mostly nondeviants in comparison to the United States and Canada.

In light of Hofstede (1980) and the following management studies, I argue that people in Asian cultures are more likely to conform to the group norm to avoid uncertainty involved in their judgments. It is likely that an increase in the degree of uncertainty relates directly to an increase in the weight of cognitive factors determining the response that takes place under the condition of social influence. Tajfel (1969) argued that a fixation of the nature of stimulus narrows down the range of alternatives subsequently sought; the greater the uncertainty, the greater also is the likelihood that information derived from a social source will contribute to the formation of such hypotheses. Wiener (1958) found that the major variable determining uncertainty in social conditions, as in nonsocial conditions, is the degree of ambiguity of stimulus. Thus, people in the culture with high uncertainty intolerance are motivated to avoid uncertainty by following group norms, whereas the opposite is true for the people in the culture with low uncertainty intolerance. Thus,

Hypothesis 2:

Stronger conformity occurs for the consumers of high uncertainty intolerable culture when they are exposed to the uniform opinion of a reference group, because they are more likely to be motivated to reduce the uncertainty involved in their decision making. However, weaker conformity is expected for the consumers of low uncertainty intolerable culture.

Confucian Values

Among Hofstede's (1980) cultural dimensions, the Confucian dynamic is the only dimension that did not surface through Hofstede's 40 country survey, but it appeared in a separate, 22-country study conducted by Bond et al. (1987). At one end, the positive pole, are values indicating a dynamic, future-oriented mentality, such as persistence, hard working, thrift, shame, and regard for relationships. At the opposite end, the negative pole, are values representing a static mentality focused on the past and present, such as reciprocation, face, and tradition. These values encourage keeping within well-known and accepted boundaries. The Confucian dynamics is not limited to cultures with a historic Confucian influence. In fact, one of the highest scoring cultures on this factor is Brazil. However, this value is, in general, prevalent in the East Asian countries, although the factor is by no means restricted to that region. Hong Kong, Taiwan, Japan, and South Korea rate the highest on this factor, whereas countries low on this factor include West Africa, Canada, and the United States (Hofstede, 1994).

In Oriental society such as South Korea, Japan, and China, many aspects of members' life are to some extent influenced by values and norms of Confucian philosophy. Because of the influence of the Western culture (due to the diffusion of Western ideas and products and the increase of communication between nations), its influence has recently been diminished as can be observed from the behavior of the young generation in Oriental society. However, Confucian influence is still strong in people's attitudes toward ethnicity (Tan & McCullough, 1985).

Confucianism is well represented by the notion of benevolence, propriety, wisdom, and obedience and these life philosophy are regarded as norms of human beings (Nivison & Wright, 1966). Especially, the major concern of Confucianism is with the correct observance of human relationships within a hierarchical society. According to Confucianists, a proper state of mind and correct conduct are necessary for a proper social order. One may ask what "a proper state of mind and correct conduct" mean anyway. Regarding this issue, Tan and McCullough (1985) argued that they are related to the following attitudes: a) do the right things so as not to lose face, b) when making important decisions consideration of family comes first, c) interact closely with relatives and friends, and d) one should not go to extremes in one's behavior.

In particular, self-image enhancing influence processes (i.e., identification and compliance) may be closely related to the Confucian values. Compliance process is operating when an individual conforms to the expectations of another to receive a reward or avoid a punishment mediated by that other. Because in Confucian cultures people are motivated to foster harmony with members of their reference groups, it is likely that they conform to the opinion of the majority. Also, because it is important for them to identify with the reference group, identification processes are expected to occur. Furthermore, as d) states, people in Confucian cultures are motivated not to be extreme: as a result, they are more likely to follow the majority opinion.

People in Confucian cultures are, in general, under more pressure to live up to the expectation of significant others so as to preserve their face. As a result, individual behavior is dictated by the necessity of maintaining the social relationship, which would result in stronger conformity under social pressure. In the light of this understanding, the following hypothesis is suggested:

Hypothesis 3:

In Confucian cultures, a self-image enhancing influence process is more likely to occur than an informational influence process because people in those cultures are strongly motivated to keep harmony with the members of a reference group.

CONCLUSION

The phenomenon of social conformity has profound implications for individuals' social and buying behavior. Accordingly, many social psychology and marketing researchers have explored the extent and characteristics of conformity to social pressure in a variety of contexts. Although these studies do not show the same results, they basically demonstrate that conformity is a widespread phenomenon. In this review, I suggested CVA (cultural values arguments) that conformity is a manifestation of certain cultural values. Identifying two major motivations of social conformity (i.e., self-image enhancing vs. information-seeking motivations), I hypothesized that collectivism/individualism, uncertainty tolerance, and Confucian values are moderating the social conformity impact in terms of magnitude and motivation type. Future studies should empirically test whether the suggested cultural values significantly intervene in the social conformity process.

Regarding the managerial implications of social conformity, I suggest the following examples in which international marketers can benefit from using the information regarding individuals' conformity to social pressure in a certain cultural region. First, consumers often purchase a product to identify with a membership or reference group by owning it. When an international marketer finds out the strong influences exerted by a certain group, such as neighborhood groups and bridge clubs, on the members of a certain culture, he or she may want to build a brand image that matches the characteristics of the reference group. Second, if people in a certain culture are strongly subject to the normative conformity process, a marketer may prefer to use a personal distribution channel. For example, one conceivable direct selling method is the party plan method, used by several U.S. consumer goods companies, such as Mary Kay Cosmetics and Tupper Ware, in which a salesperson presents and sells products to a group of customers attending a party or show in one of the customer's homes. Third, if the conformity to social norms in a certain culture is mainly characterized as the informational influence process, a marketer may benefit by emphasizing in the advertisement that the leading character in the advertisement prefers the product because it brings a great value to him or her. Finally, for a certain industry, it is often important to accelerate the diffusion of new products at an introduction stage (e.g., the software industry). A marketer in such an industry may want to enter a country in which people show strong conformity to social pressure. The information on the conformity in a certain cultural region may help a marketer make an international market entry decision.

REFERENCES

Allen, V. L. (1965). Situational factors in conformity. In L. Berkowitz (Ed.), *Advances in Experimental Social Psychology: Vol. 2* (pp. 133–173). New York: Academic Press.

Asch, S. E. (1951). Effects of group pressure upon the modification and distortion of judgment. In H. Guetzkow (Ed.), *Groups, leadership and men* (pp. 177–190). Pittsburgh, PA: Carnegie Mellon Press.

Bearden, O. W., & Etzel, M. J. (1982). Preference group influence on product and brand purchase decisions. *Journal of Consumer Research, 9,* 183–194.

Bearden, O. W., Netemeyer, R. G., & Teel J. E. (1989). Measurement of consumer susceptibility to interpersonal influence. *Journal of Consumer Research, 15,* 473–481.

Bearden, O. W., & Rose R. L. (1990). Attention to social comparison information: An individual difference factor affecting consumer conformity. *Journal of Consumer Research, 16,* 461–471.

Blake, R. R., & Mouton, J. S. (1954). Present and future implications of social psychology for law and lawyers. *Journal of Public Law.* Emory University.

Bond, M., Leung, H. K., & Wan, K. C. (1987). Chinese values and the search for culture-free dimensions of culture. *Journal of Cross-Cultural Psychology, 18,* 143–164.

Bovard, E. W. (1951). Group structure and perception. *Journal of Abnormal Social Psychology, 46,* 398Œ405.

Burnkrant, E. R., & Cousineau A. (1975). Informational and normative Influence in buyer behavior. *Journal of Consumer Research, 2,* 206–215.

Chandra, S. (1973). The effect of group pressure in perception: A cross-cultural conformity study. *International Journal of Psychology, 8,* 37–39.

Childers, L. T., & Rao, A. R. (1992). The influence of familial and peer-based reference groups on consumer decisions. *Journal of Consumer Research, 19,* 198–211.

Crutchfield, R. S. (1955). Conformity and character. *American Psychology, 10,* 191–198.

Deutsch, M., & Gerard, H. B. (1955). A study of normative and informational social influences upon individual judgment. *Journal of Abnormal and Social Psychology, 51,* 629–636.

Douglas, S. P., & Craig, S. (1995). *Global marketing strategy.* Englewood Cliffs, NJ: Prentice Hall.

Douglas, S. P., Morrin, M. A., & Craig S. (1994). Cross-national consumer research tradition. In G. Lilien, B. Pras, & G. Laurent (Eds.), *Research Traditions in Marketing* (pp. 210–218). New York: Praeger.

Ellis, E., Nel, E., & Rooyen, J. V. (1992). Conformity behavior of Afrikaans- and English-speaking adolescents in South Africa. *The Journal of Social Psychology,* 875–878.

Frager, R. (1970). Conformity and anti-conformity in Japan. *Journal of Personality and Social Psychology, 15,* 203–210.

Gergen, K. J. (1973). Social psychology as history. *Journal of Personality and Social Psychology, 26,* 309–320.

Herskovits, M. (1955). *Cultural anthropology.* New York: Knopf.

Hoffman, M. L. (1953). Some psychodynamic factors in compulsive conformity. *Journal of Abnormal Social Psychology, 48,* 383–393.

328   JUNG

Hoffstatter, P. R. (1963). Einfuhrung in die social psychology. Stuttgart: Alfred Kroner.
Hofstede, G. (1980). *Culture's consequence: national differences in thinking and organizing.* Beverly Hills, CA: Sage.
Hofstede, G. (1994). Management scientists are human. *Management Science, 40,* 4–13.
Hofstede, G., & Bond, M. H. (1984). Hofstede's culture dimensions: An independent validation using Rojeach's value survey. *Journal of Cross-Cultural Psychology, 15,* 417–433.
Howard, J. A. (1963). *Marketing: Executive and buyer behavior.* New York: Columbia University Press.
Hui, C. H., & Triandis, H. C. (1986). Individualism–collectivism: A study of cross-cultural researchers. *Journal of Cross-Cultural Psychology, 17,* 225–248.
Janis, I. L. (1954). Personality correlates of susceptibility to persuasion. *Journal of Personality, 22,* 504–518.
Kelman, H. C. (1961). Processes of opinion change. *Public Opinion Quarterly, 25,* 57–78.
Lennox, R. D., & Wolfe, R. N. (1984). Revision of the self-monitoring scale. *Journal of Personality and Social Psychology, 46,* 1349–1369.
Lewin, K. (1948). Some social psychological differences between the U.S. and Germany. In K. Lewin (Ed.), *Resolving social conflicts* (pp.3–33).. New York: Harper & Row.
Mann, L. (1980). Cross-cultural studies of small groups. In H. C. Triandis & R. W. Brislin (Eds.), *Handbook of cross-cultural psychology, Vol. 5,* (pp.155–210). Boston, MA: Allyn & Bacon.
Miniard, P. W., & Cohen, J. B. (1983). Modeling personal and normative influences on behavior. *Journal of Consumer Research, 10,* 169–180.
Nakano, C. (1970). *Japanese society.* Berkeley, CA: University of California Press.
Nivision, D. C., & Wright, A. F. (Eds.). (1966). *Confucian in action.* Palo Alto: Stanford University Press.
Park, C. W., & Lessig, V. P. (1977). Students and housewives: Differences in susceptibility to reference group influence. *Journal of Consumer Research, 4,* 102–110.
Ralston, D., Gustafson, D. J., Cheung, F. M., & Terpstra, R. H. (1992). Eastern values: A comparison of U.S., Hong Kong and PRC managers. *Journal of Applied Psychology, 77,* 664–671.
Sherif, M. (1935). A study of some social factors in perceptions. Arch. Psychol. vol.37
Sherif, M. (1936). *The psychology of social norms.* New York: Harper.
Sojka, Z. J., & Tansuhaj, P. (1995). Cross-cultural consumer research: A twenty-year review. *Advances in Consumer Research, 22,* 120–127.
Tajfel, H. (1969). Social and cultural factors in perception. In G. Lindzey & E. Aronson (Eds.), *Handbook of social psychology, Vol. 3,* Reading, MA: Addison-Wesley.
Tan, C. T., & McCullough, J. (1985). Relating ethnic attitudes and consumption values in an Asian context. *Advances in Consumer Research, 12,* 122–125.
Timaeus, E. (1968). Untersuchungen zum sogenannten konformen Verhatten. *Zeitschrift fur Experimentelle und Angewandte Psychologie, 15,* 176–194.
Tse, D. K., Lee, K., Vertinsky, L., & Wehrung, D. A. (1988). Does culture matter? A cross-cultural study of executives' choice, decisiveness, and risk adjustment in international marketing. *Journal of Marketing, 52,* 81–95.
Tylor, E. B. (1874). *Primitive culture.* London: Murray.
Venkatesan, M. (1966). Experimental study of consumer behavior conformity and independence. *Journal of Marketing Research, 3.*
Vitell, S., Nwachukwu, S. L., & Barnes, J. H. (1993). The effects of culture on ethical decision-making: An application of Hofstede's typology. *Journal of Business Ethics, 12,* 753–760.
Waterman, A. S. (1984). *The psychology of individualism.* New York: Praeger.

Whittaker, J. O., & Meade, R. D. (1967). Social pressure in the modification and distortion of judgment: A cross-cultural study. *International Journal of Psychology, 2,* 109–113.

Wiener, M. (1958). Certainty of judgment as a variable in conformity behavior. *Journal of Social Psychology, 48,* 257–263.

Yip, S. G. (1992). *Total global strategy.* Englewood Cliffs, NJ: Prentice Hall.

Zimbardo, P.G. (1960) Involvement and communication discrepancy as determinants of opinion conformity. *Journal of Abnormal and Social Psychology, 60,* 86–94.

CHAPTER TWENTY

The Impact of Media and Culture on the Consumption Values of Women in China and Taiwan

Tsai-Ju Liao
Providence University

Lien-Ti Bei
National Chengchi University

With the increasing growth of women's consumption power in both China and Taiwan, more and more managerial practices are focusing on the female market so as to gain more market shares. However, under the influence of Confucius, a woman is taught to obey her father before marriage, obey her husband after getting married, and then obey her son as a widow. A woman belongs to the family and should not have any intellectual self-determination. On the other hand, according to the communists, women should "hold up half of the sky"; after being inundated with communist ideology for more than 50 years, women were empowered to be equally responsible in society. Yet during the further acculturation of Western individualism in the 1990s, women started to behave however they wanted and enjoyed an independent role free from misogynistic ancient values. How all these conflicting philosophies influence women's consumption values in China is one of the purposes of this study.

In addition, noting how the combination of traditional Confucian thought with modern individualistic and materialistic values plays out among Taiwanese women is a focus of this study. Confucius' philosophy was strongly recommended by the government in the 1770s and is still in the textbooks of both elementary and high schools. However, Western culture was introduced to Taiwan society beginning in the 1960s, deeply influencing women through the dissemination of female independence and equality in Hollywood movies and TV programs. Therefore, the combination of traditional Confucianism with modern individualism has demonstrated interesting consumption values among women in Taiwan that is worthy of study.

Clearly, cultural context invariably influences women's attitudes toward themselves, their family, society, and, of course, their consumption values. Taiwan is more industrialized than China and had contact with Western countries much earlier than China. Although some researchers have studied Chinese consumer society (Lee & Tse, 1994; Tse, Belk, & Zhou, 1989; Tse, Sin, Yau, & Yu, 1999), few researchers have paid attention to the sequential impact of different values on consumption values (Cheng, 1997). For this reason, this study explores the influence of foreign mass media on traditional Confucian values and the consequential impact on related consumption values in both China and Taiwan.

CONCEPTUAL FRAMEWORK

Yang (1981) argued that even among the most rapidly modernizing segment of the Chinese population, there is a tendency for people to act primarily in accordance with the anticipated expectations of others and, more broadly, social norms rather than with their internal wishes or personal attributes. Social norms are the influence of the well-known intellectual philosophy of Confucianism. Traditional values have had an enduring historical and cultural continuity (see Bond, 1986). No matter where Chinese are, their behaviors will always follow the ancient rules.

The family environment (Scanzoni & Fox, 1980; Thornton, Alwin, & Camburn, 1983) and social norms influence how the attitudes toward gender roles are socialized. Confucianism directs a woman how to behave properly, not to act against traditional norms, and to obey her husband. Serving her parents-in-law carefully and taking care of her family have become the most important responsibilities for women under traditional Confucian education.

Women's Opinion

Markus and Kitayama (1991) suggested that constructs of the self could be separated into an independent view and an interdependent view. The independent view is related to concepts of the self, such as self-actualization; expressing one's unique set of needs, rights, and capacities; developing one's distinct potential; autonomy; and being self-contained. In this study we define self-determination from the independent view, deriving from a belief in the wholeness and uniqueness of each person's configuration of internal attributes (Johnson, 1985).

On the other side, the interdependent view insists that one's self be fundamentally connected to other human beings; that is, a collective and connected relationship. To reveal the context of connection with others in more detail, we instead use family opinion and societal opinion to represent the interdependent view.

Traditional Chinese attitudes, pertaining to a hierarchical ranking of authority and status distinctions in the family (Ho, 1994) and a pervasive application of a moral norm, are the primary standards against which people are judged (Ho, 1996). Everyone should behave appropriately—that is, suitably for one's status in society.

Bond's (1996) empirical study on China, Hong Kong, Taiwan, and Singapore found that these Chinese cultural groups all focus on their hierarchy and disciplines. Unfortunately, a woman in Chinese society has inherited the legacy of traditional values that severely discriminates against her compared to men (Veronica, 1996).

Even though there are wide geographical and ideological differences in China and Taiwan, both are influenced by Confucianism and share many similar traditional values. Chinese women are educated to think that men belong to society and women belong to the family. In Chinese society, women tend to follow others' expectation in living their life. Daughters are destined at birth to be married into another family. A wife could be divorced for failing to bear sons or failing to obey and serve her parents-in-law (Veronica, 1996). Under all these pressures of other people's expectations, a woman is educated to look after her family as her first priority. Therefore, a woman's opinions are strongly tied to her family. In other words, women place much greater value on the family than on themselves.

Political and Economic Revolution

Under Chinese communism, women are educated to contribute themselves to the country at the expense of a private life. Women cultivated by Marxist ideology pursue equal rights, employment, and the opportunity to participate in the political arena. Women also have the equal right to accept education and be treated equally in the labor force. They are educated to be independent and treated equally, not for themselves but for their country. They are expected to contribute themselves to society rather than the family such that their patriotism is augmented even as they devalue traditional family values. Therefore, the opinion of society, meaning to what extent people are contributing to the country and society generally, has extremely strong value in China.

In the 1970s the PRC implemented a four-modernization plan (emphasizing the development of agriculture, industry, technology, and national defense) after the Cultural Revolution in the preceding decade. The four-modernization plan incorporated many aspects of capitalism into the PRC economy. Nonetheless, the government still pursued the equality of women. Women are encouraged to participate in the labor market and to strive for independence, which became a politically correct issue. The proportion of working women increased dramatically, reaching 44.80% in 1994 (*The People's Daily*, 1995, quoted in Tan, 1997).

Although both communism and capitalism emphasize the importance of gender equality, they have some differences. Communism proclaimed that women should be independent and contribute what they have earned to the country. By contrast, capitalist doctrine holds that women should be economically independent and consider their self-value first. Even in the beginning, after they were impelled to open their doors and agree on gender equality, the Chinese government under communism still did not encourage people to uphold Western style consumerism and the attendant wasteful habits: chasing after material possessions, hoarding money, or, more generally, becoming a consumer society (Tse, Belk, and Zhou, 1989).

As time passed, women began reevaluating their roles in society, especially during the economic revolution. After China opened its doors, women have had more opportunities and have endorsed Western style individualism; they have begun to perceive an alternative identity, different from the roles ascribed by the communist state. These different ideologies are gradually changing the identity of women in China.

To examine more thoroughly the different cultural influences on women's opinions, we divided women's opinions into three categories: autonomy, family constraints, and social influence. The prior discussion suggests that women's opinions in the two cultures are likely to differ and they are hypothesized as:

H_{1-1}: Women in Taiwan maintain more positive attitudes toward autonomy than women in China due to westernization and modernization.

H_{1-2}: Women in Taiwan maintain less positive attitudes toward family constraints than women in China due to westernization and modernization.

H_{1-3}: Women in China maintain more positive attitudes toward social influence than women in Taiwan due to the cultivation of communism.

Foreign Mass Media

Advertisers have historically portrayed women as depending on men, incapable of participating in important activities or making decisions, and having a limited array of traditional work and nonwork roles (Courtney & Whipple, 1983; Wagner & Banos, 1973). Most women's roles in magazine advertisements are found to be restricted to those of a highly recreational, familial, or decorative nature (Courtney & Whipple, 1983).

Mays and Brady (1990) compared the portrayals of women in seven general readership magazines between 1975 and 1985 and found that women were shown less often in the home and more often in social and business settings. Women's roles in the media were not only less family oriented but also demonstrated a higher degree of autonomy. Kerin, Lundstrom, and Sciglimpaglia (1979) suggested that due to an increasing proportion of women in the professional workforce there would be an increasing emphasis on contemporary roles for women in advertisements in the 1980s. They also forecasted that advertising would contain the use of more role blending (i.e., scenes in which no sex dominates), role switching (i.e., purchase or use of a product portrayed by the opposite gender and defying the normal stereotype), and dual roles (i.e., portrayal of women in both traditional and nontraditional roles simultaneously). Lysonski (1983) denoted similar results: Advertisers in magazines between 1974–1975 and 1979–1980 increasingly portrayed women as career oriented, participating in nontraditional activities, and less dependent on men.

We expect that mass media, especially foreign mass media, will bring a fresh outlook to the concept of independence and will positively influence women's social roles and self-perceptions. Conversely, the value of independence stemming from foreign mass media will contradict the constraints on women by traditional familial structures. Therefore, we expect there will be a negative effect of foreign mass media on traditional family values.

H_{2-1}: Foreign mass media has a positive effect on women's attitudes toward autonomy.

H_{2-2}: Foreign mass media has a negative effect on women's attitudes toward family constraints.

Beginning in 1978, China changed sharply to a market orientation. They went from having no advertising to having a contemporary advertising superstructure with all the tools of modern media in use (Tse et al., 1989). Advertisements appeared in newspapers and magazines, on radio and television, and in outdoor locations.

Before the political reforms in 1978, China's national newspaper (e.g., *The People's Daily*) and its magazines (e.g., *China's Women*) did not carry any advertising except for government slogans and announcements. With the increasing volume of advertising nowadays, women have more chances to access Western culture and individualism. However, China's government neither gave up communism nor accepted capitalism completely. China's government has still declared the communist spirit as everyone's core value through the use of media. They only implemented a capitalist economics and intervened in the process to achieve the desired economic development. Therefore, foreign mass media may negatively but slightly shape women's attitudes toward social influence.

Women in Taiwan, on the other hand, have had more opportunity to learn individualism from Western culture. After terminating the restrictive 38-year martial law, Taiwan's government dissolved their strict social controls and formally inaugurated modern trends in Taiwan. Collectivism and social dogma were no longer the central values in textbooks. More and more foreign influence came into Taiwan through mass media. People started to absorb Western notions of individualism through foreign mass media. Therefore, we hypothesize that women are influenced by foreign mass media and have lowered their consideration of social or state values.

H_{2-3}: Foreign mass media has a negative effect on women's attitudes toward social influence.

Consumption Value

Although the two countries have the same ethnic culture and speak the same language, differences in socioeconomic standards and political ideologies are reflected in the value-building process.

Literature on consumer behavior has noted for some time now that cultural values are powerful forces in shaping consumers' motivations, lifestyles, and product choices (Tse, Wong, & Tan, 1988). Generally, a value system is sets of beliefs, attitudes, and activities to which a culture or subculture subscribes (Rokeach, 1973). As described before, foreign mass media influences attitudes and the construction of new values. Advertisements emphasize utilitarian values, the promise of a better life, and focus on the development of state as a consumption theme in China. Advertisements in Taiwan illustrate more hedonistic and utilitarian values than those in China (Tse et al., 1989). Hedonism involves fun, gratification (e.g., an exciting life), and pleasure (Campbell, 1987) and results in an endless and ultimately unfulfilling quest for novelty, primarily through consumption. Advertising philosophies are likely to cause or reflect differences in the values consumers seek to enact with their purchases and, accordingly, the ways that advertisers choose to communicate to consumers (Tse et al., 1988). We desire to explore whether women's opinions mediate the effect of the foreign mass media on consumption values. Thus, the impact of women's opinions on their consumption values is discussed in the following sections.

This study focuses on how cultural values affect the consumption behavior of women. Cultural values are dynamic, and they originate from the ethnic and social groups to which people belong. They are also affected by the economic, political, and technological environment that people live in (Tse et al., 1988). Due to the influence of cultural values, consumers perceive some product attributes to be more important than others and hence make purchase decisions reflecting the cultural values of these attributes. Although common cultural values are the same in different Chinese countries, consumers' purchase behaviors across the Taiwan Strait reflect different consumption values due to the changing environment in China versus Taiwan. Thus, Tse, Wong, and Tan (1988) also noted that a consumer's social and cultural environment affects his or her preference.

Sheth, Newman, and Gross (1991) identified five consumption values influencing consumer choice behavior. They are function values, emotional values, epistemic values, social values, and conditional values. This study focuses on function values, epistemic values, and social values. Moreover, we separated social values into family values and patriotic values. Conditional values are not discussed because the focus of this study is on the impact of the level of economic development and communist ideology.

The functional value is traditionally presumed to be the primary driver of a consumer's choice (Sheth et al., 1991). That is, goods must provide consumers with basic needs, such as physical needs and safety needs, which derive from such characteristic attributes as reliability, durability, and price (Ferber, 1973). The functional value is the basic consumption value that somehow exists in all purchases and is controlled in this study.

According to Sheth and his colleagues (1991), emotional values are associated with emotional responses and are often related to an aesthetic value, whereas epistemic values correspond to arousing curiosity, providing novelty, and satisfying a desire for knowledge. These two consumption values are combined into the fashion pursuing value based on the nature of the clothing purchase in this study. A woman may be more likely to pursue a fashion trend to present herself in a particular way and to satisfy her own aesthetic needs.

Social values are associated with one or more specific social groups. Products have been known to possess a symbolic or a conspicuous consumption value in excess of their functional utility (Veblen, 1899). Social values affect consumer choices resulting from interpersonal communication and information dissemination. There are two values, patriotic values and family values, identified in this study. Ethnocentrism offers an explanation for why consumers pursue patriotic values. That is, ethnocentrism views one's own in-group as possessing proper standards of behavior and as offering protection against apparent threats from out-groups (Brislin, 1993). Consumers with ethnocentric tendencies then refuse to purchase foreign-made products (Jill, Etenson, & Morris, 1998; Sharma, Shimp, & Shin, 1995; Shimp & Sharma, 1987). On the other hand, regarding family values, the Confucian influence dictates that consumers prefer to buy products that facilitate contact with their families. The product not only should be good for the individual buyer but also should satisfy his or her family values.

Autonomy to Consumption Value

Functional value is the fundamental requirement for a product. Technical criteria, such as assessing the physical attributes and performance of a product, are the basic criteria in choosing a given brand over competing ones. Women with a strong sense of independence may care about the functional value more because they would like to prove their consumption power and demonstrate a high living standard by purchasing products of high quality. This power indirectly demonstrates their autonomy.

Women with professional careers and a more independent attitude have more access to information. While accessing Western culture, they are likely to be influenced by hedonistic consumption values and individualism. In other words, when compared with traditional women, modern women are more likely to accept a youthful and fashionable lifestyle. They are more likely to read fashion-oriented and cosmopolitan magazines, especially if they work. In sum, individualism encourages women to think for themselves, not for their families. Such a woman focuses more on her own independence and on being fashion oriented and less on family-oriented values.

H_{3-1}:   Autonomy has a positive effect on women's functional values, a positive effect on their fashion-oriented values, and a negative effect on their family-oriented values.

Family Constraint to Consumption Value

A woman identifying family as her first responsibility considers the benefits of her family as her first priority when making any decision. Women with a positive attitude toward family constraints should care more for the practical function of products to bring the maximum utility to their families. However, women with strong orientations to family tend to care for fashion-oriented value less because they focus on the benefits of the family. Even when buying clothes for themselves, traditional housewives consider if the clothes are suitable for their status in the family and if they can facilitate contact with their families. Only then do they rarely focus on the fashion-oriented value.

H_{3-2}: Family constraints have a positive effect on women's functional values, a negative effect on their fashion-oriented values, and a positive effect on their family-oriented values.

Social Influence to Consumption Value

Women more influenced by society are likely to choose those domestic products presenting their commitment to their country. When they are concerned about their contributions to society, they demonstrate their patriotic spirit through their purchasing behaviors. For example, they may choose domestic-made products, which match the group press.

H_{3-3}: Social influence has a positive effect on women's patriotic value.

Control Variables: Demographic Factors

Many researchers have found that a woman's gender identity is correlated with certain demographic variables, such as age, marital status, and occupation. Those having higher sense of femininity tend to be older, married with children, and employed in lower paying jobs (Reynolds, Crask, & Wells, 1977). Educated women in the homemaker-only role may feel a sense of relative deprivation in their social status. Economic criteria may also influence their purchasing criteria. Therefore, age, educational level, marital status, presence of children, and the percentage of family income contributed by women are treated as control variables in this study.

According to the review of previous studies, the conceptual framework of this study can be demonstrated as in Fig. 20.1. Briefly speaking, women's attitudes and opinions toward their sense of autonomy as women, family constraints, and society are influenced by their contact with foreign mass media. These attitudes and opinions then decide their consumption values, namely their functional, fashion-oriented, family-oriented, and patriotic values.

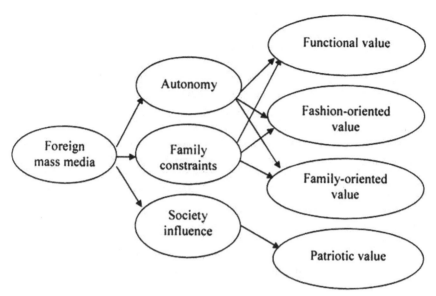

FIG. 20.1.   Empirical model. One-group representation of a two-group model.

METHOD

Survey Procedure and Samples

Our survey was conducted in Beijing and Taipei in 1997. Women in these two metropolitan cities are more likely to have professional careers, are more likely to have been influenced by Western culture, and harbor a wide range of opinions on the aforementioned issues. To ensure the sample is as random and representative as possible, a stratified sampling process was adopted in Taipei to collect 680 respondents. The sampling process in Beijing was administered in a similar manner with 690 respondents. All answers were anonymous.

An evening dress was used as the consumption target to examine women's concerns when purchasing for themselves. Paff and Lakner (1997) noted that a dress is linked to gender symbols and roles. Women wear an evening dress to express their personalities and define or demonstrate their roles. Therefore, among the influences on their consumption behavior toward evening dresses will be whether these women regard themselves as the first priority or still adhere to family needs.

Measurement and Analysis

The first section of the questionnaire considers women's feminine roles. Respondents are asked to express their opinions and attitudes as female individuals (i.e., autonomy), wife or mother at home (i.e., family constraints), and member of society (i.e., social influence) for 42 items. The second part measures their consumption value in buying an evening dress for a party. These two parts are measured on 5-point Likert-type scales (see Table 20.1). The last part includes foreign mass media, such as the frequency of watching foreign TV programs and reading magazines, as well as the respondents' personal background information.

This study emphasized the functional, fashion-oriented, family-oriented, and social values as constitutive of consumption values. They are evaluated from 1 as strongly unimportant to 5 as strongly important.

A constructer equation model was used to analyze the relations among foreign mass media influence and women's attitudes toward autonomy, family constraint, and social influence, and then was mapped onto their consumption values, including functional value, fashion-oriented value, family-oriented value, and patriotic value. The models were tested using the two-step structural equation procedure (Jöreskog & Sörbom, 1989) proposed by Anderson and Gerging (1988). Two-group confirmatory factor analysis (CFA) was performed to evaluate the construct validity and to test the equality of the measurement models between Taiwan and China. A two-group structural analysis was then used to test whether the structural coefficients are unequal across the two countries. Chi-square tests were done to demonstrate the differences between the constrained model and the base model (constrained models have specific paths set as equal). The empirical model is presented in Fig. 20.1.

RESULTS

Socioeconomic characteristics were age, educational level, marital status, presence of kids, living with in-laws, percentage of family income contributed by women, and household income. The majority of respondents' ages ranges from 21 to 40 years old ($\chi^2 = 55.995, p < .01$). The education of the majority of respondents was higher than junior high school. The percentage of respondents with a college or above education in Taiwan was 63.2%. Compared to 55.70% in Beijing, Taiwan was relatively higher ($\chi^2 = 31.748, p < .01$). Respondents' marital status was not significantly different across the two countries, with more than 70% married. The percentages of respondents who have children were both greater than 60% in the two places ($\chi^2 = 0.187$, n.s.). The percentage of respondents who live with parents-in-law was 36.5% in China, which is lower than 42.7% in Taiwan ($\chi^2 = 5.099, p < .01$).

Women's incomes as percentages of a family's total income wee significantly different between China and Taiwan ($\chi^2 = 169.079, p < .01$). Women in China contributed more income to the family than women in Taiwan did. The household income of the majority of respondents ranged from 701 RMB to 1700 RMB in China (60.6%) and from 20,000 NTD to 80,000 NTD in Taiwan (65.4%).

TABLE 20.1

Scale Items Used for Each Construct

Construct	Variable	Scale	Scale
Exogenous construct			
Foreign mass media	MEDIA1	1–5	Foreign TV programs
	MEDIA2	1–5	Foreign magazines and books
Endogenous constructs			
Autonomy	AUTO1	1–5	Married women have the right to decide whether to have a baby or not
	AUTO2	1–5	The women's abilities in work are better that men
	AUTO3	1–5	Women should be independent in economics
Family constraints	FAM1	1–5	Men belong to the society, while women belong to the family
	FAM2	1–5	A woman should obey her father before married, and then obey her husband after married, and then obey her children
	FAM3	1–5	Women do not need to take higher education
	FAM4	1–5	A woman should avoid having greater achievements than her husband
	FAM5	1–5	Men are more respectful than women
Social influence	SOC1	1–5	I am willing to help abused children
	SOC2	1–5	We should devote ourselves to the future of the society and country
	SOC3	1–5	Everyone should take time to be a volunteer for society and country
Functional value	INST1	1–5	Quality and quantity of the product
	INST2	1–5	Value of the product
Fashion-oriented value	FAS1	1–5	Styles can match the popularity
	FAS2	1–5	The popularity of the brand
	FAS3	1–5	New model and type
Family-oriented value	FCON1	1–5	Enhance the living quality of the familyew model and type
	FCON2	1–5	Enforcement of the contacts between the family members
	FCON3	1–5	Suitable to the status of the family
Patriotic value	PAT1	1–5	Local production
	PAT2	1–5	Local brand

Equivalence of Measurement Models Between the Two Places

The results show 13 factors for women in China and 11 factors for women in Taiwan based on the factor analysis (EFA) for the 42 items of opinion. This difference implies that women in these two places have different attitudes toward feminine roles. This study focused on the 11 items that fall in the same factors across the two places as a comparison. After EFA, CFAs were used to confirm the adequacy of the measurement model across the groups. The equivalence of the measurement model across groups was assessed by hierarchical tests (Bollen, 1989). To compare the relevance of the two constructs between the two nations, it is necessary to test whether the relevant constructs are cross-nationally invariant (Hui & Triandis, 1985).

First, the model without constraints provided a baseline chi-square for further comparisons. The results show that the model reached a partial acceptable goodness of fit with $\chi^2_{(404)} = 1219.27$, $p < .005$, RMSEA $= 0.055$, and GFI $= 0.94$, but CFI $= 0.88$ and was only at the moderate level of recommendation. Second, the factor loadings equal across the groups were constrained to test the factor loading invariance. There was a significant difference in the chi-square between the constrained model and the baseline model ($\chi^2_{(15)}$ of difference $= 48.69$, $p < .005$).

Steenkamp and Baumgartner (1998) argued that "if measurement instruments are at least partially invariant, then valid cross national comparisons can be conducted even when the ideal of full invariance is not realized" (p. 88). Partial metric invariance requires cross-country invariance of the measurement items for some items in the same constructs but not necessarily all items. Therefore, the partial measurement invariance was applied. The modification index indicated that factor loadings of the items SELF3, FAM5, and FAS3 (refer to Table 20.1) were a little high in the full item-level metric invariance. The constraints on these items were sequentially relaxed to build the final model of the partial metric invariance. The final model was found not to be significantly different from the baseline model, with $\chi^2_{(12)}$ of difference $= 27.07$, $p > .05$, the same GFI, and an improved CFI and RMSEA. Thus, partial metric invariance (with only 3 of 23 invariance constraints relaxed) was supported.

The validity of the final model was next evaluated. An examination of the final model indicated that substantial amounts of variance on the measures were captured by the latent constructs because all loadings were highly significant. This finding demonstrates convergent validity. If the confidence interval of the correlation between any two latent constructs (as shown in phi-matrix) excludes 1, then the measurement model reaches discriminant validity (Smith & Barclay, 1997). According to the phi-matrix, the results also demonstrated discriminant validity. The reliability of the construct ranged from 0.34 to 0.95. Although highly reliable measures of a test and criteria are desirable theoretically, it is not necessarily true that the predictive power of a test is maximized by maximizing the internal consistency (Crocker & Algina, 1986). Empirically, the relatively low reliability is corrected by Lisrel.

Comparison of Women's Opinions Between the Two Places

A comparison of women's opinions between the two groups is presented. Taiwanese women's opinions of autonomy were higher than those of women in China ($\chi^2 = 111.770$, $p < .01$), whereas women's opinions in China of the family constraint are higher than those of Taiwanese women ($\chi^2 = 38.801$, $p < .01$). Women's opinions of social influence were not different across these two groups ($\chi^2 = 0.395$, $p > .05$). Hypotheses 1-1 and 1-2 were supported, but Hypothesis 1-3 was not supported.

The Structural Model Testing

First, the relation among foreign mass media and women's opinions and attitudes toward feminine roles was tested. The results of the baseline two-group model with no structural constraints were $\chi^2_{(640)} = 2143.96$, GFI = 0.90, and RMSEA = 0.061. The invariance of the coefficient was tested to explore the difference in the coefficient between women in Taiwan and China, although it was not inferred in the hypothesis. Equality of structural paths was examined by systematically constraining the coefficients to be equal across groups and by comparing the constrained model with the baseline model for a significant increase in the chi-square (see Table 20.2). Each path was checked separately by constraining one but not the other to be equal across groups (i.e., first $\gamma_{Media} \to$ autonomy was equal across groups and then $\gamma_{Media} \to$ family constraints then $\gamma_{Media} \to$ social influence). The coefficients of $\gamma_{Media} \to$ autonomy were positively significant (t = 6.34) in both China and Taiwan and are the same, $\chi^2_{(1)}=0.78$, n.s. Hypothesis 2-1 was supported for both groups of women.

The significant chi-square ($\chi^2_{(1)} = 4.36$, $p < .05$) revealed the coefficients of $\gamma_{Media} \to$ family constraints = 0.57 ($p < .05$) in China versus $\gamma_{Media} \to$ family constraints = 0.10 (n.s.) in Taiwan, not like the suggestion in Hypothesis 2-2. The coefficients of $\gamma_{Media} \to$ social influence were also different ($\chi^2_{(1)} = 7.99$, $p < .05$) between women in China and Taiwan, $\gamma_{Media} \to$ social influence= 1.73 ($p < .05$) versus $\gamma_{Media} \to$ social influence = 0.31 ($p < .05$), but unexpectedly showed a positive and significant relation. Hypothesis 2-3 also was not supported.

The second set of tests evaluated the invariance of the coefficients of autonomy to consumption values. All coefficients were not significant in the chi-square test between women in China and Taiwan. The indifference of chi-square ($\chi^2_{(1)} = 3.06$, n.s.) showed that $\gamma_{Self} \to$ instrument value = 1.41 ($p < .05$) both in China and in Taiwan. Similarly, the chi-square result ($\chi^2_{(1)} = 1.28$, $p > .05$) showed $\gamma_{Self} \to$ fashion-oriented value = 1.06 ($p < .05$) both in China and in Taiwan. However, $\gamma_{Self} \to$ family-oriented value = 1.25 ($p < .05$) between China and Taiwan, with $\chi^2_{(1)} = 0.12$ (n.s.). Hypothesis 3-1 was partially supported.

Hypothesis 3-2 discusses the relation between family constraint and consumption values. Similar tests of invariance in the coefficients were conducted, and all coefficients were significantly different in the chi-square test between the two places. The coefficient for $\gamma_{Fam} \to$ instrument value was 0.59 ($p < .05$) in China but not significant in Taiwan. The coefficient for $\gamma_{Fam} \to$ fashion-oriented value is –0.24 ($p < .05$) in Taiwan but was 0.40 in China ($p < .05$). The result ($\chi^2_{(1)} = 0.12$, n.s.) showed that the coefficient for $\gamma_{Fam} \to$ family contact was not different across the

TABLE 20.2

Test for Equality of Path Coefficients Between China and Taiwan

Path Constrained Equal Across China and Taiwan	χ2 Differences: Baseline Versus Constrained Model	Comparison of Path Coefficient China versus Taiwan: χ2 Test Conclusion	Path Coefficients (T-values)	
			China	Taiwan
Foreign mass media → Autonomy	$\Delta \chi^2_{(1)} = 0.48$, ns at $p < .05$	China = Taiwan	0.78 (6.34)	
Foreign mass media → Family constraints	$\Delta \chi^2_{(1)} = 4.36$, significant at $p < .05$	China > Taiwan	0.57 (5.15)	0.10 (1.66)
Foreign mass media → Social influence	$\Delta \chi^2_{(1)} = 7.99$, significant at $p < .05$	China > Taiwan	1.73 (3.33)	0.31 (5.07)
Autonomy → Instrument value	$\Delta \chi^2_{(1)} = 3.06$, ns at $p < .05$	China = Taiwan	1.41 (5.49)	
Autonomy → Fashion-oriented value	$\Delta \chi^2_{(1)} = 1.28$ ns at $p < .05$	China = Taiwan	1.06 (5.38)	
Autonomy → Family-oriented value	$\Delta \chi^2_{(1)} = 0.12$ ns at $p < .05$	China = Taiwan	1.25 (5.55)	
Family constraints → Instrument value	$\Delta \chi^2_{(1)} = 21.09$ significant at $p < .05$	China > Taiwan	0.59 (6.94)	0.05 (1.00)
Family constraints → Fashion-oriented value	$\Delta \chi^2_{(1)} = 17.16$ significant at $p < .05$	China > Taiwan	0.40 (3.97)	−0.24 (−3.36)
Family constraints → Family-oriented value	$\Delta \chi^2_{(1)} = 0.12$ ns at $p < .05$	China > Taiwan	−0.05 (−0.97	
Social influence → Patriotic value	$\Delta \chi^2_{(1)} = 4.68$ significant at $p < .05$	China > Taiwan	0.95 (5.22)	0.39 (2.46)
Control variable Education → Fashion-oriented value	$\chi^2_{(1)} = 4.14$ significant at $p < .05$	China = Taiwan	0.07 (2.09)	−0.03 (−0.92)
Education → Family-oriented value	$\chi^2_{(1)} = 0.91$ ns at $p < .05$	China = Taiwan	−0.06 (−2.99)	
Income → Fashion-oriented value	$\chi^2_{(1)} = v1.76$ ns at $p < .05$	China = Taiwan	0.01 (0.72)	
Income → Family-oriented value	$\chi^2_{(1)} = 0.09$ ns at $p < .05$	China = Taiwan	0.01 (0.96)	
Kid → Fashion-oriented value	$\chi^2_{(1)} = 1.10$ ns at $p < .05$	China = Taiwan	−0.09 (−1.30)	
Kid → Family-oriented value	$\chi^2_{(1)} = 0.85$ ns at $p < .05$	China = Taiwan	0.07 (1.10)	
Age → Fashion-oriented value	$\chi^2_{(1)} = 1.37$ ns at $p < .05$	China > Taiwan	−0.05 (−2.57	
Age → Family-oriented value	$\chi^2_{(1)} = 0.91$ ns at $p < .05$	China = Taiwan	0.01 (0.30)	
Marital → Fashion-oriented value	$\chi^2_{(1)} = 2.76$ ns at $p < .05$	China < Taiwan	0.06 (1.04)	
Marital → Family-oriented value	$\chi^2_{(1)} = 0.03$ ns at $p < .05$	China = Taiwan	0.05 (0.85)	

two groups and surprisingly the coefficient was not significant ($t = -0.05$). These results partially support Hypothesis 3-2.

The next test assessed the invariance of the coefficient between social influence and consumption values. There was a significant difference in chi-square ($\chi^2_{(1)} = 4.68$, $p < .05$) between $\gamma_{Soc} \rightarrow$ patriotic value $= 0.95$ ($p < .05$) in China versus $\gamma_{Soc} \rightarrow$ patriotic value $= 0.39$ ($p < .05$) in Taiwan. Thus, Hypothesis 3-3 was also partially supported.

The last part tested the invariance of the coefficients between control variables and consumption values. Most control variables showed no significant relations with consumption values. Only the educational level of women was significantly related to fashion-oriented values in China (0.07, $p < .05$) and to family-contact values in both places (-0.06, $p < .05$). The age level of women was also significantly related to fashion-oriented values in both places (-0.05, $p < .05$).

DISCUSSION AND IMPLICATIONS

This study investigated the relation among foreign mass media and women's opinions and attitudes and, in turn, their consumption values in both China and Taiwan. Women in both places are influenced by their respective traditional cultures, but due to economic reformation in China and Westernization in Taiwan, women's opinions and attitudes toward their feminine roles are different and influenced by foreign mass media. This study used a two-step structural equation procedure to examine these relations both in China and Taiwan.

The results indicate that because of the influence of modernization and Westernization, women's attitudes toward autonomy is more highly valued in Taiwan than in China; conversely, their attitudes toward family constraints are stronger in China than in Taiwan. This finding may indicate that the foreign mass media has relaxed the constraint on women across the two groups. However, women have similar attitudes toward social influence across the two groups. It seems that being a volunteer for society or helping abused children has become a duty for a citizen whether she is in a capitalist society or a socialistic society.

Foreign mass media has an influential effect on autonomy and prompts women to consider their own desires more. Unexpectedly, foreign mass media does not influence women's attitude toward family constraints. The reason may be that women in China have noted in Western TV programs some negative consequences of autonomy for women, such as divorce, the difficulties of being a single mother, and social violence. They perhaps reconsidered these consequences in the light of traditional Chinese culture and tried to keep their allegiances to family values. Of course, this hypothetical explanation needs more evidence to support the content of women's contact with foreign mass media.

The study also shows a surprisingly positive effect of foreign mass media on societal values in both Taiwan and China. It is possible that women spending more time on foreign mass media may also have more contact with local media.

The local media in China is strongly influenced by communism, and the local media in both places are full of concepts concerning traditional culture. These communications all educate women to contribute more to society. Therefore, although there is high foreign mass media contact, women have a stronger society-focus concern through the influence of the local media. However, this explanation should be further examined.

As hypothesized, autonomy has positive effects on both fashion-oriented values and functional values, and the effects are stronger in Taiwan than in China. Women with positive independent attitudes tend to evaluate fashion and function more while purchasing an evening dress. However, another unexpected result is that the effect of autonomy on family-oriented value is positive in both China and Taiwan. The reason may be that women with a strong sense of autonomy do not dare to resist traditional values. In other words, women with strong independent values may consider their families' benefits more to balance their mental conflicts due to the lack of time or other contributions to the family. Thus, autonomy did not demonstrate a negative effect on the consumption of family values.

Women's opinions about family constraints negatively influence fashion-oriented consumption values in Taiwan, but not in China. It seems that women, who are limited by traditional values in China, tie a hedonic purchase, such as buying an evening dress, strongly with both instrumental and fashionable reasons. It could be a rebound for those traditional women, an idea that needs further study to explore the psychological mechanism behind the scenario.

The relation between society and patriotic values is positively significant as hypothesized in both places. This relation is stronger in China than in Taiwan, which implies that women in China consider the contribution to the society more than women in Taiwan do, even linking it to making purchase decisions. Thus, they tend to buy products made in China.

Managerial Implication

The results have some implications for managers. First, if foreign corporations want to market in China, they must notice the influences of mass media. They may add concepts of economic independence in their commercial appeals to emphasize the autonomy value and then to encourage the fashion-oriented value. Autonomy can increase fashion-oriented values and functional values. Because marketers want to target women with a sense of independence, they may more greatly emphasize fashion consumption values. Functional value is also very important for women with high autonomy and a family-constraint opinion. Therefore, managers should take this determining quality as the basic requirement of consumers.

Due to women's attitudes toward social influence having a positive effect on patriotism, the results indicate that if foreign corporations want to promote products to this segment, they may join in a venture with local partners or invest locally to attract consumers that have strong socially influenced opinions.

Most of the women's opinions toward autonomy, family constraints, and society and consumption values are different in China versus Taiwan. Douglas and Wind (1987) argued that too many barriers and external constraints, including technical standards and government regulations, would have to be ignored to make a global standardization of goods and services workable. They do not refute the existence of certain global market segments. Therefore, marketers should notice the differences between these two markets when they try to promote products in both China and Taiwan, even though consumers in these two countries inherit the same traditional Chinese culture.

Limitations and Suggestions for Future Research

Unfortunately the data set does not include the contents or types of foreign mass media received by women. This study assumed that foreign mass media contact leads to individualism. However, different media contents may have different effects on women's opinions. This is a limitation of our study and an opportunity for future research to explore the effects of different contents of foreign mass media on women in China and Taiwan. One should also be reminded that women in Beijing are more Westernized than those living in rural areas of China. The results should not be generalized or extended to all other provinces in China.

To compare the differences between the two countries, some items of women's opinions and consumption values are deleted. This deletion implicitly represents that women have distinct values in these two markets. That is, the two markets do not hold the same values according to various factors extracted from the exploratory factor analysis This study only discusses the shared factors so as to make the two data sets comparable in the structural equation analysis. Those unrevealed factors have some undiscovered meanings that should be investigated in further studies.

The partial measurement equivalence is not as good as the full invariant in this study. To make the results comparable, three items are relaxed because the full invariance model is hard to arrive at, especially in a culture comparison. However, this change somehow creates a limitation in this study.

REFERENCES

Anderson, J. C., & Gerging, D. W. (1988). Structural equation modeling in practice: A review and recommended two-step approach. *Psychological Bulletin, 103,* 411–423.

Bollen, K. A. (1989). *Structural equations with latent variables.* New York: Wiley-Interscience.

Bond, M. H. (1986). *The psychology of the Chinese people.* New York: Oxford University Press.

Bond, M. H. (1996). Chinese values. In M. H. Bond (Eds.), *The handbook of Chinese psychology* (pp. 208–226). New York: Oxford University Press.

Brislin, R. W. (1993). *Understanding culture's influence on behavior.* Fort Worth: Harcourt Brace Jovanovich.

Campbell, C. (1987). *The romantic ethic and the spirit of modern consumerism.* Oxford, England: Blackwell.

Cheng, H. (1997). Holding up half the sky? A sociocultural comparison of gender-role portrayals in Chinese and U.S. advertising. *International Journal of Advertising, 16,* 295–319.

Courtney, A. E., & Whipple, T. W. (1983). *Sex stereotyping in advertising: Sex role in advertising.* Lexington, MA : Lexington.

Crocker, L. M., & James, A. (1986). *Introduction to classical & modern test theory.* Austin, TX: Holt, Rinehart & Winston.

Douglas, S. P., & Wind, Y. (1987). The myth of globalization. *Columbia Journal of World Business, 22,*(4) 19–30.

Ferber, R. (1973). Consumer economics—A survey. *Journal of Economic Literature, 11*(4), 1303–1342.

Ho, D. Y. F. (1994). Filial piety, authoritarian moralism and cognitive conservatism in Chinese societies. *Genetic, Social and General Psychology Monographs, 120,* 347–365.

Ho, D. Y. F. (1996). Filial piety and its psychological consequences. In M. H. Bond (Ed.), *The handbook of Chinese psychology* (pp. 155–165). New York: Oxford University Press.

Hui, H. C., & Triandis, H. C. (1985). Measurement in cross-cultural psychology: A review and comparison of strategies. *Journal of Cross-Cultural Psychology, 16,* 131–152.

Jill, G. K., Etenson, R., & Morris, M. D. (1998). The animosity model of foreign product purchase: An empirical test in the People's Republic of China. *Journal of Marketing, 62,* 89–100.

Johnson, F. (1985). The western concept of self. In A. J. Marsella, G. A. De Vos, & F. L. K. Hsu (Eds.), *Culture and Self: Asian and Western perspectives* (pp. 91–138). New York: Tavistock.

Jöreskog, K. G., & Sörbom D. (1989). *Lisrel 7: A guide to the program and applications.* Chicago: SPSS, Inc.

Kerin, R. A., Lundstrom, W. J., & Sciglimpaglia, D. (1979). Women in advertisements: Retrospect and prospect. *Journal of Advertising, 8*(3), 37–42.

Lee, W., & Tse, D. K. (1994). Changing media consumption in a new home: Acculturation patterns among Hong Kong immigrants in Canada. *Journal of Advertising, 23*(1), 57–70.

Lysonski, S. (1983). Female and male portrayals in magazine advertisements: A re-examination. *Akron Business and Economic Review, 14*(3), 45–50.

Markus, H. R., & Kitayama, S. (1991). Culture and the self: Implications for cognition, emotion, and motivation. *Psychological Review, 98*(2), 224–253.

Mays, A. E., & Brady, D. L. (1990). *Women's changing role portrayals in magazine advertisements: 1955 to 1985.* Working paper, Millersville State University Series.

Paff, J. L., & Lakner, H. B. (1997). Dress and the female gender role in magazine advertisements of 1950–1994: A content analysis. *Family and Consumer Sciences Research Journal, 26*(1), 29–58.

Reynolds, F. D., Crask, M. R., & Wells, W. D. (1977). The modern feminine life style. *Journal of Marketing, 41,* 38–45.

Rokeach, M. J. (1973). *The nature of human values.* New York: The Free Press.

Scanzoni, J., & Fox, G. L. (1980). Sex roles, family and society: The seventies and beyond. *Journal of Marriage and the Family, 42*(4), 743–756.

Sharma, S., Shimp, T. A., & Shin, J. (1995). Consumer ethnocentrism: A test of antecedents and moderators. *Journal of the Academy of Marketing Science, 23*(Winter), 26–37.

Sheth, J. N., Newman, B. I., & Gross, B. L. (1991). Why we buy what we buy: A theory of consumption values. *Journal of Business Research, 22,* 159–170.

Shimp, T. A., & Sharma, S. (1987). Consumer ethnocentrism: Construction and validation of the CETSCALE. *Journal of Marketing Research, 24*(August), 280–289.

Smith, J. B., & Barclay, D. W. (1997). The effects of organizational differences and trust on the effectiveness of selling partner relationships. *Journal of Marketing, 61*(January), 3–12.

Steenkamp, J. E. M., & Baumgartner, H. (1998). Assessing measurement invariance in cross-national consumer research. *Journal of Consumer Research, 25,* 78–89.

Tan, S. (1997). Women in social development. In X. Y. Lu & L. P. Lin (Eds.), *Chinese new period—society development reports 1991–1995* (pp. 539–571). Shenyang, China: Liao Ning People Publishers (in Chinese).

Thornton, A., Alwin, D. F., & Camburn, D. (1983). Causes and consequences of sex-role attitudes and attitude change. *American Sociological Review, 48,* 211–227.

Tse, D. K., Belk, R. W., & Zhou, N. (1989). Becoming a consumer society: A longitudinal and cross-cultural content analysis of print ads from Hong Kong, the People's Republic of China, and Taiwan. *Journal of Consumer Research, 15,* 457–472.

Tse, D. K., Sin, L. H., Yau, O. H., & Yu, C. J. (1999). Resolving consumption disagreements in Mainland Chinese families: An inter-generational comparison. In R. Batra (Ed.), *Marketing issues in transitional economies* (pp. 56–71). Boston: Kluwer.

Tse, D. K., Wong, J. K., & Tan, C. T. (1988). Toward some standardized cross-cultural consumption values. *Advances in Consumer Research, 15,* 387–395.

Wagner, L. C., & Banos, J. B. (1973). A woman's place: A follow-up analysis of the roles portrayed by women in magazine advertisements. *Journal of Marketing Research, 10,* 213–214.

Veblen, T. (1899). *The theory of the leisure class.* New York: MacMillan.

Veronica, P. (1996). The past is another country: Hong Kong women in transition. *The Annals of the American Academy, 547,* 91–103.

Yang, K. S. (1981). Social orientation and individual modernity among Chinese students in Taiwan. *Journal of Social Psychology, 113,* 159–170.

CHAPTER TWENTY-ONE

Cross-Cultural Comparisons of Brand Personality in Print Media: The Case of Mainland China and Taiwan

Yung-Cheng Shen
Yuan-Ze University

Lien-Ti Bei
Chih-Yun Wu
National Chengchi University

Brand building is an undertaking of paramount importance for marketers (J. Aaker, 1997). A strong brand with high brand equity is the most important asset for the company (Keller, 1998). Brand equity comprises several different elements (D. Aaker, 1991), one of which is brand associations. One particular type of brand association is the personification of the brand, that is, brand personality. Brand personality treats a brand as a person, with unique personality traits that can be differentiated from those of competitor brands. The concept of brand personality appeared in literature a long time ago (Levy, 1959), but systematic investigations of the concept itself have not appeared until recently (J. Aaker, 1997; Alt & Griggs, 1988).

Just as human personalities can be observed through personal communications, so too can brand personalities be discerned through observance of market communications. Marketing communication programs are often designed to communicate a designated brand personality. Different cultures may value different personal characteristics. The same may be true for brand personalities in various commercial cultural environments. Some brand personalities may be more valued in one culture, whereas others are more appreciated in another culture. Mainland China and Taiwan are both heirs to a Chinese cultural tradition, but they have very different economic and political developmental histories. Taiwan experienced phenomenal economic growth during the 1970s through the 1990s. The commercial culture of Taiwan is heavily influenced by the United States, Japan, and Hong Kong. Mainland China, on the other hand, did not start to catch up with global economic developments until the late 1990s. With 50 years of political and social separations, very different social and cultural values have evolved in the two places. This difference is also reflected in the business environment (Tse, Belk, & Zhou 1989). This chapter includes a comparison of brand personalities of Mainland China and Taiwan through analyzing the content of their print ads to understand these cultural differences. The next section presents a brief review of relevant literature, followed by the study itself.

BACKGROUND LITERATURE

Dimensions of Brand Personality

Alt and Griggs (1988) were the first to study the structures of brand personalities systematically. Using three product categories with two brands in each category, they developed four dimensions to describe brand personality: extroversion, social acceptability, virtue, and potency. Later, J. Aaker (1997) conducted a much more comprehensive study on the structure of brand personalities. She collected hundreds of brands and factor analyzed their personalities. Like the Big Five in human personality (Digman, 1990), Aaker also came up with five major dimensions for brand personality: sincerity, excitement, competence, sophistication, and ruggedness. Each of the five dimensions is comprised of four facets, which in turn are constructed by a total of 42 traits. For instance, the sincerity dimension is constituted of four facets: down-to-earth, honest, wholesome, and cheerful. Each facet is related to two to three specific traits, such as original, friendly, sentimental, and family oriented. These dimensions represent a stable construct structure that can explain 93% of the variance in Aaker's data. Based on these dimensions, Aaker developed a brand personality scale (BPS) to measure the personalities of brands other than those used in Aaker's study.

Later, Aaker, Garolera, and Benet-Martinez (2001) also studied brand personalities in Japanese society. Using 10 major Japanese brands, they found five major dimensions that are slightly different from those in American society: excitement, competence, peacefulness, sincerity, and sophistication. Each dimension consists of two to four facets, which in turn are constructed by 36 traits. The major dimensional difference between the Japanese and American brand personalities is that peacefulness replaces ruggedness. Peacefulness is comprised of two facets: mildness and naivety. Mildness is related to four traits: shy, mild, mannered, and peacefulness. Naivety is related to three traits: naïve, dependent, and childlike.

Other studies try to apply the general framework of Aaker to different markets. For example, Cheng (1998) employed Aaker's measurement to apply to brands in the Taiwanese market. He came up with five dimensions that are comparable to those in Japanese society: liveliness, steadiness, peacefulness, kindness, and elegance. Although Cheng (1998) named the factors differently from those dimensions found in Japan, the content and traits are very similar in each dimension. As stated above, Taiwanese society is heavily influenced by Japanese as well as American cultures. As Mainland China, Taiwan, and Japan are all Asian countries, the study presented here employs the Japanese version of the brand personality structures (Aaker et al., 2001) to compare brand personality differences between Mainland China and Taiwan.

Brand Personality in Advertising: Cultural Differences

Advertising reflects cultural values and norms (Kuhns, 1970). People's values, beliefs, behaviors, and lifestyles in a particular culture often form the essential elements of advertising. People in different cultures have different values, beliefs, and lifestyles. Thus advertising reveals and emphasizes different concepts in different cultures. Research has generally supported the idea that different cultures entail different advertising, but there are disagreements regarding the causal factors involved. Some researchers have argued that cultural differences lead to differences in advertising (Cheng & Schweitzer, 1996; Culter & Javalgi, 1992; Ramaprasad & Hasegawa, 1992; Tansey, Hyman, & Zinkhan, 1990). In contrast, other research suggests that advertising can cause changes in cultural values. For example, Lasch (1979) argued that advertising makes up a primary consumers' value in life. Lears (1983) suggested that in the 20th century, pursuing material comfort replaced religious objectives due to advertising. Advertising provides important information about customs, entertainment, and lifestyles for consumers (Holder, 1973). Indeed, it has been further argued that understanding different consumption styles also helps the mobility of social classes (Belk & Pollay, 1985). Finally other research argues for a mutual influential relation between culture and advertising (Albres-Miller & Gelb, 1996; Kuhns, 1970). In sum, although there are controversies regarding the causal directions of influences between cultures and advertising, it seems reasonable to conclude that the two are mutually dependent.

Brand personality is an overall image description of the brand. Designated brand personalities must be delivered to consumers through marketing communications such as advertising (Batra, Lehmann, & Singh, 1993; Levy, 1959; Plummer, 1984). Because different cultures tend to advertise differently, it is thus interesting to see if brand personalities are presented differently in advertising of different cultures. Research has pointed out cultural differences in brand personalities (Aaker et al., 2001). J. Aaker (1997) also suggested that cultural differences should be taken into account when studying brand personality. However, previous research on cross-culture comparisons of brand personality has been rare (Paunonen, Jackson, Trzebinski, & Fersterling, 1992). As discussed in the beginning of this chapter, Mainland China and Taiwan have the same cultural roots but have very different economic development experiences in modern history. Thus, it is interesting to compare brand personalities manifested in the marketing communications of the two places.

THE STUDY

The study reported here employed print ads from Taiwan and Mainland China; we analyzed brand personalities by content analysis (Tse, Belk, & Zhou, 1989). The next section describes the methodology of the study in detail.

METHOD

Sampling: Print Media Selection

One major newspaper circulated in each place was used to sample ads. For Mainland China, the major newspaper *Wen Hui Bao* (*Wen Hui*) was chosen for two reasons. First, *Wen Hui* is the largest newspaper circulated in the greater Shanghai area. Its readers are quite representative of the demographic characteristics of population in Shanghai. More important, *Wen Hui* targets general readers, so it contains many commercial ads of consumer-oriented products. Compared with other newspapers that mostly serve the government, *Wen Hui* is more useful in reflecting business activities in China. Therefore, it was chosen as the newspaper from which to sample Chinese print ads.

For Taiwan, there are three major newspapers. *The China Times* is one of the oldest and the largest newspapers circulated throughout Taiwan. Its daily circulation amounts to over 1.18 million copies. There are more than 4.56 million readers of *The China Times*. These numbers make it the largest newspaper in Taiwan. Therefore, we chose *The China Times* as the newspaper from which to sample Taiwanese print ads.

Sampling Method

As China opens its gates to the world, its business activities are growing at a booming rate. More commercial activities have led to wide varieties of consumption choices. It also has led to heavy marketing communications between manufacturers and consumers. This study sampled print ads of newspapers from 1996 to 2001, during which period high gross domestic production growths in Mainland China were observed.

Print ad samples were systematically selected on the 1st, 6th, 11th, 16th, 21st, and 26th of each month. A total of 72 days were sampled each year. One print ad was selected for each day. The designated page from which the ad is sampled was chosen in turn. For example, if the first page was chosen for March 1, 1997, then the second page was chosen for March 6, 1997. The rest were taken with this general rule. All ads were bigger than 3 × 14 inches to be valid for the sample of this study. If the designated page did not have any ads, or did not have ads that fulfilled the requirements of this study, then the next page was used.

Eight major consumer product categories were chosen for ad sampling: food, drinks, grocery items, clothing, consumer durables, transportation, consumer electronics, and services. These are also the consumer products advertised most often in the newspapers.

Data Coding Schemes and Rules

Three graduate students who were unaware of the purpose of the study were recruited and trained for the brand personality coding task. Two people coded the same ads. When their codes did not agree, the third person served as the judge to decide which code should be used.

The coding scheme was based on the Japanese version of the brand personality study conducted by J. Aaker et al., (2001). To ensure the completeness of coding, we also incorporated the brand personality dimensions from the Lu (2002) study. In Lu's study, brand personalities were represented with bipolar dimensions on the trait level. There are some overlaps between Lu's brand personality structure and that of Aaker et al., but there are also differences. For instance, in the peacefulness dimension, Lu had come up with three additional traits not seen in Aaker's work: leisurely–diligent, relaxed–serious, and confident–modest. Appendix A tabulates the detailed correspondences between the two studies.

An additional personality dimension, namely, internationalization versus localization, is also coded as an independent personality dimension. As Mainland China opens its gate to the world and strives to become a major player in the world economy, internationalization is one major issue it has to deal with in the developmental process. Similarly, the issue of internationalization versus localization is also a topic of considerable controversy in Taiwan. Because of the importance of this issue, this dimension was also coded, in addition to the schemes set up by J. Aaker et al. (2001) and Lu (2001).

Coders coded each ad with respect to whether each trait exists in the sampled ads. A "1" meant the trait existed in the ad, "0" meant it did not exist, and "–1" meant the opposite trait existed. For instance, a "1" was recorded for the innovativeness trait if the trait was perceived to exist in the ad. If it was not, then a "0" was recorded. Finally, if the coders perceived that some trait opposite to innovativeness exists, such as conservativeness, then a "–1" was recorded for the trait opposite to innovative.

RESULTS

Interrater Reliability

A total of 432 advertisements were sampled and coded. The overall interrater reliability was 0.96, after practicing on the ads of 2002. Coders generally had high consensus on the presented brand personality of the sampled ads.

Comparisons of Brand Personality: Mainland China versus Taiwan:

Table 21.1 lists the average percentages of each dimension coded for both places, as well as the percentages of presence versus opposite of each dimension.

One can see that for both places, excitement was the most frequently observed personality dimension (33.5% for Mainland China, 31.5% for Taiwan), followed by competence (31.9% for Mainland China, 27.2% for Taiwan) and peacefulness (14.9% for Mainland China, 15.1% for Taiwan). Sincerity (9.7% for Mainland China, 12.1% for Taiwan) and sophistication (10% for Mainland China, 14.1% for Taiwan) were two less commonly observed dimensions.

The percentages of individual traits under the personality dimension as well as the total percentages for that dimension of Mainland China and Taiwan are tabulated in Appendix B. Chi-square tests were performed comparing the equality of percentages. When collapsed into the level of personality dimensions, the presentation of three dimensions, excitement ($\chi^2 = 1.99$), Competence ($\chi^2 = 1.29$), and peacefulness ($\chi^2 = 2.10$) were similar between the two places without any significant differences. Nonetheless, for the other two dimensions, sincerity ($\chi^2 = 6.78$, $p < 0.05$ and sophistication ($\chi^2 = 7.74$, $p < 0.05$), there were significant differences

TABLE 21.1

Percentages of Each Brand Personality Dimension for Both Places

Personality		Mainland China			Taiwan	
Excitement	33.5%	Opposite	17.3%	31.5%	Opposite	11.9%
		Presence	82.7%		Presence	88.1%
Competence	31.9%	Opposite	4.7%	27.2%	Opposite	9.6%
		Presence	95.3%		Presence	90.4%
Peacefulness	14.9%	Opposite	43.7%	15.1%	Opposite	37.9%
		Presence	56.3%		Presence	62.1%
Sincerity	9.7%	Opposite	14.3%	12.1%	Opposite	21.3%
		Presence	85.7%		Presence	78.7%
Sophistication	10%	Opposite	29.8%	14.1%	Opposite	20.7%
		Presence	70.2%		Presence	79.3%
SUM	100%			100%		

between Mainland China and Taiwan. For the sincerity dimension, Taiwanese ads (27.6%) tended to be more sincere than those of Mainland China (19.8%). For the sophistication dimension, Taiwanese ads (22.6%) also tend to demonstrate more sophistication personality than those in Mainland China (11.6%).

When each individual trait was compared, most of the traits under the personality dimension were different between Mainland China and Taiwan (except for nine traits: positive, determined, masculine, mature, peaceful, casual, warm, gregarious, and unique). The next section discusses these differences under each personality dimension in detail.

Excitement. The presence of the excitement dimension (30.8% for Mainland China; 37.4% for Taiwan) was higher than its opposite (6.4% for Mainland China; 5.1% for Taiwan). For the percentages of present traits, contemporary (54.9% for Mainland China; 65.5% for Taiwan) and friendly (43.1% for Mainland China; 57.6% for Taiwan) were two traits showing the highest percentages under this dimension, whereas brave showed the lowest percentage (16.9% for Mainland China; 10% for Taiwan). Taiwanese ads were higher than ads of Mainland China in both contemporary and friendly but lower in brave. For the opposite trait appearance, talkative (13.4% for Mainland China; 20.8% for Taiwan) and funny (35.2% for Mainland China; 18.1% for Taiwan) had the highest percentages. Mainland Chinese ads were lower in talkative, but higher in funny.

Competence. The appearance of the competence dimension (37.7% for Mainland China; 36.4% for Taiwan) was higher than its opposite (2% for Mainland China; 4.3% for Taiwan). For the presence of traits, responsible (74.1% for Mainland China; 67.1% for Taiwan), confident (66.4% for Mainland China; 73.4% for Taiwan), and realistic (85% for Mainland China; 69.7% for Taiwan) have the highest percentages. Taiwanese ads were higher in responsible, but lower in confident and realistic. For the opposite traits, restrained (14.8% for Mainland China; 23.1% for Taiwan) and serious (7.6% for Mainland China; 18.1% for Taiwan) had the highest percentages. Taiwanese ads were higher on both traits.

Peacefulness. The presence of the peacefulness dimension (15.5% for Mainland China; 21% for Taiwan) was similar to its opposite (12% for Mainland China; 12.9% for Taiwan). Peaceful (36.8% for Mainland China; 37.7% for Taiwan) and mild (24.5% for Mainland China; 41.4% for Taiwan) had the highest percentages, whereas shy had the lowest percentage (0.5% for Mainland China; 7.4% for Taiwan). Ads in Mainland China were similar to Taiwanese ads in peaceful, but lower in both mild and shy. For the opposite trait appearance, dependent (38.9% for Mainland China; 40.5% for Taiwan) and childlike (44.4% for Mainland China; 36.8% for Taiwan) had the highest percentages. Taiwanese ads were lower in childlike but similar to ads in Mainland China in dependent.

Sincerity. The presence of the sincerity dimension (19.8% for Mainland China; 27.6% for Taiwan) was higher than its opposite (3.3% for Mainland China; 7.5% for Taiwan). Humanistic (44.7% for Mainland China; 54.9% for Taiwan) and thoughtful (23.6% for Mainland China; 46.3% for Taiwan) had the highest percentages, whereas modest had the lowest percentage (1.9% for Mainland China; 1.6% for Taiwan). Taiwanese ads were higher than those of Mainland China in both humanistic and thoughtful, but similar in modest. For the opposite trait appearance, family oriented (8.8% for Mainland China; 28.5% for Taiwan) and modest (9.5% for Mainland China; 15% for Taiwan) had the highest percentages. Taiwanese ads tended to have more family flavor than ads in Mainland China.

Sophistication. The presence of the sophistication dimension (11.6% for Mainland China; 22.6% for Taiwan) was higher than its opposite (5% for Mainland China; 5.9% for Taiwan). For the presence percentages, stylish (22.5% for Mainland China; 37% for Taiwan) and unique (28% for Mainland China; 30.8% for Taiwan) had the highest percentages, with Taiwanese ads higher in stylish. Mainland China and Taiwan are most different on the extravagant dimension (34.7% for Mainland China; 3.5% for Taiwan). Rather, the opposite trait appearance, romantic (22.9% for Mainland China; 29.9% for Taiwan), had the highest percentage. Taiwanese ads were also higher than ads from Mainland China on this trait.

Internationalization Versus Localization. Both places were moderate in internationalization (46.8% for Mainland China; 53.2% for Taiwan) and lower in localization (28.5% for Mainland China; 26.2% for Taiwan). No significant difference was found in these two dimensions between the two places.

DISCUSSION AND CONCLUSION

The current study compares the print ads of Mainland China and Taiwan, the results of which reveal several facets about the similarities and differences in the brand personalities of the two cultures. First, both cultures emphasize excitement and competence the most, whereas sincerity is least expressed. Second, ads of Mainland China tend to carry more competence traits than ads of Taiwan. This finding probably has to do with its greater emphasis on the functional side of products. Taiwanese ads, however, are better at expressing excitement, sophistication, and sincerity. Both cultures are similar in emphasizing peacefulness. Third, the presence of traits is higher than their opposites for both cultures. Brand personalities usually deliver positive values that each respective culture appreciates. Negative expressions of personality traits are usually disapproved of according to the norms of cultural values. Thus, the positive presence of a personality is usually more prevalent than the negative absence of it.

This study contributes to the cross-cultural comparisons of brand personalities in several respects. First, ever since the development of major brand personality dimensions, cross-cultural comparisons of brand personalities are still rare in the literature. As J. Aaker (1997) indicated, it is a central issue in brand personality research that deserves increased research efforts. Second, as the economics of China is growing and as it becomes an economic center in the world, China's commercial activities deserve more thorough consideration. This study that compares brand personality differences between Mainland China and Taiwan serves as a first step toward this goal. Third, the finding that different personalities are exhibited disproportionately is also interesting. For instance, it is found that, in both cultures, the personalities of excitement and competence are much more prevalent in the sampled ads than other personalities. It seems that Chinese consumerist culture values these personality dimensions more than others. This finding should be taken into account when designing marketing communication messages.

Despite these contributions, this study is still limited in several respects. Only print ads in a specific time frame are covered. Other media such as TV can more vividly present brand personalities. Future studies may consider using other media and cover a broader time range. Also, as an exploratory study, this study describes and compares brand personality profiles of the two cultures, but it lacks more solid theoretical foundations to explain these differences. Future research can address the factors that lead to such observed differences in brand personalities. Finally, this study is a cross-sectional study of brand personality comparisons. Longitudinal studies should be able to reveal transitions of brand personalities as cultural changes occur.

REFERENCES

Aaker, D. A. (1991). *Managing brand equity: Capitalizing on the value of a brand name.* New York: The Free Press.

Aaker, J. L. (1997). Dimensions of brand personality. *Journal of Marketing Research, 34,* 347–356.

Aaker, J. L., Garolera, J., & Benet-Marinez, V. (2001). Consumption symbols as carriers of culture: A study of Japanese and Spanish brand personality constructs. *Journal of Personality and Social Psychology, 81,* 492–508.

Albres-Miller, N. D., & Gelb, B. D. (1996). Business advertising appeals as a mirror of cultural dimensions: A study of eleven countries. *Journal of Advertising, 25*(4), 57–70.

Alt, M., & Griggs, S. (1988). Can a brand be cheeky? *Marketing Intelligence and Planning, 6*(4), 9–16.

Batra, R., Lehmann, D. R., & Singh, D. (1993). The brand personality component of brand goodwill: Some antecedent and consequence. In D. A. Aaker & A. L. Biel (Eds.), *Brand equity and advertising* (pp. 83–96). Hillsdale, NJ: Lawrence Erlbaum Associates.

Belk, R. W., & Pollay, R. W. (1985). Images of ourselves: The good life in 20th century advertising. *Journal of Consumer Research, 11,* 887–897.

Cheng, I. H. (1998). *The effects of brand personality and product category on brand extension.* Unpublished thesis, National Central University.

Cheng, H., & Schweitzer, J. C. (1996). Cultural values reflected in Chinese and U. S. televisions commercials. *Journal of Advertising Research, 36*(3), 27–45.

Culter, B. D., & Javalgi, R. G. (1992). A cross-cultural analysis of the visual components of print advertising: The United States and the European community. *Journal of Advertising Research, 32,* 71–80.

Digman, J. (1990). Personality structure: Emergence of the five-factor model. In M. Rosenzweig & L. W. Porter (Eds.), *Annual Review of Psychology* (pp. 417–440). Palo Alto, CA: Annual Reviews, Inc.

Holder, S. C. (1973). The family magazine and the American people. *Journal of Popular Culture, 7,* 264–279.

Keller, K. L. (1998). *Strategic brand management: Building, measuring, and managing brand equity.* Englewood Cliffs, NJ: Prentice-Hall.

Kuhns, W. (1970). *Waysteps to Eden: Ads and commercials.* New York: Herder and Herder.

Lasch, C. (1979). *The culture of narcissism: American life in an age of diminishing expectations.* New York: Norton.

Lears, T. J. J. (1983). From salvation to self-realization: Advertising and the therapeutic roots of the consumer culture, 1880–1930. In R. W. Fox & T. J. J. Lears (Eds.), *The culture of consumption: Critical essays in American history* (pp. 3–38). New York: Pantheon.

Levy, S. J. (1959). Symbols for sales. *Harvard Business Review, 37*(4), 117–124.

Lu, I. A. (2002). *The perceptions of brand personality by different generations.* Unpublished thesis, National Chengchi University.

Paunonen, S. V., Jackson, D. N., Trzebinski, J., & Fersterling, F. (1992). Personality structure across cultures: A multi-method evaluation. *Journal of Personality and Social Psychology, 62,* 447–456.

Plummer, J. T. (1984). How personality makes a difference. *Journal of Advertising Research, 24*(Dec.), 27–31.

Ramaprasad, J., & Hasegawa, K. (1992). Creative strategies in American and Japanese TV commercials: A comparison. *Journal of Advertising Research, New York, 32*(Jan/Feb), 59–68.

Tansey, R., Hyman, M. R., & Zinkhan, G. M. (1990). Cultural themes in Brazilian and U.S. auto ads: A cross-cultural comparison. *Journal of Advertising, 19,* 30–40.

Tse, D., Belk, R. W., & Zhou, N. (1989). Becoming a consumer society: A longitudinal and cross-cultural content analysis of print ads from Hong Kong, the People's Republic of China, and Taiwan. *Journal of Consumer Research, 15,* 457–472.

APPENDIX A

A Comparison of the Dimensions of Brand Personality by Aaker, Garolera, & Benet-Martinez (2001) and Lu (2002).

Dimension	Aaker (2001)	Lu (2002)
Excitement	Talkative	
	Funny	Cute ↔ Mature (in Competence)
	Optimistic	
	Positive	Diligent ↔ Relaxed (in Peacefulness)
	Contemporary	
	Free	
	Friendly	Friendly ↔ Proud
	Happy	Cheerful ↔ Gloomy
	Likable	Likable ↔ Wild
	Youthful	Youthful ↔ Aged
	Energetic	
	Spirited	
		Demonstrative ↔ Restrained (in Competence)
		Creative ↔ Conservative (in Competence)
		Brave ↔ Timid
Competence	Consistent	
	Responsible	
	Reliable	
	Dignified	
	Determined	
	Confident	Confident ↔ Modest (in Peacefulness)
	Patient	
	Tenacious	
	Masculine	Masculine ↔ Feminine (in Sophistication)
		Mature ↔ Cute (in Excitement)
		Restrained ↔ Demonstrative (in Excitement)
		Realistic ↔ Romantic (in Sophistication)
		Conservative ↔ Creative (in Excitement)
		Formal ↔ Casual (in Peacefulness)
Peacefulness	Shy	
	Mild	
	Mannered	
	Peaceful	
	Naïve	
	Dependent	
	Childlike	
		Relaxed ↔ Diligent (in Excitement)
		Casual ↔ Formal (in Competence)

(continued)

Dimension	Aaker (2001)	Lu (2002)
Sincerity	Warm	
	Thoughtful	Thoughtful ↔ Sloppy
	Kind	
		Modest ↔ Confident (in Competence)
		Gregarious ↔ Independent
		Family-oriented ↔ Individualized
		Humanistic ↔ Technological
Sophistication	Elegant	Elegant ↔ Crude
	Smooth	
	Romantic	Romantic ↔ Realistic (in Competence)
	Stylish	
	Sophisticated	Sophisticated ↔ Rough
	Extravagant	Extravagant ↔ Common
		Feminine ↔ Masculine (in Competence)
		Charming ↔ Dull
		Unique ↔ Ordinary
		Fashionable ↔ Old-fashioned

APPENDIX B

The percentages of records for each dimension of brand personality in Mainland China and Taiwan.

% Brand Personality	Mainland China			Taiwan			χ^2
	Opposite	Absent	Present	Opposite	Absent	Present	
Excitement							
Talkative	13.4	44.4	42.1	20.8	40.7	38.4	8.35*
Funny	35.2	41.9	22.9	18.1	45.1	36.8	39.36**
Optimistic	0.0	80.6	19.4	0.0	72.9	27.1	7.06**
Positive	0.0	57.4	42.6	0.2	60.2	39.6	1.76
Contemporary	4.6	40.5	54.9	4.2	30.3	65.5	10.50**
Free	0.0	79.4	20.6	0.7	66.2	33.1	20.73**
Friendly	0.5	56.5	43.1	1.2	42.1	57.6	20.73**
Happy	0.9	77.8	21.3	0.0	66.9	33.1	18.60**
Likable	14.8	69.9	15.3	11.1	66.0	20.9	9.38**
Youthful	10.6	64.6	24.8	3.7	61.6	34.7	22.02**
Energetic	4.9	64.8	30.3	0.9	66.9	32.2	11.94**
Spirited	0.7	67.1	32.2	0.0	57.9	42.1	11.72**
Demonstrative	1.9	58.6	39.6	6.7	49.3	44.0	16.35**
Innovative	8.8	55.3	35.9	8.3	47.2	44.4	6.77*
Brave	0.0	83.1	16.9	0.0	90.0	10.0	8.96**
Subtotal	6.4	62.8	30.8	5.1	57.5	37.4	1.99

(continued)

Competence

Consistent	0.0	48.8	51.2	0.0	59.3	40.7	9.44**
Responsible	0.0	25.9	74.1	0.0	32.9	67.1	5.02*
Reliable	0.0	61.3	38.7	0.0	52.5	47.5	6.82**
Dignified	0.5	81.0	18.5	1.2	74.1	24.8	6.53*
Determined	0.0	67.4	32.6	0.0	69.0	31.0	0.26
Confident	0.0	33.6	66.4	0.0	26.6	73.4	4.95*
Patient	0.9	92.8	6.3	0.2	86.1	13.7	14.80**
Tenacious	0.0	97.9	2.1	0.0	88.4	11.6	30.58**
Masculine	0.0	88.2	11.8	0.5	86.6	13.0	2.30
Mature	0.0	57.2	42.8	0.2	60.2	39.6	1.88
Restrained	14.8	56.9	28.2	23.1	46.5	30.3	12.75**
Realistic	1.2	13.9	85.0	9.3	21.1	69.7	40.11**
Conservative	3.2	74.1	22.7	7.4	80.1	12.5	20.80**
Serious	7.6	45.1	47.2	18.1	46.8	35.2	25.96**
Subtotal	2.0	60.3	37.7	4.3	59.3	36.4	1.29

Peacefulness

Shy	6.0	3.5	0.5	9.0	83.6	7.4	31.49**
Mild	2.1	73.4	24.5	9.3	49.3	41.4	58.72**
Courteous	0.0	79.9	20.1	0.5	85.9	13.7	8.31*
Peaceful	0.0	63.2	6.21*				
Naïve	15.3	74.5	10.2	17.6	64.6	17.8	12.78**
Dependent	38.9	56.5	4.6	40.5	48.8	10.6	12.78**
Childlike	44.4	49.3	6.3	36.8	48.6	14.6	17.52**
Relaxed	0.5	83.1	16.4	0.0	76.2	23.8	9.19**
Casual	1.2	78.5	20.4	0.9	76.9	22.2	0.53
Subtotal	12.0	72.4	15.5	12.9	66.1	21.0	2.10

Sincerity

Warm	0.0	85.0	15.0	0.7	80.8	18.5	5.00
Thoughtful	0.0	76.4	23.6	0.0	53.7	46.3	48.89**
Kind	4.6	67.8	27.5	6.0	53.2	40.7	19.39**
Modest	9.5	88.7	1.9	15.0	83.3	1.6	6.21*
Gregarious	0.2	89.6	10.2	0.5	89.4	10.2	0.34
Family-oriented	8.8	75.7	15.5	28.5	50.7	20.8	69.61**
Humanistic	0.0	55.3	44.7	1.6	43.5	54.9	17.59**
Subtotal	3.3	76.9	19.8	7.5	64.9	27.6	6.78*

Sophistication

Elegant	3.7	81.9	14.4	1.4	67.6	31.0	36.95**
Smooth	0.9	89.4	9.7	0.7	81.0	18.3	13.22**
Romantic	22.9	71.5	5.6	29.9	52.3	17.8	44.64**
Stylish	4.9	72.7	22.5	3.9	59.0	37.0	21.98**
Sophisticated	0.5	81.3	18.3	1.6	81.7	16.7	32.02**
Extravagant	0.7	95.8	3.5	1.2	64.1	34.7	43.80**
Feminine	3.0	95.1	1.9	6.7	85.9	7.4	22.54**
Charming	7.6	88.4	3.9	9.0	72.9	18.1	46.11**
Unique	1.2	70.9	28.0	1.2	68.1	30.8	2.74
Fashionable	4.2	87.0	8.8	3.5	82.4	14.1	6.16*
Subtotal	5.0	83.4	11.6	5.9	71.5	22.6	7.74*
Internationalization	—	53.2	46.8	—	46.8	53.2	3.63
Localization	—	71.5	28.5	—	73.8	26.2	0.58

Note: ** $p < .01$; * $p < .0$

Author Index

Note: *f* indicates figure, *t* indicates table.

Subject Index

Note: *f* indicates figure, *t* indicates table.

A

Absolut Vodka ads, 79
Accessibility-diagnosticity model, 92
Advertisements, *see also* Advertising; Persuasive appeal/message
  attention moderating effects of, 76
  brand personality in, 356–358, 356*t*, 362*t*, 363*t*
  in China vs. Taiwan (*see* China vs. Taiwan)
  for Christmas cake/holiday, 49*f*, 54, 54*f*, 55*f*, 56*f*, 57*f*, 58*f*, 59*f*, 60*f*, 61*f*
  creators role in, 203–204
  familiarity and product categories, 41*t*
  fuzzy products and, 40–41
  and likeability, 194
  as "multi" advertisements, 285
  narrative format and elaboration, 75
  noise and, 194
  and presentation modality, 73
  product/endorser fit in, 196
  prototypicality of, 35, 37*t*, 38*t*, 39–40 (*see also* Prototypicality measurement)
  television, 75, 194, 285
  transformational (feel), 284–285
  women portrayed in, 206, 214–215, 334–335
  word-of-mouth vs., 91
Advertising, *see also* Advertisements; Persuasive appeal/message
  in America vs. Taiwan, 178
  beauty and, 201–202
  brand vs. category image and, 43
  celebrity endorsement in, 161–163
  Christmas cake, 55
  collectivism and, 188
  as communication vs. consumer involvement, 63
  constraints and prototypicality, 45
  creators of, 203–204, 206
  effectiveness, 180–181, 181*f*, 184–186, 184*f*, 185*f*
  experience and, 81
  familiarity and product categories, 41*t*
  functional vs. symbolic brand image, 283–284
  gender roles in, 214–215
  item and relational information, 271
  in Korea, 285
  national vs. individual differences, 188
  open-ended product status and, 63
  product category and, 41, 41*t*
  product image change and, 63
  sponsorship vs., 258
  word-of-mouth vs., 91–92, 94, 97*t*
Aesthetics and brand-self connection, x
Affect/emotion
  attitude formation and, 294–295
  attributes of images and, 292–293
  and brand-self connection, ix–xiii
  in cognitive processing, 293–295, 295*f*
  connotations of brand name and, 13

381